Company Directors

Kolkata
Eastern Law House Private Ltd.
54 Ganesh Chunder Avenue
Kolkata (Calcutta) 700 013

New Delhi
Eastern Law House Private Ltd.
36 Netaji Subhash Marg, Daryaganj
New Delhi 110 002

Company Directors

Fiduciary Duties & Liabilities under the Indian Company Law

BY

K.D. Raju

BSc, LLM, MPhil, PhD (JNU)
Fulbright Fellow, Microsoft Outstanding Young Faculty Fellow
Faculty of Law in Rajiv Gandhi School of Intellectual Property Law
IIT, Kharagpur

Kolkata New Delhi
EASTERN LAW HOUSE
2013

Published and processed by
EASTERN LAW HOUSE PRIVATE LTD.
54 Ganesh Chunder Avenue
Kolkata (Calcutta) 700 013
Tel: (033) 2215-1989/2301 Fax: (033) 2215-0491
Email: elh.cal@gmail.com • elh@cal.vsnl.net.in
www.easternlawhouse.com

ISBN 978-81-7177-261-2

Printed at
Dey's Offset, Kolkata

Dedicated

To my mother Hymavathy who is the main source of inspiration and unswerving support for my goals in life.

Preface

This book is designed for the use of company directors, corporate law practitioners, law students, business school students, company secretary students and all those who are interested in knowing the engagement of company directors.

Directors occupy a key position in a company. They hold vast powers and wide discretion in the discharge of their functions. As regards the nature of their powers almost all powers held by them are powers in trust and are exercised by them in a fiduciary capacity.

This book earnestly attempts to analyze the various aspects of the position of directors, the discretionary powers of directors and fiduciary duties, the good faith in duties and the duty of disclosure of their personal interests in the transactions entered into by the company and the areas of conflicts between their fiduciary duties and personal interests. Reference is also made to fiduciary obligation and liability for breach of trust has been made out. The prosecution of directors under various legislations has also discussed. The impact of Companies Bill 2012 in the light of economic reforms and new role of company directors in the 21st century are examined. The efficacy of the techniques for enforcing the fiduciary duties and the shortcomings thereof are discussed and suggestions are made in the light of Indian as well as foreign cases to make this work an up-to-date one. The objective of this book included:

- To identify the fiduciary duties of directors;
- To clarify the position of directors in the Indian context;

- To analyze the jurisprudence of fiduciary duties of company directors from the common law practice to the decisions of various Indian courts;
- To provide additional support to company directors, practitioners, students and other stakeholders those who want to know more about company directors;
- To identify the prosecution provisions in the Companies Bill 2012.

However, this book is not claimed to address all subjects but answering questions with regard to each and every aspect of fiduciary duties and liabilities, case laws and prosecution provisions. It is also try to demystify and explain some of the traps and legal issues relating to the role of company directors as trustees, agents of the company, employee and an officer of a company. This book does not undertake to fully discuss all the provisions of Companies Act 1956, but it covers all provisions dealing with company directors along with innovations introduced in the Companies Bill 2012.

Kharagpur
4th March 2013 K.D. RAJU

Acknowledgments

The journey through the foggy world of company director's fiduciary duties, liabilities and prosecutions has been both fascinating as well as a tedious job for the last three years. The persons who helped me to undertake this journey are too numerous to name personally. But few of them deserve special mention. I am indebted to Prof. Paul Gomez, Faculty of Law, Government Law College, Ernakulam, Kerala for his encouragement and advice during my LLM studies. All the teachers of the college are acknowledged with deep respect. My classmates in LLM class were very much supportive during the initial stages of this work.

I am thankful to Prof. (Dr.) S.V. Joga Rao, Dean, Rajiv Gandhi School of Intellectual Property Law for his inspiring guidance and leadership at the School.

I am grateful to the staffs of the Libraries of Government Law College, Ernakulam, Kerala High Court Library, Jawaharlal Nehru University, Indian Law Institute, British Council and FICCI Libraries, New Delhi, who have helped me to find the relevant materials for this study.

I would be failing in my duty if I do not acknowledge the help and assistance of my friends Shiju M.V., Dr. Ajish P. Joy and K.M. Gopakumar (JNU) for the help and support they rendered at various stages of this work.

My students, Miss Mathura Roy, Miss Apurba Kundu and Mr. Ravikant Bharadwaj at Rajiv Gandhi School of Intellectual Property Law, IIT, Kharagpur deserves special mention for their help.

The main source of inspiration and support of my work has been my mother and my brother. Without them, this work would have been anything but complete.

I am grateful to my wife Roopa and son Aravind for their sacrifice of time. Their love and affection prevented me from going astray from my preoccupation.

The editorial staffs of Eastern Law House, Kolkata spent lot of time for this project. Mr. De, his son and his team have helped me in the writing and editing process, keeping me in line and providing immediate support.

Last, but not the least, I thank the God for steadfastly supporting me and helping me to complete my works in time.

With all acknowledgements, the end result and responsibilities are mine. Any oversights and errors are mine and mine alone.

K.D. RAJU

Contents

Table of Cases

Abbreviations

AC	:	Law Reports–Appeal Cases
ACLR	:	Australian Company Law Reports
ACSR	:	Australian Corporations and Securities Reports
AGM	:	Annual General Meeting
ALD–Cri	:	Andhra Law Decisions–Criminal
All ER	:	All England Law Reports
All ER–Com	:	All England Law Reports–Commercial Cases
All ER–EC	:	All England Law Reports–European Cases
ALR	:	American Law Reports
B & Ad	:	Barnewall & Adolphus' King's Bench Reports
BCC	:	British Company Cases
BCLC	:	Butterworths Company Law Cases
BLR	:	Business Law Review
CA	:	Court of Appeal
CAO	:	Chief Accounts Officer
CBDT	:	Central Board of Direct Taxes
CBLJ	:	Corporate and Business Law Journal
CEO	:	Chief Executive Officer
CFO	:	Chief Financial Officer
Ch D	:	Law Reports–Chancery Division
CHN	:	Calcutta High Court Notes
CII	:	Confederation of Indian Industries
CIT	:	Commissioner of Income Tax
CLA	:	Corporate Law Advisor
CLB	:	Company Law Board
CLJ	:	Cambridge Law Journal
CLR	:	Commonwealth Law Reports
Co Law	:	Company Lawyer
Col LR	:	Columbia Law Review
Com LJ	:	Commercial Law Journal

CSR	:	Corporate Social Responsibility
CTC	:	Current Tamil Nadu Cases
CTO	:	Commercial Tax Officer
CWN	:	Calcutta Weekly Notes
D & FI	:	Derivatives and Financial Instruments
DIN	:	Director Identification Number
DLR	:	Directors Law Reporter
DLT	:	Delhi Law Times
EBL	:	Electronic Business Law
EBLR	:	European Business Law Review
ECC	:	European Commercial Cases
EPF	:	Employees Provident Fund
ER	:	English Reports
ESI	:	Employees State Insurance
ESOP	:	Employees Stock Option Scheme
FBT	:	Fringe Benefit Tax
FEMA	:	Foreign Exchange Management Act
FICCI	:	Federation of Indian Chamber of Commerce and Industry
FLR	:	Family Law Reports
FSR	:	Fleet Street Reports
GLR	:	Gujarat Law Reporter
Hare	:	Hare's Vice-chancellors' Reports
HL	:	House of Lords
ICR	:	Industrial Cases Reports
IDC	:	Industrial Development Consultants
ILL	:	Illinois Reports
IPC	:	Indian Penal Code
IRLR	:	Industrial Relations Law Reports (UK)
ISJ	:	Important and Selected Judgments (Banking)
ITR	:	Income Tax Reports
JBL	:	Journal of Business Law
JCC	:	Journal of Criminal Cases
JT	:	Judgment Today
KB	:	Law Reports, King's Bench Division
KLT	:	Kerala Law Times
KMP	:	Key Managerial Personnel
LIC	:	Life Insurance Corporation of India
LJ Ch	:	Law Journal Reports, New Series, Chancery–England
LJKB	:	Law Journal King's Bench
LJPC	:	Law Journal Reports, Privy Council New Series
Ll LR	:	Lloyd's Law Reports
Ll PC	:	Lloyd's Price Cases
LLJ	:	Labour Law Journal (India)

LLR	:	Labour Law Reporter
LQR	:	Law Quarterly Review
LRA	:	Law Review Association
LRC	:	Law Reform Commission
LTR	:	Thomson Legal & Regulatory Ltd.
Macq HL	:	Macqueen's Scotch Appeal Cases, House of Lords–A publication (DLA)
MD	:	Managing Director
MIC	:	Methyl Iso-cyanate
MLJ	:	Madras Law Journal
MRTP	:	Monopolies and Restrictive Trade Practices Commission
MULR	:	Melbourne University Law Review
NCLT	:	National Company Law Tribunal
NCT	:	National Capital Territory
NSWLR	:	New South Wales Law Reports
NZLR	:	New Zealand Law Reports
NZSC	:	Supreme Court of New Zealand
OPC	:	One Person Company
OR	:	Official Report
PC	:	Privy Council
PCB	:	Pollution Control Board
PNLR	:	Professional Negligence and Liability Reports
PNSC	:	Pakistan National Shipping Corporation
QB	:	Law Reports, Queen's Bench
QBD	:	Queen's Bench Division
RAC	:	Royal Automobile Club
RACL	:	Royal Automobile Club Ltd.
RACMS	:	RAC Motoring Services
RBI	:	Reserve Bank of India
RLW	:	Rajasthan Law Weekly
RPC	:	Reports of Patent, Design and Trademark Cases
SALJ	:	South African Law Journal
SC	:	Supreme Court
SCALE	:	Supreme Court Almanac
SCB	:	Standard Chartered Bank
SCC Supp	:	Supreme Court Cases (Supp).
SCC	:	Supreme Court Cases
SCL	:	SEBI and Corporate Laws
SCR	:	Supreme Court Reports
SCW	:	Supreme Court Weekly
SEBI	:	Securities Exchange Board of India
SEC	:	Securities and Exchange Commission
SFIO	:	Serious Fraud Investigation Office

SLJ	:	Service Law Journal
SLT	:	Scots Law Times
STC	:	Simon's Tax Cases
STR	:	Service Tax Review
TADA	:	Terrorists and Disruptive Activities (Prevention) Act
Tax LR	:	Tax Law Review
TLR	:	Texas Law Review
UK	:	United Kingdom
UNI	:	United News of India
US	:	United States
VST	:	VAT and Service Tax
WLR	:	Weekly Law Reports
WN	:	Weekly Notes
WTO	:	World Trade Organization

Introduction

In January 2009, the ₹ 7000 crore accounting fraud in the Indian information technology major "Satyam",[1] revealed by its Chairman's confessional statement sent a shock wave among the Indian corporate world.[2] This incident has made a black mark on the vibrant Indian corporate sector after the opening of its economy in 1991. This has compelled all stakeholders including the Government, regulators and the Industry to think of placing more riders on the Indian companies in terms of regulations. In a recent incident, one of the Hospitals in Kolkata caught fire on 9th December 2011 and more than 90 people were reported dead. Subsequently the police arrested all the directors for criminal negligence and other provisions of law.[3] The industry chambers like Confederation of Indian Industry (CII) and Federation of Indian Chamber of Commerce and Industry (FICCI) criticised this move of the State Government for arresting non-executive directors of the hospital whom are not liable for day-to-day activities of the company.[4] This incident also raises many questions of criminal liabilities of company directors in India.

Considering the key position occupied by the directors of a company, as drivers of the world economy in the 21st century, a discussion about

1 It is paradoxical that the name of the company is "Satyam" meaning "truth" and what has happened is the largest corporate fraud in the history of India.

2 *The Financial Express*, 7th January 2009. In a letter to the Satyam Board of Directors he revealed the details of the fraud. See http://www.financialexpress.com/news/satyam-fraud-full-text-of-rajus-letter-to-board/407799/, visited on 08.01.2009.

3 *Times of India Daily* online 9th December 2011.

4 *The Economic Times Daily*, 24th January 2012.

their position under the known connotations as agents, trustees and managing directors is important and necessary. The Government of India has re-introduced a new Bill in the Lok Sabha which seeks to revolutionize corporate governance in the country. This has been due since the beginning of the economic liberalization. The present Companies Act 1956 shall be substantially repealed by the proposed Companies Bill 2009 which is merged in the Companies Bill 2011. The new Bill has been presented in the Parliament with 470 sections. The new bill has incorporated sufficient changes suggested by different stakeholders to the 2009 Bill. The new law will make changes in the role of "independent" directors in the company and introduced the concept of "One Man Company" to India.[5] An analysis of the position of company directors, their duties, liabilities and responsibilities is therefore inevitable in the context of recent developments. The jurisprudence in this regard has emerged from the British cases and practices in other leading jurisdictions around the world as well.

A "corporation" in the eye of law is an abstraction and has neither mind nor a body of its own. The board of directors of a company fills this gap and is an integral part of a company. The directors are the directing mind of a company and they occupy a pivotal position in the structure of a company. Most of the functions of the company are vested with the board of directors. Even though the general meeting of share holders retains ultimate control, the day-to-day business of the company is carried out by its directors. Directors act as agents of the company enter into transactions on its behalf although they are not agents for individual shareholders or members. Directors are in fact controllers of the company's affairs. A director may be an employee, a servant or even 'worker' of the company. He or she occupies the position of a trustee, though he/she is not a trustee in the strict sense in respect of the company's properties and funds. The evolution of a company's directors as powerful administrators of the economy made them very powerful as good as controlling even their respective governments.

As aforementioned, the board of directors are now the principal organ of a company. The management of the affairs of the company is

5 *The Hindu Business Line*, 15th December 2011, available online, http://www.thehindubusinessline.com/industry-and-economy/article2717904.ece, accessed on 06.03.2012.

vested in the board of directors and all powers except those are specifically reserved for the general meeting by the Act or the articles or memorandum of association or otherwise must now be done by the board of directors vide s. 291 of the Companies Act 1956.[6]

The early legal position was that directors are not liable for the activities of the company. The House of Lords in *Wilson* v *Dickson*,[7] held:

> In the case of a company, the persons responsible would be the board of directors. There is a distinction between the board, who have the general management and control of the company, and a person appointed by the board or by the company at general meeting to do a particular class of acts ... he was not the alter ego of the company. He did not represent the company in the sense of making his fault, the fault of the company. The case of a company is analogous to the old case of a sixty-fourth owned ship. Sleeping ownership is recognized by law and is in the interest of public policy, and section 502, which is a reproduction of similar provisions in older Acts, expressly exempts a sleeping owner from responsibility. The object of the section is to restrict the doctrine of *respondeat superior* within certain defined limits.

But this position was changed with the decision of House of Lords in *Lennard's Carrying Company Ltd.* v *Asiatic Petroleum Co. Ltd.*, which explained the theory of 'directing mind' and held that:

> ... a corporation is an abstraction. It has no mind of its own any more than it has a body of its own; its active and directing will must consequently be sought in the person of somebody who for some purposes may be called an agent, but who is really the directing mind and will of the corporation, the very ego and centre of the personality of the corporation ... It must be upon the true construction of that section in such a case as the present one that the fault or privity is the fault or privity of somebody who is not merely a servant or agent for whom the company is liable upon the footing *respondeat superior*, but somebody for whom the

6 S.C. Sen, *The New Frontiers of Company Law* (Eastern Law House: Calcutta, 1971), p. 51, quoted in *Luxumi Tea Co. Ltd.* v *Pradipkumar Sarkar* (1990) Comp Cas 518 (SC).

7 [1818]2 B & Ald 2; [1915] AC 705 (HL).

> company is liable because his action is the very action of the company itself. It is not enough that the fault should be the fault of a servant in order to exonerate the owner, the fault must also be one which is not the fault of the owner, or a fault to which the owner is privy; and I take the view that when anybody sets up that section to excuse himself from the normal consequences of the maxim *respondeat superior* the burden lies upon him to do so.[8]

This decision is an extension of the theory in famous case of *Salomon* v *Salomon & Co.*,[9] in which the corporate responsibility was fixed through the doctrine of "lifting the corporate veil." The earlier position was that only employees are liable for the activities of the company and immunity was given to directors. But with this decision, the liability of a director is fixed and the principle was laid that a company works through its agents known as directors who are responsible for the day-to-day activities of the company.

Directors are held to be trustees and agents of the company. They are trustees of the properties and funds of the company which are under their control. As such their position is equal to a trustee and their duty towards the company is a fiduciary one. They can also be called as the agents of the company in as much as they can by their conduct bind the company in dealing with third parties; for example, allotment of shares, transfer of shares, investments etc. Almost all powers of directors are powers held by them in trust. The power to issue shares, to forfeit shares, to issue further capital, the power to accept or refuse transfer of shares and the general power of management are all held to be powers in trust which have to be exercised in good faith for the benefit of the company as a whole.

The articles of a company may designate its directors as governors, members of governing council or the board of management, or give them any other title. In case of associations or other bodies registered as companies under s. 25, the members of the executive committee or the governing body are directors for purposes of the Act, though they

8 [1915] AC 705 (HL).
9 [1897] AC 22 (HL).

may not be called by that name.[10] The position of directors, their duties and liabilities are complex in the modern corporate world. It is necessary to make a thorough research on the subject to analyze the role of company directors in the globalized world.

Break-up of the book

The whole work stands divided into 10 chapters. The forthcoming chapters represent and attempt to analyze the various positions of directors, their duties, and liabilities in a fiduciary capacity. The corporate accountability of directors has to be re-defined in the emerging situation, and the liability of each and every organ to be attributed in order to identify who is "managing" the company in reality. The role of the "regulator" is supreme in such situations and a regulator without "teeth" is not good for the Indian corporate sector and the further growth of the economy.

The first chapter examines the "characteristics" of company directors, qualifications, appointment, remuneration, positions, limitations, disqualifications, resignation, and removal through the analysis of various Committee Reports on corporate governance. The independent directors and their positions in a company are analyzed in the light of various company laws and judicial decisions of various forums. The Companies Act 1956 makes serious attempt to define their position. Section 2(13) of the Act provides that "director includes any person occupying the position of a director, by whatever name called". They are called sometimes as agents and sometimes as trustees and managing partners. They are however not servants or employees of the company. There is no precise definition of the term Directors. The company law of England or those of any other Common Law countries have not made any attempt to define it other than giving a vague explanation. The Courts also have made some vain attempts to define the same. Being an artificial person, the company cannot act for itself. It is the directors who act for and on behalf of the company. The general principles of the law of principal and agent thus regulate in most respects the relationship of the company and its directors. Again a company cannot look after its property and conduct its money transactions, as these are

10 Section 25 provides for registration of companies with an objective of charitable purposes, in furtherance of art, science, commerce, culture, etc.

being entrusted with the directors. So they can rightly be considered as trustees of the company. They are only treated as trustees of company's money and property and trustees of the powers entrusted to them, and not in all aspects.

Again the company being an artificial person cannot be held liable for wrongful acts which require the requisite *mens rea*. Here the actions and intentions of the directors are treated at par with that of a company and are considered in effect as the very actions and intentions of the Company. Thus directors are treated as organs of the company, for whose action the company is held liable just as natural persons. So, directors can be treated as agents, trustees, members and organs of the company.

A company is described as a group of persons associated together for attaining a common object. On registration the company is regarded as an entity separate from its members. Though a legal entity in the eye of law, it is an artificial person; it cannot act on its own. So the entire management of the company is vested with the Board of Directors. They are described as the central organ or the brain of the body corporate. Their powers and functions are co-extensive with that of the company and are exercised in their personal discretion. Chapter 2 is devoted to analyze the position and possibilities of directors under different names like agents, trustees, employees, managers, members of the company and organs of the company.

Chapter 3 is devoted to analyze the powers of directors and director board of companies. The directors have wide discretion, like the general powers of management and control. The issue and transfer of shares, the further issue of shares, debentures, declaration of dividends, the acquisition, holding and disposal of property, capital and money, monetary transactions like borrowing, lending and investment, power to enter into contracts for and on behalf of the company are all powers exercised by them in their personal discretion. This discretion cannot be exercised arbitrarily and must be exercised in good faith and for the best interest of the company.

The doctrine of "fiduciary duties" was developed by common-law judges and was later incorporated in the company laws of most of the nations. Most important among them are the duty of trust, duty of good faith and the duty to consider the beneficial interest of the company. As a fiduciary, directors have a duty towards the company, shareholders, employees, and creditors, in addition to the director's limitations in using their discretion, duty of good faith and *bona fides*, duty to promote the interest of the company, duty to use due diligence and skill, duty to reveal conflicts of interest and profits, fiduciary obligation and abuse of confidence, the powers in purchase of shares etc. These are dealt with in Chapter 4.

A fiduciary must not place himself in a situation where his personal interests conflict or may likely to conflict with his duties towards his *cestui que trust*. The Indian Companies Act contemplates certain circumstances where the duties and personal interests of the directors may come into conflict with each other. Contracts with the company are the major area in which a director may have a personal interest which may come into conflict with the interest of the company. A director is not expected to conduct a business competing with that of the company. He should not abuse or misappropriate the properties and funds of the company.

A fiduciary is not expected to make secret profits by using his position held. They are not entitled to receive any benefit which they would not have reaped but for some misuse of their special position. This also includes various forms of secret profits and equitable principle and statutory duty of disclosure of such interests.

The first and foremost duty of every person in fiduciary position is to act with honesty. They should not abuse the confidence reposed in them. Abuse and misappropriation of corporate opportunities, fraudulent transfer of controlling block of shares, assisting mischievous takeover bids and sharing proceeds of such takeover bids may all be quoted as instances of abuse of confidence. Chapter 5 deals with all these aspects and the related procedures to be followed.

The main question is: who is liable for illegal activities of a company? The liabilities for various activities of the companies are fixed with directors. These liabilities include their negligence, liability for breach of warranty of authority, liability for breach of contract, liability in tort, liability in company's debts, liability for negligent advice, liability for frauds and liability for insider trading. Chapter 6 is devoted to discuss the breach of various fiduciary duties of directors.

Prosecution of directors for illegal activities, which are contained in a pool of legislations like the Companies Act 1956, criminal law,

Negotiable Instruments Act 1881, Food Adulteration Act 1954, pollution laws, labour laws, tax laws, etc. are dealt in Chapter 7.

The fiduciary duties which the directors owe to the company make them liable for breach of trust when these duties are violated or disregarded. In such situations, general principles of equity and common law come to the rescue of the company and its share holders. In case of a breach of fiduciary duties by the directors, the major remedies available to the injured in a case of a breach of fiduciary duties are injunctions, compensation, restoration of property, rescission of the contract in question, and summary dismissal. These and related remedies are described in Chapter 8.

Chapter 9 deals with the 21st century's innovation in Company Law through Companies (Amendment) Bill 1997, Companies (Second Amendment) Bill 1999, Companies (Amendment) Bill 2000, Companies (Amendment) Bill 2003, Companies Bill 2008 and Companies Bill 2009. The 2009 Bill has again resurfaced in the name of "The Companies Bill 2011". The new Bill is expected to change the entire realm of company law administration in India. But it is only possible after it becomes an Act.

Chapter 10 is devoted to analyze the efficacy of the techniques of enforcing the fiduciary duties of directors and the major drawbacks and shortcomings in the present system of enforcement. The undue adherence to the corporate entity, principle, exclusion clauses incorporated in the articles of companies, growing professionalism in the management of companies, exemption and release of directors from liability by the Company and above all, the procedural limitations are all hindrances in enforcing the duties of directors. As a whole the chapter is critical, suggestive and conclusion of the study.

1

Company and its Directors

1.1 The company

The word 'company' is an amalgamation of Latin words, 'Com' meaning 'with or together' and 'Pains' meaning 'bread'. Originally, it has taken from the French word 'companio' referred to a group of people who took their meals together or one who eats bread with you.[1] A company is nothing but a group of persons who have come together or who have contributed money for some common purpose and have incorporated themselves into a distinct legal entity in the form of a company for a particular purpose.[2] Under Halsbury's *Laws of England* the term 'company' has been defined as a collection of many individuals united into one body under special denomination, having perpetual succession under an artificial form and a common seal.[3] The Bombay High Court in *Pannaji Devichand* v *Senaji Kapurchand,*[4] it was held that a syndicate of more than 20 people joined together to do "business" outside the purview of s. 4(2) of the Companies Act 1913 was held as illegal. The company is a group of people who is authorized to do business under the established law.

In short, a company is a juristic personality run by directors on behalf of shareholders. A company is indeed a person, but a juridical person and the directors as a body endow the juridical person with human face that can act and react. A company is thus a potentially complex organization, which is assimilated into the pre-existing

1 http://thinkexist.com/dictionary/meaning/company, visited on 10.06.2009.
2 wordnet.princeton.edu/perl/webwn, visited on 06.06.2009.
3 Halsbury's *Laws of England*, 4th Ed., vol. 9, para 1204.
4 (1934)4 Comp Cas 444.

individualistic framework of the law by pursuit of fiction and analogy with a natural person.[5] The most important legal fiction in a company is that it is a different 'legal personality' from its promoters, and directors of the company.[6] The Privy Council also confirmed this position in *E.B.M. Co. Ltd.* v *Dominion Bank,*[7] it was observed that "the distinction should be clearly marked, observed and maintained between an incorporated company's legal entity and its actions, assets, rights and liabilities on the one hand and the individual share-holders and their actions, rights and liabilities on the other". According to the Indian Penal Code the definition of word "Person" includes a company,[8] which is not a natural person having its own body, mind and soul. Its activities are instituted, regulated, controlled and activated by directing hand and mind of natural persons. The company hence is always called as a juristic person, a separate legal entity distinct from its promoters or directors.

According to the proposed new comprehensive company law: "company means a company incorporated under this Act or under any previous company law."[9] It included another category; "Small Company" as:

> "Small company" means a company, other than a public company,—
>
> (1) whose paid-up share capital does not exceed such amount as may be prescribed and the prescribed amount shall not be more than five crore rupees; or
>
> (2) whose turnover as per its last profit and loss account does not exceed such amount as may be prescribed and the prescribed amount shall not be more than twenty crore rupees...[10]

Another category of company proposed by the new law is "one person company", it defines: "One Person Company" means a company which has only one person as a member.[11] Section 2(11) of the Companies Bill 2011 defines a company as:

5 *Assistant Commissioner, IT* v *Velliappa Textiles Ltd.* AIR 2004 SC 86; (2003)11 SCC 405; 2004 Cr LJ 1221.
6 *Salomon* v *Salomon & Co. Ltd.* [1897] AC 22; [1895-97] All ER Rep 9.
7 (1937)7 Comp Cas 448; AIR 1937 PC 729.
8 Section 11.
9 Section 2(1)(*t*) of 2009 Bill and s. 2(20) of the 2011 Bill.
10 Section 2(1)(*zzzg*) of 2009 Bill.
11 Section 2(1)(*zzk*) of 2009 Bill.

"Body corporate" or "corporation" includes a company incorporated outside India, but does not include—

(*i*) a co-operative society registered under any law relating to co-operative societies; and

(*ii*) any other body corporate (not being a company as defined in this Act), which the Central Government may, by notification, specify in this behalf.

The Indian Supreme Court (SC) held that a company cannot have the status of a citizen under the Constitution of India in *State Trading Corporation of India* v *CTO*.[12] A company is an artificial person and it can work only through directors.[13] The human agency through which the affairs of the company are managed is called 'directors.' The Bombay High Court also held that a company registered under the Indian Companies Act is a legal person, separate and distinct from its individual members. Hence, a shareholder, a depositor or a director is not entitled to move a petition for infringement of the rights of the company unless by the action impugned his rights are also infringed. The natural persons who are directing mind of the company are the administrators of a company, i.e., directors or by whatever name they are called. The relationship between managers and shareholders are completely governed by a contract. The shareholders in a large establishment don't have the ability or incentive to manage the day-to-day affairs of a company. Consequently, they in turn elect directors and who in turn appoint officers to run the company.[14]

In *Lee* v *Lee's Air Farming Ltd.*,[15] the appellant's husband was working as chief pilot of the company and held 2,999 out of 3000 shares and appointed himself as sole governing director. He was killed in an air crash when working for the company. The question was whether he could be considered as a "worker" under the Workmen Compensation Act of 1922 (NZ) and Mrs. Lee be entitled to compensation. The Court of Appeal (NZ) held that he was not a worker and Mrs. Lee was not entitled to compensation. She successfully appealed and the Lordships followed the decision in *Salomon*'s case and held that the company was distinct from the deceased. The company

12 AIR 1963 SC 1811; (1963)33 Comp Cas 1057 (SC).

13 *Ferguson* v *Wilson* [1866] LR 2 Ch App 77.

14 Mark E. Van Der Weide, *Against Fiduciary Duties to Corporate Stakeholders*, Delware Journal of Corporate Law, vol. 21, pp. 21-86.

15 [1961] AC 12.

and the deceased were separate legal entities. There can be a contract between the company and the sole director for employment. Hence, Mrs. Lee succeeded in claiming the compensation from the company for the death of her husband as a worker of the company, even though he himself was the major shareholder and sole director. It is clear that company is a separate legal personality from its shareholders and directors.

1.2 Company Directors

The Companies Act 1956 defines "director includes any person occupying the position of director, by whatever name called."[16] The British Companies Act 1985 also provides almost the same definition. It provides that "it shall include any person occupying the position of a director, by whatever name called."[17] It is not the name by which a person is called but the position he occupies and the functions and duties which he discharges that determine whether in fact he is a director or not. His function as a director is most important rather than by whatever name he is called.[18] They can be called governors, members of governing council, or the board of management.[19] Section 303 (1) of the Companies Act (British) provides that any person with whose directions or instructions the board of directors is accustomed to act is also deemed to be a director. However, if a person illegally occupies the position of a director, without being lawfully appointed, he cannot be treated as a director.[20] An executive of a company who is named as Executive Director, but not a member of a board is not a director designated under the Act.

The Andhra Pradesh High Court in *Deen Dayalu* v *Sri B.P. Reddy*,[1] held that a manager or any other managerial personnel is, however, not a director. In *Global Drugs (P) Ltd.* v *M. Venkatnarayana,*[2] it was held that a director is an individual lawfully appointed to the Board of Directors of a company which is duly constituted to direct, control and supervise the affairs of a company. In all cases, it is not the name

16 Section 2(13).
17 British Companies Act 1985, s. 741(1).
18 *In Re, Forest of Dean Coal Mining Co.* [1878]10 Ch D 450.
19 Pennington, *Company Law*, 5th Ed., p. 609.
20 *Dean* v *Hiesler* [1942]2 All ER 340 (KB).
1 (1984)2 Comp LJ 396.
2 (2008)141 Comp Cas 935; (2008)84 SCL 120 (AP).

but the position and functions that determine the real status of a director. Sub-section (25) of s. 2 of the Act defined 'managing agent' and the provision was deleted by the amendment in 2000.[3] Sub-section (26) of s. 2 included 'managing director' also as a director of a company.[4] Section 2(30) of the Act defines 'officer' that includes director as well.[5] The board of directors comprises directors as a body acting collectively except where individual duties and powers are conferred on or delegated to individual directors.[6] The board of directors is the 'directing mind' of the company. The Companies Act specifies where the company itself is to act both as principal and the agent and where the board of directors is to act on its behalf. The Companies Bill 2009 defines directors as "director" means a director appointed to the Board of a company, and includes a deemed director.[7] The 2011 Bill defines a director as "director means a director appointed to the Board of a company".[8] If a person who has been appointed as a director but not consented to be the director, cannot be called as a director.[9] A "deemed director" means a person under whose advice, instructions or directions,

3 (The section reads) Prior to deletion s. 2(25) was as: "managing agent means any individual, firm or body corporate entitled, subject to the provisions of this Act, to the management of the whole, or substantially the whole, of the affairs of a company by virtue of an agreement with the company, or by virtue of its memorandum or articles of association, and includes any individual, firm or body corporate occupying the position of a managing agent, by whatever the name called."

4 "managing director means a director who, by virtue of an agreement with the company or of a resolution passed by the company in general meeting or by its Board of directors, or by virtue of its memorandum or articles of association, is entrusted with substantial powers of management which would not otherwise be exercisable by him, and includes a director occupying the position of managing director, by whatever name called." Wordings in a quotation cannot be changed?

5 This provision was modified by the Companies (Amendment) Act 2000. Prior to its amendment it stood as: "officer" includes any director, managing agent, secretaries and treasurers, manager or secretary; where the managing agent or the secretaries and treasurers are a firm, also includes any partner in the firm; and where the managing agent or the secretaries and treasurers are a body corporate, also includes any director, managing agent, secretaries and treasurers or manager of the body corporate; but, save in ss. 477, 478, 539, 543, 545, 621, 625 and 633 does not include an auditor.

6 Clause (6).

7 Section 2(*zi*) of the Companies Bill 2009 and s. 2(34) of the Companies Bill 2011.

8 Section 2(34) of the Companies Bill 2011.

9 *British Empire Match Co. Ltd., Re* [1888]59 LT 291. See also *Laljibhai C. Kapadia* v *Lalji B. Desai* (1973)43 Comp Cas 17 (Bom).

the Board of Directors is accustomed to act, but does not include a person who has been engaged by the company to advise it in a professional capacity.[10] The "Board of Directors" or "Board", in relation to a company, means the collective body of the directors of the company.[11]

A director is an agent of the company for the conduct of business of the company. The directors' major role is to approve the commercial roles and strategies of the company with a view to make profit.[12] The directors carry out the company's management functions and they speak as a company.[13] According to s. 2(30) of the Companies Act, the definition of an "officer" includes any director, manager or secretary or any person in accordance with whose direction or instructions the Board of Director's or any one or more of the directors is or are accustomed to act. As agents or officers of the company, directors have a fiduciary relation with the company, its shareholders and investors.[14] Directors are bound to use fair and reasonable diligence in discharging the duties and to act honestly, and with such care as may be reasonably expected from, having regard to their knowledge and experience. Express liability would usually arise only when a director has personally guaranteed the performance of a contract. As far as fiduciary duties are concerned, any breach by directors would make them liable. Directors would be liable for negligence, breach of trust, misfeasance, and *ultra vires* actions and for misappropriation of funds of the company. The Kumaramangalam Birla Committee on Corporate Governance characterizes directors as:

> The board of a company provides leadership and strategic guidance, objective judgment independent of management to the company and exercises control over the company, while remaining at all times accountable to the shareholders. The measure of the board is not simply whether it fulfills its legal requirements but more importantly, the board's attitude and the manner it translates its

10 Section 2(*ze*) of the Companies Bill 2009.

11 Section 2(*j*) of the Companies Bill 2009, s. 2(10) of the 2011 Bill retains the same definition.

12 Barbara Mescher and Bryan Howieson, *Corporate Governance Law Review,* vol. 1:1, 2005, p. 98.

13 *Tesco Supermarkets Ltd.* v *Nattrass* [1972] AC 153; [1971]2 WLR 166; *Hamilton* v *Whitehead* [1988]166 CLR 121.

14 *Darvall* v *North Sydney Brick and Tile Co. Ltd.* [1987]16 NSWLR 212; 12 ACLR 537.

awareness and understanding of its responsibilities. An effective corporate governance system is one, which allows the board to perform these dual functions efficiently. The board of directors of a company thus directs and controls the management of a company and is accountable to the shareholders.[15]

1.3 Minimum number of Directors

The Companies Act requires that a minimum number of directors to be appointed in a company according to the nature of the company from the date of its incorporation.[16] But if the number goes below the statutory minimum, the Board cannot be held unless the remaining directors co-opt[17] one or more directors so that the quorum could be met. In the case of a company happened to be directorless, the power of management would revert back to the company in general meeting.[18] The Companies Act 1956 provides that:

> Every public company (other than a public company which become such by virtue of s. 43A) shall have not less than three directors. Provided that a public company having:
>
> (*a*) a paid-up capital of five crore rupees or more;
>
> (*b*) one thousand or more small shareholders,
>
> (*c*) may have a director elected by such small shareholders in the manner as may be prescribed.
>
> *Explanation.* For the purpose of this sub-section "small shareholders" means a shareholder holding shares of nominal value of twenty thousand rupees or less in a public company to which this section applies.[19]
>
> 2. Every other company shall have at least two directors.[20]

---

15 Kumaramangalam Birla Committee Report on Corporate Governance, para 6.1, available on http://web.sebi.gov.in/commreport/corpgov.html, visited on 20.01.2009.

16 Section 252 of the Companies Act 1956.

17 The co-option should be exercised in the best interest of the shareholders. *A. Anantalakshmi Ammal* v *Indian Trades and Investments Ltd.* (1952)22 Comp Cas 324; AIR 1953 Mad 467 (Mad).

18 *Alexander Ward & Co Ltd.* v *Samyang Navigation Co. Ltd.* [1973]3 LT (Notes) 80 approved in appeal by the House of Lords (1975)1 WLR 673.

19 This proviso to sub-sec. (1) was inserted by Companies Amendment Act 2000. The provisions are of directory in nature. The rules were framed in 2001 (Companies Appointment of Small Share Holders Director) Rules 2001.

20 Section 252 of the Companies Act 1956. The Companies Bill 2008, included one Person Company with a single member, s. 2(*zzk*).

3. The directors of a company collectively are referred to in this Act as the "Board of Directors" or "Board."

The Companies Bill 2009 provides that:

A company may be formed for any lawful purpose by any—

(*a*) seven or more persons, where the company to be formed is to be a public company, or

(*b*) two or more persons, where the company to be formed is to be a private company, or

(*c*) one person, where the company to be formed is to be a One Person Company,

by subscribing their names or his name to a memorandum in the manner prescribed and complying with the requirements of this Act in respect of registration:

Provided that the memorandum of a One Person Company shall indicate the name of the person who shall, in the event of the subscriber's death, disability or otherwise, become the member of the company:

Provided further that it shall be the duty of the member of a One Person Company to intimate the Registrar the change, if any, in the name of the person referred to in the preceding proviso and indicated in the memorandum within such time and in such form as may be prescribed, and any such change shall not be deemed to be an alteration of the memorandum.[1]

Section 3(1) of the Companies Bill 2011 follows the same provision on formation of a company.

In case the first directors are not appointed by the promoters of a company, subscribers of the memorandum shall be deemed to be the directors of the company until the directors are duly appointed. This provision can be found in s. 282 of the British Companies Act 1985 which states that "(1) Every company registered on or after 1st November 1929 (other than a private company) shall have at least two directors; (2) Every company registered before that date (other than a private company) shall have at least one director; (3) Every private company shall have at least one director". Usually the number of directors of a company will be provided in the articles of association. In such a situation, a smaller number cannot act unless the articles also provide that they can act notwithstanding vacancies.[2]

1 Section 3(1) of the Companies Bill 2009.

2 *In Re, Scottish Petroleum Co.* [1883]23 Ch D 413; *Bank of Syria* [1900]2 Ch 272, appeal, [1901] Ch 115 (CA).

1.4 Maximum number of Directors and limitations

There is no limit to the maximum number of directors in a company in the Indian law.[3] The increase in the number of directors of a public company is regulated by s. 259. Where a minimum number is fixed by the statute, if the number falls below the minimum number, the remaining directors cannot act. The business completed after the number fell below the minimum was held to be invalid.[4] The strength of the board includes the number of directors who are actually holding the office excluding the vacancies. However, it is valid to delegate all the powers of the board of directors to a single named person who is a director of the company and the directorship is within the valid period.[5]

The annual general meeting can reduce the number of directors from the maximum prescribed in articles of association. In order to reduce the number in such circumstances, alteration of articles is not required.[6] If the articles of a company provide that the number of directors may be varied by the general meeting by an ordinary resolution, then the articles need not be altered by a special resolution.[7] But the manner or mode of appointment being dependent on the memorandum or articles or agreement or resolution of the company or of the boards of directors, any slightest change or variation in it will bring the case under the provisions of s. 268 requiring Central Government approval. Small shareholders can elect their representative according to the prescribed rules framed in 2001. The candidate has to be elected same way as other candidates.[8]

No person can be a director in more than 15 companies at a time.[9] This rule does not extend to a person being the manger of a company other than the 15 companies of which he is a director. This includes

3 The maximum number of directors prescribed in the Companies Bill 2008 is, for public companies, twelve excluding the directors nominated by the lending institutions.

4 *In Re Sly, Spink & Co.* [1911]2 Ch 430; *Re, Alma Spinning Co.* [1880]16 Ch D 681.

5 *Whitehouse* v *Carlton Hotel Pty. Ltd.* [1897]70 Aust LR 251 (Aust).

6 *Gur Prasad Kapoor* v *Rameshwar Prasad* (1933)3 Comp Cas 153; AIR 1933 All 344.

7 *Ramkrissen* v *Satyacharan* AIR 1950 PC 81; 20 Comp Cas 133.

8 See the 'appointment' section for their qualifications and disqualifications.

9 Section 275. Prior to the Companies (Amendment) Act 2000, the ceiling was 20 companies.

public as well as private companies.[10] This prohibition also does not extend to the holding of directorships in other corporate bodies, being foreign companies, as they do not come within the definition of "company" under s. 2(10) and s. 3 of the Act. However, his liberty can be curtailed by a contract of exclusive service. He can be precluded by contract and is already bound by a fiduciary duty not to pass on confidential information from one company to the other.[11] The Kumaramangalam Birla and Narayana Murthy Committee on Corporate Governance suggested ceiling on a director to become member in different committees of a company also.

Presently, a director cannot be a member in more than 10 committees or act as Chairman of more than five committees across all companies. It is mandatory for every director to inform the company about the committee positions he occupies in other companies. Any director holding office in more than 15 companies shall be punishable with a fine which may extend to ₹ 50000.

1.5 Appointment of Directors

The first directors of a company are usually named in its articles of association, or the articles provide that the first directors shall be appointed by the subscribers of the memorandum and articles. Where the articles do not provide for the appointment of first directors, the subscribers to the memorandum, who are individuals, shall be deemed to be the first directors of the company subject to the regulations of the company's articles. Section 254[12] of the Act provides that subscribers to the memorandum are deemed to be directors. Where the subscribers are directors, under such an article they hold office until the first directors are actually appointed.[13]

First directors can also be appointed by naming them in the articles of association. In that case, the subscribers to the memorandum will not be the directors of the company. When there are no validly appointed directors functioning, the shareholders have the right to appoint

10 Section 278.

11 *On the Street Pty Ltd.* v *Cott* [1990]3 ACSR 54 (Aust).

12 Section 254 of the Act provides: "In default of and subject to any regulations in the articles of a company, subscribers of the memorandum who are individuals, shall be deemed to be the directors of the company, until the directors are duly appointed in accordance with section 255."

13 *Morley (John) Building Co.* v *Barras* [1891]2 Ch 386.

directors at the annual general meeting.[14] A meeting is not necessary if all the subscribers concur with the appointment.[15] If the articles are silent as to the appointment of directors, or do not specifically provide for appointment of directors otherwise than in a general meeting, then the directors are to be appointed in general meeting by the shareholders.[16] Individual subscribers of the memorandum shall be deemed to be the directors even though they do not hold qualification shares, though the articles of the company require that qualification shares must be held in order to be appointed as directors. This is because qualification shares are required to be held only for being appointed as directors and not for being deemed to be directors.[17]

Section 253 stipulates that no body corporate, association or firm shall be appointed as director of a company, and only an individual can be appointed. The Supreme Court pointed out the importance as to why it is necessary that only an individual should be director of a company in *Oriental Metal Pressing Works (P) Ltd.* v *Bhaskar Kashinath Thakoor.*[18] Pointing out the reason for the legislative restriction, the Court emphasized that the office of a director is to a certain extent an office akin to a trust and therefore it was felt desirable that some individual human being should be available as a field of accountability. It is difficult to fix responsibility for the failure to carry out the trust, and it might be difficult to fix that responsibility if the director is a corporation or an association of persons.

No director shall be appointed or reappointed if he has not been allotted a Director Identification Number (DIN) according to s. 266B.[19] It is a statutory requirement to have every appointment and re-appointment of any individual as a director of a company. However, under the English law a company or other body corporate can be appointed as director of another company.[20] New Zealand law doesn't

14 *Viswanathan (B.N.)* v *Tiffins Barytes Asbestis & Paints Ltd.* (1953)23 Comp Cas 29.

15 *Re Great Northern Salt & Chemical Works, ex p Kennedy* [1890]44 Ch D 472.

16 *Swapan Das Gupta* v *Navin Chand Suchanti* (1988)3 Comp LJ 76 (Cal).

17 A.M. Chakraborti, *Company Law,* 1994, p. 815.

18 (1961)31 Comp Cas 143; AIR 1961 SC 573.

19 This provision has been *inserted* by the Companies (Amendment) Act 2006.

20 *Bulawayo Market & Officers Co. Ltd., Re* [1907]2 Ch 458.

permit the partners of a firm collectively to be appointed as directors.[21] But the representative of a firm may be elected or nominated as a director.[1] In the early 1930s the investment in companies was based on the goodwill of the directors. Their functions at that point of time were explained as two fold:

> Their names act first as the bait by which the public is induced to acquire the shares of the company, and, secondly, after the company has been formed, as a means of preserving confidence. Though the 'prestige of the aristocracy' even in conservative England is not what it used to be, nevertheless, at company meetings 'the medieval glamour still shines bright, and the average shareholder dearly loves a lord.[2]

Directors have to retire by rotation at every annual general meeting. They will be those who have been longest in office since their last appointment, but as between persons who became directors on the same day, those who are to retire shall, in default of and subject to any agreement among themselves, be determined by lot. The annual general meeting will appoint directors in place of every director who retires.[3] If the company wants to increase the number of directors beyond the prescribed limit, it has to pass special resolution to that effect. Section 259 stipulates that prior sanction of the Central Government is necessary to increase the number of directors in certain cases.[4]

21 *Commercial Management Ltd.* v *Registrar of Companies* [1987] 1 NZ LR 744.
1 *Motion Picture Assn., in re.* (1984)55 Comp Cas 375 (Del).
2 William O. Douglas, *Directors' Who do not Direct*, Harvard Law Review, vol. 47(8), 1934, p. 1318.
3 Section 257 of the Act.
4 Section 259: In the case of a public company or a private company which is a subsidiary of a public company, any increase in the number of its directors, except—
 (*a*) in the case of a company which was in existence on the 21st day of July, 1951, an increase which was within the permissible maximum under its articles as in force on that date, and
 (*b*) in the case of a company which came or may come into existence after that date, an increase which is within the permissible maximum under its articles as first registered,

shall not have any effect unless approved by the Central Government; and shall become void if, and in so far as, it is disapproved by that Government:

Provided that where such permissible maximum is twelve or less than twelve, no approval of the Central Government shall be required if the increase in the number of its directors does not make the total number of its directors more than twelve.

1.6 Retirement of Directors

The retirement of directors by rotation shall be made at the annual general meeting.[5] However, it does not prevent the adoption by a company of regulations providing for any preliminary mode of election such as choosing the candidates by postal voting, or ballot or otherwise and then submitting those chosen for approval by the annual general meeting, provided that such procedure does not contravene any provisions of the Act. A person who is not a retiring director shall be eligible for appointment to the office of a director at any general meeting.[6] The power of increasing or reducing the number of directors is vested with the board of directors and they have to make a proposal for the same to the general body. A shareholder can make a proposal of this kind through a requisition.[7] In the absence of any provision in the articles, directors of an independent private company are entitled to continue until removed under s. 284.[8]

A company is not bound to appoint the maximum number of directors fixed by the articles. It can appoint the number of directors between the minimum and the maximum prescribed in the articles of association by resolution at general meeting.[9] If the number of directors authorized by the articles of association is seven and there are only five directors functioning, appointment of two more directors does not require a separate resolution of the company as it is implicit in the resolution to increase the number.[10] Any irregular appointment can be corrected by a subsequent ratification by the general body meeting. When an increase in the number of directors involve an alteration of the articles, a special resolution is necessary for the purpose.[11] In any public company or a private company which is a subsidiary of a public company, any increase in number of its directors exceeding twelve requires Central Government's permission.[12] Increasing the number

5 Section 256 of the Act.

6 Section 257 and the Companies (Amendment) Act 1988, s. 45 vide GSR No. 559(E), dated 10.06.1988.

7 *Ravi Shankar Taneja* v *Motherson Triplex Tools P. Ltd.* (2001)4 Comp LJ 102.

8 *S. Labh Singh* v *Panaser Mech. Works (P) Ltd.* (1987)61 Comp Cas 618.

9 *Pazhamalai (S)* v *Aruna Sugars Ltd.* (1984)55 Comp Cas 500 (Mad).

10 This view has been expressed by Bhasme, J, of the Bombay High Court in *Laljibhai C. Kapadia* v *Lalji B. Desai* (1973)43 Comp Cas 17 (Bom).

11 *Ram Kissendas Dhanuka* v *Satya Charan Law* (1950)20 Comp Cas 133.

12 Section 259.

of directors to fifteen also requires approval of the Central Government.[13]

1.7 Small shareholders' Director

There are special rules pertaining to the election of small shareholders' director. A public company may by its own motion be able to appoint a director. Alternatively, not less than one-tenth of the total number of small shareholders (not less than 100 shareholders) may propose the name of a small shareholder for appointment as a director. In either case, the appointment should be with the approval of the small shareholders.[14]

In the developed countries like the US and European countries like Scandinavian nations, Germany, Luxembourg and Austria, the workers participation in the director board of companies was talked about.[15] This is basically with a social objective of integrating workers' interest in decision making of the companies and in the management. However, this particular practice is not yet experimented in India so far.

The directors are not personally liable for acts committed in the course of business even though their appointments are irregular. The case of *British Asbestos Co. Ltd.* v *Boyd,*[16] was a case of defective appointment and the Court held that the irregularities in the appointment and subsequent acts of the directors irregularly appointed were validated by s. 108 and s. 67 of the Companies Act. In this case s. 89 provided the circumstances under which the office of a director shall be vacated. One of the directors, Boyd had vacated office and the contingent irregularities were not brought to the notice of the defendant company. The irregularities complained of consisted in acting as

13 *Vinod Kumar Mittal* v *Kaveri Lime Industries Ltd.* (2000)2 Comp LJ 354 (CLB).

14 Election of a small shareholder of a public company has to be made by postal ballot in accordance with the postal ballot rules [Rule 4(4)]. Such director cannot hold office in more than two companies at a time. He cannot be appointed as managing director or whole-time director. The term of office of small share holders' director is a maximum period of 3 years. He may be re-elected on the expiry of his tenure for another period of 3 years [sub-rules (6), (7) of Rule 4) of the Companies (Passing of the Resolution by Postal Ballot) Rules 2001.

15 Tove H. Hammer, Steven C. Curral and Robert N. Stern, *Worker Representation on Boards of Directors—A Study of Competing Roles*, Industrial and Labour Relations Review, vol. 44(4), 1991.

16 [1903]2 Ch 439.

director, convening meetings of the company ordinary and extra-ordinary, signing balance-sheets, recommending directors for re-election, etc. On the finding that there was no evidence that the directors including Boyd and Reed had not acted in good faith in all they did, the Court held that the irregularities were condoned by s. 67 of the Act and s. 108 of the Companies Act.

The Companies Bill 2009 provides that:

> Section 132. (1) Every company shall have a Board of Directors consisting of only individuals as Directors and shall have—
>
> (*a*) a minimum number of three directors in the case of a public company, two directors in the case of a private company, and one director in the case of a One Person Company; and
>
> (*b*) a maximum of twelve (replaced as 15 Directors by the Companies Bill, 2011) Directors, excluding the Directors nominated by the lending institutions.

The 2009 bill stipulates that one of the directors shall at least be a person ordinarily resident in India.[17]

1.8 Qualifications

An individual who is an adult and of sound mind having contractual capacity can be a director. A lunatic, an undisclosed bankrupt, and persons suffering from legal disabilities cannot be appointed as directors. No body corporate, association or firm shall be appointed as a director of a company, and only an individual shall be so appointed. There is no bar to appoint a foreigner as a director except an alien enemy. The Companies Act has not prescribed any academic or professional qualifications for directors. The Act does not also impose any share qualification on the directors, unless the company's articles contain a provision to that effect. Usually, the articles may provide for a minimum share qualification. The subsidiaries of a public company have fixed minimum number of share qualification under section 270 which provides:

(*i*) each director must take his qualification shares within 2 months after his appointment;

17 *Explanation.* For the purposes of this sub-section, "ordinarily resident in India" means a person who stays in India for a total period of not less than one hundred and eighty-two days in a calendar year. Same provision followed in the Companies Bill 2001 in s. 149(2).

(*ii*) the nominal value of the qualification shares must not exceed ₹ 5000 or the nominal value of one share where it exceeds ₹ 5000; and

(*iii*) share warrants will not count for the purposes of share qualification.

If a director fails to obtain his qualification shares within two months, he vacates office automatically on the expiry of two months after the date of his appointment. If he works as a director after two months he shall be liable to pay a fine which may extend to ₹ 500 for every day until he stops acting as such.[18] However, the articles of a company cannot compel a person to hold qualification shares before he is not elected as a director nor can these require him to obtain qualification shares within a shorter period than two months after his appointment.

Presently, permission of the Reserve Bank of India (RBI) is not required for a foreigner to be appointed as a director of an Indian company.[19] It was held in *Oriental Metal Pressing Works Pvt. Ltd* v *Bhaskar Kasinath Thakoor* by the SC that "the office of a director is to be extent an office of trust, there should be somebody readily available who can be held responsible for the failure to carry out the trust and it might be difficult to fix that responsibility if the director was a corporation or an association of persons".[20] There would be no perpetual management. Assignment of an office of director is also void even if it is passed by a special resolution of the company.[1] However, if the managing director had power under the articles of the company to appoint a person to be the managing director in succession to him, and in exercise of that power he had appointed somebody, it is valid under s. 255 of the Act.

The regulations of a company allowed the managing director (MD) to appoint 'any person' in his place, either *inter vivos* or by a testament. The appointment of a new MD, conveyed by the testament of the former, was contested. The court opined that under s. 312 of the Companies Act 1956 the word 'assignment' did not mean the same as 'appointment'. Moreover, s. 255 allows appointment of directors

18 Section 272.
19 Press Release 2005-2006/142. Dt. 2-8-2005.
20 (1960)30 Comp Cas 682 (SC).
1 Section 312 specifically forbids assignment of an office of director.

otherwise than by the company. It was held that the appellant had lawfully appointed the new MD in accordance with the powers given to him.[2]

1.9 Independent Directors

Now-a-days the role of independent directors is drawing wide attention especially in the context of public companies. The independent director is hailed as a way of improving the monitoring of corporate management and the quality of decision-making by corporate boards.[3] The fraud committed by the chairman and other directors of the premier Indian IT Company, "Satyam Computers" raises many questions of independent directors and their role in the administration and corporate governance of Indian Inc. The ₹ 7000 crore financial fraud was unveiled by the confessional statement of its chairman & managing director.[4] It points towards the need of urgent reform of Indian Companies Act and a watch on the functioning of giant Indian companies. It was reported that more than 340 independent directors resigned from Indian companies after the "Satyam" incident in 2009 January up to May, in order to save their reputation.[5] This shows the urgency to define the independent director's role, rights and liabilities in a company.

1.9.1 *SEBI's role and independent Directors*

SEBI has revised Clause 49 of the Listing Agreement of Companies,[6] which requires appointment of independent directors:

(*a*) By all entities seeking listing for the first time, at the time of listing.

(*b*) By all listed entities having a paid up share capital of ₹ 3 crores and above or net worth of ₹ 25 crores or more at any time in the history of the company. These companies shall be

2 *Oriental Metal Pressing Works* v *Bhaskar Kashinath Thakoor* AIR 1961 SC 573.

3 Katherine Hall and Suzanne Le Mire, *Independent Directors: Problem or Solution*, Monash Business Review, vol. 2:3, November 2006, paper available at http://www.buseco.monash.edu.au/mbr/assets/issue-five/independent-directors.pdf, visited on 21.01.2009.

4 *The Hindu Daily*, 9th January 2009.

5 Directordatabase.com, visited on 14.05.2009.

6 Revised SEBI/MRD/SE/31/2003/26/08 of dt. 26.08.2003.

required to comply with the requirement of the clause on or before 31st March 2004.[7]

The board of directors of the company has a combination of non-executive and executive directors. The number of independent directors would depend on whether Chairman is executive or non-executive. In case of non-executive chairman, at least one third of the board should comprise of independent directors and in case of an executive chairman, at least half of board should comprise of independent directors. Clause 49 also mandates firms to constitute an audit committee, with one of the directors as its members, and submit quarterly compliance report to the stock exchanges.

1.9.2 *Birla and Murthy Committee on Corporate Governance and Independent Directors*

The Kumaramangalam Birla Committee on Corporate Governance described the importance of independent directors and defined independence as under:

> Among the non-executive directors are independent directors, who have a key role in the entire mosaic of corporate governance. The Committee was of the view that it was important that independence be suitably, correctly and pragmatically defined, so that the definition itself does not become a constraint in the choice of independent directors on the boards of companies. The definition should bring out what in the view of the Committee is the touchstone of independence, and which should be sufficiently broad and flexible. It was agreed that "material pecuniary relationship which affects independence of a director" should be the litmus test of independence and the board of the company would exercise sufficient degree of maturity when left to itself, to determine whether a director is independent or not. *The Committee therefore agreed on the following definition of "independence." Independent directors are directors who apart from receiving director's remuneration do not have any other material pecuniary relationship or transactions with the company, its promoters, its management or its subsidiaries, which in the judgment of the board may affect their independence of judgment. Further, all*

7 It was extended up to 31th December 2005. http://www.sebi.gov.in/circulars/2005/dil0105.html, visited on 03.03.2009.

pecuniary relationships or transactions of the non-executive directors should be disclosed in the annual report.[8]

The Committee constituted by the Securities Exchange Board of India (SEBI) under the chairmanship of N.R. Narayana Murthy also defined who an independent director is. The report describes that:

> "*Explanation* (*i*): For the purpose of this clause, the expression 'independent director' shall mean non-executive director of the company who:
>
> (*a*) apart from receiving director's remuneration, does not have any material pecuniary relationships or transactions with the company, its promoters, its senior management or its holding company, its subsidiaries and associated companies;
>
> (*b*) is not related to promoters or management at the board level or at one level below the board;
>
> (*c*) has not been an executive of the company in the immediately preceding three financial years;
>
> (*d*) is not a partner or an executive of the statutory audit firm or the internal audit firm that is associated with the company, and has not been a partner or an executive of any such firm for the last three years. This will also apply to legal firm(s) and consulting firm(s) that have a material association with the entity;
>
> (*e*) is not a supplier, service provider or customer of the company. This should include lessor-lessee type relationships also; and
>
> (*f*) is not a substantial shareholder of the company, i.e. owning two percent or more of the block of voting shares."

In short, it can be said that an independent director is independent in judgment and no material or pecuniary relationship with the promoters. In UK, the Cadbury Report on Corporate Governance defines the independence as: "Apart from their directors' fees and shareholdings, they should be independent of management and free from any business or other relationship which could materially interfere with the exercise of their independent judgement".[9] Various reports attribute common fiduciary duties with independent directors. While each of the directors

8 The Committee recommended that "the non-executive directors, i.e. those who are independent and those who are not, help bring an independent judgement to bear on board's deliberations especially on issues of strategy, performance, management of conflicts and standards of conduct. The Committee therefore lays emphasis on the calibre of the non-executive directors, especially of the independent directors".

9 See www.independentdirector.co.uk, visited on 21.01.2009.

in the board represents the company as a whole and should be in a position to participate objectively and independently, the independent director (who is also a non-executive director) is there specifically to provide independent judgment and outside experience and objectivity. He is not subordinated to operational considerations on all issues which are brought to the board. In other words, he must be independent of management, that is, he must recognize the division between the board and management and not become involved in management issues or in managing the implementation of board policy. That is precisely why he may not be an officer of the corporation, nor provide any services, nor receive any significant income for other professional services to the corporation. Neither may he be related to an officer or in a senior management position of the corporation. Possibly the following role can be assigned to the independent directors:

1. Contribute to and constructively challenge development of company strategy.
2. Scrutinize management performance.
3. Satisfy them that financial information is accurate and ensure that robust risk management is in place.
4. Meet at least once in a year with the chairman or executive directors–and there should be a statement in the annual report saying whether such meetings have taken place.
5. Be prepared to attend AGMs and discuss issues relating to their roles (especially chairmen of committees).
6. Have a greater exposure to major shareholders (particularly the senior independent director).[10]

The Companies Bill 2009, defines independent director as:

"Independent director", in relation to the company, means a non-executive director of the company, other than a nominee director. According to s. 2(47) of the Companies Bill 2011, "independent director means an independent director referred to in sub-sec. 5 of s. 149". His qualifications prescribed are of a person of integrity and possesses relevant expertise and experience. He should not have any

10 Pawan Agarwalla, *http://www.legalservicesindia.com/articles/cor.htm,* visited on 23.01.2009.

relationship or transaction with the company, subsidiary, associated company, promoters or directors of the company. A personnel who had been employee of the company in any of the three consecutive preceding financial years cannot become an independent director. An earlier auditor or company secretary of the company or its subsidiary or associated company cannot become an independent director. An independent director shall not be entitled to any remuneration, other than sitting free, reimbursement of expenses for participation in the board and other meetings.[11]

In the present corporate situation in India, the independent directors have a crucial role in the administration and business of a company. All these recommendations and committee reports[12] in and outside India suggested reform in constitution of the board of directors. However, the Satyam fiasco raises the question of how well this reform strategy works in practice. Presently, independent directors are nominated by the management and are at the mercy of the promoters. So, the independence of the directors is "more a myth than a reality."[13] Many agree to this statement and it is high time to put huge penalties on all directors of the erring companies including the independent directors like in the US Sarbanes Oxley Act 2002 which provides for $5 million fine for individuals, $25 million for entities and prison term up to 20 years.

1.10 Additional Directors

> Section 260 provides that: *Nothing in sections 255, 258 or 259 shall affect any power conferred on the Board of directors by the articles to appoint additional directors:*
>
> Provided that such additional directors shall hold office only up to the date of the next annual general meeting of the company:
>
> Provided further that the number of the directors and additional directors together shall not exceed the maximum strength fixed for the Board by the articles.

This is an emergency provision and power given to the directors for appointing additional directors. The appointment lapses when the shareholders would normally assume control over the appointment or

11 Section 132(5) of the Companies Bill 2009.
12 For example, *Higgs Committee Report in UK*, 2003.
13 *Rediff News*, 14th January 2009.

the removal of directors at their ordinary general meeting.[14] The powers given under this section are applicable to public as well as private companies. But if there is no power given in the articles, the Board cannot appoint additional directors.[15] Appointment of an additional director does not amount to a contract nor is it an arrangement by or on behalf of the company.[16] Where the number of directors is reduced to one, it has been held that he can appoint additional directors.[17] The Board cannot appoint additional directors exceeding the number prescribed in the articles of association. An additional director can hold office only up to the date of the next annual general meeting of the company. If the meeting is not held or could not be called is not an excuse for an additional director to continue in office.[18] In *P. Natarajan* v *Central Government*[19] it was held that the provision for additional director is one which is meant to enable the companies to have the benefit of the services of a person, who otherwise is suitable for serving on the board, and whose presence in the board is desirable in the interests of the company, till the time the next annual general meeting is held.

Appointment of a non-resident Indian as director does not require Central Government sanction, but RBI sanction will be required before any shares are allotted to him. The section does not give decisive guidelines as to when the directors exactly vacate office rather it says till the next annual general meeting. It is not necessary that all annual general meetings happen within one year period. Hence, the period should be fixed to one year whether the annual general meeting happens or not.[20] The casual vacancies can be filled by the Board at a meeting of the Board and not by means of a resolution or otherwise. Any such person appointed could hold office only up to the date which the director in whose place he is appointed would have held office.[1] Casual

14 *Topandas Mohanlal Advani* v *Yeotmal Electric Supply Co.* (1940)10 Comp Cas 113, 139.
15 *Needle Industries (India, Ltd.)* v *Needle Industries Newey (India) Holdings Ltd.* AIR 1981 SC 1298.
16 *Madras Tube Co. Ltd.* v *Hari Kishore Somani* (1985)1 Comp LJ 195 (Mad).
17 *Zimmers Ltd.* v *Zimmer* (1951) WN 600.
18 *Krishna Prasad Pilani* v *Colaba Land and Mills Company* (1959)29 Comp Cas 273.
19 (2004)51 SLC 76 (Mad).
20 Reliance can be placed on *Eyre* v *Milton Proprietary Ltd.* [1936]2 Ch 244.
1 Section 262.

vacancy means that 'any vacancy which occurs by reason of death, resignation, disqualification, failure of an elected director to accept the office or for any other reason than retirement by rotation'.[2] It means that the power of the board to fill casual vacancies extends only up to the next annual general meeting. This power should be exercised in good faith in the interest of the company as a whole.[3]

Section 142 of the Companies Bill 2009 provides that:

> The articles of a company may confer on its Board of Directors the power to appoint any person, other than a person who fails to get appointed as a director in a general meeting, as an additional director at any time who shall hold office up to the date of the next annual general meeting or the last date on which the annual general meeting should have been held.[4]

The board of directors can appoint a person in accordance with the articles of association, by a resolution passed by the company in general meeting not being a person holding any alternate directorship for any other director in the company, to act as an alternate director during his absence for a period of not less than three months from India.[5]

1.11 Shadow Directors

British Companies Act 1985, s. 741(2) provides that "in relation to a company, 'shadow director' means a person in accordance with whose directions or instructions the directors of the company are accustomed to act. However, a person is not deemed a shadow director by reason only that the directors act on advice given by him in a professional capacity."[6]

2 *Cf. Srinivasan (M.K.)* v *Subramanya Ayyer (W.S.)* (1932)2 Comp Cas 147.

3 *Anantha Lakshmi Ammal (A.)* v *Indian Trades & Investment Ltd.* (1952)22 Comp Cas 324.

4 The same provision was inducted in s. 161(1) of the Companies Bill 2011 as well without any changes.

5 Section 142(2) of Companies Bill 2009 and s. 161(2) of the Companies Bill 2011.

6 Sub-section (3) of the British Companies Act 1985 provides that "For the purposes of the following provisions of this Act, namely—s. 309 (directors' duty to have regard to interests of employees), s. 319 (directors' long-term contracts of employment), ss. 320 to 322 (substantial property transactions involving directors), [s. 322B (contracts with sole members who are directors), and] ss. 330 to 346 (general restrictions on power of companies to make loans, etc., to directors and others connected with them), (being provisions under which shadow directors are treated as directors), a body corporate is not to be treated as a shadow director of any of its subsidiary companies by reason

In *Hydrodam (Corby) Ltd, Re*[7] Millet, J. took the view that in nearly all cases, the two categories (shadow director and a *de facto* director) were mutually exclusive. It was observed that "a *de facto* director...is one who claims to act and purports to act as a director, although not validly appointed as such. A shadow director by contrast, does not claim or purport to act as director. On the contrary, he claims not to be a director. He lurks in the shadows, sheltering behind others who, he claims, are the only directors of the company to the exclusion of himself". Section 251 of the British Companies Act 2006 defines shadow director in relation to the company means a person in accordance with whose director or instructions the directors of the company are accustomed to act.

There is no mention about shadow directors in the Indian Companies Act. However, s. 7 talks about deemed directors.[8] For certain purposes, the Companies Act 1956 treats as director the person in accordance with whose directions or instructions the board of directors of a company is accustomed to act.[9] It means that such persons do not acquire any rights or powers in connection with the management of the company. Such provisions have been addressed under the English law as "shadow directors". The 'person' in accordance with whose directions or instructions, the board of directors is accustomed to act need not necessarily be an individual.[10] It can be a body corporate. As per definition of the General Clauses Act 1897, person "shall include any company or association or body of individuals, whether incorporated or not."

The intention of the Companies Act 1956 was to bring different category of persons like professional advisers like solicitors, auditors etc. in this category. But s. 7 makes it clear that such persons by reason only of giving advice in their professional capacity does not come

---

only that the directors of the subsidiary are accustomed to act in accordance with its directions or instructions".

7 [1994]2 BCLC 180 (Ch D).

8 Except where this Act expressly provides otherwise, a person shall not be deemed to be, within the meaning of any provision in this Act, a person in accordance with whose directions or instructions the Board of directors of a company is accustomed to act, by reason only that the Board acts on advice given by him in a professional capacity.

9 Sections 305(2) and 308 of Companies Act 1956.

10 Sastri Committee Report, para 24.

within this category. Only when this advice acquires "the potency of directions or instructions" to the Board of Directors then such persons are considered as shadow directors.[11] The role of a wife will be decided based on whether she undertook functions independently or she participated in the affairs of the company in a subordinate role, or she assumed the status of a company director and exercised her powers as a director.[12] Section 2(76)(*vii*) defines related party as "any person on whose advice, directions or instructions a director or manager is accustomed to act." This provision have close similarity with s. 251 of the British Companies Act 2006. But these category of persons are termed as "related party" not as "shadow directors" in the Indian law.

Under s. 239(1)(*c*) of the Companies Act 1956 empowers the inspectors to investigate into the affairs of a company whose board of directors are accustomed to act according to the direction and instructions of the directors of the company whose affairs are being investigated. Section 305(2) talks about the duty of shadow director to disclose particulars of appointment or relinquishment of the office of director, managing director, etc. of any other company. Section 308 provides for disclosure of shareholdings by shadow directors. The fiduciary duties are also apply to shadow directors.[13]

1.12 Managing Director

The office of the managing director is the most important managerial post in a company. Section 2(61) includes Chief Executive Officer or Managing Director as a "key personnel" in a company.[14] The Managing Director has an ostensible authority to act on behalf of the company.[15]

The appointment of whole-time directors or managing director or manager is entrusted with the board of directors. Section 2(26) of the Companies Act 1956 defines a Managing Director as: "Managing Director means a director who, by virtue of an agreement with the

11 *Secretary of State for Trade and Industry* v *Deverell* [2000]2 BCLC 133 (CA).
12 *Gemma Ltd.* v *Davies* [2000]2 BCLC 281 (Ch).
13 *Yukong Line Ltd.* v *Rendsburg Investments Corp. of Liberia* [1998]1 WLR 294; [1998]4 All ER 82 (QBD); [1998]2 BCLC 485. See also *Union of India* v *Playworld Electronics Pvt. Ltd.* (1989)3 SCC 181; AIR 1990 SC 202; *State of U.P.* v *Renusagar Power Co.* (1988)4 SCC 59; AIR 1988 SC 1737.
14 Companies Bill 2011.
15 *Freeman* v *Buckhorst* [1964]2 Comp LJ 36; (1964) Com Cas 405 (CA).

company or of a resolution passed by the company in the general meeting or by its board of directors or by virtue of its memorandum or articles of association, is entrusted with substantial powers of management which would not otherwise be exercisable by him, and includes a director occupying the position of a managing director, by whatever name called"[16] A person who is already a director can be appointed as a whole time or managing director. Section 291 vests the board with the powers of management. The managing director is fully answerable to the board of directors. If any person (an outsider) with a technical qualification has to be appointed as managing director, first he has to be appointed as an additional director. If he is appointed as an additional director, he can continue in the office only up to the next annual general meeting according to s. 260. If he is not re-appointed by the annual general meeting, he will automatically vacate his office of managing director or whole time director. If a managing director is appointed for five years and he is liable to retire by rotation, he cannot continue to hold office as managing director or full time director after the expiry of three years unless he is re-appointed as a director under s. 251(1) and (2) for another two years. Small share holders' director of a public company elected according to s. 252(1) shall be treated as a director for all purposes except for the appointment as managing director or full time director.[17]

1.12.1 *Managing Director as an employee*

The Managing Director may have a dual role to play in certain circumstances. In *Ram Prashad* v *CIT, New Delhi*,[18] it was held that he may be a director as well as an employee. It depend upon his nature of work and his employment terms. The nature of his work can be ascertained from the articles of association of the company. In *Joginder Singh Palta* v *Time Travel (P) Ltd.*,[19] held that a Managing Director

16 Section 2(54) of the Companies Bill 2011 provides that "managing director" means a director who, by virtue of the articles of a company or an agreement with the company or a resolution passed in its general meeting, or by its Board of Directors, is entrusted with substantial powers of management of the affairs of the company and includes a director occupying the position of managing director, by whatever name called.

17 Rule 4(8) of Companies (Appointment of Small Shareholders' Director) Rules 2001.

18 (1972)42 Comp Cas 544; AIR 1973 SC 637; (1972)2 SCC 696.

19 (1984)56 Comp Cas 103 (Cal).

is an employee and hence no injunction can be issued against the company restraining managing director's removal as it is a contract of employment and no court of law will enforce an employment agreement. But in *Sardar Harpreet Singh* v *CIT*,[20] Allahabad High Court held that a joint managing director is not an employee.

A person cannot be a managing director of more than one company at a time. But for an appointment in another company, a specific notice must be given to all the directors and the appointment has to be made by a resolution in the board. Otherwise a person cannot be appointed as a managing director in another company. On the other hand there is no prohibition in the Companies Act 1956 for appointing more than one managing director in a company as far as substantial powers[1] are entrusted to more than one person in a company according to s. 2(26) of the Act. The Central Government may permit any person to be appointed as a managing director of more than two companies if satisfied that it is necessary for proper working of several companies, and should function as a single unit.[2]

1.13 Remuneration to Directors

Every company recognises the need to attract, retain and incentivize executives with the appropriate skills and talent to manage and develop the strategies of the company. Every company has attractive individual-based packages for the directors according to their experience and expertise. Director's remuneration shall be fixed according to the articles of association or by a resolution (special resolution if the articles so require), passed by the company in general meeting. It means that the amount of remuneration will depend on the terms of the articles and the directors' service contracts (if any).

The payment of remuneration to directors is regulated by various provisions under the Companies Act 1956. Section 198 specifies the overall limit of remuneration payable to directors, while s. 269 specifies that the remuneration payable to a managing or whole-time director is paid in accordance with the provisions of Schedule XIII or else

20 (1991)91 CTR (All) 43; (1991)55 Taxman 97.

1 The Supreme Court of India in *Meenakshi Mills* v *V. Vishvanatha Sastri* AIR 1955 SC 13; (1955)1 SCR 787 held that the word substantial has no fixed menaing.

2 *Desein (P) Ltd.* v *Elektrim India Ltd.* (2001)3 Comp LJ 459; (2001)43 CLA 141; (2001)32 SCL 393 (CLB).

necessary approval is obtained by the concerned company from the Central Government. Section 309, *inter alia*, specifies the mode of payment of remuneration to ordinary directors. However, these provisions are applicable only in the case of a public company or a private company that is a subsidiary of a public company. It means that private companies are free to offer any 'remuneration' to its directors. After 1988 amendment to the Companies Act, remuneration paid to the director or managing director is vested with the shareholders. Previously the sanction of the Central Government was necessary and the companies were prevented from paying any fancy amount to the directors in the name of 'remuneration.' Statutory restriction on managerial remuneration is a special feature of company law in India. The Indian Companies Act 1913 included s. 87C which put restrictions on managerial remuneration as a proportion of the net profits without specifying any percentage of the net profits. In *CLB* v *Upper Doab Sugar Mills Ltd.*,[3] Supreme Court held that the CLB has the power to fix the ceiling on the remuneration of the managing director. The amendment made to the Act in 1988 has provided statutory guidelines in the form of Schedule XIII to the Companies Act, 1956 for the Appointment and Remuneration of Managerial Personnel.

The remuneration of director comes from two sources: fees paid to them by way of fees for attending each meeting of the board or of any committee thereof. A director who is in whole time employment of the company or a managing director or an executive director, may be paid remuneration either by way of a monthly payment or at a specified percentage of net profits of the company or partly by one and partly by the other. A company can pay a maximum of five per cent of the net profits of the company for a particular year, except with the approval of the Central Government and 10 per cent for all the managing/whole-time directors put together. Other benefits are determined according to the service contract entered into by them as managers with the company.[4] The statutory limit of remuneration was fixed in s. 198 and s. 309 of the Companies Act 1956.

Companies are also allowed to pay remuneration to its managerial personnel in the years where the company has no profits or when the

3 (1977)47 Comp Cas 173.

4 Gower & Davies, *Principles of Modern Company Law,* Thomson, London, 2008, p. 381.

profits are not adequate by way of salary, dearness allowance, perquisites and any other allowances, depending on the effective capital of the company. Company's effective capital has to be calculated to determine the amount that can be paid to the managerial personnel. A company cannot lawfully pay commission to a director for placing shares unless the director has thereby performed such special services as are authorized by the articles to be the subject of remuneration.[5] If a director is paid remuneration at a certain percentage of the profits of the company and the director ceases to hold the post before the close of the financial year, he shall be entitled to a proportionate share of such remuneration for the period during while in his office as director. A company cannot set-off against fee due to a director of the company the amount of unpaid calls due by the director to the company.[6] A company is entitled to a lien on the shares held by the directors in respect of remuneration wrongly paid to the directors.[7]

If a director is not properly appointed he cannot claim the remuneration to which a director is entitled, even though he believes himself to have been properly appointed and actually serves the company.[8] However, he is entitled to reasonable sum as a *quantum meruit*[9] for the services which he has already rendered.[10] If the director's service contract entitled him to remuneration only if he served for a full year and he vacated office during the year, it was held that he was entitled neither to remuneration nor a *quantum meruit* for his period during which he had served.[11] If the director is paid on an early basis and his services are lawfully terminated before the expiry of the period, he cannot claim remuneration on *quantum meruit* basis.[12] The director gets all the remuneration as a director and not as a member. He can prove his debt along with other ordinary creditors.[13] A company carrying on business can give remuneration by voting in a general meeting, a

5 *Ural Caspian Oil Corporation Ltd.* v *Hume-Schweder* (1913) The Times, 31st July.
6 *Punjab Electric Power Co.* v *Suraj Kishan* (1936)6 Comp Cas 390.
7 *Sri Meenakshi Mills Ltd.* v *Callianjee & Sons* (1935)5 Comp Cas 103.
8 *Woolf* v *East Nigel Gold Mining Co.* [1905]21 TLR 660.
9 It means that as much as he has deserved.
10 *Craven-Ellis* v *Canons Ltd.* [1936]2 KB 403.
11 *Re London and Northern Bank, Mcconnell's Claim* [1901]1 Ch 728.
12 *Boston Deep Sea Fishing & Ice Co.* v *Ansell* [1888]39 Ch D 339; *London & Northern Bank, In re* [1901]1 Ch 728.
13 *Ex. P. Beckwith* [1898]1 Ch 324; *Dover Coalfields Extension Co.* [1908]1 Ch 65.

sum to directors for the past services.[14] In *Bushell* v *Faith*,[15] the House of Lords held that the defendants must pay on the basis of *quantum meruit* not only for the services rendered in the past according to the agreement between the parties but also for the services rendered after declaring the agreement invalid.

In the case of *in re, Consolidated Nickel Mines Ltd.*,[16] the question considered was whether a director who continued to performs his duties after the expiry of office was entitled to remuneration as director. The Court held that the directors vacated their office on the last day on which the General Meeting for the year could have been held and were not entitled to any remuneration for the subsequent period. Sargant, J. makes the following observation:

> A director on his appointment does not ordinarily step into an office which is perpetual unless terminated by some act, but into an office the holding of which is limited by the terms of the Articles ... The duty of the directors was to call a meeting in 1906 and 1907 and they cannot take advantage of their own fault in that respect and say that they still remained directors.

The total managerial remuneration payable by a public company or a private company which is a subsidiary of a public company to its directors and its manager in any financial year must not exceed 11 per cent of the net profits of the company calculated in accordance with the provisions of ss. 349, 350 and 351.[17]

Similarly, the law stipulates that if a company has no managing director or a whole-time director then it can pay a maximum of three per cent of its net profit for the year as remuneration to non-executive directors. However, if a company has even one managing or whole-time director then the remuneration payable to non-executive directors cannot exceed one per cent of the net profits of the company for that financial year.

In the case of a director who is in the whole-time employment of the company or a managing director may be paid remuneration either by way of a monthly, quarterly or annual payment with the approval

14 *Hampson* v *Price's Patent Candle Co.* [1876]45 LJ Ch 437.
15 [1970]2 WLR 272.
16 [1914]1 Ch 883.
17 Section 198 of the Companies Act 1956.

of the Central Government or by way of commission if the company by special resolution authorizes such payment. Such special resolution as per sub-sec. (4) shall not remain in force for a period of more than five years; but may be renewed, from time to time, by special resolution for further periods of not more than five years at a time. Remuneration payable to such directors cannot exceed:

(*a*) if the company has a managing or whole-time director or a manager, one per cent, of the net profits of the company in any financial year;

(*b*) in any other case, three percent of the net profits of the company.

If any director earns remuneration from a company in excess of the above limits without prior approval of the Central Government, he shall refund the excess to the company and until such repayment hold the money in trust with him.

The fulltime directors are usually remunerated by a salary with or without a percentage of the company's profits to a bonus dependent on minimum profits being earned by the company as an addition. Part time executive directors of a company are remunerated by an annual salary, which is always more modest than remuneration of the company's full-time executive directors.

Every managerial personnel are entitled to a remuneration not exceeding the limits specified in the tables given in s. 11 of Part II of Schedule XIII of the Companies Act 1956.

In addition to the above, the managerial personnel are entitled for the following perquisites which are not to be considered for the above ceiling:

(*i*) Contribution to provident fund, superannuation fund or annuity fund to the extent these either singly or put together are not taxable under the Income-tax Act 1961,

(*ii*) Gratuity payable at a rate not exceeding half a month's salary for each completed year of service, and

(*iii*) Encashment of leave at the end of the tenure.

If the company proposes a remuneration exceeding these limits the prior approval of the Central Government would be required. Sitting fees to directors for attending meetings of the Board or any other committee are ordinarily considered as remuneration within the purview of s. 309(2) but the express exclusion under s. 198(2) has to be taken into consideration for the calculation of remuneration under the Companies Act 1956.

1.13.1 *Stock options*

Rule 4.3 of the Securities and Exchange Board of India (Employee Stock Option Scheme And Employee Stock Purchase Scheme) Guidelines 1999 provides that "A director who either by himself or through his relative or through any body corporate, directly or indirectly holds more than 10 per cent of the outstanding equity shares of the company shall not be eligible to participate in the employees stock option scheme (ESOP)." Therefore, a non-executive director is eligible for allotment of shares under the ESOPs scheme.

Effective capital means the aggregate of paid-up share capital (excluding share application money or advances against shares) amount, if any, standing to the credit of share premium account, reserves and surplus excluding revaluation reserve, long term loans and deposits repayable after one year (excluding working capital loans, overdrafts, interest due on loans unless funded, bank guarantee, etc., and other short term arrangements) as reduced by the aggregate of any investments (except in the case of investment by an investment company whose principal business is acquisition of shares, stock, debentures or other securities), accumulated loss and preliminary expenses not written off.

Moreover, the Central Board of Direct Taxes (CBDT) has clarified through a circular that the benefit arising out of ESOP issued to non-employees will not be liable to Fringe Benefit Tax (FBT). "However, in such cases, the taxability of such benefits in the hands of the non-employees will be determined in accordance with the existing law," it says.

Further, the circular has given a relief to those companies which purchase securities from the market and given them to employees. The expenditure incurred by a company on purchasing shares would be allowable as a deduction in computing its taxable income. A large number of listed companies opt for this route. But, the companies allotting shares from their own share capital will not be able to claim it as a deduction, since no expenditure has been incurred. Subsequently, if the employer recovers the FBT from the employee, it will not be treated as his income.

Section 178 of the Companies Bill 2011 provides number of guidelines in fixing the remuneration to directors. Board of Directors of every company has to constitute a Nomination and Remuneration Committee consisting of three or more non-executive directors out of which not less than one half shall be independent directors to formulate policy on remuneration. Such Committee must ensure that:

(*a*) the level and composition of remuneration is reasonable and sufficient to attract, retain and motivate directors of the quality required to run the company successfully;

(*b*) relationship of remuneration to performance is clear and meets appropriate performance benchmarks; and

(*c*) remuneration to directors, key managerial personnel and senior management involves a balance between fixed and incentive pay reflecting short and long term performance objectives appropriate to the working of the company and its goals.[18] The Supreme Court in *Central Bank of India* v *Their Workmen*,[19] held that remuneration is a reward, recompense, pay for services rendered.

1.13.2 *Remuneration to Foreign Director*

The legal framework for appointment and remuneration of foreign nationals still remains complex, despite the enactment of Foreign Exchange Management Act 1999 (FEMA) in the post liberalization era. The heterogeneous legal positions in different laws have to be given a careful thought before engaging the services of foreign national to facilitate repatriation and effective tax planning.

Foreign nationals employed in India may like to repatriate best part of their income to their family residing abroad. Salary earned by foreign nationals, being considered as current account transaction, is regulated by the Foreign Exchange Management (Current Account Transactions) Rules 2000. Repatriation by a foreign national resident in India[20] but not permanently resident in India is allowed up to the net salary of the person or up to US$ 1,00,000.

18 Section 178(4) of Companies Bill 2011.

19 AIR 1960 SC 12; (1959)29 Comp Cas 367; (1960)1 SCR 200.

20 The residential status of a foreign national will be determined according to s. 6 of the Income Tax Act 1961.

A foreign national may open bank accounts in India and receive funds from abroad. He is allowed to repatriate 75 per cent of his net earnings after tax deductions and after his employment is approved by the Government and the exchange control authorities. If employment is for a short duration, such approvals are not necessary, provided the amount of remittance is within the approved limits.[1]

A national of a foreign state could continue to be an employee of foreign company and posted in Indian operations on deputation to the joint venture or branch in India. In such cases they are not employees of Indian company and are allowed to open, hold and maintain foreign currency account with bank outside India.

1.14 Disqualifications of Directors

The Act does not provide for any qualifications to become a director, but it mentions the disqualifications. Section 274 enumerates various circumstances under which a person is ineligible to be appointed as a director. It provides that:

274. (1) *A person shall not be capable of being appointed director of a company, if,*

(*a*) he has been found to be of unsound mind by a Court of competent jurisdiction and the finding is in force;

(*b*) he is an un-discharged insolvent;

(*c*) he has applied to be adjudicated as an insolvent and his application is pending;

(*d*) he has been convicted by a Court[2] of any offence involving moral turpitude and sentenced in respect thereof to imprisonment for not less than six months, and a period of five years has not elapsed from the date of expiry of the sentence;

(*e*) he has not paid any call in respect of shares of the company held by him, whether alone or jointly with others, and six months have elapsed from the last day fixed for the payment of the call;

(*f*) he has been disqualified by a Court/Tribunal[3] in pursuance of section 203. Section 203 empowers the Court/Tribunal to restrain fraudulent persons from managing companies, unless the leave of the Court/Tribunal has been obtained for his appointment;

1 See http://www.indianembassybudapest.org/index.php?option=com_content&id=38, visited on 28.06.2009.

2 The words "in India" *omitted* by Act 65 of 1960, s. 93 (w.e.f. 28-12-1960).

3 *Inserted* by Companies (Second Amendment) Act 2002.

(g) such person who is already a director of a public company which:—

(A) Has not filed the annual accounts and annual returns for any continuous three financial years commencing on and after the first day of April, 1999.

(B) Has failed to repay its deposit or interest thereon on due date or redeem its debentures on due date[4] or pay dividend and such failure continues for one year or more.

(2) The Central Government may, by notification in the Official Gazette, remove:—

(*a*) the disqualification incurred by any person in virtue of clause (*d*) of sub-section (1) either generally or in relation to any company or companies specified in the notification; or

(*b*) the disqualification incurred by any person in virtue of clause (*e*) of sub-section (1).

(3) A private company which is not a subsidiary of a public company may, by its articles, provide that a Person shall be disqualified for appointment as a director on any grounds in addition to those specified in sub-section (1).

A director disqualified under s. 274(1) shall not be eligible to be appointed as a director of any other public company for a period of five years. The Bombay High Court, in *Snowcem India Ltd.* v *Union of India*,[5] held that s. 274(1)(*g*) is not in violation of Arts. 14 & 19(1)(*g*) and 21 of the Constitution of India. The Court explained the objective of inserting the section was to serve a larger public interest and did not violate the fundamental rights or any other rights of the petitioner. A private company which is not a subsidiary of a public company may, by its articles, provide that a person shall be disqualified for appointment as a director on any grounds in addition to those specified above. Section 275 mandates that no person shall, save as otherwise provided in s. 276, hold office at the same time in more than fifteen companies. Section 276 gives option to decide the fifteen companies in which a person wishes to retain his directorship. However, s. 278 provides that in computing this number of fifteen directorships, those of the following will be omitted:

4 *Inserted* by Department Circular dated 14-01-2002. In *Essar Oil Ltd., in re* (2005)63 SCL 126 (Guj), it has been held that default for repayment starts from due date and cannot be postponed on the basis of a scheme submitted for repayment, awaiting disposal.

5 (2005)60 SCL 50.

(*i*) Private companies (other than subsidiaries or holding companies of public companies);

(*ii*) Unlimited companies;

(*iii*) Associations not carrying on business for profit or which prohibit payment of a dividend; and

(*iv*) Alternate directorships (i.e., he is appointed to act as a director only during the absence or incapacity of some other director).

The disqualification to appoint as small shareholders' director is provided in r. 5 of Companies (Appointment of the Small Shareholders' Director) Rules 2001. All the disqualifications described in s. 274(1) are applicable to this special category as well. The non-payment of deposit or redeem debentures or continuous default in filing of annual returns and accounts does not cast a disability on the director candidate. It means that small shareholders' director does not incur the disqualification on the ground of continuous default by the company under cl. (*g*) of the s. 274(1).[6]

The Central Government through wide powers conferred by cl. (*b*) of s. 642(1) has made certain rules to carry out the purpose of s. 271(1)(*g*). These Rules[7] provide that:

1. Whenever a company fails to file the annual accounts and annual returns, as described in sub-clause (A) of clause (*g*) of sub-section (1) of section 274, persons who are directors on the last due date for filing the annual accounts and the annual returns for any continuous three financial years commencing on and after the first day of April, 1999, shall be disqualified.

2. If a company has failed to repay any deposit, irrespective of the enactment, rules or regulations under which the deposits have been accepted by the companies, or interest thereon, or redeem its debentures, or pay any dividend declared on the respective due dates, and if such failure continues for one year, as described in sub-clause (B) of clause (g) of sub-section (1) of section 274, then the directors of that company shall stand disqualified immediately on expiry of that one year from the respective due dates:

---

6 This provision was *inserted* by the Companies' Amendment Act 2000.

7 Companies (Disqualification of Directors under s. 274(1)(*g*) of the Companies Act 1956) Rules 2003.

Provided that all the directors who have been directors in the relevant year, from the due date to the expiry of one year after the due date, will be disqualified:

Provided further that disqualification on account of the reasons cited under this Rule shall also apply to the reappointment as a director.

3. *Duty of statutory auditor to report on disqualification:*

(*a*) It shall be the duty of statutory auditor of the appointing company as well as disqualifying company, as required under section 227(3)(*f*) to report to the members of the company whether any director is disqualified from being appointed as director under clause (*g*) of sub-section (1) of section 274 and to furnish a certificate each year as to whether on the basis of his examination of the books and records of the company, any director of the company is disqualified for appointment as a director or not.[8]

(*b*) It shall be the duty of the statutory auditors of the "disqualifying company" as required in section 227(3)(*f*) to report to the members of the company whether any director in the company has been disqualified during the year from being re-appointed as director, or being appointed as director in another company under clause (*g*), of sub-section (1) of section 274.

4. *Duty of company to intimate disqualification.* Whenever a company fails to file the annual accounts and returns, or fails to repay any deposit, interest, dividend, or fails to redeem its debentures, as described in clauses (A) and (B) of clause (g) of sub-section (1) of section 274, the company shall immediately file a return in duplicate in Form 'DD-B', prescribed under these rules for this purpose, to the Registrar of Companies, furnishing therein the names and addresses of all the Directors of the company during the relevant financial years:

Provided that names of such directors who have been exempted from application of s. 274(1)(*g*) by the Central Government, from time to time, shall be excluded.

Provided further that no unusual abbreviations or short forms shall be used in filling up the Form 'DD-B', which shall give such details as may be necessary to distinguish and identify each director without any ambiguity.

---

8 Auditor cannot submit a report about disqualification of directors under s. 274(1)(*g*) on the basis of statement supplied by company alone; he has to examine and even he has to make an independent enquiry about collected materials from other sources to submit such report. *Pawan Jain* v *Hindustan Club Ltd.* (2005)62 SCL 610 (Cal).

5. *Failure to intimate disqualification shall render director as officer in default.* When a company fails to file the Form 'DD-B' as above within 30 days of the failure that would attract disqualification under Section 274(1)(g), officers of the company listed in section 5 of the Companies Act, 1956 shall be officers in default.

6. *Names of the disqualified directors on the web-site etc.*:

(*a*) the Central Government shall place on the web-site of the Department of Company Affairs the names and addresses and such other details including names and details of the companies concerned, as may be necessary, in respect of all the disqualified directors.

(*b*) The Central Government may also publicize the names of disqualified directors in such manner as it may consider appropriate.

(*c*) The Central Government shall take such steps as may be required to update its web-site to ensure that name of the person, in whose respect disqualification period has expired after 5 years, is deleted from the web-site.[9]

7. *Duty of every director.* Every director in a public company registered under the Companies Act, 1956 shall file Form 'DD-A', prescribed under these Rules, before he is appointed or re-appointed.

8. *Punishment for contravention of the rules.* If a company or any other person contravenes any provision of these rules for which no punishment is provided in the Companies Act, 1956, the company and every officer of the company who is in default or such other person shall be punishable with fine which may extend to five thousand rupees and where the contravention is a continuing one, with a further fine which may extend to five hundred rupees for every day after the first, during which the contravention continues.

All disqualifications to become a director are applicable to managing directors as well.[10] When compared to disqualifications of managing director, only the past five years of directorship or management will be taken into account; but there is no time-limit is prescribed for managing directors. He must be good character throughout his lifetime for the consideration of a managing director. The Central Government

9 In view of non-filing of declaration prescribed in statutory form [under s. 274(1)(*g*)] by any of directors seeking appointment and reappointment, said director is not automatically disqualified; before a person is declared to be disqualified by auditor or any other person, a view has to be formed whether grounds mentioned in section 274 have been proved without any doubt. See *Pawan Jain* v *Hindustan Club Ltd.* (2005)62 SCL 610 (Cal).

10 Section 267 of the Companies Act 1956.

can remove such disqualification in case of managers under s. 385(2), but not in the case of a managing or full-time director. If any director is appointed as manager of one company, he cannot be a manager or employee of any other company, if he is appointed for full time.

1.14.1 *Common grounds for disqualification*

The Companies Bill 2009 and Companies Bill 2011[11]included most of these grounds in the proposed law. It can be summarized the common grounds as:

1. A person found to be of unsound mind by a court of competent jurisdiction;
2. a person he is an undischarged insolvent;
3. a person has applied to be adjudicated as an insolvent and his application is pending;
4. has been convicted by a Court of any offence involving moral turpitude and sentenced in respect thereof to imprisonment for not less than six months, and a period of five years has not elapsed from the date of expiry of the sentence;
5. an order disqualifying him for appointment as a director has been passed by a Court or Tribunal;
6. a person has not paid any calls in respect of any shares of the company held by him;
7. a person has been convicted of the offence dealing with related party transactions at any time during the last preceding five years;
8. a person has not obtained Director Identification Number (DIN); and
9. a person has failed to repay the deposits accepted by it or pay interest thereon or to redeem any debentures on the due date or pay interest due thereon or pay any dividend declared.

1.14.2 *Insolvency of Director*

The Bombay High Court in *Jayesh Ramniklal Doshi* v *Carbon Corporation Ltd.*[12] elaborately discussed the question of insolvency

11 Section 164 of the Companies Bill 2011.
12 (1993)76 Comp Cas 748 (Bom).

and consequent disqualification to become a managing director. In this case the defendant was working as managing director and in an earlier proceeding the Apex Court granted an opportunity to the defendant No. 2 to repay his creditors and on such repayment had directed that the insolvency proceedings would stand discharged. The plaintiff contends that defendant No. 2 is not entitled to function as a managing director of the first defendant-company by reason of the statutory prohibition contained in s. 267(*a*) of the Companies Act 1956.

Section 385(2) of the Act empowers the Central Government to remove the disqualification incurred by a manager by virtue of the provisions contained in s. 385(1) of the Act. In the case of a managing director, the provisions of the Act are more stringent as no power is conferred on the Central Government or any other authority to remove the disqualification similar to the power conferred under s. 385(2) of the Act in the case of managers incurring similar disqualification. In the case of managing directors, a person who has at any time been adjudged as an insolvent is disqualified from being appointed or continued as managing director of a company for his lifetime. Whereas in the case of a manager such disqualification operates only if the person concerned was adjudged as an insolvent within the preceding five years.

By pointing the legislative history of this provision, the legislative object in enacting s. 267 of the Act, the recommendation of the joint Committee on the Companies Bill 1953, categorically stated that:

> The Committee feel that the provision should be stiffer in the case of the managing director than in the case of a manager and have, therefore, omitted the provision found in original clause 285(2) (section 385) for the removal of the disqualification imposed by the clause. The limitation of the disqualification to a period of five years has also been removed.

The court was of the view: "In such a case, it cannot be said that the order of discharge of insolvency operates with retrospective effect as if the debtor was never adjudged insolvent and the order of adjudication is to be treated as non-existent from inception. An order of discharge of insolvency does not mean setting aside of the insolvency from inception. In this setting, the appellate order would merely mean that the order of adjudication is terminated from the date of completion of payments specified in the appellate order. In other words, discharge of insolvency does not mean nullification of insolvency from inception." The court conceded that he would be eligible for being elected or re-appointed as a director because the disqualification stated in s. 283

blows over. In view of s. 267 of the Companies Act, the defendant No. 2 was not entitled to continue as managing director of the company.

The above single Bench judgment was reversed in *Mukul Harkisondass Dalal* v *Jayesh Ramhiklal Doshi*;[13] the trial judge issued an injunction against the company from permitting defendant No. 2 to act as managing director or director and defendant No. 2 was further restrained from receiving any salary, perquisites, benefits or privileges from the company as managing director or director. The Division Bench was of the opinion that the effect of the Supreme Court order was not merely a discharge of the insolvent but also a discharge of the proceedings itself. The Court observed: "The result of the finding of the trial judge is that although the insolvency proceedings are set aside, the appellant will be treated as being adjudged insolvent for his entire life. It is impossible to put such a construction on the order of the Supreme Court as it would lead to unusual results. In our judgment, the impugned order cannot be sustained and the grant of injunction was inappropriate". Accordingly the Court reversed the single Bench decision.

For a director to be insolvent within the meaning of this section it is not necessary that there should be a definite act of insolvency done on a particular date; it is sufficient evidence from which the court can find that the director is insolvent.[14]

An un-discharged bankrupt to act as a director of a company is considered as an offence under the Company Directors Disqualifications Act 1986.[15] The offence is one of absolute liability, and it is no defense for the bankrupt to prove that he honestly but mistakenly believed that he had been discharged from bankruptcy by the effluxion of time since the bankruptcy order was made against him.[16] Section 164(1)(*b*) of Companies Bill 2011 is also provides that an undercharged insolvent is not eligible to be appointed as a director of a company. In the case of discharge of insolvency, he would become qualified again for appointment as director.[17]

13 (1997)88 Comp Cas 808 (Bom-DB).

14 *Re London & Countries Asset Co. Ltd.* v *Brighton Picture Polance Ltd.* [1915]2 KB 493.

15 Section 11(1) and (2).

16 *R* v *Brockley* [1994]1 BCLC 606.

17 *Jayesh Ramniklal Doshi* v *Carbon Corp. Ltd.* (1993)76 Comp Cas 748, 762 (Bom).

1.14.3 *Moral turpitude*

Managing director of a company who has been convicted for an offence involving moral turpitude cannot continue as a managing director.[18] The *Black's Law Dictionary* defines *moral turpitude* as meaning "Conduct that is contrary to justice, honesty, or morality." Moral turpitude means a conduct contrary to justice, honesty, modesty, good morals or contrary to what a man owes to society. It includes black-marketing, profiteering, hoarding, adulteration and other malpractices.[19] Moral turpitude means, in general, shameful wickedness—so extreme a departure from ordinary standards of honest, good morals, justice, or ethics as to be shocking to the moral sense of the community. It has also been defined as an act of baseness, vileness, or depravity in the private and social duties which one person owes to another or to society in general, contrary to the accepted and customary rule of right and duty between people.[20]

Moral turpitude includes an act which is shameful, licentitious, lewd or unchaste. It will also include black marketing, profiteering, hoarding, adulteration and other anti-social acts. It means a conduct contrary to justice, honesty, modesty or good morals and contrary to what a man owes to fellow men or to society in general. Drunkenness at public place leading to criminal conviction amounts to moral turpitude.[1] The standard of moral turpitude is clear that, anything against public interest or rule of public policy is amount to moral turpitude.[2] The SC consistently took the same view that the expression 'moral turpitude' is not defined anywhere but it means anything done contrary to justice, honesty, modesty or good morals. It implies depravity and wickedness of character or disposition of the person charged with the particular conduct.[3] In *Mangali* v *Chhakki Lal*.[4] SC had drawn some guidelines for the test:

(*i*) Whether the act leading to a conviction was such as could shock the moral conscience of society in general.

18 Section 164(1)(*d*) of the Companies Bill 2011.
19 C.R. Datta, *Company Directors,* (Eastern Law House, 1977), p. 7.
20 *American Encyclopedia of Law*, vol. 13 online available in http://webpac.lincolnlibraries.org:2048/public/westlaw.html, visited on 11.06.2010.
1 *Durga Singh* v *State of Punjab* AIR 1957 Punj 97.
2 *Pullman's Palace Car Co.* v *Central Transp. Co.* 65 Fed 158 (161).
3 *Baleshwar Singh* v *District Magistrate and Collector, Banaras* AIR 1959 All 71.
4 AIR 1963 All 527.

(*ii*) Whether the motive which led to the act was a base one, and

(*iii*) Whether on account of the act having been committed, the perpetrator could be considered to be of a depraved character or a person who was to be looked down upon by the society.

Section 267(*c*) and s. 283(1)(*e*) of the Companies Act 1956 make a bar to the appointment of a managing director convicted of an offence involving moral turpitude. This was held in *Rama Narang* v *Ramesh Narang*. In this case the managing director was convicted under ss. 114, 120B and 420 of Indian Penal Code 1860 and s. 267 of Companies Act 1956. The respondent contended that s. 267 was not attracted because of interim order passed in appeal filed by him before appellate court against conviction. The court held that the post of managing director comes to an end the moment the order of conviction is recorded. The case reached before the SC and it categorically held that "On a plain reading of this section it seems clear to us from the language in which the provision is couched that it is intended to be mandatory in character. The language is plain, simple and unambiguous and does not admit of more than one meaning, namely, that after the commencement of the Companies Act, no person who has suffered a conviction by a court of an offence involving moral turpitude shall be appointed or employed or continued in appointment or employment by any company as its managing or whole-time Director".[5] The SC dismissed the appeal. The decision made it very clear that no one can be appointed as a managing director or whole time director if there has been at any time in his life a conviction for an offence involving moral turpitude. Section 164(1)(*d*) and s. 167(1)(*f*) of the Companies Bill 2011 also provides for the same disqualification of a director.

1.15 Vacation of office of the Director

Under s. 283 of the Companies Act 1956 the office of the director shall become vacant if:

(*a*) he fails to obtain within the time specified in sub-section (1) of section 270, or at any time thereafter ceases to hold, the share qualification, if any, required of him by the articles of the company;

(*b*) he is found to be of unsound mind by a Court of competent jurisdiction;

5 *Rama Narang* v *Ramesh Narang* (1995)83 Comp Cas 194 (SC); (1995)2 SCC 513; JT 1995(1) SC 515.

(*c*) he applies to be adjudicated an insolvent;

(*d*) he is adjudged an insolvent;

(*e*) he is convicted by a Court of any offence involving moral turpitude and sentenced in respect thereof to imprisonment for not less than six months;

(*f*) he fails to pay any call in respect of shares of the company held by him, whether alone or jointly with others, within six months from the last date fixed for the payment of the call unless the Central Government has, by notification in the Official Gazette, removed the disqualification incurred by such failure;

(*g*) he absents himself from three consecutive meetings of the Board of directors, or from all meetings of the Board for a continuous period of three months, whichever is longer, without obtaining leave of absence from the Board;

(*h*) he (whether by himself or by any person for his benefit or on his account), or any firm in which he is a partner or any private company of which he is a director, accepts a loan, or any guarantee or security for a loan, from the company in contravention of section 295;

(*i*) he acts in contravention of section 299;

(*j*) he becomes disqualified by an order of Court under section 203;

(*k*) he is removed in pursuance of section 284; or

(*l*) having been appointed a director by virtue of his holding any office or other employment in the company, he ceases to hold such office or other employment in the company.

(2) Notwithstanding anything in clauses (*d*), (*e*) and (*i*) of sub-section (1), the disqualification referred to in those clauses shall not take effect—

(*a*) for thirty days from the date of the adjudication, sentence or order;

(*b*) where any appeal or petition is preferred within the thirty days aforesaid against the adjudication, sentence or conviction resulting in the sentence, or order until the expiry of seven days from the date on which such appeal or petition is disposed of, or

(*c*) where within the seven days aforesaid, any further appeal or petition is preferred in respect of the adjudication, sentence, conviction, or order, and the appeal or petition, if allowed, would result in the removal of the disqualification, until such further appeal or petition is disposed of.

(2A) Subject to the provisions of sub-sections (1) and (2), if a person functions as a director when he knows that the office of director held by him has become vacant on account of any of the disqualifications, specified in the several clauses of sub-section (1), he shall be punishable with fine-which may extend to five thousand rupees for each day on which he so functions as a director.

(3) A private company which is not a subsidiary of a public company may, by its articles, provide, that the office of director shall be vacated on any grounds in addition to those specified in sub-section (1).

The office of a director will be automatically vacated on the happening of any events mentioned in the section. The board of directors has no power to waive any of the conditions or condone the offence.[6] All directors in public companies as well as in private companies will come under the purview of the section. However, this section does not deal with the retirement of directors.[7] If a director fails to obtain qualification shares within the prescribed time limit is a valid reason. Mere claim of right to shares is not enough.[8] If the company is not permitting any director to register his shares, his office cannot be vacated.[9] Paying the debt cannot wipe out the fact of insolvency from a director.[10] Automatic vacation of his office will takes place when a director fails to pay the call money due from him singly or jointly with others within six months from the last date fixed for the payment of the call.[11] His office will be vacated automatically if he fails to disclose his interest in any of the company's transactions.[12] If a director is not attending three consecutive meetings, his office will be vacated.[13] The three months period will starts from the date of the first meeting from which the director absents himself.[14] The word

6 *Bodega Company Ltd., In re* [1904]1 Ch 276; *Glossop* v *Glossop* [1907]2 Ch 370.
7 *B.R. Kundra* v *Motion Pictures Association* (1976)46 Comp Cas 339 (Del).
8 *Coal Products (P) Ltd.* v *Ram Autar Jalan* (1969)39 Comp Cas 223 (Cal-DB).
9 *Ram Autar Jalan* v *Coal Products (P) Ltd.* (1970)40 Comp Cas 715 (SC).
10 *Jayesh Ramniklal Doshi* v *Carbon Corporation Ltd.* (1993)76 Comp Cas 748.
11 *Hind Iran Bank Ltd.* v *Raizada Jagannath Bali* (1959)29 Comp Cas 418 (Punj).
12 *Kuldip Singh Dhillon* v *Paragon Utility Financiers Pvt. Ltd.* (1988) Comp Cas 19 (32) (P&H).
13 *D. Srinivasan* v *H.S. Vishvanath* (2007)75 SCL 59 (CLB-Chennai).
14 *Vinod Kumar Mittal* v *Kaveri Lime Industries Ltd.* (2000)2 Comp LJ 354 (CLB).

'absent' implies voluntary or deliberate absence and does not cover cases of absence due to reasons like illness beyond the control.[15] In *Vijay Krishan Jaidka* v *Jaidka Motor Co. Ltd.*,[16] it was held that where there was no proof that notices of board meetings were served on directors, directors could not be removed on the ground that they abstained from attending meetings. Where a person is appointed as director by virtue of his employment in the company, his directorship will cease automatically on the termination of his employment.[17]

Section 148(1) of the Companies Bill 2009 and s. 167(1)(*f*) of the Companies Bill 2011 also followed the earlier suit and included all old provisions as a disqualification and a reason for vacating a director's office.

1.16 Resignation of Directors

There is no express provision in the Companies Act 1956 that deals with the resignation of a director similar to that of a managing agent in s. 342. The Act, however, indirectly recognizes the right of resignation through the provisions in s. 318(3)(*a*) and s. 318(3)(*b*), of a managing director or a whole time director. If any provision in the articles permits the director to resign at any time, the resignation will take effect without any need for acceptance by the board. If a director is contracted to act for a fixed period of time, violation of any agreement will make him liable for damages. If there is no provision in the articles of association, a director can resign without serving a proper notice.[18] However, the ordinary procedure of resignation of an agent or an officer must be followed.

In the absence of any provision in the artiles or the terms of appointment of a director, the ordinary rules of common law as regards resignation by an officer or agent must be followed.[19] In *T. Murali* v *State*,[20] the court opined that "even in the absence of a provision in respect of resignation under the Act or under the articles of association

15 *In Re London and Northern Bank, Macks Claim* [1900] WN 114.
16 (1996)10 SCL 244 (CLB); *Bagri Cereals (P) Ltd., In re* (1997)5 Comp LJ 145 (Cal).
17 *Sunil K. Alagh* v *Britania Industries Ltd.* (1993)11 Corpt LA 68 (Bom).
18 *OBC Caspian Ltd.* v *Thorp* [1998] SLT 653 (Scot).
19 LVV Iyer, *Guide to Company Directors: Powers, Rights, Duties, Liabilities & Corporate Social Responsibilities*, 3rd Ed. 2011, Butterworths-Wadhwa: Nagpur, p. 997.
20 (1976)46 Comp Cas 613 (Mad).

of the company; the resignation tendered by the director or managing director unequivocally in writing will take effect from the time when such resignation is tendered". It was also held that "So far as the Indian Companies Act is concerned, this has followed the pattern of the British law relating to companies. If there is any provision in the articles giving right to a director to resign at any time, the resignation will take effect without any need for its acceptance by the board or the company in the general meeting. In the absence of any such provision relating to the resignation in the memorandum or articles of association, it is well settled that a resignation once made takes effect immediately when the intention to resign is made clear".[1]

In Halsbury's *Laws of England*, 4th Ed., vol. 7, page 316, in para 536 under the heading "Resignation", it is stated as follows:

> Where by the articles a director has power to resign at any time, his resignation takes effect independently of acceptance by the other directors or the company. Where the articles of association of a company provide that the office of a director is to be vacated *ipso facto* if by notice in writing to the company a director resigns office, an oral resignation if accepted by the company is valid.

In Palmer's *Company Law*, 21st Ed., page 543, under the heading "Resignation," it is stated as follows:

> A director can at any time resign his office, and usually the articles make express provision accordingly. If he communicates his resignation to the company, for instance by a notice upon the company served in the manner provided by section 437, his resignation is effective. A resignation once made cannot be withdrawn, except with the consent of the company.

Ultimately the court held that "I see that there is no obligation under the Companies Act requiring a director, even if he is the only director, to co-opt another in case he intends to resign his office. After going through the provisions of the Act, I find there is nothing to show that such a co-option is a condition precedent for a director validly tendering his resignation. The power of co-option is only an enabling provision to co-opt so as to have the quorum for holding the meeting. There is no specific article in the articles of association of this company

1 The same position was followed in *S.S. Lakshmana Pillai* v *ROC* (1977)47 Comp Cas 652 (Mad).

that it is imperative on the part of the outgoing director to co-opt another director before he leaves his office. So this contention also fails".[2]

In *Saumil Dilip Mehta* v *State of Maharashtra*,[3] it was observed that a director could not evade his obligations by severing his connection with the company. Whereas a director has tendered his resignation and board of directors has accepted it and has acted on it, such a director cannot be held liable for liability incurred by said company after date of acceptance of his resignation except the liability which has been incurred by him for purchase of shares of said company and nothing more. The judicial decisions are consistently conclusive that a director who submitted his resignation will be deemed to have resigned from the date of resignation.[4] However, a resignation addressed to a third party shall have no effect other than the company.[5] In *Saumil Dilip Mehta* v *State of Maharashta*,[6] it was held that a director can resign simply by sending a letter to the Chairman or Secretary of the company, expressing his intention to resign from the post of the director of the company.

Section 149 of the Companies Bill, 2009 and s. 168 of the Companies Bill 2011, provides procedures for resignation of a director. A director can resign from his office by giving a notice in writing to the company and the Board with intimation to the Registrar. Where all the directors of a company resign from their offices, or vacate their offices under s. 148 (2009 Bill) or s. 167 (2011 Bill), the promoter or, in his absence, the Central Government shall appoint the required number of directors who shall hold office till the directors are appointed by the company in general meeting.

1.17 Removal of Directors

A director appointed under the Act can be removed by shareholders, Central Government and Company Law Board (CLB). The articles of a company may authorize the appointment of a director for any period, however long or short, and the appointment is valid if made consistently

2 *Ibid.*, para 29 of the Judgment.
3 (2002)39 SCL 102 (Bom).
4 *Abdul Haq* v *Katpadi Industries Ltd.* AIR 1960 Mad 482.
5 *Registrar of Companies* v *Orissa Paper Products Ltd.* (1988) Comp Cas 460 (Ori).
6 (2002)39 SCL 102 (Bom).

with the articles. Thus, a director may hold office at will, and be removable under the terms of the articles at any time by the other directors or by the members of the company in general meeting.[7] Section 284 recognizes the inherent right of the shareholders to remove the directors appointed by them. In *Tarlok Chand Khanna* v *Raj Kumar Kapoor,* it was held that section 284 is designed to enable the shareholders to control the directors by their removal. It is not even necessary that there should be proof of mismanagement, breach of trust, misfeasance or other misconduct on the part of the directors. The British Companies Act 2006 also empowers the shareholders to remove a director under s. 168 by ordinary resolution at any time. Section 150 of the Companies Bill 2009 and s. 169 of the Companies Bill, 2011 provides that the director, not being a director appointed by the tribunal, can be removed by the company by a special resolution. A special notice shall be required of any such resolution for the removal of a director under this section. Any director removed under this section is eligible to get compensation or damages according to his employment contract.

However, in *Queen Kuries & Loans (P) Ltd.* v *Sheena Jose*,[8] it was held that the notice must disclose the grounds on which the director is proposed to be removed. The disclosure of the ground for removal is a matter of substance and not of form because the directors concerned are entitled to make a representation in writing against their removal at the meeting. Omission to serve a special notice on the directors sought to be removed constitutes denial of their statutory right of reply and in the absence of such notice to the directors, any resolution for their removal would be vitiated by such omission.[9] The SC in *LIC* v *Escorts*,[10] held that the requisitionists could not be compelled to state the grounds for removal of directors. A director's office is held vacant when his period of office expires. Neither the members nor the board of directors of a company have an inherent power to remove directors before the normal expiration of their period of office in the absence of a power to do so in the articles.[11]

7 Section 284.
8 (1993)76 Comp Cas 821.
9 *S. Varadarajan* v *Udhayem Leasing & Investments (P.) Ltd.* (2005)62 SCL 315 (CLB-Chennai).
10 AIR 1986 SC 1370.
11 *Imperial Hydropathic Hotel CO, Backpool* v *Hampson* [1882]23 Ch D 1.

A director or a managing director can be removed by the general meeting under s. 284 of the Companies Act other than the directors appointed under s. 408. The shareholders can exercise this power any time by passing an ordinary resolution at a meeting of shareholders of the company. A director may cease to hold office by retirement, dismissal, removal or by vacating office. The only remedy available to the director is to claim compensation for breach of contract, if any, for his pre-mature removal. The amount of compensation will always depends upon the terms of appointment.[12] The courts have consistently held that no injunction will be issued against the company either to prevent it from removing the director or to compel it to reinstate.[13]

Central Government's approval is required only for the appointment of a managing director and not for his removal.[14] Where the articles of association confer powers to the board of directors to remove the managing director or other directors, such power is not affected by the provisions of s. 284.[15] This section is not attracted if directors are removed *en block* under s. 402 as part of the action against oppression and mismanagement.[16] It has been held that if a director has sent malicious complaints to governmental authorities which resulted in raids on the company's premises and the authorities found nothing wrong in the records, is a good ground to remove a director under the section.[17] However, this section does not affect the power of the board of directors to revoke the appointment of a director or a managing director made by the board.[18] The right of representation of the removed director was discussed elaborately by the Bombay High Court in *Escorts Ltd.* v *Union of India.*[19] The Court was of the view that when a meeting

12 *Nelson* v *James Nelson & Sons Ltd.* [1914-15] All ER Rep 433.

13 *Life Insurance Corporation of India* v *Escorts Ltd.* (1986)59 Comp Cas 548; *Sardar Gulab Singh* v *Punjab Zamindar Bank Ltd.* (1941)11 Comp Cas 301.

14 *Pyare Lal Gupta* v *Agarwal (D.P.)* (1983)53 Comp Cas 586.

15 *Home Chaudhary (A.K.)* v *National Textile Corporation U.P. Ltd.* (1984)48 Fac LR 96-101 (All-DB).

16 *Shoe Specialties Ltd.* v *Standard Distilleries and Breweries (P) Ltd.* (1997) Comp LJ 243.

17 *Vinod Kumar Mittal* v *Kaveri Lime Industries Ltd.* (2000)36 CLA 474 (CLB-PB).

18 *Major General Shanta Shamsher* v *Kamani Brothers* AIR 1959 Bom 201; *S. Varadarajan* v *Venkateswara Sovent Extraction (P) Ltd.* 80 Comp Cas 693 (Mad).

19 (1985)57 Comp Cas 241 (Bom).

is requisitioned by the shareholders for a director's removal, the requisitionists must disclose the grounds under which they want to proceed, and the director must be given a chance to explain to the shareholders. The court held that the notice served which did not specify the grounds failed in its purpose. The Court also observed that when the shareholders change the combination of board of directors and the future of the company, the power of removal must be exercised in good faith and must be in the interest of the company.

The Bombay High Court judgment was reversed by the SC in *Life Insurance Corporation of India* v *Escorts Ltd.*[20] Court observed that:

> Thus, we see that every shareholder of a company has the right subject to statutorily prescribed procedural and numerical requirements, to call an extraordinary general meeting in accordance with the provisions of the Companies Act. He cannot be restrained from calling a meeting and he is not bound to disclose the reasons for the resolutions proposed to be moved at the meeting. Nor are the reasons for the resolutions subject to judicial review. It is true that under section 173(2) of the Companies Act, there shall be annexed to the notice of the meeting a statement setting out all material facts concerning each item of business to be transacted at the meeting including, in particular, the nature of the concern or the interest, if any, therein, of every director, the managing agent, if any, the secretaries and treasurers, if any, and the manager, if any. This is a duty cast on the management to disclose, in an explanatory note, all material facts relating to the resolution coming up before the general meeting to enable the shareholders to form a judgment on the business before them. It does not require the shareholders calling a meeting to disclose the reasons for the resolutions which they propose to move at the meeting. The Life Insurance Corporation of India, as a shareholder of Escorts Limited, has the same right as every shareholder to call an extraordinary general meeting of the company for the purpose of moving a resolution to remove some directors and appoint others in their place. The Life Insurance Corporation of India cannot be restrained from doing so nor is it bound to disclose its reasons for moving the resolutions.[1]

20 1985 SCR Supl (3) 909; AIR 1986 SC 1370.
1 *Ibid.*, p. 918.

The SC relied on the judgment in *Bentley-Stevens* v *Jones,*[2] where it was held that a shareholder had a statutory right to move a resolution to remove a director and that the court was not entitled to grant an injunction restraining him from calling a meeting to consider such a resolution. The proper remedy of the director was to apply for a winding up order on the ground that it was "just and equitable" for the court to make such an order. In the case of *Ebrahimi* v *Westbourne Galleries Ltd.,*[3] a similar view was held that the absolute right of the general meeting to remove the directors was recognized and it was pointed out that it would be open to the director sought to be removed to ask the company court for an order for winding-up on the ground that it would be "just and equitable" to do so.

Despite the view held by the Supreme Court, we can find change in legal interpretations. In *Bhankerpur Simbhaoli Beverages (P) Ltd.* v *P.R. Pandya,*[4] the Punjab & Haryana High Court held that where the directors sought to be removed are not given the opportunity for making a representation which is their statutory right under this section, the resolution passed for removal would be of no effect.

In the case of *Nazir Hoosein* v *Darayus Bhattena,*[5] SC held that an appointment of a chairman or directors made in contravention of the articles is void and is not regularized by mere acquiescence, and consequently resolutions carried by the casting vote of such a chairman are inoperative.

The following directors cannot be removed by the shareholders in general meeting:

(1) A director appointed by the Central Government under s. 408;

(2) A director of a private company holding office for life on 1st April 1952;

(3) Director elected by the principle of proportional representation under s. 265;

(4) Directors appointed by Central Government under Industries (Development & Regulation) Act 1951;

2 [1974]2 All ER 653.
3 [1972]2 WLR 1289; [1972]2 All ER 492, 500 (HL).
4 (1996)86 Comp Cas 842 (P&H).
5 AIR 2000 SC 2427.

(5) Special directors appointed under Sick Industrial Companies (Special Provisions) Act 1985;

(6) Directors appointed by financial institutions under statutory powers;

(7) Nominee directors; and

(8) Directors appointed by Company Law Board (Tribunal) under s. 402.

In *S. Varadarajan* v *Venkateswara Solvent Extraction Pvt. Ltd.*,[6] it was held that shareholders cannot have the authority to remove the director who has been appointed by an authority other than the body of shareholders. A director appointed by Central Government under section 408 cannot be removed by shareholders. Section 284 applies to both public as well as private companies. The article cannot provide that a director cannot be removed; it will be contrary to s. 9 of the Companies Act 1956.[7] In other jurisdictions like in the US, the shareholders cannot remove the directors in the absence of any provisions in the statutes, articles of incorporation, or by-laws authorizing the stockholders' action, and the removal of the directors before the expiration of the term is void.[8] It therefore follows that the power of the stockholders to remove directors is dependent entirely upon the provisions of the statutes of the State, the articles of incorporation, and the by-laws of the corporation. Thus, if the statute provides that directors may be removed by the stockholders, without doubt the directors may be so removed, even though the directors' term has not expired.[9]

Under s. 388B, the Central Government has the power to make a reference to the CLB (Tribunal) against any managerial personnel. The power can be exercised where, in the opinion of the Central Government, there are circumstances suggesting:

6 (1992)9 CLA 39 (Mad).

7 *Tarlok Chand Khanna* v *Raj Kumar Kapoor* (1983)54 Comp Cas 12 (Del); *Paramanadn Choudhary* v *Smt. Shukla Devi Mishra* (1990)67 Comp Cas 45 (MP).

8 *State* v *Kylmanen* (Minn) [1929]226 NW 401.

9 *State* v *Horan* 22 Wash 197; 60 Pac 135; *People ex rel Manice* v *Powell* 201 NY I94; 94 NE 634; *Nathan* v *Tompkins* 82 Ala 437; 2 So 747; *Toledo Traction, Light and Power Co.* v *Smith* 205 Fed 643; See also *Power of Shareholders to Remove Directors*, Michigan Law Review, vol. 28, No. 5, 1930, pp. 617-618.

(1) that any person concerned in the conduct and management of the affairs of a company is or has been in connection therewith guilty of fraud, misfeasance, persistent negligence or default in carrying out his obligations and functions under the law, or breach of trust; or

(2) that the business of a company is not or has not been conducted and managed by such person in accordance with sound business principles or prudent commercial practices; or

(3) that a company is or has been conducted and managed by such person in a manner which is likely to cause, or has caused, serious injury or damage to the interest of the trade industry or business to which such company pertains; or

(4) that the business of a company is or has been conducted and managed by such person with intent to defraud its creditors, members or any other persons or otherwise for a fraudulent or unlawful purpose or in a manner prejudicial to public interest.

Under s. 388C, the Tribunal can pass an interim order in the interest of the members or creditors of the company or in the public interest or *suo motu* or on the application of the Central Government. The interim order may direct the concerned managerial personnel not to discharge any of the functions of the office until further order. The Tribunal can further order the appointment of a suitable person to perform the duties of the personnel concerned and specify the terms and conditions thereof.

At the conclusion of the hearing of the case, the Tribunal shall record its decision stating therein specifically as to whether or not the respondent is a fit and proper person to hold the office of director or any other office connected with the conduct and management of any company (s. 388D). On the basis of the findings of the Tribunal, the Central Government may, by order, remove from office any director, or any other person concerned in the conduct and management of the affairs of a company against whom where there is a decision of the Tribunal (s. 388E).

If the Tribunal receives a complaint against a company under ss. 397 or 398 against oppression and mismanagement of a company's affairs, the Tribunal may order for the termination or setting aside of an agreement with the company and any director. Such manager, director or managing director shall not be entitled to serve the company without the leave of the Tribunal. He shall also be not entitled to claim any compensation from the company for the loss of office [s. 407(*a*)].

In January 2009 the Central Government has intervened in the tainted "Satyam" and the Company Law Board has issued order to the existing directors of the board restraining them from exercising their functions. The Government also removed two directors from "Maytas" Infrastructure Company run by the sons of the tainted "Satyam" chairman.[10]

Before removing a director the following formalities should be completed or to make a check list:[11]

(1) A special notice as required under sub-sec. (2) of s. 284 was given to the company to remove a director.

(2) The company has sent forthwith a copy thereof to the director concerned and the director was provided opportunity to be heard on the resolution at the meeting.

(3) The representation, if any, made by concerned director has been notified to the members on the request of the director along with the notice of the resolution and if a copy of the representation was not sent because it was received too late or because of company's default, it was read out at the meeting on the request of the director.

(4) The director who was removed from office was not re-appointed as a director by the board of directors.

(5) The company has electronically filed e-form No. 32[12] with the Registrar of Companies within 30 days from the date of removal.

(6) Any order was passed by the Company Law Board for removal of director.

(7) Notify the change in directorships to all the stock exchanges where the company is listed.

10 http://www.business-standard.com/india/news/govt-moves-clb-to-supersede-boardsmaytas-firms/349395/, visited on 20.03.2009.

11 www.icsi.edu, visited on 20.12.2011.

12 *Inserted* vide GSR 56(E), dated 10.02.2006, see MCA 21 Initiation Guide, Appendix 1A.

1.18 Conclusion

Directors are the key personnel in a company, and their appointment, functions, disqualification and removal should be in accordance with best international practices. Since the economic liberalization in 1991, Indian Government came up with a number of amendments to the Companies Act 1956. However, the same is still not materialized due to opposition, mainly from the industrial houses. Directors are the driving force and brain of the "legal personality" like a company. Directors are dealing with enormous functions like economic, business and financial in the capacity of agents, employees, trustees and many more. The recent financial fraud revealed in an Indian IT company, "Satyam" cannot be seen in isolation. There should be proper control and regulation over such persons who control the giant financial dealing and only an efficient 'watch dog' can identify and prevent such fraud on the shareholders adversely affecting the whole economy of the country. The Securities and Exchange Board of India (SEBI) is not amply equipped to monitor efficiently the inside activities of the companies. The qualification and level of professional ethics should be raised to higher levels, so that the glory of Indian companies can be back. The proposed Bill may be an experiment by taking into consideration of all experiences in the past in a company administration which have to be passed in the Parliament as soon as possible. It may spell out the role of company directors more clearly and may fix liabilities firmly. Next chapter discusses the position of directors elaborately.

2

Position of Directors

2.1 Directors—position and possibilities

It is intricate to explain the position of directors in a company, as the Companies Act 1956 also has not tried to bestow or explain either intentionally or deliberately. Clause (13) of s. 2 of the Act states that a 'director' includes any person occupying the position of a director by whatever name called. Section 253 stipulates that only individual shall be appointed as a director. As observed by Subba Rao, J: "They are described sometimes as agents, sometimes as trustees and sometimes as managing partners of a company. They are professional men hired by the company to direct its affairs".[1] But they are not servants of the company as such as, Lush, J held, director is not a servant of any master and he cannot be described as a servant of the company or of anyone.[2] Director is not an employee of the company, but nothing prevents a director from working as an employee in a different capacity in the company in which he is a director; in such cases he is treated at par with other employees of the same position in that company.[3] However, in *Deen Dayalu, T.* v *Sri Bezwada Papi Reddy*, the Andhra Pradesh High Court held that a director is not a manager or any other managerial personnel of a company.[4] But in case of the *Global Drugs (P) Ltd.* v *M. Venkatnarayana*, the Court held that a director is an individual lawfully appointed to the Board of Directors of a company

1 *Ramchand & Sons Sugar Mills* v *Kanhayalal* (1966)2 Comp LJ 224; AIR 1966 SC 1899.
2 *Moriarty* v *Regent's Garage & Engineering Co.* [1921]2 KB 766.
3 *Lee* v *Lee's Air Farming Ltd.* [1961] AC 12.
4 (1984)2 Comp LJ (AP) 396; AIR 1984 AP 162.

which is duly constituted to direct, control and supervise the affairs of a company.[5]

In the above case, Madhava Rao and Sardar Ali Khan, JJ opined that "a plain reading of the above definition clause in our view clearly indicates that 'manager simpliciter' does not include a director. It means that 'manager' includes an individual who, subject to the superintendence, control and direction of the board of directors, has the management of the whole, or substantially the whole of the affairs of a company and includes a director or any other person occupying the position of a manager, by whatever name called and whether under a contract of service or not. *But every director cannot be a manager, and every manager cannot be a director.* In the absence of any evidence, it cannot be said that a director is functioning or discharging the duties as manager. In the affidavit filed in support of the writ petition nothing is stated indicating that directors are appointed as managers. This is a question of inquiry".[6]

Similar views were expressed by the English Courts, in *Shaw & Sons (Salford) Ltd.* v *Shaw*,[7] by Greer, LJ as follows:

> A company is an entity distinct alike from its shareholders and its directors. Some of its powers may, according to its articles, be exercised by directors; certain other powers may be reserved for the shareholders in general meeting. If powers of management are vested in the directors, they and they alone can exercise these powers. The only way in which the general body of shareholders can control the exercise of powers by the articles in the directors is by altering the articles, or, if opportunity arises under the articles, by refusing to re-elect the directors of whose actions they disapprove. They cannot themselves usurp the powers which by the articles are vested in the directors any more than the directors can usurp the powers vested by the articles in the general body of shareholders.

A director is under no disability in working as an employee in his own company, is affirmed in the above case. In *Lee's* case the managing director was working as pilot in the same company. After his death in

5 (2008)141 Comp Cas 935 (AP); (2008)84 SCL 120 (AP).
6 Emphasis added.
7 [1935]2 KB 113.

plane crash while acting as a pilot, his widow could recover compensation under Workmen's Compensation Act. But the different status is recognized only where sufficient proof of employment apart from being a director is available. But the whole burden of proof is with him.[8] Thus in *Parson* v *Albert J. Parsons Ltd.,*[9] the Court of Appeal disallowed a person's claim for compensation for his unfair dismissal from the directorship of a company for want of clear proof of his appointment as an employee under the company.

The position of directors is described thus: "Directors are not only agents but they are in some sense and to some extent, trustees or in the position of trustees. No doubt, their position differs considerably from that of the trustees of a marriage settlement or will, and it is well settled that the strict rules applicable to such trustees do not apply in all respects to directors... Nevertheless, it is impossible now to dispute the proposition that they are in some sense trustees, that proposition having been established by a long series of cases."[10]

The SC laid down the test as to whether or not a managing director is an employee in *Ram Prasad* v *CIT*:[11]

> "...though an agent as such is not a servant, a servant is generally for some purposes his master's implied agent, the extent of the agency depending upon the duties or position of the servant. It is again true that a director of a company is not a servant but an agent inasmuch as the company cannot act in its own person but has only to act through directors who *qua* the company have the relationship of an agent to its capacity... A servant acts under the direct control and supervision of his master. An agent, on the other hand, in the exercise of his work is not subject to the direct control or supervision of the principal, though he is bound to exercise his authority in accordance with all lawful orders and instructions which may be given to him from time to time by his principal. But this test is not universal in its application and does not determine in every case, having regard to the nature of employment, that he is a servant. A doctor may be employed as

8 Ibid., *Lee* v *Lee's Air Farming Ltd.* [1961] AC 12.
9 (1978) IRE 456; Noted (1978) JBL 61; 1979 ICR 271.
10 Palmer's *Company Precedents,* 17th Ed., Part I, pp. 512-14.
11 (1972)42 Comp Cas 544 (599); AIR 1973 SC 637; (1972)2 SCC 696.

> a medical officer and though no control is exercised over him in respect of the manner he should do the work nor in respect of the day to day work, he is required to do, he may nonetheless be a servant if his employment creates a relationship of master and servant. Similar is the case of a chauffeur who is employed to drive the car for his employer."

The court has of the opinion that "the managing director and the company may be similar to a person who is employed as a servant or an agent for the term 'employed' is facile enough to cover any of these relationships. The nature of his employment may be determined by the articles of association of a company and/or the agreement if any, under which a contractual relationship between the director and the company has been brought about, where under the director is constituted an employee of the company, if such be the case, his remuneration will be assessable as salary under s. 7. In other words, whether or not a managing director is a servant of the company apart from his being a director can only be determined by the articles of association and the terms of his employment. A similar view has been expressed by the Scottish Court of Session in *Anderson* v *James Sutherland (Peterhead) Ltd.*,[12] where Lord Normand held that:

> "... As managing director is a party to a contract with the company and this contract is a contract of employment; more specifically I am of the opinion that it is a contract of service and not a contract for services. There is nothing anomalous in this; indeed it is a commonplace of law that the same individual may have two or more capacities, each including special rights and duties in relation to the same thing or matter or in relation to the same persons."[13]

The nature of the employment may be decided by the articles of association and the agreement between the company and the managing director. The fact that apart from being a managing director, he is given the liberty to work for the company as an agent which is indicative of his employment as a managing director not being that of an agent. The

12 [1941] Scottish Cases 203.

13 http://www.executiverights.com.au/employment-law-case-watch/, visited on 11.07.2010.

terms of employment can only be decided by looking into the articles of association and contractual relation between the company and the managing director.

A director of a company, only by that reason or capacity, is not a servant of the company.[14] He is a person who is doing business for the company, but not on ordinary terms.[15] But that does not prevent a director from entering into a contractual relationship with the company. The relationship may be created either by service agreement or by the articles themselves.[16] However, it was also held that the question of employee will depend upon the facts of the case.[17]

Thus it is very difficult to explain the exact legal position of the directors of a company. The Companies Act also makes no serious effort to define their position. The Act states only so much that "director includes any person occupying the position of a director, by whatever name called."[18]

The decision of various courts has also not yet clearly defined the nature of the office of a director. It is rarely that the court has seemed to recognize that directors may occupy two positions regulated by entirely different principles. They are that of officers of the company appointed under the provisions of its constitution, and that of employees or agents of the company serving under express or implied contracts or service or as agents of the company. Most probably only his contract of service can shed light on his status in a company.

So to sum up, the position of a director is varied as he can rightly be considered as a trustee or commercial trustee, an agent, a managing partner, an indivisible organ of the company and what not, and each of his roles deserves to be examined separately.

2.2 Directors as agents

A company being an artificial person cannot act on itself. It must, therefore, act through some agents who are called, in the eyes of law,

14 *CIT* v *Armstrong Smith* (1946)14 ITR 606, 609 (Bom); *L. Armstrong Smith* (1946)16 Comp Cas 172 (Bom).
15 *CIT* v *Lady Navajbhai R.J. Tata* (1947)15 ITR 8, 11 (Bom).
16 *CIT* v *Armstrong Smith* (supra).
17 *CIT* v *Travancore Manufacturing Co.* (1982)133 ITR 818 (Ker).
18 Section 2(13).

agents of the company for which they act. Directors are agents of the company; they are special agents; they have such powers vested in them by the memorandum and articles. The general principles of agency, therefore, govern the relations of directors and of persons dealing with the company through its directors. A director is an agent of the company for the conduct of business of the company. As agents or officers of the company, directors have a fiduciary relation with the company and its shareholders.

Directors' position as agents of the company is well recognized as early as the decision in *Ferguson* v *Wilson*[19] in 1866, when the Court opined that "The company is not a natural person; it can act only through directors and the case is, as regards those directors, merely the ordinary case of principal and agent". It means that companies can only act through natural people employed to act as its agents. Consequently, where directors enter into contracts on behalf of the company, it is the company and not the directors, who are liable thereunder.[20] The principle of limited liability protects shareholders and not directors, and a director is as responsible for his own torts as any other servant or agent.[1] In *Trevor Ivory Ltd.* v *Anderson,*[2] the personal liabilities of directors were discussed elaborately by a New Zealand Court.

In this case *Trevor Ivory Ltd.* had contracted to provide horticultural advice to the Andersons who were orchardists. The advice was provided by Mr. Trevor Ivory, the sole director and shareholder of *Trevor Ivory Ltd.* The advice was negligent and caused the loss of the Andersons' raspberry crop. The Andersons sought damage not only from the company but from Mr. Ivory, suing him in the tort of negligent misstatement.

The Court unanimously dismissed the claim against Mr. Ivory. It has been held that when a company makes a negligent statement in the course of the business which damages the interests of the other party, it is the company that is subject to liability and not the director-controller of the company, even if it is he who made the statement on

19 [1866] LR 2 Ch App 77; 15 LT 230.

20 *Elkington & Co.* v *Hurter* [1892]2 Ch 452; *Belvedere Fish Guano Co.* v *Rainham Chemical Works* [1921]2 AC 465; *Smith* v *Hull Glass Co.* [1852]11 CB 897.

1 Hardie Boys, J *in Morton* v *Douglas Homes Ltd.* [1984]2 NZLR 548.

2 [1992]2 NZLR 517 (CA).

behalf of the company. The general rule does not apply in those exceptional cases where there is evidence that the director in question assumed individual personal responsibility.

Thus the relations subsisting between the company and its directors are those of the principal and agents and are governed by the general principles of agency. The company is liable for all its contracts entered between the directors and third parties on behalf of the company.

In *Automatic Self Cleansing Filter Syndicate Co. Ltd.* v *Cuninghame*,[3] the court observed that company is the principal or employer; the directors are agents or servants. Every principal or employer has a right to the obedience of his agents or servants in the case of all lawful commands. In the case of a company there is a great difficulty in making its wishes known, and directors are properly allowed a free hand; but when it does make known its wishes the directors must obey, in the absence of fraud and oppression.

The above decision was followed in *Horcal* v *Gatland Ltd.*, where it was held that directors have a positive duty to disclose breaches of fiduciary duty. A failure by a director of a company, as opposed to an employee, to disclose an earlier breach of fiduciary duty would render an agreement terminating his contract of service (on terms advantageous to the director) void on the grounds of mistake.[4]

In this case the company agreed to award a director a 'golden handshake' of £5,000 on the termination of his employment. Subsequently it was found that the director had acted in breach of his fiduciary duty to the company, in that he had appropriated the benefit of a contract with a customer. The company unsuccessfully sought repayment of the sum on the ground that he had failed to disclose that appropriation, which would have justified his dismissal for misconduct.

On appeal it was held that such an agreement was not avoided where at the time of the agreement the director had formed an intention to deprive the company of the profits of a contract, but he had not then done anything to implement that intention. Hence the appeal dismissed.[5]

3 [1906]2 Ch 34 (CA).
4 [1984] BCLC 549 (CA); [1984] IRLR 288 (CA).
5 http://www.lawteacher.net/cases/comp13.htm/file-21.php, visited on 08.02.2009.

In *Industrial Development Consultants* v *Cooley,*[6] the director's liabilities to account for the profits were discussed. Mr. Cooley was an architect and the managing director of IDC. The Eastern Gas Board has a lucrative contract going, to design a depot in Letchworth, but they told Mr. Cooley that they did not want to give it to his firm. Mr. Cooley told IDC that he felt a bit poorly and could he resign from his job on early notice. He resigned and got handsomely compensated. IDC found out the truth and they sued him for breach of his duty of loyalty. Citing Roskill, J, as quoted, *Parker* v *Mc Kenna,*[7] James, LJ said, at p. 124:

> I do not think it is necessary, but it appears to me very important, that we should concur in laying down again and again the general principle that in this court no agent in the course of his agency, in the matter of his agency, can be allowed to make any profit without the knowledge and consent of his principal; that that rule is an inflexible rule, and must be applied inexorably by this court, which is not entitled, in my judgment, to receive evidence, or suggestion, or argument as to whether the principal did or did not suffer any injury in fact by reason of the dealing of the agent; for the safety of mankind requires that no agent shall be able to put his principal to the danger of such an inquiry as that.

A director must account to the company for all of the company's property in his control. He is liable to account to the company for any unauthorized profits made by him by virtue of his office. This rule is absolute and independent of any question of fraud or absence of good faith and it matters not that the company itself could not have made the profits which the director made.[8]

Section 182 of the Indian Contract Act 1872 says that "An agent is a person employed to do any act for another or to represent another in dealings with third persons. The person for whom such act is done, or who is so represented, is called the principal." Where one employs another to do an act for him or to represent him in dealings with third parties, the person so employed is called an agent.

Section 2(13) of the Companies Act 1956 defines that "director includes any person occupying the position of a director by whatever

6 [1972]1 WLR 443; [1972]2 All ER 162.
7 [1874-75] LR 10 Ch App 96.
8 *Weber Feeds Ltd.* v *Weber* [1979]24 OR (2nd) 754 (Ont CA).

name called". Company directors can be called the agents of the company to do various functions on behalf of the company.

Thus, director is an individual lawfully appointed by the board of directors of a company which is duly constituted to direct, control and supervise the activities and affairs of a company. Directors of a company are, in the eye of law, agents of the company for which they act and the general principles of the law of principal and agent regulate in most respects the relationship of the company and its directors.[9] The test of agency is whether the person is purporting to enter into transaction on behalf of the principal or not. In order to constitute an agency, it is not necessary to have a formal agreement. As far as fiduciary duties are concerned, any breach by directors would make them liable. Directors would be liable for negligence, breach of trust, misfeasance, and *ultra vires* actions and for applying the funds of the company for such acts.

As per Lord Cranworth, LC in *Aberdeen Railway Co.* v *Blaikie Bros*:

> A corporate body can only act by agents, and it is, of course, the duty of those agents so to act as best to promote the interests of the corporation whose affairs they are conducting. Such agents have duties to discharge of a fiduciary nature towards their principal. And it is a rule of universal application that no one, having such duties to discharge, shall be allowed to enter into engagements in which he has, or can have, a personal interest conflicting or which possibly may conflict, with the interests of those whom he is bound to protect... So strictly is this principle adhered to that no question is allowed to be raised as to the fairness or unfairness of the contract entered into...[10]

In this case the director, Mr. Blaikie, was entrusted with the task of negotiating a contract to buy iron chairs for his railway company; he bought them from a firm in which he was the principal partner. This prompted Lord Cranworth, LC to lay down the celebrated statement that "no one having fiduciary duties to discharge shall be allowed to enter into engagements in which he has a conflicting personal interest". His Lordship explained that Mr. Blaikie's duty to obtain the chairs at

9 *Somayazula* v *Hope Prodhome & Co.* [1963]2 An WR 112.
10 [1854]1 Macq. HL 461; [1843-60] All ER Rep 249 (PC).

the lowest possible price conflicted with his personal interest (as seller) to obtain a price 'as high as possible'.[11]

The directors are the persons to whom the duties of managing the general affairs of the company are delegated. A corporate body can only act through agents, and it is of course the duty of those agents so to act as best to promote the interests of the corporation whose affairs they are conducting. Such agent has to discharge duties of a fiduciary nature towards their principal.

A director of a company is not necessarily the agent of the company or of its shareholders, but the true position of the directors of a company may be that of an agent of the company with powers and duties of carrying on the whole of its business, subject to the restrictions imposed by the articles of association.

As company is an artificial person, it can only contract through its agents; the normal mode of signing is to use the words 'on behalf of' so and so company before the signature of the agent signing, and if an agent so signs, no personal liability will attach to him. Directors are agents of the company to the extent of the authority delegated to them. Hence, where directors make a contract in the name of, or purporting to bind the company, it is the company–the principal–which is liable on it and not the directors. The directors are not personally liable unless it appears that they took personal liability.

Directors are not personally liable under a contract which is lawful if they have made in the proper exercise of their authority. Directors purchased goods for their company and agreed with the supplier to allot him debentures for the price. Before the debentures could be issued, the company went into liquidation. The supplier was held not liable to make the directors personally liable under the contract.[12] However, if they had contracted in their own names, they would have been personally liable. Where chief executive of the company executed promissory note and borrowed amount for company's sake, it could not be said that amount was borrowed by him, in his personal capacity.[13]

11 Rebecca Lee, *In Search of the Nature and Function of Fiduciary Loyalty: Some Observations on Conaglen's Analysis*, Oxford Journal of Legal Studies, 27, 2007, p. 327.

12 *Elkington & Co.* v *Hurter* [1892]2 Ch 452.

13 *Kirlampudi Sugar Mills Ltd.* v *G. Venkata Rao* (2003)42 SLC 798 (AP); 2003(2) ALT 550; (2003)114 Comp Cas 563 (AP).

Whereas surety was furnished by directors in their personal capacities and not for and on behalf of company, company could not be sued for the amount of surety.[14] Directors are personally liable where they exceeded their authority.[15] A transaction by the directors beyond their powers but within the powers of the company can be ratified by a resolution of the company or even by acquiescence.[16] Shareholders can by their assent ratify acts of directors which are *intra vires* the company, though they may not be *intra vires* the board of directors.[17]

In the case of *Port Canning Land Investments Reclamation and Docking Company Ltd.*,[18] it was held that "directors are better designated as agents of the company than as trustees... but, as regards the shareholders; they are clothed with a fiduciary character." The directors of a company are not in a fiduciary position towards the shareholders individually.[19]

It has also been held that directors are not exactly trustees except in a very limited sense like in the case of *Albert Judha* v *Ramapada Gupta*.[20] The Calcutta High Court held that directors are liable as trustees for breach of trust, if they mis-applied the funds or committed breach of by-laws. Their position differs considerably from ordinary trustees and it is futile to apply the entire law of Trust and the whole body of rules enunciated by the Court of Equity defining the rights and liabilities of the trustees, to determine the rights and liabilities of a director. The conduct of the directors is to be measured with reference to the character of the undertaking for which they are appointed to manage and conduct. In the case of an ordinary commercial company, a director does not commit a breach of trust when he, in the usual course of business, sells or purchases goods from another company in which the director had interest. He is only liable for breach of trust when he misapplies the fund and misappropriates any assets. In the instant case, the plaintiff as managing director has neither

14 *H.P. State Electricity Board* v *Shivalik Casting (P) Ltd.* (2003)115 Comp Cas 310 (HP); (2004)50 SCL 212 (HP).

15 *Weeks* v *Propert* [1873] LR & CP 427.

16 *Bhajekar* v *Shinkar* (1934)4 Comp Cas 434 (Bom); (1934)36 Bom LR 483.

17 *Balasaraswathi Ltd.* v *A. Parameswara Aiyer* (1956)26 Comp Cas 298 (Mad); AIR 1957 Mad 122.

18 (1871)6 Beng LR 278.

19 *Re, Richmond Gate Property Co. Ltd.* [1965]1 WLR 335.

20 AIR 1959 Cal 715; (1960)30 Comp Cas 582.

misappropriated the funds nor the assets of the company nor is he alleged to have committed any breach of bye-laws.

The Court observed that "there is no statute prohibiting contracts between two companies, one private and another public, with some common shareholders and common directors. The two companies in law are two different persons, even though they have some common shareholders or directors. Section 86F of the Companies Act does not, in my judgment, contain any such prohibition. On the contrary, it expressly states that a director, with the consent of the other directors, can enter into a contract with a partnership or private company in which he is a partner or shareholder or director. The section does not seem to recognise any public policy prohibiting contract between a private and public company with some common shareholders or directors. Not a single decision has been cited in which any Court, either in India or in England has held that such a contract between a public company and a private company with a common director is void on the ground of public policy. At best, in one case the Court refused to enforce such a contract and held that it is voidable and public company was relieved of the contractual obligation on equitable grounds. No case has been cited in which after the contract has been fully performed the Court directed restitution of the benefit on the ground that the contract was void."

In *Imperial Hydropathic Hotel Company* v *Humpson*, it has been held that directors are agents of the company and they are trustees for the company but not in the full sense of the terms.[1] In contracts entered by them, the directors act as agents, they having no personal liability.[2] But they are not agents for individual members of the company.[3]

The articles of association of a company may provide for the delegation of functions to the extent to which it is permitted under Indian Companies Act. They have to act within the scope of their authority given by the articles and all acts done by them while acting

1 [1882]23 Ch D 1 (12); 49 LT 147; *Regal (Hastings) Ltd.* v *Gulliver* [1942]1 All ER 378 (387).

2 *Wilson* v *Bury (Lord)* [1880]5 QBD 518; *Cargill* v *Bower* [1878]10 Ch D 502 (513); *Pudukkottah Textiles Ltd.* v *B.R. Adityan* (1975)1 MLJ 356.

3 *Gramaphone & Typewriter Ltd.* v *Stanley* [1908]2 KB 89.

within the scope of their authority are binding on the company though done with improper motive or to derive some wrongful benefit for themselves provided that the outsider acted *bona fide* and without notice.[4] In certain cases, a director might be in breach of duty if he delegates to others, the matters for which the board of directors as a whole had to take responsibility. Directors are ultimately entrusted with the management of the company; they cannot entirely divest themselves of their responsibility by delegation. The company can ratify an act done by the directors though in excess of their authority provided such act is within the powers of the company.

In *Re, County Life Assurance Co.*,[5] the Court considered the question of liability of directors in acts done within the purview of articles of the company. In this case the promoter of a life assurance company, who was also named as managing director in the Articles, continued to carry on business in spite of the fact that the three nominated directors in the Articles expressly prohibited the managing director to carry on the business and they refused to act as directors. The managing director thereupon proceeded to choose fresh directors in place of those who declined to act. The company issued a number of policies and the policies *ex facie* were in order and were consistent with the Articles. The company was wound up and in the winding up proceedings the question arose whether the policy was binding on the company.

Giffard, LJ held that "an outsider was not expected to know the indoor management of the company and could not be and was not aware that anything irregular had taken place". The learned Lord Justice upheld the claim under the policy with the following observation: "The company is bound by what takes place in the usual course of business with a third party where the third party deals *bona fide* with persons who may be termed '*de facto*' directors, and who might so far as he could tell have been directors '*de jure*' as well".

Directors have no liabilities if their acts come within the scope of the powers conferred on them. Thus in *Elkington & Co.* v *Hurter*,[6] the plaintiff supplied certain goods to a company through its Chairman who promised to issue him a debenture *in lieu* of price. But before the

4 *Hambro* v *Burnard* [1904]2 KB 10.
5 [1870] LR 5 Ch App 288.
6 [1892]2 Ch 452; 66 LT 764.

issue the company went into liquidation. It was held, he was not liable to the plaintiff. And also in *Trevor Ivory Ltd.* v *Anderson,*[7] it has been held that:

> When a company makes a negligent statement in the course of the business which damages the interests of the other party, it is the company that is subject to liability and not the director-Controller of the company, even if it is he who made the statement on behalf of the company. This general rule, however, does not apply in those exceptional cases where there is evidence that the director in question assumed individual personal responsibility.

The fiduciary obligation continues even after a person has ceased to be a director. But these obligations will remain limited. Ex-directors should not exploit 'corporate opportunity' in which the company has any 'interest or expectancy'.[8]

The cardinal principle of law of agency, that the notice to agent in the course of business amounts to notice to the principal,[9] is also applicable to the case of directors in their relation with the company. A director being placed in a controlling position in a company supposed to know all the important dealings of the company and fully representing his company in dealing with other persons, and therefore knowledge acquired by him while acting in the course of his duties is a sufficient notice to the company. This relation between the company and its directors is illustrated in *T.R. Pratt (Bombay) Ltd.* v *M.T. Ltd.*[10]

In the above case there were three companies namely S. Co., M.T. Co., and P. Co. For many years S. Co. had been financing P. Co. All the transactions of loan were entered through the agency of M.T. Co., which held almost all the shares in P. Co., and its directors were also the directors of P. Co. and this fact was known to the directors of S. Co. For a loan granted by S. Co., to M.T. Co., an equitable mortgage was created on the property of P. Co. In the winding up of P. Co., it was held that the official liquidator was entitled to avoid the equitable

7 [1992]2 NZLR 517 (CA).

8 Pearlie Koh, *Once a Director, Always a Fiduciary?* 62 Cambridge Law Journal 403.

9 Section 299 of Indian Contract Act 1872.

10 AIR 1938 PC 159; (1938)8 Comp Cas 137. See also *N. Bella Gowder* v *Tehsildar, Coonoor* (1969)71 ITR 26.

mortgage as the S. Co., through its directors, had the knowledge of the facts.

But notice to director will amount to notice to the company only if the director is, like an agent, bound in the course of his duty to receive the notice and to communicate it to the company. It was held in *Hampshire Land Co., Re,*[11] that where one person is an officer of two companies, he has personal knowledge of both the companies unless he is under a duty to receive the notice and communicate it to the other. In India the Bombay High Court also held the same view in a similar case.[12]

Even the directors as agents make the company liable for contempt of court. The SC, in *Vineet Kumar Mathur* v *Union of India,* directed the company in 1993 to close down the plant as the Pollution Control Board (PCB) refused to certify on the ground of non-fulfillment of required standards. The company runs for a period of 4 days in 1993 after the court order. The Court held that running the company even with the consent of the PCB was a violation of the court's order. A compensatory fine of ₹ 5 Lakhs was imposed beside costs on the company.[13]

The exemption of directors from personal liability is available not only in matters connected with contracts entered between the company and third person. But it also extended to other liabilities of the company; for example, the director of a company is not liable for the failure of the company to pay taxes and other arrears. Thus in the case of *Re, Desi Raju Venkata Krishna Sarma,*[14] a company failed to pay its sales tax for the year 1948-49 which was an offence punishable under the Madras General Sales Tax Act. The court convicted a director of the company, imposed fine and directed that the arrears of tax should be recovered from him. But the High Court reversed the order and held that directors being agents of the company there could be no personal obligation on them to pay the taxes payable by the company. However, s. 179 of the Income Tax Act 1961 imposes personal liability for tax arrears upon every director of a private company who cannot prove

11 [1896]2 Ch 743.
12 *Meenakshi Mills Ltd.* v *Ratilal Thakkar* AIR 1941 Bom 108.
13 (1996)20 CLA 213 (SC); (1996)7 SCC 714.
14 (1954)5 STC 448; (1955)25 Comp Cas 32 (AP).

that the default was not due to his neglect, misfeasance or breach of duty. This position is upheld in *N. Bella Gowder* v *Tehsildar, Coonoor*.[15]

Section 226 of the Indian Contract Act 1872 assumes that the contracts or act of the agent is one, which, as between the principal and third person, is binding on the principal. If the contracts is entered into, or act done professedly on behalf of the principal and is within the scope of the actual authority of agent, there is no difficulty. With regard to contracts and acts which are not actually authorized, the principal may be bound by them on the principle of estoppel, if they are within the scope of the agent's ostensible authority; but in no case is he bound by any unauthorized act or transaction with respect to persons having notice that the actual authority is being exceeded. Therefore no act done by an agent in excess of his actual authority is binding on the principal with respect to persons having notice that the act is unauthorized. An agent who was appointed by a power of attorney, borrowed money on the faith of a representation made by him that the power gave him full authority to borrow and misapplied it. The agent produced the power, which did not authorize the loan, but the lender did not read it, and made the advance in reliance on the agent's representation. It was held that the lender must be taken to have had notice of the terms of the power and that the principal was not bound by the loan.[16]

The s. 238 of the Indian Contract Act, which deals with effect on agreement of misrepresentation or fraud by agent, makes the principal bound by such acts of the agent having same effect as though the principals had committed the fraud or misrepresentation. But misrepresentations made or frauds committed by agents in matters that do not fall within their authority do not affect their principals.[17] A director of a company is not necessarily an agent of the company or its shareholders. If he acts as an agent he must specifically say so. So, in his written statement if a director did not raise such a plea, he is deemed to have acted on his personal capacity. So a suit against him alone is not barred by ss. 230 and 235 of the Contract Act.[18]

Thus it can be summarized that the directors of a company are its agents in all respects when the relation between the principal and

15 (1969) Comp LJ 34; (1968)1 MLJ 444; (1969)71 ITR 26 (Mad).
16 *Jacobs* v *Morris* [1902]1 Ch 816.
17 http://EzineArticles.com/?expert=Stuti_Bansal, visited on 26.01.2009.
18 *Raja Ram Jaiswal* v *Ganesh Parshad* AIR 1959 All 29.

agent as envisaged by the Indian Contract Act is considered. Judicial opinion also substantiates the position of directors as agents of the company. Thus in *Sadar Gulab Singh* v *Punjab Zamindara Bank Ltd.*,[19] upholding the removal of a director, the court held that:

> It would be contrary to public policy to impose upon an unwilling person or agent whom he does not wish to employ, because an agent can always bring an action for damages.

The Court in this case recognized the position of a director as that of an agent while upholding the removal of a director by the company who was not desirable to the company. But it should be remembered that they are the agents of the institution of company and not of its individual members. But the relationship of principal and agent may arise between a director and a member of the company due to special circumstances.[20]

The contractual obligation with the company is well explained in *Turquand's* case,[1] as stated in Halsbury's *Laws of England*,[2] and quoted in *Kanssen's* case,[3] in the following terms:

> But persons contracting with a company and dealing in good faith may assume that acts within its constitution and powers have been properly and duly performed, and are not bound to enquire whether acts of internal management have been regular... One of the fundamental maxims of the law is the maxim '*omina praesumuntur rite ease acta.*' It has many applications. In the law of agency it is illustrated by the doctrine of ostensible authority. In the law relating to corporations its application is very similar. The wheels of business will not go smoothly round unless it may be assumed that that is in order which appear to be in order. But the maxim has its proper limits. An ostensible agent cannot bind his principal to that which the principal cannot lawfully do. The directors or acting directors or other officers of a company cannot bind it to a transaction which is *ultra vires*. Nor is this the only

19 AIR 1942 Lah 47.
20 *Allen* v *Hyatt* [1914]30 TLR 444. Also see *Shyam Sundar Jalan* v *State* (1977)47 Comp Cas 61 (Cal).
1 [1856]6 E&B 327 (Exch Ch).
2 Hailsham Edition, Volume V, p. 423.
3 [1946] AC 459; [1946]1 All ER 586.

> limit to its application. It is a rule designed for the protection of those who are entitled to assume, just because they cannot know, that the person with whom they deal has the authority which he claims. This is clearly shown by the fact that the rule cannot be invoked if the condition is no longer satisfied that if he who would invoke it is put upon his inquiry. He cannot presume in his own favour that things are rightly done if inquiry that he ought to make would tell him that they were wrongly done.

This presumption of regularity in the internal management of the company in favour of an outsider dealing with the company is due to the fact that an outsider has no right to look at the indoor management of the company. This rule has been followed in a number of decisions some of which has been already noticed. This rule of indoor management was also applied by a Division Bench of the Bombay High Court in the case of *D. Pudumjee and Co.* v *N.H. Moos*,[4] reported in with the following observation:

> Persons contracting with the company are bound to know, or are precluded from denying that they know, the constitution of the company and its power as given by statute and Memorandum and Articles but they are not affected with notice of all that is contained in the register of directors kept as required by s. 87 of the Act. Notwithstanding the provisions of s. 87, the appointment of directors will remain a part of the 'indoor management' of the company and it would hardly conduce to the facility of business if outsiders are compelled to search the register and find for themselves whether a person who was permitted to act as director of the company for some length of time was also its director *de jure*.

The Madras High Court, in *Puddokottah Textiles Ltd.* v *B.R. Adityan*, observed that normally a director is not an agent of the company but where he acts as a director-in-charge and corresponds with another party to bring about a contract he will act as an agent. As such the liability is of the company and not the agent personally.[5]

The SC held that "the director of a company is not a servant but an agent inasmuch as a company cannot act in its own person but only

4 AIR 1926 Bom 28; (1925)27 Bom LR 1218.

5 *Puddokottah Textiles Ltd.* v *B.R. Adityan* (1975)88 Mad LW 688, 790.

through its directors, who qua the company have a relationship of an agent to the principal".[6] A managing director is not in a true sense a managing agent of the company, he may be a director and an agent, and sometimes he may both be a director and an employee. He has not only the persona of a director but also the persona of an employee or an agent depending on terms of his employment and the company's articles of association.

In *Lee Behrens & Co., Re*, it was observed that directors are elected representatives of the shareholders engaged in directing the affairs of the company on its behalf. As such directors are agents of the company but they are not employees or servants of the company. However, there is nothing in law to prevent a director from accepting employment under the company under a special contract which he may enter into with the company.[7] Where a director accepts employment under the company under a separate contract of service, in addition to the directorship, he is also treated as an employee or servant of the company. Directors are also treated as officers of the company for certain matters and are bracketed with the manager, secretary, etc. for this purpose.

In *Ferguson* v *Wilson*,[8] Turner and Cairns, LJJ pointed out that the directors are agents of the company. The company cannot itself act in its own person; it can only act through directors and the case is, as regards the directors merely the ordinary case of principal and agent, for whenever an agent is liable the directors would be liable. In some sense and to some extent, the directors are no doubt in the position of trustees. In *York and North Midland Ry. Co.* v *Hudson*,[9] Roumilly, MR observed:

> Directors are persons selected to manage the affairs of the Company for the benefit of the shareholders. It is an office of trust, which if they undertake, it is their duty to perform fully and entirely.

6 *Ramprasad* v *Commissioner of Income Tax* AIR 1973 SC 637; (1972)42 Comp Cas 544; *Commissioner of Income Tax* v *Manmohan Das* AIR 1966 SC 798; (1966)2 SCR 531; (1966)59 ITR 699.

7 (1932)2 Comp Cas 588.

8 [1866]2 Ch App 77.

9 [1845]16 Beav 485.

This twofold character of the directors has been well expressed by Lord Selbourne in *Great Eastern Railway Company* v *Turner*[10] in these words:

> The directors are the mere trustees or agents of the company-trustees of the company's money and property; agents in the transactions which they enter into on behalf of the company.

Sir George Jessel, MR, in the case of *Re, Forest of Dean, Coal Mining Co.*,[11] observed that "directors have sometimes been called as trustees or commercial trustees, and sometimes they have been called managing partners, it does not matter much what you call them so long as you understand what their real position is, which is that they are really commercial men managing a trading concern for the benefit of themselves and of all the shareholders in it. They stand in a fiduciary position towards the company in respect of their powers and capital under their control... a director is the managing partner of the concern, and although a debt is due to the concern I do not think it is right to call him a trustee of that debt which remains unpaid, though his liability in respect of it may in certain cases and in some respects be analogous to the liability of a trustee. So much for the question of unpaid debts."[12]

In *Aberdeen Railway Company* v *Blaikie*,[13] the head note reads: The director of a railway company is a trustee, and as such is precluded from dealing on behalf of the company with himself or with a firm of which he is a partner. According to Lord Cranworth, "A corporate body can only act by agents, and it is of course the duty of those agents so to act as best to promote the interests of the corporation whose affairs they are conducting. Such agents have duties to discharge of a fiduciary nature towards their principal, and it is a rule of universal application that no one having such duties to discharge shall be allowed to enter into engagements in which he has or can have a personal interest conflicting, or which possibly may conflict, with the interests of those whom he is bound to protect."

10 [1872] LR 8 Ch App 149.
11 [1878]10 Ch D 450.
12 See *Parker* v *McKenna* [1874-75] LR 10 Ch App 96; *Boardman* v *Phipps* [1966]3 All ER 721 (HL); [1967]2 AC 46; [1966]3 WLR 1009; *Horcal* v *Gartland* 1984 BCLC 549 (CA).
13 [1854]I MacQ 461.

2.3 Directors as trustees

A company, as already been stated, being an artificial person cannot manage its affairs or look after its properties or conduct its money transactions. The entire management of a company is entrusted with the director board and the managing director. So their position seems analogous with that of trustees or constructive trustees. But they are not properly being called trustees as the terms envisaged by the Indian Trusts Act 1882.[14] A trustee is a person who is vested with the legal ownership of assets which he administers for the benefit of another or others. Directors are regarded as trustees of the company's assets and of the powers that vest in them because they administer those assets and perform duties in the interest of the company and not for their own personal advantage. The duties of loyalty which the law requires of directors were developed by the courts by analogy with the duties of trustees. The concept developed prior to the British Joint Stock Companies Act 1844, when most of the companies were unincorporated and the validity of companies depended on a deed of settlement. The directors were entrusted with duties of trustees and even a distinction drawn between private trustees and managing board of trustees. The court of equity considered directors as trustees of company property. Further the courts extend this analogy to apply the label "trustee" to anyone in a fiduciary position.[15]

Trust is created always for and is annex to a property called 'trust property.' Directors' obligation, on the other hand, is not limited to the property of the company alone. It is extended to the whole management of the company. The directors are trustees of the company and not of individual shareholders of the company.[16] "Directors are subject to various duties, both common law and statutory. At a very fundamental level, these duties are directed at four well-defined objectives: to compel directors to act in accordance with the strict terms of their mandate; to compel them to exercise care and skill in carrying out their various functions; to compel them to use their wide discretionary

14 Section 3 of the Indian Trusts Act defines Trust as an obligation annexed to the ownership of property, and arising out of confidence reposed in and accepted by the owner, or declared and accepted by him, for the benefit of another, or of another and the owner.

15 Gower and Davies, *Principles of Modern Company Law,* (Thomson: London), 2008, p. 496.

16 *Percival* v *Wright* [1902]2 Ch 421.

powers in good faith and for proper purposes; and, finally, to compel them to act loyally in advancing the interest of their company."[17]

As per James, LJ the distinction between a director and a trustee is that; a trustee is a man who is the owner of the property and who deals with it as principal, as owner and as master, subject only to an equitable obligation to his *cestuie que trust*. The office of the director is that of a paid servant of the company.[18]

As their fiduciary duty, directors are expected to display good faith towards the company, in their dealings with or on behalf of the company. They are liable as trustees for breach of trust if they misapply the funds or commit breach of bylaws.[19] Fiduciary duties are concerned with the concept of loyalty and honesty and not with competence.[20] The said fiduciary duties are, however, owed to the company and the company alone and not to shareholders.

Although directors are not properly speaking trustees, yet they have always been treated as trustees of a company's money and property and trustees of powers entrusted to them. This is because of the peculiar position held by them. They are considered and treated as trustees of company's money which comes to their hands and trustees of company's properties which are actually under their control. They have always been held liable to make good to the company for moneys which they have misapplied upon the same footing as if they were trustees.[1] Again in *Baker* v *Gibbons*[2] it was held that:

> The trusteeship of directors extends not merely to the property of the Company, but also to the moneys of the Company, trade secrets and other items of intellectual property, the existence or particulars of *which* may be within the personal knowledge of the directors.

Another reason why directors have been described as trustees is the peculiar nature of this office. "The directors are selected to manage the

17 Sarah Worthington, *Corporate Governance: Remedying and Ratifying Directors' Breaches,* [2000]116 LQR 640.

18 *Smith* v *Anderson* [1880]15 Ch D 247 (CA).

19 *Albert Judah Judah* v *Ramapada Gupta* AIR 1959 Cal 715; (1960)30 Comp Cas 582.

20 *Extrasure Travel Ins. Ltd.* v *Scattergood* [2000]1 BCLC 598 (Ch D).

1 Per Lindley, LJ in *Re Lands Allotment Co.* [1894]11 Ch 616 (631).

2 [1972]11 WLR 693.

affairs of the company for the benefit of the share holders. It is an office of trust, which if they undertake, it is their duty to perform fully and entirely."[3] In the case of *Fateh Chand Kad* v *Hidsons (Patiala) Limited*[4] it was held that "a director stands in a fiduciary position to this company." Some of their duties to the company are of the same nature as those of a trustee. But in every case he is not regarded as a "trustee" in every single sense of the term. There is no legal guidance available on the extent to which a director is regarded as "trustee". Under s. 11 of the Indian Trusts Act 1882, it is the duty of the trustee to execute the trust reposed in him by fulfilling the purpose of the trust, etc. Under s. 46 of the same Act, a trustee who has once accepted the trust cannot afterwards renounce it except with the permission of the relevant Court, or the permission of the beneficiary or by virtue of a special power in the instrument of trust. This provision specifically refers to the resignation of a trustee.

The main elements of the directors' fiduciary duties are in the following categories:

- The directors must remain within the scope of the powers which have been conferred upon them.
- The directors must act in good faith to promote the success of the company.
- They must exercise independent judgment.

The other three categories are rule against directors putting themselves in a position in which their personal interests conflict with their duty to the company. The directors are prevented from doing business with the company in the following circumstances:

1. Out of a transaction with the company.
2. Out of the directors' personal exploitation of the company's property, information or opportunities.
3. Out of the receipt from their party of a benefit for exercising their directorial functions in a particular way.

3 Romily, MR, in *York & North Midland Railway Co.* v *Hudson* [1853]61 Beav 485; 22 LJ Ch 529.

4 (1957)27 Comp Cas 240.

2.4 The scope of trust (the beneficial interest)

Directors are not trustees in the strict sense of the term. They stand in a fiduciary relationship to the company and therefore may be called as quasi-trustees or constructive trustees. They hold a fiduciary position towards the company and have been considered and treated as:

(*a*) Trustees of a company's money and property; and

(*b*) Trustees of the powers entrusted to them.

The directors of a company are considered as trustees of the company's money and property in the sense that they must account for all the company's money which comes to their hand or all the properties which are actually under their control. Their position as trustees has been recognized by courts and they have been at several times held liable to make good to the company for the moneys which they have misapplied.[5] In *Horcal* v *Gartland Ltd.*,[6] it was held that "The failure by the directors to disclose a breach of his fiduciary duty would have rendered void the agreement with the company terminating his directorship and disentitled him from receiving compensation for the termination." *In Re Sharpe*[7] directors were held liable to replace capital which was taken by them in paying interest *ultra vires* the company. Again in *Selangor United Rubber Estates Ltd.* v *Cradock (No. 3)*,[8] the directors have been held trustees of the money standing to the credit of the company's bank account which they operate.

Again it may be noted that, a director's liability for the misuse of money does not come to an end with his death. Their liability is extended to their legal representatives and such cause of action survives against them. In *Ramaswamy Iyer* v *Brahmayya & Co.*,[9] the Madras High Court held that "The directors of a company are trustees for the company, and with reference to their power of applying funds of the company and for misuse of the power they could be rendered liable as

5 Per Lord Selborne, LC in *Great Eastern Railway Co.* v *Turner* [1872]8 Ch App 149 (152); also see Lindley, LJ *In Re, Hands Allotment Co.* [1894]1 Ch 616, p. 631.

6 [1984] BCLC 549 (CA); [1984] IRLR 288 (CA).

7 [1892]1 Ch 154: [1891-4] All ER Rep Ext 1974.

8 [1968]1 WLR 1555; [1968]2 All ER 1073; [1968]2 Lloyd's Rep 289; [1968]112 SJ 744 (Ch D).

9 (1966)1 Comp LJ 107 (Mad).

trustees and on their death the cause of action survives against their legal representatives."

In *R.K. Dalmia* v *Delhi Administration*, the SC held that directors as agents and trustees of the company who can be held liable under section 409 of the Indian Penal Code for criminal breach of trust with respect to the securities and funds of the company.[10]

Besides the money and property under their control, the directors are also trustees of the powers entrusted to them. They are considered as trustees of the powers entrusted to them in the sense that they must exercise their powers honestly and in the interest of the company and its shareholders and not in their own interest and if any loss is caused to the company because of their lack of care or otherwise they must make good to the company for such loss. In *Chevalier-II Iyyappan* v *Dharmodayam Co., Trichur,*[11] director's proposal to construct a building on the company's land at his own cost and hand it over back as trust property was accepted by the company. After the construction the directors created a trust by putting himself in the position of lessee of the premises. Supreme Court held that this is in breach of the fiduciary obligation. The Court observed that "when the director making the offer for creating a trust he was not merely an agent of the company but was also a trustee of the assets of the company and as such could not do anything in regard to assets of the company which would prejudicially affect its rights. The offer and the acceptance of the terms of the trust deed being wholly different from what had now been executed by the director and from the manner in which the new trust had been constituted into a lessee of the company without the company's agreement it was not possible for a court in equity to accept the new trust. The amount spent by the director having been returned to him he had suffered no loss. In these circumstances it was impossible to say that there were any equities in his favour which he was entitled to enforce by way of defence to the suit". In this case the SC recognized the fiduciary position of the directors in relation to the properties of the company.

Again in *Piercy* v *S. Mills & Co.*[12] the directors of a company had the power to issue the unissued shares of the company. The company

10 (1962)32 Comp Cas 699 (SC).
11 AIR 1966 SC 1017; (1963)1 SCR 85.
12 [1920]1 Ch 77.

was in no need of further capital, but the directors made a fresh issue to themselves and their supporters with a view to maintain the control over the company. It was held that the allotment of fresh shares was invalid and void. Thus after a thorough examination of the nature of the powers of directors of a company, it can rightly be concluded that all powers of directors are powers of trust.[13] The power to make calls,[14] to forfeit shares,[15] to issue further capital,[16] general powers of management[17] and power to accept or refuse transfer of shares,[18] are all powers in trust which have to be exercised in good faith for the benefit of the company as a whole.[19] It is a well settled principle that the directors are trustees of the moneys and property of the company.

2.5 Directors as trustees of the company

In Palmer's *Company Law*, the relationship with a company and director is explained as the fiduciary relationship of a director with the company; the director is not usually a trustee for individual shareholders. Thus, a director may accept a shareholder's offer to sell shares in the company although he may have information which is not available to others and the contract cannot be upset even if the director knew of some fact which made the offer an attractive proposition.

In *Percival* v *Wright*, the plaintiffs offered to sell their shares, and the defendants, the chairman of the board and two other directors agreed to buy them at £ 12.10s. per share. After completion of the transfer, it was found that at that point of time the board had been negotiating with an outsider for the sale of the company's whole undertaking at a price which represented well over £12.10s. per share, but the information was not shared with the plaintiffs.

13 See Berle, "*Corporate Powers as Powers in Trust*" where the learned writer enlists the powers of a director which have been held as powers in trust.
14 *Alexander* v *Automatic Telephone Co.* [1900]2 Ch 56 (CA).
15 *In Re Export Trading Co.* [1879]12 Ch 191.
16 *Nanalal Zaver* v *Bombay Life Association Co.* AIR 1950 SC 172; (1950) SCR 391; (1950)20 Comp Cas 179.
17 Per Romer, J, *In Re Equitable Fire Insurance Co. Ltd.* [1925] Ch 407 at p. 426; 133 LT 520.
18 *Bajaj Auto Ltd., Poona* v *Firodia* (1970)2 SCC 550; (1971)41 Comp Cas 1; AIR 1971 SC 321.
19 *In Re Smith and Fawcett Ltd.* [1942] Ch 304; [1942]1 All ER 542 (CA).

The directors of a Company bought shares from the plaintiff shareholders when negotiations for the sale of the Company's undertakings to another at a very high price were in progress. But they did not disclose this fact to the plaintiff. Afterwards the negotiations proved to be abortive, but the plaintiffs claimed that the non-disclosure was a breach of the fiduciary duty entitling them to repudiate the sale. The plaintiffs claimed that the directors stood in a fiduciary position towards them as shareholders. The Court held that "There was no such fiduciary duty towards the individual share holders and therefore, the directors were not bound to disclose negotiations which ultimately proved abortive".

In his judgment Swinfen-Eady, J said that there is no question of unfair dealing in this case. The directors never approached the shareholders with the view of obtaining their shares. The shareholders approached the directors and fixed the price at which they were desirous of selling.[20] It is clear that the courts have been reluctant to impose a duty on officers of a corporation not to do insider trade. The learned Judge held that management of a corporation does not owe a fiduciary duty to shareholders to avoid misusing corporate information for its own benefit – their only duty was to the company.[1]

The general principle regarding the fiduciary position of directors is that, they are trustees of the company and not of individual shareholders or outsiders. This principle was laid down in *Percival* v *Wright*[2] and still remains as the basic proposition.

In Pennington's *Company Law* it is stated: Directors owe no fiduciary or other duties to individual members of their company in directing and managing the company's affairs, acquiring or disposing of assets on the company's behalf, entering into transactions on its behalf, or in recommending the adoption by members of proposals made to them collectively. If the directors mismanage the company's affairs, they incur liability to pay damages or compensation to the company or to make restitution to it, but individual members cannot recover compensation for the loss they have respectively suffered by the consequential fall in value of their shares, and they cannot achieve this

20 Palmer's *Company Law*, 23rd Ed., p. 848.

1 *Percival* v *Wright* [1902]2 Ch 421; *Peskin* v *Anderson* [2001]1 BCLC 372 .

2 [1902]2 Ch 421. See also *Ramaswamy Iyer* v *Brahamayya & Co.* (1966)1 Comp LJ 107.

indirectly by suing the directors for conspiracy to breach the duties which they owed the company. However, there may be certain situations where directors do owe a fiduciary duty and a duty to exercise reasonable skill and care in advising members in connection with a transaction or situation which involves the company or its business undertaking and also the individual holdings of its members.[3] Therefore, the upshot of the above discussions is that the directors are in a position of a trust. They must confirm to the probity and their conduct should be above suspicion.

The Report of the High-Powered Expert Committee on Companies and MRTP Acts (1978) succinctly expresses the legal position of the directors as:

> Directors are appointed to act in the interests of the company and an important area of their legal responsibility stems from the law of Trusts – they have a fiduciary relationship with the Company. The duties arising from the relationship are well defined viz., to exercise their powers for the benefit of the Company, to avoid a Conflict of interests and a duty not to restrict their right to freely and fully exercise their duties and powers. In addition to their fiduciary duties, directors also owe a duty of care to the Company not to act negligently in the management of its affairs, the standard being that of a reasonable man looking after his own affairs.[4]

The rule in *Percival* v *Wright* though still represents the general principle, certain statutory provisions make it incumbent upon the directors to hold a fiduciary position towards the shareholders. Now there is a statutory obligation on the directors to disclose any profit occurring from the transfer of shares, property undertaking to the shareholders.[5] Contrary views also can be seen in cases like *Jones* v *Dumbrell.*[6]

Situations where directors are considered to be holding fiduciary position towards shareholders also received judicial recognition in many

3 Pennington's *Company Law*, 6th Ed., pp. 608-09.

4 Sachar Committee, See also P.V. Krishna Rao and K.P. Sastry, *Restrictive Trade Practices Policy in India*, The Journal of Industrial Economics, Vol. 37(4), 1989, pp. 427-435.

5 Section 193 of English Companies Act of 1948 and ss. 319-321 of the Indian Companies Act 1956.

6 [1981] VR 119, Supreme Court of Victoria (Aust).

cases.[7] The House of Lords in *Erlanger* v *New Sombrero Phosphate Company*, looked it differently and it is somewhat obvious that the relationship of a promoter and controller to his company is considerably different to that between a director and a shareholder. Nonetheless, Mahon, J expresses the view that:

> the essential basis of a breach of fiduciary duty is the improper advantage taken by the defendant of a confidence reposed in him either by, or for the benefit of, the plaintiff. When one considers the relationship between the shareholders in a limited company and the directors entrusted with the management... it appears ... that in any transaction involving the sale of shares between director and shareholder the director is the repository of confidence and trust necessarily vested in him by the share-holder, or by his legal status, in relation to the existence of information affecting the true value of those shares. I say this because a shareholder who is not a director has not in the absence of any special provision in the articles, any right to intervene in the management of the company...[8]

The Court in *Percival* v *Wright* disallowed shareholders' claim on the place of premature disclosure. This decision left scope for the Court to hold that when negotiations reach a certain stage of maturity director's disclosure of profit to the selling shareholders would be necessary. In such a situation the directors owe a fiduciary obligation towards the selling shareholders and failing in their duty of disclosure would cast liability on them.[9] This principle found application in *Allen* v *Hyatt*,[10] where the directors of a company represented to the shareholders that their consent is necessary to effect an amalgamation and induced the shareholders to give them the option to purchase their

7 See *Erlanger* v *New Sombrero Phosphate Company* (1878)3 App Cas 1218; and *Gluckstein* v *Barnes* [1900] AC 240; [1900]69 LJCH 385; [1900]82 LT 393; [1900]16 TLR 321 and J.H. Gross, *Company Promoters,* (1972) Chapter 6.

8 See also *Lynall* v *I.R.C.* [1971]3 All ER 914; [1972] AC 680 particularly Lord Reid at p. 919, nor in public companies, *Crabtree* v *Hinchcliffe* [1971]3 All ER 967; [1971]3 WLR 821. See also *Barry A.K. Rider, Percival* v *Wright. "Per Incuriam," The* Modern Law Review, vol. 40(4), (July 1977), pp. 471-476.

9 *Robert H. Mannheim in the Texas Gulf Sulphur Complaint* (1966), Journal of Business Law, 284.

10 AIR 1914 PC 246; (1914)30 TLR 444 (PC).

shares. They exercised the option, carried out the amalgamation and made profit. It was held that:[11]

> The directors were the trustees of this profit for the benefit of the share holders. They cannot always act under the impression that they have no duty to individual share holders. No doubt the duty of the directors is primarily one to the company itself. But the facts of the present case show that the directors had to hold themselves out to the individual shareholders as acting for them.

It is clear that where the directors have specifically undertaken to act as the shareholder's agents, a duty will be owed to individual shareholders.[12] The directors' position is well settled through a series of decisions by various courts. In *Regal (Hastings) Ltd.* v *Gulliver,* Lord Russell of Killowen observed as under: "Directors of a limited company are the creatures of a statute and occupy a position peculiar to themselves. In some respects they resemble trustees, in others they do not. In some respects they resemble agents, in others they do not. In some respects they resemble managing partners in others they do not". The said judgment quotes from Principles of Equity by Lord Kames & Henry Homes. In one sentence, the entire concept is conveyed. The sentence runs: "Equity prohibits a trustee from making any profit by his management, directly or indirectly. Ultimately the issue in each case will depend upon facts of that case."[13]

This position was followed by Indian courts as well. In *National Textile Workers' Union* v *P.R. Ramakrishnan,*[14] the Supreme Court held that the directors of a company are its agents and they stand in a fiduciary relationship to the company. The duties of good faith which are imposed by this fiduciary relationship are virtually identical with those imposed on trustees. The directors are generally expected not to place themselves in a position where their duties towards the company conflict with their personal interests.

The directors are trustees of the money with the company as well on behalf of the shareholders. The money so kept in the separate bank account is held by the company for and on behalf of the subscribers in a fiduciary capacity. Such amounts do not form part of the general

11 The judgement of the Lord Chancellor.
12 *Allen* v *Hyatt* AIR 1914 PC 246; (1914)30 TLR 444 (PC).
13 [1942]1 All ER 378 (HL).
14 AIR 1983 SC 75; (1983) 53 Comp Cas 184 (SC); (1983)1 SCC 228.

assets of the company. The relationship between the applicants and the company in respect of the application money so held in accordance with sub-sec. (3) is that of 'bailors and bailee and not of creditors and debtor.'[15] Where a director is a trustee for the qualification shares, *his cestui que* trust is not entitled to the amount of the remuneration given to the director.[16]

This position was confirmed in *Bajaj Auto Ltd.* v *N.K. Firodia*,[17] and later in *Life Insurance Corporation* v *Escorts*,[18] the nature of the power of the directors and scope of scrutiny by the court were explained: "Discretion implies just and proper consideration of the proposal in the facts and circumstances of the case. In the exercise of that discretion, the directors will act for the general interest of the shareholders because the directors are in a fiduciary position both towards the company and towards every shareholder. The directors, are therefore required to act *bona fide* and not arbitrarily and not for any collateral motive". This position is confirmed in *Shailesh Prabhudas Mehta* v *Calico Dying & Printing Mills Ltd.*[19]

A company is a juristic person and it acts through its directors who are collectively referred to as the board of directors. An individual director has no power to act on behalf of a company of which he is a director unless by some resolution of the board of directors of the company specific power is given to him/her. Whatever decisions are taken regarding running the affairs of the company, they are taken by the board of directors. The directors of companies have been variously described as agents, trustees or representatives, but one thing is certain that the directors' action on behalf of a company in a fiduciary capacity and their acts and deeds have to be exercised for the benefit of the company. They are agents of the company to the extent they have been authorized to perform certain acts on behalf of the company. In a limited sense they are also trustees for the shareholders of the company. To the extent the powers of the directors are delineated in the Memorandum and Articles of Association of a company, the directors

15 *Raymond Synthetics Ltd.* v *Union of India* AIR 1992 SC 847; (1992)73 Comp Cas 762 (SC). See Palmer's *Company Law*, 24th Ed., para 24.31; 1955(1) WLR 1080 (1085).
16 *Dover Coalfields Extension Co.* (1908)1 Ch 65.
17 AIR 1971 SC 321; (1971)41 Comp Cas 1 (SC); (1971)2 SCR 40.
18 AIR 1986 SC 1370; (1986)59 Comp Cas 548 (SC).
19 (1994)3 SCC 339; (1994)80 Comp Cas 64 (SC).

are bound to act accordingly. As agents of the company they must act within the scope of their authority and must disclose that they are acting on behalf of the company. They have a duty to make full and honest disclosure to the shareholders regarding all important matters relating to the company. It follows that in the matter of issue of additional shares, the directors owe a fiduciary duty to issue shares for a proper purpose. The fiduciary capacity, within which directors have to act, enjoins upon them a duty to act on behalf of a company with utmost good faith, utmost care and skill and due diligence and in the interest of the company they represent.[20]

In *Sangramsinh P. Gaekwad* v *Shantadevi P. Gaekwad (Dead) Through LRs*, it was observed that the director acts in a fiduciary capacity *vis-à-vis* the company. It was also observed that the court is bound to look at the business realities of the situation and not to confine to a narrow legalistic view. The interest of the company should be paramount, and isolated incidents may not be enough but there should be continuous oppressive conduct, for consideration to fix liability.[1]

In a recent decision on *J.K. Paliwal* v *Paliwal Steels Ltd.*,[2] regarding the role of directors in terms of ss. 397 and 398, the Company Law Board (CLB) held that the role of directors was well settled and they were the trustees of the company. Thus, the CLB opined that the directors were required to act on behalf of the company in a fiduciary capacity and their acts and deeds have to be exercised for the benefit of the company. In this case the Board found that the directors are failed to act as trustees. This decision was followed in the subsequent case and the SC held that the directors are trustees of the company and their acts and deeds must be for the benefit of the company.[3]

To sum up, under certain circumstances where a great trust and confidence is placed on or where the circumstances require utmost good faith to be shown by the directors towards the shareholders, it is incumbent on the directors to act for the benefit of the individual

20 *Dale and Carrington Invt. (P) Ltd.* v *P.K. Prathapan* (2004)122 Comp Cas 161 (SC); (2005)1 SCC 212.

1 AIR 2005 SC 809; (2005)123 Comp Cas 566 (SC).

2 (2007)5 Comp LJ 279 (CLB); (2008)141 Comp Cas 624 CLB; (2008) 81 SCL 121 (CLB).

3 *M.S.D.C Radharamanan* v *M.S.D Chanderaseker Raja* (2008)143 Comp Cas 97, 114; AIR 2008 SC 1738; (2008)6 SCC 750.

shareholders. After all, shareholders are the real beneficiaries of directorial trust; and it is in consonance with the norms of corporate democracy to see their rights being protected.

2.6 Social trustees

A company is an economic institution constituted solely for the purpose of the economic needs of its members. It has neither charitable purpose to be served nor any social cause to be upheld. Joint Stock companies emerged during when individualism and *laissez faire*[4] economic concepts were the chief political and economic ideologies. However, with the dawn of twentieth century, collectivism and the concept of welfare state began to emerge. Their impacts left nothing untouched and corporate management and control was not an exception to the sweeping changes in the attitude towards private enterprise.

Thus the role of a corporation in the modern society is something different from what it was in the previous century. Its role has also to be changed with the changing society. The modern company should function not simply as an economic machine designed to churn out profits for its shareholders, but rather as an institution which owes social responsibilities to a wide circle of interest.[5] The social character of a company received the recognition of the Supreme Court in *Chiranjiv Lal* v *Union of India*[6] where the court observed:

> A corporation which is engaged in the production of a commodity vitally essential to the community, has a social character of its own and it must not be regarded as the concern primarily or only of those who invest money in it.[7]

Thus it can be summarized that a modern company is essentially a Social Institution with a social purpose and the beneficiaries of a modern company are not shareholders alone. The investing persons,

4 An economic theory from the 18th century that is strongly opposed to any government intervention in business affairs.

5 R.C. Benthin, *The Range of a Company's Interest*, (1969)86 SALJ 155. The concept of the Company as social institution is developed in the works such as George Goyder, *The Future of Private Enterprise* (1951); *The Responsible Company* (1961); D.L. Mazumdar, *Towards a Philosophy of the Modern Corporation Asia,* (1967).

6 AIR 1951 SC 41 (59); 1950 SCR 869; (1951)21 Comp Cas 33 (SC).

7 Per Mukherjee, J.

labourers, consumers and the general public, etc, are all beneficiaries of the company. So those who look after the affairs of the company are not trustees of the shareholders alone, rather they are social trustees. A business executive once declared: "I am the trustee of the Institution and not merely the attorney of the investor".[8]

Thus, the brief discussion on the position of directors as trustees can be summarized as follows: Although directors are loosely called trustees, they are not trustees in the strict sense of the term. The correct view is that they stand in a fiduciary relationship to the company and are really only "quasi-trustees" because: (*a*) the company's money and property are only under their control and not vested with them but in the company itself; and (*b*) their duties of care are not onerous as those of trustees.

2.7 Directors as managers or employees

In *Lee* v *Lee Air Farming Ltd.,* it was held that a director is neither an employee nor a servant of the company unless he is working as such in a different capacity.[9] Directors are not managers of the company in the strict sense of the term. A manager is a paid executive of the company and is subject to the superintendence, control and directions of the board of directors.[10] He is a servant of the company and not part of the company. A director on the other hand is an integral part of the company. He is not a servant of the company.[11] Directors are not servants of the company and are not entitled to remuneration unless provided for in the articles.[12] However, although the directors are not managers of the company properly, under certain circumstances they are treated as officers of a company.[13] For example, the Companies Act indirectly permits a director to be appointed as an officer of the company by providing that no director of a company shall hold any office or place of profit under the company or under any subsidiary

8 Joseph L. Weiner, *The Barle-Dodd Dialogue of the Concept of the Corporation,* (1964)64 Col LR 1458.
9 [1961] AC 12 (PC).
10 Section 2(24).
11 *In re Newspaper Proprietary Syndicate Ltd.* [1900]2 Ch 349; 83 LT 341; *Ram Prashad* v *Commissioner of Income Tax, Delhi* (1972)2 SCC 696; AIR 1973 SC 637; 1973 SCR 3985.
12 *Whitehall Court Ltd.* [1887]56 LT 280; *Dunston* v *Imperial G.L.&W. Coke Co.* [1831]3 B & Ad 125.
13 Section 314(1).

of the company except with the consent of the company by a special resolution. It means that a director is expressly included in the definition of an 'officer'.[14] Again a director holding the office of manager or in the whole time employment of the company is entitled to get compensation for loss of office.[15]

Auditor appointed full time for the purpose of auditing the accounts of the company is an officer of the company under the English Law.[16] But the Indian law says the other way round. It was held that where an auditor retained only to carry out an audit function without appointment is not an officer within the meaning of the Act.[17]

Directors as such are not employees or servants of the company directly. It will depend upon the service or employment agreement with the company. A managing director or whole time director holds such a double role.[18] It means that quite apart from his office of director he becomes entitled to remuneration as an employee of the company. He is a person doing business for the company.[19]

Apart from these exceptional circumstances, directors are treated as officers of the company for certain matters also under the Companies Act. A director has to perform his functions with reasonable care. He has to attend with due diligence and caution the work assigned to him. He need not exhibit in the performance of his duties a greater degree of skill that may reasonably be expected from a person of his knowledge and experience.[20] The AP High Court in *Deen Dayalu T.* v *Sri Bezawada Papi Reddy*, it was held that a director is not a manager or any other managerial personnel.[1] But the recent cases shows a deviation from the traditional principles. In *Neufeld* v *Secy. of State, Enterprises and Regulatory Reform*, the court held that there was no reason why a person who was a shareholder and a director of the company could not also be an employee under a contract of employment with the company

14 *Pravin Sankalchand Shah* v *D.B. Dalal (Official Liquidator)* (1967)37 Comp Cas 317 (Bom).
15 Section 318.
16 *R.* v *Shacter* [1960]1 All ER 61; [1960]2 QB 252; [1960]2 WLR 258.
17 *Mutual Reinsurance Co. Ltd* v *Post Marwick Mitchell & Co.* [1996] BCC 1010; [1997]1 BCLC 1 (CA).
18 *CIT* v *Armstrong Smith* (1946)14 ITR 606 (Bom).
19 *Hutton* v *West Cork Railway Co.* [1883]23 Ch D 654.
20 *In re Brazilian Rubber Plantations & Estates Ltd.* [1911]1 Ch 425; 103 LT 697. Not liable for ignorance of trade practices.
1 (1984)2 Comp LJ 396 (AP); AIR 1984 AP 162.

even when his shareholding gave him a total control of the company. If there is a genuine employment contract, there was no alternate conclusion that he was an employee.[2]

Thus it may be summed up that, though directors are not properly be callèd or construed to be managers of the company, their position resemble to that of managers in a company.

2.8 Directors as members of the company

A company is an association of persons called shareholders who constitute money or money's worth (called shares) to a common stock called share capital and employ it in some common trade or business. Shareholders are, thus, its members. Its affairs are managed by persons called directors. They are only professional men hired by the company to direct its affairs. They are not members of the company though they are an integral part of the organizational structure of a company.

However, an article of a company may provide that a certain number of shares will have to be held by each director.[3] In that case directors are also treated as members of the company. In theory shareholders are the owners of the company and all of them are entitled to get an equitable treatment. But the so called corporate democracy in actual practice is a mere sham to cover the private character of public companies. In most cases the whole company is in the hands of few people who conduct its affairs as their family matters. This was what exactly happened in the case of "Satyam" an IT major where the Chairman, Mr. Ramalinga Raju used the company along with his family members as a family property even though they were the minority shareholders. The directors hold key positions in the Company as – the Chairman, Managing Director and majority of directors are either themselves or their supporters. They hold the vast majority of shares and can effectively control the management of the company. Actually the directors who hold the majority of shares are the true owners of the company; and their fraternity holding the positions of directors in rotation would ensure their control over the company.

Again, in most cases the promoters of the company who are also the subscribers of the memorandum are also seen to be in the controlling

2 [2009]2 BCLC 273 (CA). See also *Clark* v *Clark Constrution Initiatives Ltd.* [2009] BCLC 665; [2008] ICR 635.

3 Section 270 of the Companies Act 1956.

position of the company. Thus, it can be summarized that in most cases public companies are actually only partnerships and their directors are also their effective members.

2.9 Directors as organs of the company

Trading on joint account has a very long history. But its importance increased only in the twentieth century. During eighteenth and nineteenth century its role in business affairs was very minor one. In the end of twentieth century a wide transformation was seen due to globalization and liberalization in India and large joint stock companies emerged with large capital pooling and massive production. This change was due to the growth of international marketing and consumption. Thus corporations play a major part in the economic life of the country. Woodrow Wilson aptly remarked: "There was a time when corporations played a very minor part in our business affairs, but now they play the chief part, and most men are the servants of the corporations".[4]

This growing importance of corporations gives them enormous power to affect the lives of shareholders, labourers, consumers and the general public. But company being an artificial person could not be held liable in many circumstances in the part for wrongful acts involving certain mental elements. But this notion of exemption of corporations from criminal liability is gradually fading by giving way to the changed belief that the range of corporate responsibility almost corresponds with that of an individual.[5] But now the offending corporations cannot escape from the consequences of penal liability.

Again it may be noted that when fixing liability on the company for the actions of the directors, the intentions of those persons whose acts caused the injury is considered as the intentions of the company. "Hence certain persons are treated as the organs of the company, for whose actions the company is held to be liable just as natural person is for the action of his limbs".[6]

4 *The New Freedom* 24 (1967) Jaico.

5 C.R.N. Winn, *Criminal Liability of Corporations* (1929)3 Camb LJ 398.

6 Talukdar, J in *Gopal Khaitan* v *State* AIR 1969 Cal 132 at 138; (1969)39 Comp Cas 150.

This organic character of a company has been explained very well in *H.L. Bolton (Engineering) Co. Ltd.* v *T.J. Graham & Sons*[7] by Lord Justice Denning in the following words:

> A company may in many ways be likened to a human body. It has a brain and a nerve centre which holds the tools and act in accordance with directions from the centre. Some of the people in the company were servants and agents who are nothing more than hands to do the works, and cannot be said to represent the mind or will. Others are directors and managers who represent the directing mind or will of the company and ... is treated by the law as such.

Thus "the modern directors are something more than mere agents or trustees. The board is also correctly recognized to be a primary organ of the company".[8] In *Bath* v *Standard Land Co.* case, Neville, J observed that "the board of directors is the brain and the only brain of the company which is the body and the company can and does act only through them."[9]

Hidayatullah, J was of the opinion that, "When the brain functions the corporation is said to function."[10] Similarly, Greer, LJ, said in *Fanton* v *Denville* that "a general manager of a business is regarded as the 'alter ego' of the company, and it would responsible for his personal negligence."[11]

Thus it is now well accepted that a company is liable as the same footing as that of a natural person for the actions of officers of the company and whose intentions are intentions of the company itself.

In *Panorama Developments (Guildford) Ltd.* v *Fidelis Furnishing Fabrics Ltd.,*[12] a company has been held liable for the hire of car which was engaged by the secretary for his personal purposes while operating from the office of the company. Commenting upon the growing importance of the Secretary, Lord Denning, MR said:

7 [1957]1 QB 159; 1956 WLR 804; [1956]3 All ER 624 at 630.

8 R.C. Beuthin, *The Range of a Company's Interests* (1969)86 SALJ 155 (156).

9 [1911]1 Ch 618.

10 *State Trading Corporation* v *C.T.O.* AIR 1963 SC 1811 (1832); (1963)33 Comp Cas 1057.

11 [1932] KB 309 at 329.

12 [1971]13 WLR 440; [1971]13 All ER 16 (CA).

> A modern secretary is not a mere clerk but an officer of the company with extensive duties and responsibilities and has authority to sign contracts connected with the administrative side of a company's affairs and has ostensible authority to enter into a wide range of contracts. In that respect his position has altered materially since the nineteenth century.

Another factor which influenced the organic conception is that outsiders have no chance of notice as to how and by whom the company's internal machinery is handled. In such situations persons who are responsible for the irregularities are considered as part of the company and the company may be held liable. Thus a company may be held responsible for the statements in a prospectus issued by the board of directors.[13] On such situations company is held liable, like an ordinary person. Such circumstances compel the courts to identify a company with its members. In the circumstance the court would say, "where the responsible person is in the controlling position of the company, it would not be right to say that there were two persons or two minds."[14]

Thus, the modern directors are something more than mere agents or trustees or employees. The organic theory[15] of corporate treats them as organs of the company for whose actions the company is to be held liable just as a natural person is for the action of his limbs. His corporate rights are distinguished from individual rights; it is because they are controlled by this distinctive will. The Corporation as a person distinct from its members is not a fiction, but a reality.[16]

2.10 Conclusion

To conclude the discussion about the position of directors, their role in a modern company is varied with vast possibilities. They act as the managers/agents and trustees of the company. To sum up, we may

13 Palmer's *Company Law*, 20th Ed. 1959, p. 165.

14 *R.* v *McDonnell* [1966]1 All ER 193; [1966]1 QB 233.

15 The fiction theory has been strongly assailed in recent times by the German Jurists, who insist that the distinctiveness of the corporate personality is as real as the individuality of a physical person. The fiction theory maintains that the attribute of personality, involving unity of violation, belongs to the individual only, and the application of the term to composite bodies must rest upon a figure of speech adopted for convenience of reasoning.

16 Ernst Freund, *The Legal Nature of Corporations,* The University of Chicago, 1896, p. 14.

quote, Jussel, MR, who said: Directors have sometimes been called as trustees or commercial trustees, and sometimes they have been called managing partners; it does not matter what you call, the real position is that they are really commercial man managing a trading consortium for the benefit of themselves and of all the shareholders in it. They stand in a fiduciary position towards the company in respect of their powers and capital under their control.[17]

17 *In Re Forests of Dean Coal Mining Co.* [1878]10 Ch D 450.

3

Powers of the Board of Company Directors

3.1 Introduction

The board of directors and the shareholders in general meeting are the two primary organs of the company. But the powers of the general meeting of a company are limited. The general meeting has only minute role or no role at all in the day-to-day business of the company. Thus the powers of management of the affairs of the company are vested with the board of directors.[1] The board is responsible for conduct of the general operations of company in accordance with the articles of association. The board is recognized as the body of operation of companies from the beginning of the development of company law.[2] The board thus becomes the operational organ of the company.[3] The board of directors sometimes compared to an advisory board. The director board delegates most of its powers to individual directors to manage the company as agents. The over-all control and powers of directors is done only in accordance with the memorandum and articles of association of the company. Unless the directors are acting contrary to the memorandum and articles, the powers of conducting the management and affairs of the company are vested in them.[4] Every company is entitled to their collective wisdom. In furtherance of their collective·wisdom, one or more duties may assign to one director or a

1 Section 291 of the Act deals with general powers of the Board.

2 Gower and Davies, *Principles of Modern Company Law,* (Thomson: London), 2008, p. 411.

3 A. Ramaiya, *Guide to the Companies Act,* (Butterworths Wadhwa: Nagpur), 2010, p. 3538.

4 *Artens* v *Salmon* [1909] AC 442; *John Shaw & Sons (Salford) Ltd.* v *Shaw* [1935]2 KB 113; *Scott* v *Scott* [1943]1 All ER 582 (Ch D).

committee of directors or managing director or manager or other principal officers. The directors exercise these powers either directly or through officers subordinate to them. Mostly they are known as "power elite" in the society.[5]

The board of directors of a company can exercise all the powers of a company except those which are expressly required to be exercised by the company in general meeting, under the Companies Act, according to the memorandum and articles of the company. The directors, however, are to exercise their powers *bona fide* in the interest of the company. The powers of directors cannot be overridden even by the company in general meeting and they cannot interfere with the decision of directors. If the power of management is vested with the directors, nobody can overturn the decisions of directors. Under s. 291 of the Companies Act 1956 empowered the directors to do all the things that the company can do. This power includes the right to issue preference shares, borrow money, and all that power necessary for the management of the company. Section 292(2) of the Act deals with powers to be exercised by the Board only at meeting. That provision vests with the Board the power to do acts by means of resolution passed at meetings of the Board in respect of matters stipulated therein. A reading of the aforesaid provision shows that power to issue additional shares is not one such power which is conferred on the board of directors.

The Board thus becomes the working on behalf of the company. In their domain of power there can be no interference, not even by the shareholders. The manner in which the directors are to exercise their powers depends on the company's articles. The Act provides that in respect of the matters listed in s. 292, the Directors must sit together at a Board meeting, the company is entitled to their collective wisdom. The Act goes further and specifies in s. 293 a number of powers which the directors must exercise only with the consent of shareholders in general meeting. The Act thus makes managerial powers exercisable in three ways: (1) Powers which can be put to use in accordance with the Articles; (2) a set of powers which can be exercised only at a board

5 See Mayer N. Zald, *The Power and Functions of Boards of Directors: A Theoretical Synthesis*, The American Journal of Sociology, vol. 75(1), (July 1969), pp. 97-111.

meeting; and (3) another set of powers exercisable with the consent of shareholders in general meeting.[6]

The power to sell the property of the company is vested with the board of directors. If the directors feel that it is not in the interest of the company to sell its assets it is not bound to do so.[7] The directors can sue on behalf of the company and be sued. The directors cannot contract for depriving themselves of the power to control a manager so as to confer powers on him to the exclusion of them.[8] The directors and shareholders has to follow the directions given by the general meeting, but if it is not in the interest of the company they are not bound to act or adopt a particular line of action at the instance of the shareholders.[9] The directors and shareholders in a joint meeting are primary organizations of the company between whom the company's powers are divided.

Subject to the provisions of Companies Act, the Board of directors of a company shall be entitled to exercise all such powers, and to do all such acts and things, as the company is authorized to exercise and do.[10] The board of directors of a company shall exercise the following powers on behalf of the company, and it shall do so only by means of resolutions passed at meetings of the Board:

- the power to make calls on share holders in respect of money unpaid on their shares;
- the power to issue debentures;
- the power to borrow moneys otherwise than on debentures;
- the power to invest the funds of the company;
- the power to make loans;
- to diversify the business of the company;
- to approve amalgamation, merger or reconstruction; and

6 *I.T. Cube India (P.) Ltd.* v *I.T. Cube Inc.,* para 14 of the Karnataka High Court Judgment dated 13.03.2006; see http://www.indiankanoon.org/doc/694761/, visited on 25.08.2010.

7 *Pothan* v *Hindustan Trading Corp. P. Ltd.* (1967)37 Comp Cas 226 (Ker).

8 *Horn* v *Henry Faulder & Co.* [1908]99 LT 524.

9 *Automatic Self Cleansing Filter Syndicate Co. Ltd.* v *Cuningham* [1906]2 Ch 34.

10 Section 291 of the Companies Act 1956.

- to take over the company or a thorough controlling or substantial stake in another company.[11]

Acceptance of deposits of money from the public by banking company in the ordinary course of its business repayable on demand or otherwise and withdrawable by cheque, draft, order or otherwise or the placing of moneys on deposit by a banking company with another banking company on such conditions as the board may prescribe, shall not be deemed to be borrowing of moneys or making of loans by a banking company for the purpose of these provisions.

These provisions also do not apply to borrowings by a banking company from other banking companies or from the Reserve Bank of India or any other banks. In respect of dealings between a company and its bankers, the exercise by the company of its powers to borrow money otherwise than on debentures shall mean the arrangement made by the company with its bankers for the borrowing of money by way of overdraft or cash credit or otherwise and not the actual day-to-day operation of overdrafts, cash credit or other accounts.

Every resolution delegating the power referred to in cl. (*c*), (the power to borrow moneys otherwise than on debentures) shall specify the total amount outstanding at any one time up to which moneys may be borrowed by the delegate. Every resolution delegating the power referred to in cl. (*d*) (the power to invest the funds of the company) shall specify the total amount up to which the funds may be invested, and the nature of the investments which may be made, by the delegate. Every resolution delegating the power referred to in cl. (*e*) (the power to make loans) shall specify the total amount up to which loans may be made by the delegate, the purposes for which the loans may be made, and the maximum amount of loans which may be made for each such purpose in individual cases.

The directors as being placed in the controlling position of a company can exercise all such powers and can do all such things which the company is authorized to exercise and do.[12] A company, on the other hand, is authorized to exercise all those powers and to do all those things, subject to the provisions of the Companies Act or any other Act, which its memorandum and articles permit to exercise or do. Thus it

11 *Inserted* in the Companies Bill 2008.
12 Section 291(1).

can be said that directors' powers are co-extensive with that of the company.

As regards the nature of the powers exercised by directors it can be said that almost all the powers are in trust and are exercised by them in their personal discretion. These powers are so vast and as extensive as it is impossible to enumerate all of them. Yet reference may be made about the important areas in which directors have wide discretion and utmost good faith is required. This discretionary power deserves to be discussed in detail because utmost honesty and good-faith, which are expected from a fiduciary, are required in the exercise of powers in which the incumbent has discretion.

The modern doctrine was expressed in *John Shaw & Sons (Salford) Ltd.* v *Shaw*[13] by Greer, LJ as follows:

> A company is an entity distinct alike from its shareholders and its directors. Some of its powers may, according to its articles, be exercised by directors, certain other powers may be reserved for the shareholders in general meeting. If powers of management are vested in the directors, they and they alone can exercise these powers. The only way in which the general body of shareholders can control the exercise of powers by the articles in the directors is by altering the articles, or, if opportunity arises under the articles, by refusing to re-elect the directors of whose actions they disapprove. They cannot themselves usurp the powers which by the articles are vested in the directors any more than the directors can usurp the powers vested by the articles in the general body of shareholders.

3.2 Section 291—general powers of the Board

> 291. *General powers of the Board.* (1) Subject to the provisions of this Act, the Board of directors of a company shall be entitled to exercise all such powers, and to do all such acts and things, as the company is authorised to exercise and do:
>
> Provided that the Board shall not exercise any power or do any act or thing which is directed or required, whether by this or any other Act or by the memorandum or articles of the company or otherwise, to be exercised or done by the company in general meeting:

13 [1935]2 KB 113.

Provided further that in exercising any such power or doing any such act or thing, the Board shall be subject to the provisions contained in that behalf in this or any other Act, or in the memorandum or articles of the company, or in any regulations not inconsistent therewith and duly made thereunder, including regulations made by the company in general meeting.

(2) No regulation made by the company in general meeting shall invalidate any prior act of the Board which would have been valid if that regulation had not been made.

The following restricted powers can be exercised only with the consent of the company by a special resolution under the Companies Bill 2008:

1. to invest otherwise in trust securities the amount of compensation received by it as a result of any merger or amalgamation;
2. to borrow money exceeding that the digit of its paid-up share capital and free reserves, apart from temporary loans obtained from the companies bankers in the ordinary course of business;
3. to remit, or these time for the repayment of, any debt due from the director;
4. to contribute to charitable and other funds as donation in any financial year and amount in excess of 5% of the coverage net profits in the proceeding financial years.

The Companies Bill 2011 provides that the Board of Directors can exercise such powers mentioned in the memorandum and articles of association of a company. Clause 179 list out such powers as:

(*a*) to make calls on shareholders in respect of money unpaid on their shares;

(*b*) to authorise buy-back of securities under clause 68;

(*c*) to issue securities, including debentures, whether in or outside India;

(*d*) to borrow monies;

(*e*) to invest the funds of the company;

(*f*) to grant loans or give guarantee or provide security in respect of loans;

(*g*) to approve financial statement and the Board's report;

(*h*) to diversify the business of the company;

(*i*) to approve amalgamation, merger or reconstruction; and

(*j*) to take over a company or acquire a controlling or substantial stake in another company.

3.3 Management and control of the board

The fundamental principle relating to the administration of a company is that its board of directors should direct and control its affairs. The directors are persons selected to manage the affairs of the company. They are not mere agents of the company. There was a time when it seems to have been generally assumed that the general meeting is the company whereas the directors are merely the agents of the company subject to the control of the company in general meeting. Under s. 293 of the Act, the powers of the directors must exercise only with the consent of the shareholders in general meeting. The Act makes managerial powers exercisable in three ways (1) powers which can put to use in accordance with the articles; (2) a set of powers which can be exercisable only at board meetings; and (3) a set of powers which can be exercisable with the consent of shareholders in general meetings. In the modern time, institutional investors play a crucial role in the management of companies. The nominees of these investors in the director boards can truly act as independent oversight over the active management and monitor it.[14]

Thus in *Isle of Wight Railway* v *Taharuddin,*[15] the court refused an application by the directors of a statutory company for an injunction restraining the holding of a general meeting, one purpose of which was to appoint a committee to reorganize the management of the company. The court in this case held that "it is a very strong thing indeed to prevent shareholders from holding a meeting is the only way in which they interfere, if the majority of them think that the course taken by the directors, in a matter *intra vires* of the directors, is not for the benefit of the company."[16]

14 Edward S. Adams, *Corporate Governance after Enron and Global Crossing: Comparative Lessons for Cross-National Improvement*, 78 Indian Law Journal, 723, 2003.

15 [1883]25 Ch D 320 (CA).

16 Per Cotton D.T. at p. 329.

However, in *Automatic Self Cleansing Filter Syndicate Co. Ltd.* v *Cuninghame,*[17] the Court of Appeal made it clear that the director's powers to manage and control the affairs of the company entirely depend on the construction of the articles and that where powers had been vested in the board the general meeting could not interfere with their exercise. The articles were held to constitute a contract by which the members had agreed that "the directors and directors alone shall manage".[18] Hence, unless and until their powers were curtailed by extra ordinary resolution or an alteration of the articles they could ignore resolutions of the general meeting on matters of management.

The modern doctrine regarding the powers of the directors in managing and controlling the affairs of the company has been expressed in *Shaw & Sons (Salfard) Ltd.* v *Shaw*[19] as follows:

> If the powers of management are vested in the directors, they and they alone can exercise these powers. The only way in which the general of the shareholders can control the exercise of the powers vested by the articles in the directors is by altering their articles.[20]

The above said rule was followed by India in *M.P. & V. Works* v *M. Murarka.*[1] In *Suburban Bank (Pvt) Ltd.* v *Thariath,*[2] the court held that members were not allowed to interfere in the directors' discretion.

With regard to directors' powers of management and control, Lindley, LJ relies on partnership principles and argued that the position of the directors were analogous with that of a partner to whom all powers of management were delegated by the partnership deed and with whom the court would therefore not interfere. However, the directors cannot delegate further the powers to managers or managing agents. These include:

(*i*) The power to issue debentures;

(*ii*) The power to make calls on shareholders in respect of moneys unpaid on shares of the company;

17 [1906]2 Ch 34 (CA).
18 Per Cozens-Hardy, LJ at 11.44.
19 [1935]2 KB 113; [1935] All ER Rep 456 (CA).
20 Per Greer, LJ at p. 134.
1 AIR 1961 Cal 251; (1961)31 Comp Cas 301.
2 AIR 1968 Ker 206; (1968)38 Comp Cas 13.

(*iii*) The power to borrow moneys except within limits previously fixed by the directors at a board meeting;

(*iv*) The power to invest the funds of the company; and

(*v*) The power to make loans except within limits previously fixed by the directors at a board meeting.

The general rule is that except where express provision is made that the powers of a company in respect of any particular matter are to be exercised by the company in general meeting, in all other cases, the board of directors are entitled to exercise all its powers. The House of Lords in *Quin & Axtens, Limited* v *Salmon,*[3] it was held that if the resolution in general meeting is against the letter and spirit of the articles of association, the company must be restrained from acting upon it.

The powers of the directors are expressly stated by the Court of Appeal in *Automatic Self Cleansing Filter Syndicate Co. Ltd.* v *Cuninghame.*[4] Court observed that:

> the management of the business and the control of the company shall be vested in the directors, who, in addition to the powers and authorities by these presents expressly conferred upon them, may exercise all such powers and do all such acts and things as may be exercised or done by the company, and are not hereby or by statute expressly directed or required to be exercised or done by the company in general meeting; but subject nevertheless to the provisions of the statutes and of these presents, and to such regulations, not being inconsistent with these presents, as may from time to time be made by extraordinary resolution, but no regulation shall invalidate any prior act of the directors which would have been valid if such regulation had not been made.

The powers of the board of directors can be grouped under three heads:

1. Powers exercisable only at meetings of the board. These comprises:

    (*a*) The power to authorize buy-back of shares referred to in the first proviso to s. 77A(2)(*b*);

3 [1909] AC 442.
4 [1906]2 Ch 34 (CA).

(*b*) The filling of casual vacancies on the board [s. 262];

(*c*) The power to make calls on shareholders [s. 292(1)(*a*)];

(*d*) The power to issue debentures and borrow moneys otherwise on debentures [s. 292(1)(*b*)];

(*e*) The power to invest the company's funds and make loans [s. 292(1)(*d*) and (*e*)];

(*f*) The delegation of the power to borrow and to invest and make loans can also be effected only by means of resolutions passed at meetings of the Board [s. 292(1) proviso (2)(3) and (4)];

(*g*) The power to make political contributions [s. 293(*a*)].

(*h*) Giving consent to contracts of company with any director or his relative, firm, private company etc. [s. 297].

(*i*) Appointing as managing director or manager a person who is managing director or manager of another company [ss. 316 and 386].

(*j*) The power to sanction inter-corporate loans/investments or giving of guarantee or providing security [s. 372-A].

(*k*) The power to make a declaration in case of proposal for voluntary winding up [s. 488].

2. Powers exercisable only with the consent of the company in general meeting:

   (*a*) The power to sell, lease, otherwise dispose of the whole or part of the undertaking of the company [s. 293(1)(*a*)];

   (*b*) Power to remit debt due by a director [s. 293(1)(*b*)];

   (*c*) Power to invest compensation amounts received on compulsory acquisition of any of its properties [s. 293(1)(*c*)];

   (*d*) Power to borrow in excess of capital and reserves of the company [s. 293(1)(*d*)];

   (*e*) To contribute to charities [s. 293(1)(*e*)];

   (*f*) The power to appoint sole-selling agents [s. 294(2)].

3. All other powers which, subject to the provisions of the Act, the company is authorized to exercise. These may be exercised

either at meetings of the board or by circular resolutions (s. 289) or by delegating the same to committees or others.

If the directors misuse their powers, the resulting transaction is voidable and not void.[5] The courts are generally reluctant to grant an injunction against a company to restrain it from excluding a director from office or from interfering with the exercise of his functions, particularly when the shareholders who have the power to remove a director have resolved to exclude him from management.[6]

Under s. 293 there are restrictions on the powers of the board.[7] The board of directors of a public company, or of a private company which is a subsidiary of a public company, shall not, except with the consent of such public company or subsidiary in general meeting:

- sell, lease or otherwise dispose of the whole, or substantially the whole, of the undertaking of the company, or where the company owns more than one undertaking, of the whole, or substantially the whole, of any such undertaking;
- remit, or give time for the re-payment of, any debt due by a director except in the case of renewal or continuance of any advance made by a banking company to its director in the ordinary course of business;
- invest, otherwise than in trust securities, the amount of compensation received by the company in respect of compulsory acquisition of any such undertaking as is referred to in clause (a), or of any premises or properties used for any such undertaking and without which it cannot be carried on or can be carried on only with difficulty or only after a considerable time;
- borrow moneys, where the moneys to be borrowed together with the moneys already borrowed by the company, (apart from temporary loans obtained from the company's bankers in the ordinary course of business) will exceed the aggregate of the paid-up capital of the company and its free reserves; or

5 *Glover* v *Willert* [1996]20 ACSR 182 (SC).

6 *Harben* v *Philips* [1883]23 Ch D 14 (CA); *Bain Bridge* v *Smith* [1889]41 Ch D 462 (CA); *Browne* v *L.A. Trinidad* [1887]37 Ch 1 (CA).

7 Section 293.

- contribute, to charitable and other funds not directly relating to the business of the company or the welfare of its employees, any amounts the aggregate of which will, in any financial year, exceed fifty thousand rupees, or five per cent of its average net profits during the three financial years immediately preceding, whichever is greater.

The resolutions under cls. (*d*) and (*e*) above must specify the total amount up to which the board may borrow or the total amount which may be contributed in a financial year. Temporary loans mean loans repayable on demand or within 6 months from the date of the loan such as short term cash credit arrangements, the discounting of bills and the issue of other short term loans of a seasonal character, but does not include loans raised for the purpose of financial expenditure of a capital nature.

Any resolution passed by the company permitting any transaction such as is referred to in cl. (*a*) may attach such conditions to the permission as may be specified in the resolution, including conditions regarding the use, disposal or investment of the sale proceeds which may result from the transaction.

The acceptance by a banking company, in the ordinary course of its business, of deposits of money from the public, repayable on demand, or otherwise, and withdrawable by cheque, draft, order or otherwise, shall not be deemed to be a borrowing of moneys by the banking company within the meaning of cl. (*d*).

No debt incurred by the company in excess of the limit imposed by clause by cl. (*d*) shall be valid or effectual, unless the lender proves that he advanced the loan in good faith and without knowledge that the limit imposed by that clause had been exceeded.

The Companies Bill 2011 stipulates that if the board of directors wants to dispose off substantial undertaking of the company, which exceeds twenty percent of the investments of the company, borrow money which will exceed the aggregate of its paid up share capital and free reserves apart from temporary loans, they can do it only with the consent of the company by a special resolution.[8]

8 Section 180 of the Companies Bill 2011.

In *New Fleming Spinning and Weaving Co. Ltd.* v *Kessowji Naik,*[9] it has been observed that directors are responsible for the management of the company whereby under the articles of association the business is to be conducted by the board with the assistance of an agent. They cannot divest themselves of their responsibilities by delegating the whole management to the agent and abstaining from all enquiries. If the latter proved unfaithful under such circumstances the liability is theirs just as much as if they themselves had been unfaithful.

The Court observed that:

> "My conclusion is that, (*a*) although the directors are not trustees in every sense of the term, they stand in a fiduciary relation towards their shareholders with respect to the funds and the business placed in their charge, (*b*) It follows that they are liable to be sued for a breach of trust, in case they have not dealt with the property and watched over the business as carefully as a man of ordinary prudence would deal with such property and watch over such business if they were his own."[10]

The above observation made it clear that directors are liable for breach of trust and they have to look after the business of the company as a prudent man of reasonable diligence. Most of the English cases also support the view that directors are trustees of assets of the company.[11]

The Supreme Court in *Smt. Laxmi Devi Newar* v *East India Investment Company (P) Ltd.,*[12] laid down three tests to examine whether the board of directors are exercised the discretionary powers properly or not are: (*i*) whether the discretionary powers have been exercised in the interest of the company; (*ii*) whether they were exercised on wrong principle, and (*iii*) whether there

9 ILR (1885)9 Bom 373.

10 See also *Central Calcutta Bank Ltd., Re* (1959)29 Comp Cas 437; AIR 1959 Cal 625.

11 See also *Ramasami* v *Streeramulu Chetti* ILR (1896)19 Mad 149. The relationship of trustee and *cestui que trust* subsists between the Directors of Joint Stock Companies and the shareholders, it being held in such cases that misfeasance by a Director was a breach of trust. The same position was adopted in *In re Forest of Dean Coal Mining Co.* [1878]10 Ch D 450; see also *In re Exchange Banking Co.* LR [1882]21 Ch D 519; see also *in re National Funds Assurance Co.* LR 10 Ch D 118 and *In re Oxford Benefit Building and Investment Society* LR 35 Ch D 502.

12 (2007)137 Comp Cas 617 (CLB).

were exercised *mala fide* or for a oblique motive or for a collateral purpose.

The modern rule regarding the management of a company's affairs is that, in the absence of clear and specific provisions in the articles, the members in the general meeting cannot give directions on how the company's affairs to be dealt by the directors in their conduct of the business. The rule applies even as regards matters not specifically delegated to the directors provided they are not specifically reserved to the general meeting by the Act or the articles.

3.4 Allotment and transfer of shares

3.4.1 *Allotment*

At common-law, the allotment of shares was a matter of management and so, subject to restrictions in the company's articles, a matter for the board to decide.[13] Allotment means the appropriation of the shares of a company by the directors to a particular person. Allotting shares, making calls, forfeiting shares, accepting or rejecting transfers, etc. are powers in trust. A valid allotment can be effected only if the minimum subscription amount has been subscribed and the application money has been received in cash. If the minimum subscription has not been received and the money received from the applicant is not repaid, the directors become personally liable for the amount with interest unless the default is not due to their negligence or misconduct.

As regards the power of allotment, it may be said that, it is primarily falling upon the directors. This duty of the directors cannot be delegated except in accordance with the provisions of the articles. In *Bank of Peshawar Ltd.* v *Madho Ram,*[14] an allotment made by a general manager under an improper delegation by the directors was held to be invalid. But where the articles so provided an allotment made by secretaries and treasurers held to be regular and valid.[15] Again the allotment can be made by the directors only through a resolution of the board. The Gujarat High Court in *Smt. Shantadevi Pratapsingh Gaekwad* v *Sangramsinh P. Gaekwad,*[16] held that power of the directors to issues

13 http://www.companylawclub.co.uk/topics/faq045.htm, visited on 20.07.2009.
14 AIR 1919 Lah 351; 51 IC 812.
15 *Pasurala Sanyasi* v *Guntur Cotton, Jute & Paper Mills Co.* AIR 1915 Mad 325; 26 IC 349.
16 (2002)37 SLC 339; (2002)109 Comp Cas 533 (Guj) (DB).

shares to the members of the company is a fiduciary power to be exercised by them *bona fide* for the general advantage of the company and the directors are not entitled to use their power of issuing merely for the purpose of maintaining their control over the affair of the company or merely for the purpose of altering a majority shareholding.

The CLB in *Goldmark Enterprises Ltd.* v *Pondy Metal and Rolling Mills (P) Ltd.*,[17] held that the directors who are empowered by the articles to allot shares at their discretion must (*i*) exercise their powers with utmost good faith for the benefit and interest of the company; (*ii*) to ensure fair play in action and corporate management; and (*iii*) act *bona fide* in the exercise of their responsibilities in further issue of shares. It was also observed that the notice of a meeting of the company should be given to every member of the company whose name appears on the register of members. Increasing the capital from ₹ 125 lakhs to 225 lakhs, the directors utilized fiduciary powers of the shares not for the benefit of the company but for the purpose of consolidating the *de facto* controlling power of the respondent group by allotting shares in favour of the fourth respondent, in exclusion of majority shareholder is which could not be allowed. The directors were not entitled to use their powers of issuing shares for the purpose of defeating the wishes of the existing majority shareholders. Such issue of further shares converting the majority into a minority was a grave act of oppression.

In *Shree Krishna Agency Ltd.* v *CIT*,[18] it was held that even if absolute discretion is given to the directors, it does not confer any uncontrolled or unrestricted discretion. They cannot act arbitrarily or capriciously. The SC in *Bajaj Auto Ltd* v *N.K. Firodia*[19] it was held that when the directors have absolute and uncontrolled discretion to decline registration of transfer of shares, such discretion should be exercised *bona fide,* in the interest of the company/shareholders and not arbitrarily or for a collateral purpose.

The above position was upheld by the SC in *Indian Chemical Products Ltd.* v *State of Orissa.*[20] Court held that even if the Board had absolute

17 (2007)136 Comp Cas 598.
18 (1971)82 ITR 372 (SC).
19 AIR 1971 SC 321; (1971)2 SCR 40; (1971)41 Comp Cas 1.
20 AIR 1967 SC 253; 1966 SCR 380.

powers in the matter of registration of transfers, such powers should be exercised reasonably and in good faith and the court can control the discretion if they act capriciously or in bad faith.

The CLB in *Binani Metals Ltd.* v *Gallant Holdings Ltd.*, it was observed that directors owe a fiduciary duty to the shareholders of the company to issue shares for a proper purpose. Directors are not entitled to use their powers of issuing shares merely for the purpose of maintaining their control of themselves and their friends or the affairs of the company or merely troll of themselves and their friends, the affairs of the company or merely for the purpose of defeating the wishes of the existing majority of shareholding. In the present case it was alleged that the respondents *mala fide*, illegally and without following the process of law or without any notice to the existing members allotted shares to himself and his family members.

The CLB held that the respondents had issued additional shares with an intention to reduce the majority shareholding of the petitioners to equal shareholding and the allotment of additional shares was done with the object of gaining control of the company by becoming majority shareholders. In meetings passing such resolutions were held illegal, without the knowledge of petitioners, without giving proper notices and without following proper procedure. Therefore, allotment of additional shares in meetings were unauthorized an invalid and was to be set aside.[1]

It is the settled law that in the matter of issue of additional shares, the directors owe a fiduciary duty to issue shares for a proper purpose. This duty owed by the respondents to the shareholders of the company was breaching the act of the board of directors introducing majority of the petitioners with *mala fide* intention and is an act of oppression.[2] The doctrine of "proper purpose" requires that directors has to prove the necessity of increase in capital shareholdings and investment. In the matter of issue of shares, the directors have a fiduciary duty to shareholders of the company to issue shares for a proper purpose. The fiduciary capacity within which director has to act enjoins upon them a duty to act on behalf of the company with utmost care and skill and due diligence and in the interest of the company. They have a duty to make full and honest

1 (2008)143 Comp Cas 31 (CLB).

2 *Dale and Carrington Investment (P) Ltd.* v *P.K. Prathapan* (2004)122 Comp Cas 161; (2005)1 SCC 212.

disclosure to shareholders regarding all important matters relating to the company. The shares issued for maintenance and acquisition of control over the company is an extraneous purpose, and, therefore, cannot be upheld.

In *Needle Industries (India) Ltd.* v *Needle Industries Newey (India) Holdings Ltd,*[3] the Supreme Court referred to an old English decision with approval in *Punt* v *Symons and Co.,*[4] in which, it was held that:

> there shares had been issued by directors, not for a general benefit of the company, but for the purpose of controlling the shareholders of the greater number of shares by obtaining a majority of voting power, they owed to be restrained from holding the meeting at which the votes of the new shareholder where to have been used.

Again in *Piercy* v *S. Mills and Co. Ltd.,*[5] the same principle applied and holding that:

> the basis of both cases is, as I understand, that directors or not entitled to use their powers of issuing shares merely for the purpose of maintaining their control of the control of themselves and their friends of the affairs of the company, or merely for the purpose of defeating the wishes of the existing majority of shareholders.

All these cases proved that the directors cannot use their powers of issue of shares merely for an extraneous purpose or maintenance of acquisition of control over the affairs of the company. And also the motive for the allotment of the shares should not be *mala fide.*

3.4.2 *Transfer of shares*

Free transferability of shares is one of the main advantages of an incorporated company. The directors are not bound to register a transfer unless the application complies with the requirement of s. 108.[6] A company is not under any obligation to register a transfer of shares unless the instrument of transfer is (*i*) properly filled in, (*ii*) duly filled by the transfer and transferee, (*iii*) properly stamped,

3 (1981)51 Comp Cas 743; (1981)3 SCC 333; AIR 1981 SC 1298.
4 [1903]2 Ch 506 (Ch D).
5 [1920]1 Ch 77 (Ch D).
6 *Hemlata Saha* v *Stadmed P Ltd.* (1964)2 Comp LJ 75; (1964)34 Comp Cas 875 (Cal).

and (*iv*) such stamp ease duly challenged before it is delivered to the company.[7] If any changes or transferred or registered in contravention of section 108, the share register may be rectified by the court.[8] Where the directors have absolute discretion under the articles to refuse the registration of transfer, this discretionary power should not be exercised arbitrarily or *mala fide* or for collateral motive but in the general interest of the shareholders and the company.[9] If the directors feel that a particular transaction is not covered by the provisions of this section, the directors can deviate from that rule and take a decision which is equitable and fair to both parties.

However, the company may make regulations in its articles imposing fetters upon the right of transfer. The articles of private companies contain more rigorous restrictions on the right of its members to transfer shares. The directors of private companies have greater control over the transfer of shares. Thus in *Borland's Trustee* v *Steel Bros,*[10] it was held that if the articles of the company requiring that on the insolvency of a member, his shares would be transferred at a fair value to a nominee of the company directors were held to be valid.[11] The principle and position of directors was explained by the court in *Percival* v *Wright.*[12] In this case it was held that management of a corporation does not owe a fiduciary duty to shareholders to avoid misusing corporate information for its own benefit, rather their only duty was to the company.

Swinfen Eady, J said (at 425-27) that:

> ... It is urged that the directors hold a fiduciary position as trustees for the individual shareholders, and that, where negotiations for sale of the undertaking are on foot, they are in the position of trustees for sale ... It is contended that a shareholder knows that the directors are managing the business of the company in the

7 *Coronation Tea Co. Ltd., in re* (1962)32 Comp Cas 568; AIR 1961 Cal 528.

8 *Greene* v *Greene* [1949]1 All ER 167.

9 *Bajaj Auto Ltd.* v *N.K. Florida* AIR 1971 SC 321; (1971)2 SCR 40; (1971)41 Comp Cas 1.

10 [1901]1 Ch 279.

11 With reference to *Whitmore* v *Mason,* the court followed the judgment in this case Wood, VCJ held that "Where there is a *bona fide* intention to secure the going on of the concern, by the other parties handing over to the creditors all that the creditors ought to take, I cannot conceive there is any fraud on the bankruptcy laws" 2 J&H 204, 216.

12 [1902]2 Ch 421.

> ordinary course of management, and implicitly releases them from any obligation to disclose any information so acquired. That is to say, a director purchasing shares need not disclose a large casual profit, the discovery of a new vein, or the prospect of a good dividend in the immediate future, and similarly a director selling shares need not disclose losses, these being merely incidents in the ordinary course of management. But it is urged that, as soon as negotiations for the sale of the undertaking are on foot, the position is altered. Why? The true rule is that a shareholder is fixed with knowledge of all the directors' powers, and has no more reason to assume that they are not negotiating a sale of the undertaking than to assume that they are nor exercising any other power . . . I am therefore of opinion that the purchasing directors were under no obligation to disclose to their vendor shareholders the negotiations which ultimately proved abortive. The contrary view would place directors in a most invidious position, as they could not buy or sell shares without disclosing negotiations, a premature disclosure of which might well be against the best interests of the company. I am of opinion that directors are not in that position.

The directors in a private limited company are expected to make a disclosure to shareholders of such a company when further shares are being issued.[13] *Prima facie*, company's shares are freely transferable. Unless the company's regulations otherwise provide, the shareholder is entitled to transfer his shares to whom he likes. But the company's regulations may place restrictions on the right to transfer. These restrictions may in practice either in the form of giving the existing members a right to pre-emption in the purchase of the share or by centering a direction on the directors to refuse to pass transfers.

It is well accepted that, where the company's regulations confer discretion on the directors with regard to the acceptance of transfers, this discretion, like all the directors powers, is a fiduciary one. The directors are entitled to reject the transfer only on certain prescribed grounds on the true construction of the regulations. If it is proved that they have rejected the transfer on any ground other than those which

13 *Dale & Carrington Investment (P) Ltd.* v *P.K. Prathapan* (2004)122 Comp Cas 161 (SC); (2005)1 SCC 212; (2004)54 SLC 601 (SC).

are stated in the regulations, the court will interfere.[14] They may be asked to show on which are of certain prescribed grounds that they have acted.[15] But they cannot be asked to explain their reasons for rejecting the transfer of shares on these grounds.[16] Unless the articles of the company otherwise provide, the directors are not bound to state their reasons for rejecting the transfer.[17] But if the directors have stated their reasons for rejecting the transfer the court will investigate them to the extent of seeing whether they have acted on the right principles and will overrule their decision they have acted upon considerations which should not have weighed by them.[18] If the regulations are so constructed to give the directors an unfettered discretion, the court will only interfere with it on the ground of bad faith.[19] Although the regulations of the company give the directors the power to refuse to register transfer of shares, the manner in which the directors exercise this power and what extent the court can interfere deserve full consideration.

It is already stated that the directors have full direction with regard to the registration of transfer of shares. But they must exercise their discretion *bona fide* in what they consider is in the best 'interest of the company'. Court is not in a position to understand and decide the best interest of the company. When the directors consider a particular action is in the best interest of the company and they acted *bona fide*, the court would not be justified in interfering in the discretion of the directors. What matters is the 'good faith' and '*bona fide* action' of the directors and not the judgment of the court. If the directors have done in the best of their judgment, the court cannot substitute their judgment with its own. In the absence of evidence to the contrary, the court will take it for granted that the directors have acted reasonably and in good faith.[20] The exercise by the directors of discretionary powers will not

14 *Re Bede Steam Shipping Co.* [1917]1 Ch 123 (CA); 115 LT 580; 33 TIR 13.

15 *Sutherland* v *British Cominions Land Settlement Corpu* [1926] Ch 746.

16 *Ibid.*

17 *Berry Stewart* v *Tottenham Hotspur Football Co.* [1935] Ch 718, The Jenkins Committee recommended that directors should be required to state reasons, if asked, when they refused to register the personal representatives of a deceased shareholder: Cmnd. 1749 para 210.

18 Re, *Bede Steam Shipping Co.* (supra).

19 *Charles Forte Investments Ltd.* v *Amanda* [1964] Ch 240 (CA); *Re Hafuer* [1943] IR 264 (Ir SC).

20 *Gresham Life Assurance Society, Ex-parte Penney* [1872]8 Ch App 446.

be interfered with unless it is proved that they have acted with some improper motive or arbitrary or capriciously.[1]

The above said principle was laid down *in re Smith & Fawcett Ltd.*,[2] where the directors refused to register the transfer of all shares but agreed to register the transfer of some, on the condition that if the transferor would sell the balance to one of the directors at a certain price. It was held that this was insufficient evidence of *mala fideness*, and the court would not be justified in interfering in the discretion of the directors. The courts observed; "the directors must exercise their discretion *bona fide* in what they consider—not what a court may consider—is in the interest of the company".[3]

The directors have the power to issue shares at par even if the market value is above par. Such discretionary powers vested in the directors are in the nature of fiduciary powers and must be exercised in good faith.[4] The power to issue further shares must be for the benefit of the company. If it is detriment to the company, the court can intervene and prevent the directors from doing so. The directors are not chargeable with *mala fideness* or breach of trust merely because in promoting the interest of the company they were also promoting their own. However, the mere circumstance that the directors derive benefits as shareholders by reason of the exercise of their fiduciary power to issue shares, will not vitiate the exercise of that power.[5]

In *Hogg* v *Cramphorn Ltd.*,[6] the directors had issued shares with special voting rights to the trustees of a scheme set up for the benefit of the company employees in an attempt to forestall a takeover bid. While Buckley, J had accepted that the directors had acted in good faith, and they honestly believed that what they had done would benefit the company, his Lordship observed nonetheless that, "an essential element of the scheme, and indeed its primary purpose was to ensure control of the company by the directors and those whom they could

1 *Cannon* v *Trask* [1875] LR 20 Eq 669.

2 [1942] Ch 304; [1942]1 All ER 542.

3 Per Lord Greene *Tett* v *Phoenix Property and Investment Co. Ltd.* 1985 BCLC 599 at 621.

4 *Needle Industries (India) Ltd.* v *Needle Industries Newey (India) Holdings Ltd.* (1981)51 Comp Cas 743; AIR 1981 SC 1298.

5 *Nanalal Zaver* v *Bombay Life Assurance Co. Ltd.* (1950)20 Comp Cas 179; (1950) SCR 391.

6 [1967] Ch 254; [1966]3 WLR 995; [1966]3 All ER 420.

confidently regard as their supporters. Power to issue shares was fiduciary and if it was, 'exercised for an improper motive, the issue of these shares is liable to be set aside." The issue of shares was accordingly declared invalid. However, since the directors' breach of duty rendered their action voidable rather than void, it was capable of ratification by the shareholders in general meeting. The action was stood over and the allotment was later ratified. This decision had excited a measure of controversy in English and Australian Law.[7]

The practice in some countries leave the issuance of bonds entirely at the discretion of the company's board of directors, based on the assumption that the managers will have an incentive to obtain the best terms available, so shareholder approval is not necessary. A second group of countries, in contrast, look with greater suspicion on issuance of bonds. Some countries prohibit issuance of bonds for a period of time (up to 3 years) after the company's formation and require shareholder approval thereafter. Others limit the nominal value of bonds issued without a guarantee from a third party to the amount of the company's charter capital.[8]

The Madras High Court in *Coimbatore Kamala Mills Ltd.* v *T. Sundaram,*[9] it was held that if a director is refused transfer of shares, the company was bound to specify which of the grounds mentioned in the article was the ground on which the directors declined to register a transfer. Even though the directors did not specify the ground on which they had declined to register the transfer, the court should not grow unfavourable inferences against them. The presumption would be that directors had acted *bona fidely* and the onus would be on the

7 Buckley, J's recognition in *Hogg* that subjective honesty of purpose was not always sufficient, launched proper purposes as a separate test. The Court of Appeal in *Bramford* v *Bramford* relied upon *Hogg* as an accurate statement of the law; [1970] Ch 212; [1974]48 ALJ 319 at 321.

8 For example, under Paragraph 2 of Art. 33 of the Russian law on joint stock companies, a company issues bonds by decision of the company's board of directors, unless otherwise established in the company's charter. In France, a company cannot issue bonds during its first two years of existence and as long as its charter capital has not been entirely paid. From a practical point of view, a rule that a company cannot issue bonds during the first three years of its existence is not of great importance, since capital market rules would usually not allow companies to issue bonds during this period anyway.

9 (1950)20 Comp Cas 61; AIR 1950 Mad 725.

person challenging their action to establish the lack of *bona fides* and the impropriety on their part. The court observed that "were a discretion as to the registering transfers is by the articles given to the directors, the court will not control the exercise of such discretion, unless it is proved that the directors are not exercising it *bona fide* or are acting, in other words, oppressively, capriciously or corruptly or in some way *mala fide*". The court cited the decision *in re Smith and Fawcett Ltd.,*[10] in which it was held that "the directors may act any time in their absolute and uncontrolled discretion refuse to register any transferor of shares". If the action of the director was not *bona fide*, it will be arbitrary and illegal.

The CLB considered the question of nomination of additional directors and the director board in *ABP Ltd.* v *United News of India (UNI).*[11] In this case, the first respondent company was incorporated under s. 25 of the Companies Act 1956, with the main object to publish views regarding Indian and foreign affairs. Article four of the Articles of Association of the respondent company provided for allotment of shares only to owners of newspapers. The company was in a financial crisis and the committee to suggest measures for revival of the company suggested additional incorporation of capital. The unsubscribed shares were allotted to the fourth respondent in this case for a consideration of ₹ 5 Crores. For nominees of the committee, where appointed us additional directors of the respondent company at a board meeting. A petition filed under ss. 397 and 398 of the Act the petitioner alleged that the allotment of shares to the company had changed the character of the respondent company as it did resulted in creation of absolute majority, and the company was forced to transfer the management and control to the fourth respondent in this case.

The CLB held that both the allotment of shares as well as the changing the composition of the board would have lasting effect and therefore could be agitated in a petition under s. 397 or s. 398 of the Act. The petitioners alleged that the character of the company was changed due to decisions taken by the board of directors of the company, could be in kind of the petition. Every shareholder had the right to ensure that the character of the company was not changed

10 [1942]1 All ER 542.
11 (2008)142 Comp Cas 688 (CLB).

irrespective of whether it was the normal company or a company incorporated under s. 25 of the Act. According to Article 4 of the Articles of Association of the respondent company and the board of directors of the company could not allot shares other than to members. Moreover, the CLB found that allotment of majority shares to a single entity and appointment of a large number of nominees on the board of the company such important items on which decisions could not have been taken without including it in the agenda. There was lack of transparency in the procedure of allotment of shares in the respondent company. Hence, the allotment of shares to the fourth respondent company was null and void.

In *Howard Smith Ltd.* v *Ampol Petroleum Ltd.*,[12] the Privy Council held that directors cannot use their fiduciary powers to create any majority. Even though the company wants funds, the mode and manner adopted by the company allotment of shares is questionable.

The above position was confirmed by the Supreme Court in *Dale and Carrington Investment Pvt. Ltd.* v *P.K. Prathapan.*[13] The Court held that, it is the fiduciary responsibility of directors to make full disclosure before making allotment of shares. Without being included in the agenda, the board cannot increase the capital.[14]

The appointment of additional directors may lead to a situation of oppression and mismanagement. The CLB considered this question in *Chander Mohan Jain* v *CRM Digital Synergies Pvt. Ltd.*[15] In this case the respondent company was incorporated with the objective of taking over the business of a firm, which was engaged in the business of BPO. The petitioner, the majority shareholder, and the second respondent, the minority shareholder, were the only shareholders and directors of the respondent company. The partnership deed provided that only the partners of the firm should be the shareholders and directors of the company. As the petitioner was residing abroad, the second respondent was in control of the company, the petitioner engaging to agreement with the only customer of a company to sell his shares. The petition under ss. 397 and 398 of the Companies Act

12 [1974]1 All ER 1126 (PC); [1974]2 WLR 689; [1974] AC 821.

13 (2004)122 Comp Cas 161 (SC); (2005)1 SCC 212.

14 *Martin Castelino* v *Alpha Omega Shipmanagement Pvt. Ltd.* (2001)104 Comp Cas 687.

15 (2008)142 Comp Cas 658.

1956, the majority shareholder alleged that he had not been allowed to convene the board meeting to appoint additional directors to overcome the deadlock situation in the company. Secondly, the second respondent was guilty of financial mismanagement and siphoning off funds by payment of huge remuneration to her sun and husband. And the extra ordinary general meeting held under the direction of the CLB, the appointment of two additional directors was approved. The second respondent challenged the appointment of the two directors on the ground that the appointments were in violation of the partnership deed by which the business of the partnership was taken over by the company.

The CLB held that the provisions of the partnership deed not having been incorporated in the articles of association of the company, the petitioner was entitled to have his representatives on the Board under Art. 37 of the articles of association of the company. However, there should be justification to appoint outsiders on the board when there were only two shareholders who where the directors of the company. In such a case, there were only two directors in the company, the shares could not be transferred without the consent of the second respondent. The CLB found that the appointment of additional directors could be detrimental to the interest of the second respondent, who was a minority partner. Equitable consideration would overweigh the rights under the articles if the exercise of the rights resulting disastrous consequences against a partner in a partnership firm. Any decision taken by the reconstituted board has no effect. The court observed that if the majority shareholder doesn't have any interest in the affairs of the company and ready to sell his shares, the first option of purchasing shares should be given to the minority shareholder.

The CLB in *Smt. Laxmi Devi Newar (since deceased)* v *East India Investment Company (P) Ltd.,*[16] held that the articles of association of a company is a contract between the members and the company and the members *inter se*, the articles have to be construed in the manner in which they are understood by the members and company. If the power to dispense with production of probate was with the board, no individual director could have instead, asked for indemnity before the board considered the application and decided to call for indemnity

16 (2007)137 Comp Cas 617 (CLB).

and the decision was liable to be set aside. An act done by an individual director can only be ratified when a person who would have been competent to do such act. If the power is with the board, an individual director cannot act and later on such act done by an individual director cannot be ratified by the board if the memorandum not permits so.

The company had to ensure at all times, that its register reflects that names of persons to whom shares are transferred, which one can claim, only when one obtains probate in one's favour. If the will was under challenge, there was no certainty of obtaining probate and consequently no certainty to the position of execution. When the challenge to the will was in the public domain, no fair and sensible person could have exercised the discretionary powers to waive production of probate. The CLB observed that under the company law, knowledge of a director is the knowledge of the company itself.[17] The parties involved in the transmission they are closely associated with each other; inescapable conclusion was that they had acted in concert to get the shares transmitted in favour of the second respondent without production of probate by *mala fide* exercise of the board's discretionary powers.[18]

The vast body of case law on the scope of the directors' discretion in the registration of the transfer of shares contemplates – certain circumstances in which the court may interfere in the matter. Following grounds are held to be some of them:

3.4.2.1 BONA FIDE INTENTION

The rule *In Re Smith* is that the directors' discretion with regard to the acceptance of the transfer, like all the directors' powers, is a fiduciary one to be exercised *bona fide* and in good faith. The longed sequence of this rule is that they must exercise their power of refusal in good faith with *bona fide* for the benefit of the company and not for any collateral purpose.[19] Hence, the refusal to register a transfer must appear to have proceeded from an honest desire to benefit the company. Courts will not sustain a *mala fide* refusal of registration

17 *Pushpa Vadera* v *Thomas Cook (India) Ltd.* (1996)87 Comp Cas 921; (1995)4 Comp LJ 143.

18 This is the famous case of disputed will made by the deceased Mrs. Priyamvada Devi Birla in the name of Shri R.S. Lodha.

19 *Ibid*, p. 306.

of a transfer.[20] The court has to decide whether in exercising their power, the directors are acting oppressively, capriciously or corruptly or in some other way *mala fide*.[1] Where the directors propose to allot shares for an improper purpose, or not *bona fide* in the interests of the company then a member has standing to bring action to prevent the proposed allotment.[2] If the company in good faith gives effect to an agreement between the parties by making alterations in the register of members, the ratification of the register cannot be said to be illegal and void *ab initio*. Where a company has recognized the transfer of shares to a stranger and has register the transfer of undertaking, the transferee as a director on the basis of a transfer deed duly signed by the transferor along with a letter from him, subsequently the registration of the transfer cannot be challenged as *ultra vires* on the ground that certain formality laid down in the article of association of the company had not being followed.

3.4.2.2 IRRELEVANT CONSIDERATION

The regulations of the company may prescribe certain grounds on which a transfer may be rejected by the directors. If the regulations do not give unlimited freedom to the directors and prescribe certain grounds only on which a transfer may be rejected, the court can interfere if the directors have rejected the same on their grounds.[3] When they are rejecting a transfer, it is incumbent on them as trustees to specify the grounds on which they have declined a transfer.[4] However, the court would not entertain any adverse presumption regarding the relevancy of grounds if the directors do not furnish any grounds for rejection.[5] But a refusal based on extraneous considerations was held

20 *Re Gresham Life Ass. Society* [1872] LIZ 8 Ch App 446, 452; 28 LT 150; also *In Re Coal Port China Co.* [1895]2 Ch 404; [1895-9] All ER Rep Ext 2021; also *In Re Bell Bros.* [1891]65 LT 245; [1891]7 TLR 689.

1 *Harinagar Sugar Mills* v *Syam Sundar* AIR 1961 SC 1669 (1675); (1961)31 Comp Cas 387; also *Indian Chemical Products Ltd.* v *State of Orissa* (1966)2 Comp LJ 64; AIR 1967 SC 253; (1966)36 Comp Cas 638.

2 *Prem Seth* v *National Industries Corporation Ltd*, AIR 2001 Del 285; (2001)103 Comp Cas 1011 (Del).

3 *In Re Bede S.S. Co. Ltd.* [1917]1 Ch 123.

4 *Coimbatore Kamala Mills Ltd.* v *T. Sundrain* (1950)20 Comp Cas 61 (Mad); AIR 1950 Mad 725.

5 *Muthapa Chettiar* v *Salem Rajendra Mills* (1955)25 Comp Cas 283; (1955)2 Mad LJ 535.

to be wrong.[6] Again it was held that "the directors in refusing a transfer must have regard to those considerations and those only which the articles on their true construction permit them to take into consideration. However, the directors have an unfettered discretion; it is difficult for the Company Law Board (CLB) to interfere".[7]

3.4.2.3 INADEQUATE REASONS

The courts may enquire into the grounds upon which the directors have acted in rejecting a transfer, but do not ask the directors to furnish reasons for their refusal on these grounds.[8] Where the directors disclosed no reasons for their refusal to pass a transfer, the court expressed its helplessness in the matter.[9] If the directors have voluntarily stated the reasons the court will investigate upon them and may set aside it if they do not seem to be sufficient to justify their decisions.[10]

Thus the whole range of case laws on the subject upholds the principle that "the interest of the company" is the sole determining factor upon which the acceptance or refusal of the registration of a transfer of shares depends. If the entrance of a particular person seems to be against the interest of the company, then the directors are empowered to refuse a transfer of shares from existing member to that person. The ulterior motive of the existing directors to see themselves in the controlling position and to defect a take-over bid can no longer be considered as a ground for rejecting the transfer. Thus in *Jalpaiguri Cinema Co. Ltd.* v *Pramath Nath Mukherjee,*[11] the articles of the company had empowered the directors to refuse a

6 *Babulal Chouthani* v *Western India Theatres* (1958)28 Comp Cas 565; AIR 1957 Cal 709.

7 *Mathrubhumi Ltd.* v *Vardhman Publishers Ltd.* (1992)73 Comp Cas 80 Ker; (1992)1 Comp LJ 234 (Ker). See also *Bajaj Tempo Ltd* v *Bajaj Auto Ltd.* (1994)80 Comp Cas 618 (CLB).

8 *Sutherland* v *British Cominious Land Settlement Corpn.* [1926] Ch 746.

9 *Mathew Machael* v *Teekoy Rubbers (India) Ltd.* (1982) Tax LR 2493 (Ker); (1983)54 Comp Cas 88.

10 *In Re Smith & Fawcett Ltd.* [1942] Ch 304 (CA); *Re Bede S.S. Co* [1917]1 Ch 123; *Mathew Machael* v *Teekoy Rubbers (India) Ltd* (1990)69 Comp Cas 145 (Karn) (DB); *Mathesan* v *Nath Singh Oil Co. Ltd.* 18 JCZ 481; *Bajaj Auto Ltd.* v *Firodia* (1970)2 SCC 550; AIR 1971 SC 321; (1971)14 Comp Cas 1.

11 (1971)41 Comp Cas 678 (Del). Also *South Indian Bank* v *Joseph Michael* (1978)48 Comp Cas 368.

transfer of partly paid shares to a person of whom they would not approve. In the exercise of this power they rejected a transfer of fully paid shares on the ground that transferee had bought them for the purpose of acquiring control of the company and not for investment. This was held to be *ultra vires* the articles of the company.

Thus it was made clear in many cases that the motive of the transferee is irrelevant. It was held that a refusal on the ground that the transferee was a person who had no interest in the particular business of the company is not a sound one.[12] Again the regulations of the company give the directors only power to refuse to register a transfer and do not make their passing of transfers a condition precedent to registration. Normally transfers have to be passed by directors. The transferee is entitled to get his shares registered unless the directors decide to reject. Registration is the general rule and normal practice, whereas rejection is only an exception. It is one of the normal right of a shareholder that he should have the freedom to deal with his shares. So "any limitation on the right of transfer must be strictly complied with".[13]

It is well accepted that the directors can refuse the registration only where the articles or the regulations of the company empower them to do so. It was held that, "in construing the relevant provisions in the articles it is to be borne in mind that one of the normal right of a shareholder is the right to deal freely with his property and to transfer to whomsoever he pleases, and this right cannot be cut down by uncertain language or doubtful implications."[14] Thus, the Calcutta High Court held that the refusal of the directions of a company to register a transfer in favour of a company where they had the power to exclude undesirable persons was beyond their authority.[15]

Again the directors cannot be permitted to reject transfer of shares on frivolous grounds. Thus in *M.M. Anandram* v *Mysore Lachia Setty & Sons (P) Ltd.*, the directors were not permitted to reject a duly executed transfer only on the ground that there was a family dispute between the transferor and two sons.[16] Again, the directors were not

12 *In Re Bede Steam Shipping Co.* [1917]1 Ch 123.

13 Per Pennycuick, J, *In Re Swaldale Cleaners* [1968]1 WLR 1710; [1968]3 All ER 619 (CA).

14 *Ibid*, Per Lord Greene in *Re Smith*.

15 *Master Silk Mills (P) Ltd.* v *D.I.L Mclua* (1980)50 Comp Cas 365 (Guj).

16 (1985)58 Comp Cas 162 (Kant).

allowed to reject a transfer on the ground that the share certificate submitted along with the instrument of transfer was of greater number of shares than those transferred.[17]

As regards the manner of exercising the directors' discretion with regard to the registration of transfers, they must exercise their right to decline a registration only by passing a resolution to that effect at the board meeting. It means that individual directors cannot act on their own account. A mere failure in passing a resolution due to a deadlock or lack of quorum or something else is not an excuse to decline a transfer. Thus in *Moodie* v *W&F Shephere (Bookbinders) Ltd.,*[18] where the two directors disagreed and neither had a casting vote; the House of Lords held that registration must proceed.[19]

The right to transfer shares is a normal right of shareholders; and the transferee is entitled to get two shares registered unless the directors resolve otherwise. Thus if the directors do not resolve to decline to register, the shares are deemed to have been registered. So the power of refusal must be exercised within a reasonable period.[20] Section 111 of Indian Companies Act provides that the company shall send notice of the refusal to the transferee and the transferor within two months from the date on which the instrument of transfer or the intimation of such transmission was delivered to the company. Again it was held that this power is incapable of being exercised by reason of delay.[1] However, the Madras High Court upheld a rejection notified after two and a half months.[2] Similarly where the directors have the power to veto a transfer they will lose it if it is not exercised within a reasonable time after the transfer application forwarded.[3]

Thus the court has the power to interfere where the directors had exceeded the power conferred upon them. However, directors have an

17 *Kumar Exporters (P) Ltd.* v *Naini Oxygen Acetylene and Gas Ltd.* (1985)58 Comp Cas 97 (All). See also *Joseph Michael* v *Travancore Rubber and Tea Co Ltd.* (1986)59 Comp Cas 898 (Ker).

18 [1949]2 All ER 1044 (HL).

19 Also *Ramesh Chandra* v *Jogini Mohan* ILR 47 Cal 90; *Mahinuddin'g* case AIR 1928 Mad 571; *Babulal Chonkhani* v *Western India Theaters Ltd.* AIR 1957 Cal 709; (1958)28 Comp Cas 565.

20 *Sheperd's* case [1866] LR 2 Ch App 16.

1 *In Re Joint Stock Discount Co.* [1886] LR 3 EQ 77.

2 *In M.G. Amrithalingam* v *Gudiathan Textiles Pvt. Ltd.* (1972)42 Comp Cas 350.

3 *Re Swaldale Cleaners* [1968]I WLR 1710; [1968]3 All ER 619 (CA).

unfettered discretion in refusing transfer. In such circumstances the court can neither ask for nor are directors bound to disclose either the grounds or the reasons to refuse a transfer. However, the courts can interfere on clear proof of bad faith.[4]

3.5 Issue of debentures and declaration of dividends

Debentures[5] are issued by the board of directors.[6] But they can do this only by means of resolutions passed at the meeting of the board.[7] Debentures are issued by the directors usually in the form a certificate under the seal of the company. However, the case of *British India Steam Navigation Co.* v *Commissioners,*[8] shows that the seal is not necessary. There can be a debenture certificate merely signed by the directors and did not bear the company's seal was held valid. A public company may, however, require the approval of shareholders to borrow money in excess of the aggregate of its paid up capital and free reserves.[9]

As regards the declaration of dividends, the terms on which dividends are payable and the method of declaring them depend entirely on the provisions of the articles. However, in practice, dividends are declared by resolutions of the shareholders in general meeting in accordance with recommendations of the directors. Again they are empowered, before recommending any dividend, to set aside out of the profits any sum as a 'reserve funds'.[10] Such fund is, again, applicable at the discretion of the directors for any purpose to which profits may be applied.

4 *Re Smith & Fawcett* [1942] Ch 304 (CA); *Re Hafuer* [1943] IR 264; *Charles Forte Investment* v *Ananda* [1964] Ch 240 (CA).

5 Debentures have been defined under s. 2(12) of the Act to include debenture stocks, bonds and any other securities of the company whether constituting a charge on the company's assets or not.

6 A debenture is an instrument of debt executed by the company acknowledging its obligation to repay the sum at a specified rate and also carrying an interest. It is only one of the methods of raising the loan capital of the company. A debenture is thus like a certificate of loan or a loan bond evidencing the fact that the company is liable to pay a specified amount with interest and although the money raised by the debentures becomes a part of the company's capital structure, it does not become share capital.

7 Section 292(1)(*b*) of the Companies Act 1956.

8 [1881]7 QBD 165.

9 Section 293(1)(*d*).

10 Article 87 of Table A.

Further, besides the power of declaration of dividends and reservation out of the profit, the directors are empowered to declare interim dividends between two general meetings. Again it is open to the directors to rescind the resolution before payment. A mere declaration of interim dividends does not create any debt enforceable against the company until the directors fix a date for the payment.[11] Again, in *Vazir Sultan Tobacco Co.* v *C.I.T.*,[12] has been held that a mere recommendation of a dividend by the directors does not have any effect by itself unless approved in the general meeting. However, when a winding up procedure has commenced, a dividend cannot be payable.[13]

All these rules regarding the declaration of dividends will go to show that, although the shareholders in general meeting retain the ultimate theoretical control, the real control is vested in the directors. The shareholders have no say in the matter of interim dividends.[14] As regards final dividends for, the year they can only reduce the amount recommended by the directors and cannot raise it. But all these depend on the articles of the company.

3.6 Property, capital and money

Directors are trustees of the undertakings and property of the company. The money and other assets of a company cannot be employed for any purposes other than those pertaining to the objects specified in the memorandum of association of the company, or purposes incidental to those objects. The board of directors may sell, lease or otherwise dispose of the whole or substantial part of the property or undertaking of the company. However, they can do it only with the consent of the shareholders in general meeting if it is in accordance within the mandate of the articles.[15] Again the company in general meeting may empower the directors for the use, disposal or investment of the proceeds of such transactions. Further, the directors may divest the profit of the company after giving dividends, to for requiring properties for the company and may use them in new undertakings. The directors also have the power to make payments out of the company's funds

11 *Potel* v *IRC* [1971]2 All ER 504 (Ch D).
12 (1981)4 SCC 435 (455).
13 *Re W. Foster & Sons Ltd.* [1942]1 All ER 314 (Ch D).
14 *Scott* v *Scott* [1943]1 All ER 582.
15 Section 293(1)(*a*), Companies Act 1956.

consequent to the business of the company authorized by the memorandum of association, like payment of pensions to officers and other staff.

Courts usually used the *ultra vires* doctrine to find out whether a particular activity is within the memorandum of association, within powers of the directors and whether it is for the interest of the company and shareholders.[16] The Judges examined gratuitous and undervalued transactions of directors with care. *In Re, Lee, Behrens & Co Ltd.*[17] Eve, J discussed this position elaborately.

The case concerned a pension agreement concluded between a company and the widow of a longstanding and now deceased managing director of the company. A question arose as to whether this agreement was *ultra vires* the company. Clause 3 of the company's memorandum contained a power to provide for the welfare of persons in the employment of the company or formerly in its employment, and the widows and children of such persons by granting money or pensions etc. Eve, J interpreted this power narrowly and held that the agreement fell outside of the powers of the company.

He restricted the use of 'express or implied powers' by introducing three tests that needed to be satisfied in order for a transaction to fall within the scope of a power and as a result be considered to be *intra vires*. These tests are:

1. Is the transaction is reasonably incidental to carrying on the company's business?
2. Whether the transaction is a '*bona fide* transaction'?
3. Whether the transaction is done for the benefit and to promote the prosperity of the company?[18]

These three tests, if they had been adopted universally by the courts, would have transformed the *ultra vires* doctrine from involving questions as to the interpretation of the company's objects and powers into an enquiry into the benefits the company received through the

16 *In Re, George Newman & Co* [1895]1 Ch 674 at page 689; *In re Walters Deed of Guarantee. Walters' "Palm" Toffee, Limited* v *Walters* [1933]1 Ch 321 at page 322; see also Lord Wedderburn, *Ultra Vires in Modern Company Law*, (1983)56 MLR 204 at 207-8.

17 [1932]2 Ch 46.

18 *Ibid,* pp. 46-51.

transaction. Later decisions, however, have not wholeheartedly adopted Eve, J's three tests. The tests were applied in some later cases, but distinguished in others. The pattern that emerges from the later cases is that *Re Lee, Behrens*[19] was applied in cases where undervalue transactions involved shareholders and distinguished in cases where such transactions involved third parties. This pattern can be seen with the cases of *Re W&M Roith Ltd,*[20] where a pension agreement was considered to be *ultra vires* the company, and *Re Horsley & Weight,*[21] where a retirement policy was considered to be *intra vires.*

In Re, W&M Roith Ltd.[1] and *Re Horsley & Weight*[2] case, applied the tests in *Re Lee, Behrens* and agreed with the liquidator that the arrangement was not entered into for the benefit of the company but to provide for the widow of the director concerned. Other examples showing an application of the tests in *Re Lee, Behrens* along these lines are *Ridge Securities* v *IRC*[3] and *Charterbridge Corporation* v *Lloyds Bank.*[4]

The rule in *Re Lee, Behrens* was overruled in *Rolled Steel Products (Holdings) Ltd.* v *British Steel Corporation Ltd.*[5] In this case Rolled Steel gave a guarantee and debenture to another unrelated company, British Steel. One effect of the transaction was that the majority shareholder of Rolled Steel was released from a substantial part of a liability that arose under a personal guarantee he had given earlier to British Steel. Vinelott, J found at first instance that the transaction was *ultra vires* in a 'wider sense'. It fell within the scope of the powers of the company but it was entered into for an unauthorized purpose. This reasoning was rejected by the Court of Appeal which held that the transaction was not *ultra vires*. Slade, LJ found that the three tests suggested by Eve, J *In re Lee, Behrens'* should now be recognized as being of no assistance, and indeed positively misleading, when the relevant question is whether a particular gratuitous transaction is within the company's corporate capacity. To this extent the tests should

19 [1932]2 Ch 46.
20 [1967]1 All ER 427.
21 [1982]3 WLR 431; [1982]3 All ER 1045 (CA).
1 [1967]1 All ER 427.
2 [1982] Ch 442.
3 [1964]1 All ER 275.
4 [1970] Ch 62.
5 [1984] BCLC 466; [1985]3 All ER 52.

be ... finally laid to rest, though they may well be helpful in considering whether or not in any given case directors have abused the powers vested in them by the company.[6]

Rolled Steel's guarantee and debenture were found to be *intra vires*, but were nevertheless declared invalid because the directors of Rolled Steel had entered into the transactions in breach of the company's articles and in breach of their duties and because British Steel knew of this. A particular transaction falls within the objects of a company depends upon true construction of the company's memorandum. The court finally in this case held that the company's funds cannot be applied to making *ex gratia* payments as such.

Gratuitous payments or presents made of a company's moneys in India are, as a rule *ultra vires* except so far as they are permitted by the Companies Act 1956. Remuneration cannot be paid as *ex gratia*.[7] The shareholders-directors of a company cannot sit together under an agreement to distribute the company's money for repayment of their loans to the company and to distribute the remainder proportionately to their shareholding. The agreement was held to be not enforceable being in violation of directors' fiduciary duties to promote the interests of the company instead of their own. The agreement ignored the interests of creditor's altogether and had the effect of bringing about an informal winding up of the company.[8] The shareholders of a company formed a new company and agreed to provide funds to it on informal basis. There was no clear indication whether the money was supplied by way of loans or capital contribution. It was held that though there was no share allocation, the amounts advanced partook of the nature of the company's capital. They were not refundable to the providers of the funds. The company had subsequently gone into liquidation. The funds were divisible among shareholders only after payment of debts.[9]

The directors of a company, holding majority shares, formed a new company to which they proposed to divert the company's distribution rights. This amounted virtually to a misappropriation of the company's

6 [1986]1 Ch 246 (288).
7 *Halt Garage (1964) Ltd. Re* [1982]3 All ER 1016.
8 *Mac Pherson* v *European Strategic Bureau Ltd.* [2002]2 BCLC 683 (CA); [2002] BCC 39.
9 *Kellar* v *Williams* [2000]2 BCLC 390 (PC).

property. The members were purporting to accept the directors proposed course of action. They, at a meeting of the company, being in majority, passed resolutions dismissing the plaintiff as director and terminating his employment as managing director and general manger. The court granted an interim injunction against the proposed course of conduct. The court observed that:

(1) The grant of an interlocutory injunction depended, not upon the application of a set of fixed rules, but rather upon the decision whether, having regard to such factors as may be relevant in that case, it was, in the discretion of the court, appropriate to grant the relief sought. The defendant had established, on the affidavit evidence before the court, that the action proposed by the defendants was likely to amount to a breach of fiduciary duty, even though the company had, in general meeting, purported to accept that action.

(2) Difficulty and uncertainty in the assessment of damages was a relevant factor in deciding whether to grant an interlocutory injunction: if the defendants, in seeking to obtain the distributorship for themselves, had acted in breach of their fiduciary duty, they would be liable to account to the company for any profit made thereby: ascertainment of those profits could be extremely difficult, particularly if the new company had additional capital or if different shareholders became involved in that company. The volatile nature of the computer business also made the assessment of damages more problematic. The defendants, by proposing to obtain for themselves the company's most valuable asset, had forced the plaintiff to take legal action; and thus, the fact that the issue of an interlocutory injunction might put pressure on the defendants to purchase the plaintiff's shares on terms favourable to the plaintiff, for otherwise there was a danger that the distributorship might be granted to a third party, was no reason for refusing the grant of that interlocutory injunction.[10]

Further, the directors of a company have extensive powers with regard to the raising, maintenance, alteration, increase, reduction,

10 *Edney* v *Commodore Computer (NZ) Ltd.* [1985] LRC (Comm) 767 (NZ High Court).

further issue, conversion and disposal of capital. They raise capital by issuing shares and debentures. They can increase the capital by asking the shareholder to pay such portion of the uncalled capital. However, the directors in the exercise of raising, alteration and reduction of capital are strictly under the control of the shareholders.

If it is proved that the company's funds are diverted to extraneous purposes, it was held that the court has jurisdiction to pass an order for repayment to the company itself not only against members, former members or directors allegedly involved in the unlawful diversion, but also against third persons who had knowingly received or improperly assisted the wrongful diversion.[11] An injunction was issued to prevent foreign collaborators of a Sri Lankan company to draw payments from the company for the construction of a hotel in a manner which amounted to siphoning foreign exchange from the country and from the hands of the company.[12]

The directors of a company have wide range of powers in handling the surplus profit of the company. They may set aside any sum as a reserve fund out of profit before declaring dividends. They may use it in the business of the company. Further, they can recommend for the conversion of any amount standing to the credit of profit and loss account, reserve fund account or any other fund available for distribution up to capital.[13]

The trusteeship of directors extends not merely to the property of the company, but also to the moneys of the company, trade secrets and other items of intellectual property, the existence or particulars of which may be within the personal knowledge of the directors.[14] The money borrowed by the company under *ultra vires* transactions cannot be recovered from the company unless the money can be traced according to the rules laid down in *Sinclair* v *Brougham*. Their money is borrowed under an *ultra vires* transaction, it can be recovered by the lender only if the company puts the money into a separate account or the money is used to purchase a particular asset. Their money borrowed has been mixed up with other moneys and in the strict sense cannot be traced,

11 *Lowe* v *Fahey* [1966]1 BCLC 262 (Ch D); [1996] BCC 320.
12 *Amerakekara* v *Mitsui & Co. Ltd.* [1992] LRC (Comm) 636 (Sri Lanka SC).
13 Article 96 of Table A.
14 *Baket* v *Gibbons* [1972]1 WLR 693. http://www.lawteacher.net/cases/comp12.htm/file-97.php, visited on 12.02.2009.

the lender is entitled to a charge on the mixed fund with other claimants according to their respective amounts. The directors who receive the money on ultra-vires transactions stand in a fiduciary position towards the lenders with the result that the money is treated as if it were a trust property. Except in the hands of *bona fide* purchaser for value, the principle of trust can be enforced for the recovery of the money, provided it can be identified, by a charging order. Such right of lender can be enforced against any volunteer and anybody else receiving the trust property with notice. Where money has been spent in discharge of the company's debts legally payable the lender is entitled to the rights of the creditor who's debt has been paid and claim subrogation.[15]

It has been held in *Ciro Citterio Menswear Plc. (in Administration)*[16] that a loan to a director in contravention of the provisions of the Act did not automatically make the director a constructive trustee. A loan to a director in itself is not a misapplication of company money. If a loan is voidable, it stands until avoided. It means that property in the money paid under the loan passes to the borrower. The Judge found that such a concept is inimical to the existence of a constructive trusteeship, or any form of tracing claim, at least in the absence of special circumstances. That view is supported by the speech of Lord Goff in *Guinness Plc.* v *Saunders.*[17]

The Court observed that:

> The principal question in this part of this case is whether an unlawful loan gives rise to constructive trusteeship at any stage. I take as a starting point that a loan to a director is not of itself the sort of transaction that is inevitably a misapplication of company moneys. There is nothing inherently wrong with such a transaction in the abstract. It may or may not be a misapplication on any particular set of facts, but it is not, as such, a breach by a director of his trusteeship of company assets.

Accordingly the Court not allowed the administrator to claim equity in the property purchased with the loan amount on the footing that the director was a constructive trustee. On the other hand, directors

15 *Harris Calculating Machine Co.* [1914]1 Ch 920; *Reversion Fund & Insurance Co.* v *Maison Cosway Ltd.* [1913]1 KB 364.
16 [2002]2 All ER 717; [2003]113 Comp Cas 688 (Ch D).
17 [1990]2 AC 663 at 698; [1990]2 WLR 324; [1990]1 All ER 652.

are considered as express, rather than constructive trustees, when they are handling company's money.[18] An offshoot of the principle that corporate fund is in essence a trust fund is the principle that a person who receives any part of such a fund under a misapplication becomes a constructive trustee as such accountable to the company. The appropriate person to apply to the court for repayment of misappropriated fund of a company is not the shareholders, but the company itself.[19]

Where the funds of a company were diverted to another company to enable the two sons of the managing director to enable them to acquire control over that company, the two sons were not allowed to be charged with conspiracy and criminal breach of trust because they were not even the directors of the company at that time. Some corporate insiders or the company itself should have been linked and charged with the conspiracy and breach of trust.[20]

Again, the directors of a company have wide range of powers with regard to custody and disbursement of the company's money. They have full control over the money which comes to their hands and they keep it as trust for the company. They keep books of account. Every director has the right to inspect the books of account during business hours.[1] They lay reports and documents before the shareholders at every annual general meeting. Thus they have absolute control over the income and expenditure of the company.

The distinction between directors and trustees stems from the fact that directors unlike trustees deal with the property of the company as its agents, so to speak and not as the owner thereof. A director being governed by the provisions of the Companies Act and the articles of the company has greater flexibility in dealing with third parties than a trustee normally would.[2]

18 *Re Forest of Dean Coal Mining Co.* [1878]10 Ch D 450, 452, per Jessel, MR; *Re Sharpe* [1980]1 WLR 219; *Re Bennett* [1892]1 Ch 154; *Re Lands Allotment Co.* 70 LT 286 (290), per Lindley, LJ and 283, per Kay, LJ; *Soar* v *Ashwell* 69 LT 587, per Bowen, LJ; *The Selangor (No. 3)* case [1968]2 All ER 1073 (1091-1094).

19 *Russel* v *Wakefield Waterworks Co.* [1875] LR 20 Eq 474.

20 *Ashim K. Roy* v *Bipinbhai Vadilal Mehta* (1998) Comp Cas 1; (1997)103 Cr LJ 4651.

1 Section 209(4); *K.K. Kanagasaba* (2001) Comp Cas 596 (Mad); (2001)3 MLJ 596 (Mad).

2 Cf. *Smith* v *Anderson* [1880]15 Ch D 237 (CA).

The directors have a fiduciary duty in sale of assets. If the directors sold the company assets due to its financial difficulties to continue with the business, and keeping the business alive along with getting employment with the purchaser for the whole of the company workers along with directors is in good faith. The directors are under a duty to see that they do not leave the creditors in a worse position.[3] Once insolvency becomes likely, the directors must protect the interests of the creditors, not the shareholders.[4] At the same time the common law cases expresses the same sentiments. Directors are not entitled to sell the company's assets to save their jobs and those of other employees so that the creditors are put into a worse position than would be the case on liquidation.[5] However, a sale which is an honest attempt to save the business would not be considered to be in breach of the director's duty.[6]

3.7 Borrowing, lending and investment

The directors of a company, may, subject to the provisions of the memorandum borrow money by means of resolution passed at the meetings of the board. The Allahabad High Court in *Dehra Dun-Mussoorie Electric Tramway Co. Ltd.* v *Jagmandar Das,*[7] considered the question of the liability of the company in money borrowed by the managing director. In this case the managing director borrowed ₹ 25,000 from the respondent on a mortgage deed executed in 1923. The money was utilized for the necessary purposes of the company. The petitioner company argues that they are not bound by the mortgage deed for various reasons. The trial court held that the mortgage was binding upon company and decreed the plaintiffs' suit.

The court observed that the board of directors undoubtedly had power under the articles of Association to borrow money for the purposes of the company and to secure the loan by a mortgage. The articles of association of the company which lays down that "the board may delegate any of their powers, rather than covers to borrow and make

3 *Welfab Engineers, Re* [1990] BCLC 833 (Ch D).
4 *West Mercia Safetywear Ltd.* v *Dodd* [1988] BCLC 250.
5 *Re Ipcon Fashions Ltd.* [1989]5 BCC 773.
6 *Re CU Fittings Ltd.* [1989] BCLC 556 and *Re Welfab Engineers Ltd.* [1990] BCLC 833.
7 (1931) Comp Cas 227.

calls, to committees consisting of such number or members of their body are is they think fit". Under this article the board are expressly prohibited from delegating their power to borrow money. At the same time the managing agent was given the extensive powers to conduct and manage the business and affairs of the company and he was given power "to enter into old contracts and to do all other things usual, necessary or desirable in the management of the affairs of the company". The respondents contend that the proper of entering into contracts would include the power of contracting loans.

The court held that the articles must be read as they hold and is an article specifically restricts the board from delegating its powers of borrowing, the other article giving lots of powers to the managing director could not be interpreted so as to give the managing agent unrestricted powers of borrowing money on behalf of the company. If the managing agent did anything in the usual course of business, authorized under the ordinary rules of agency to obtain temporary accommodation from the bank for the purpose of protecting the interest of the company, he is well within his powers. The court observed that although the managing agent had no power to borrow money on behalf of the company, he was nevertheless authorized to incur temporary loans in an emergency, for protecting the interest of the company. Even though the managing agent exceeded his powers in obtaining the loan to meet an emergency, his action was never repudiated, but, on the contrary, was clearly ratified by the board of directors; so the court held that the company cannot escape liability on the ground that the managing agent had no authority to raise the loan.

The courts also observed that, even though the mortgage was executed by the managing director was without proper of the rescission from the board of directors. Even in the absence of a properly convened meeting to pass a resolution to authorize the managing director to execute the mortgage deed, thè plaintiff had no reason to suppose that the resolution had not been properly passed and was not binding upon the company.

The court referred the case of the *British Royal Bank* v *Turquand,*[8] in which it was held that the directors of the company were authorized in certain circumstances to give bonds but the company sought to

8 [1856]6 Ellis and Blackburn 327.

escape liability on the ground that there had been no resolution authorizing to making of the bond in suit. It was held that the plaintiff was entitled to judgment had been a right to presume that there had been a resolution at a general meeting authorizing the borrowing of money on the bond.

This position was confirmed in an Indian decision of *Ram Baran Singh* v *Mufassil Bank Limited.*[9] It was held that a company is liable for all acts done by directors even though unauthorized by it, provided such acts are between the apparent authority of the directors and not *ultra vires* of the company. Peoples dealing with a managing director bona fidely entitled to assume that he has all such powers as he purports to exercise, they are powers according to the constitution of the company, a managing director can have.[10] Accordingly the court confirmed the trial court decree granting to the plaintiffs a simple money decree to be realized in due course of liquidation. All these early decisions clearly points out that a company is liable for the activities of managing director who borrowed money for the legitimate interest of the company.

The director of a company to which Art. 73 of Table A of the Companies Act of 1913 applies, have power to borrow on behalf of the company up to the issued capital of the company and beyond with the consent of the shareholders. It has been held in *Balasaraswathi Ltd.* v *Parameswara Iyer,*[11] that it was not necessary where the directors borrowed be owed the share capital that the consent of the shareholders should necessarily be obtained in a general meeting. The object of Article 73 was to ensure the interest of shareholders and not to ensure compliance with any metaphysical requirements and that there was no point in setting up the company as an entity apart from the shareholders. Even if no meeting was held it was within the powers of the shareholders to ratify without a formal meeting any borrowing in excess of capital. It was accordingly held that were the only shareholders of the company joined in borrowing a certain sum of money for purchasing assets of the company and the some borrowed was beyond the share capital the company was liable to pay the full amount of the debts.

9 AIR 1925 All 206.

10 See also *Biggerstaff* v *Rowatt's Wharf Ltd.* [1896]2 Ch D 93 (E).

11 (1956)26 Comp Cas 298; AIR 1957 Mad 122.

A creditor dealing with a trading company is required by law to be conversant with the terms of its memorandum and articles of association and no more. If it is found that the transaction or long into in which the creditor is entering is not barred by the charter of the company or its Articles of Association, and could be entered into on behalf of the company by the person negotiating it, then the creditor is entitled to assume that all the formalities required in connection with that have been complied with. If the transaction in question could be authorized by the passing of a resolution, such an act is a mere formality, and the *bona fide* creditor in the absence of any suspicious circumstances is entitled to proceed on the assumption of its existence. A transaction entered into by the borrowing company under such circumstances cannot be defeated merely on the ground that no such resolution was in fact passed, as the passing of such resolution is a mere matter of indoor or internal management. Where the act is not *ultra vires* the statute or the company such a creditor would be entitled to assume the apparent or ostensible authority of the agent to be a real or genuine one. He could assume that such a person had the power to represent the company and he is in fact advance the money on such assumption; he would be protected by the doctrine of internal management. A loan was advanced to a director of a company acting, according to the assumption of the lender, on behalf of the company. This director was also a director of the managing agent of the borrower company, and, besides, the entire powers of the managing agency had been vested in him by a resolution of its board of directors. The articles of the borrower company contained nothing which could have prevented the director from borrowing money on behalf of the company.

In Buckley on the Companies Act (12th Edition) the law relating to indoor management is stated at p. 375 as follows:

> "Outsiders are bound to know what Lord Hartherley called the 'external position of the company; but are not bound to know its 'indoor management'. If persons are held out as and act as directors, and the shareholders do not prevent them from so doing outsiders are entitled to assume that they are directors, and as between the, company and such outsiders, the acts of such directors, *de facto* will bound the company."

In *Re, David Payne & Co. Ltd.; Young* v *David Payne & Co. Ltd.,*[12] it was laid down that where a company has a general power to borrow money for the purposes of its business, a lender is not bound to enquire into the purposes for which the money is intended to be applied. At page 613, Buckley, J's view is given as follows:

> "The borrowing being effected, and the money passing to the company, the subsequent application of the money is a matter in which the directors may have acted wrongly; but that does not affect the principal act, which is the borrowing of the money."

The Allahabad High Court in *Lakshmi Rattan Cotton Mills Co. Ltd.* v *J.K. Jute Mills Co. Ltd.,*[13] held that an act of a director in borrowing the money bound the company, that it did not matter that there was no resolution of the board of directors of the borrower company authorizing the director to borrow this money on behalf of the company, and that the lender was protected by the doctrine of internal management. Once the payment of a long is received by the company, the receipt of the money itself is a benefit to the company, and the creditor is not concerned with what is done with the money by the company subsequently.

Were the last amount of money has been borrowed and is shown in the balance sheet of the company, it cannot be believed that the shareholders, who approved the balance sheet, where oblivious of the fact of the want of authority of the person responsible for the inflow of such a large sum into its coffers, and the approval of the balance sheet by the shareholders would amount to ratification of the borrowing.

But the board of directors can borrow money only with the consent of the shareholders in the general meeting if the money to be borrowed exceeds the paid up share capital of the company and its free reserves.[14] However, the directors have an unfettered freedom to borrow if borrowing is incidental to the particular business of the company.[15] A trading company must always have an implied power to borrow money for its business purposes.[16] The Madras High Court

12 [1904]2 Ch 608 (I).
13 (1957)27 Comp Cas 660; AIR 1957 All 311.
14 The Companies Act, s. 293(1)(*c*).
15 *Re Introductions Ltd.* [1969]2 WLR 791; [1969]1 All ER 887.
16 *Rolled Steel Products (Holdings) Ltd.* v *British Steel Corporation* [1986] Ch 246; [1985]3 All ER 52.

in *G.V. Films Ltd.* v *Jaswant Chand,*[17] held that if a managing director borrowed money, the company is bound to repay it.

In Halsbury's *Laws of England* (Third Edition), Vol. 6, page 299, para 603, it is stated that:

> "Apart from ratification, the company will be answerable for any property which has come into its possession through the unauthorized acts of the directors."

Again the directors have the power to make loan and invest the funds of the company. However, they can lend money to another company only by a special resolution of the company authorizing such lending if the lending company and the borrowing company are under the same management and the loan exceeds such percent of the aggregate of the subscribed capital and its free reserves of the lending company as may lie prescribed by the resolution.[18]

As regards the power of investment fit other companies by purchasing shares, the board of directors may invest in shares or in debentures of another company up to such percent of the subscribed capital of the other company as may be prescribed by the investing company.[19] Again the directors may invest an amount exceeding than the prescribed one if it is sanctioned by a resolution of the investing company in general meeting and with the approval of the Central Government.

In a joint Hindu family, if the manager is borrowed the money on his personal capacity, the court considered the question whether the company is liable to pay the loan in *Mst. Mangal Bahu* v *Jaitly and Company.*[20] The court held that the mere fact that the company benefited was not by itself sufficient to bind the company. Before the company could be held liable, it must be found not only that money came into their hands but that it was in effect put into their hands by the manager of the joint Hindu family. Thus, the company is not liable for the payment of the loan.

17 (2007)137 Comp Cas 411 (Mad).

18 Section 370(1) as amended in 1988 by the Companies (Amendment) Act 1988.

19 Section 372(1).

20 (1946)16 Comp Cas 214.

The Bombay High Court discussed the case of unauthorized borrowing by the directors of the company in *T.R. Pratt (Bombay) Ltd.* v *E.D. Sassoon & Co., Ltd.*[1] If the managing director of a company is director of two companies, his personal knowledge of both the companies and the knowledge which he has acquired as an officer of one company will not be imputed to the other company unless he has some duty imposed on him to communicate his knowledge to the company sought to be affected by the notice and some duty imposed on him by that company to receive the notice.

The court held that it is his duty to communicate to the first company any material fact affecting that company which came to his knowledge as director of the other two companies and notice of any such fact could be imputed to the first company. If the directors of a company borrowed money, unauthorized, which never became the property of the company but remained the property of the lenders. In a case where the borrowing is *ultra vires* the directors, but not *ultra vires* the company, the money could be recovered by the lender in an action for money had and received. There cannot be any ratification by a company of an unauthorized act unless the company had full knowledge of all the circumstances attending the transaction or adopted the transaction with the intention to adopt it under any circumstances.

3.8 Power of contract

The power of contract comes within the purview of the general power of management. However, a company may empower any person as its attorney to execute deeds on its behalf. Again the power of directors to enter into contracts on behalf of the company is limited to a certain extent by the articles and resolutions of the company. Further the consent of the board of directors is necessary for the making of any contracts in which a particular director is interested.[2]

The powers conferred upon the directors by the statute, memorandum and articles and the general meeting of the company will assume that they are not directors of the company alone. But virtually directors have full control over the management of the company. Directors are the custodians of the company's securities and assets. They keep its

1 (1936)6 Comp Cas 90; AIR 1938 PC 159.
2 Section 297(1).

moneys and maintain its capital. They protect both the investor and creditor. So they require contractual powers to engage in different activities of the company.

3.8.1 *Individual powers*

An individual director has no power to act on behalf of the company. He is only one of the members of the body of directors called the 'board.' He has powers only to the extent of what delegated by the board or given to him in accordance with the articles.[3] If the power to institute a suit is not specifically conferred on a director, he has no authority to institute a suit on behalf of the company. Such a power can be conferred by the board by passing a resolution. In *Sankaranarayanan (K.N.)* v *Shree Consultations P. Ltd.,*[4] it was held that a petition for prevention of oppression and mismanagement filed by a single director on behalf of the company without the approval of the board of directors was not competent. The invalidity cannot be cured by a subsequent ratification. In *Apple Valley Resort* v *HP State Electricity Board,*[5] it was held that the powers of the company are to be exercised by the board of directors except as may be provided otherwise. Individual directors have only such powers as may be vested in them specially.

A single director's action against the company to prevent it from merging with another company was dismissed. He has neither authorized by the board nor under authority from the articles. His allegation was that the directors were acting at the behest of the holding company that was not caring for the interest of the subsidiary and the directors of the subsidiary were under a fiduciary obligation to protect the interests of the subsidiary which they were sacrificing. The court refused to give interim relief at the suit of an unauthorized person. However, it was observed that the directors not to act as the puppet of the holding company but to give to the company the benefit of their independent action.[6] The appointment of receivers does not remove the powers from the directors.[7]

3 Cf. *Nibro Ltd.* v *National Insurance Co. Ltd.* (1991)70 Comp Cas 388 (401); AIR 1991 Del 25.

4 (1994)80 Comp Cas 558 (Mad); (1993)II MLJ 298.

5 (2004)118 Comp Cas 328 (HP).

6 *Ferruccio Sias* v *Jai Manga Ram Mukhi* (1993)12 CLA 212 (Del); (1994)1 Comp LJ 345 (Del).

7 *Hawkesbury Development Co Ltd* v *Landmark Finance Pty Ltd.* [1969]92 WN (NSW) 199 (209).

3.8.2 *Power to make loans*

The power of the board to disburse loans to the directors is subject to s. 293. The board cannot pass any loan without the consent of the company in general meeting. The board is not, however, bound to exercise the powers, even though; the company passes resolutions in respect of such powers.[8] A resolution passed by the company in general meeting asking the directors to make an advance of money to the shareholders pending the declaration of a dividend was held to be not binding on the directors and the court refused to pass any order compelling the directors to implement the resolution.[9] The consent of the company in general meeting may be in the shape of a formal resolution in a general meeting.[10]

Section 295 refers to an indirect loan to a director, what it means is that the company shall not give loan to a director through the agency of one or intermediaries. The word 'indirectly' cannot be used to convert into a 'loan' something which is not in substance a loan.[11] In *Ciro Citterio Menswear Plc. (in admn.) Re,* the question arose as to whether an unlawful loan by a company to its directors would automatically make the director a constructive trustee for the amount of the loan. The court said that it was not so. Accordingly the company and the administrators were not entitled to claim the equity in the property in which the director invested the loan amount. The section does not prohibit loans or advances to a trust in which directors are trustees. Where a director of a banking company dishonestly sanctioned a loan in the name of a person who was an employee of his family firm, on the death of the director, the right of action survived against the sons of the directors as the money was utilized by the joint family firm.[12]

3.8.3 *Power to make political contributions*

A company, other than the Government company has been in existence for less than three financial years, contribute any amount directly or

8 *Pothen* v *Hindustan Trading Corporation (P) Ltd.* (1967)37 Comp Cas 226 (Ker).

9 *Scott* v *Scott* [1943]1 All ER 582.

10 *Bamfird* v *Bamford* [1970] Ch 212.

11 *Fredie Ardeshir Mehta* v *Union of India* (1991)70 Comp Cas 210 (Bom).

12 *People's Bank of North India Ltd.* v *Lala Har Gopal* (1935)5 Comp Cas 275 (Lah).

indirectly to any political party, to any person for political purposes, provided that the amount may be the delegate of the amount which may be so contributed by the company in any financial year shall not exceed 5 per cent. Provided that no such contribution shall be made by a company unless a resolution authorizing the making of such contribution is passed at a meeting of the board of directors, be deemed to be the justification in law for the making and acceptance of the contribution authorized by it.

On the other hand, a donation or subscription or payment caused to be given by a company on behalf of its account to a person who, by his knowledge, is carrying on any activity which, at the time of such donation can reasonably be regarded as likely to affect public support for political power shall also be deemed to be contribution of the amount of such donation, for a political purpose.

Is the amount of expenditure incurred, directly or indirectly by a company called unadvertised bench in any publication in the nature of their brochure, pamphlet or the like, shall also be deemed to be a political contribution if it is going to be advantageous to a political party for political purposes.

Every company shall disclose in its profit and loss account any amount contributed by to any political party to any person for political purposes during the financial year. If any person making any contribution in contravention of the provisions of s. 161 of the Companies Bill 2008 provides for punishment to the company with fine which may extend to 5 times the amount so contributed at every officer who is in default shall be punishable with imprisonment for a 10 which may extend to 6 months and with fine which may extend to 5 times the amount so contributed.

3.9 Doctrine of ultra vires

The memorandum of association commends the object and purposes for which the company has been incorporated and for which the moneys of the shareholders or members may be spent. The powers of the board of directors and the general meeting are restricted in this respect. Any act of the directors or general meeting will be held invalid if it is not covered by the objects clause of the memorandum. Such an act called *ultra vires* (beyond the powers or lack of power) the memorandum or the Act. The director's power is relevant in deciding whether the transaction is *ultra vires*, the memorandum has to be construed for this purpose.[13] The term *ultra vires* signifies a concept distinct from 'illegality'. In the loose or the widest sense everything that is not warranted by law is illegal but in its proper or strict connotation 'illegal' refers to that quality which makes the act itself contrary to law. The term *ultra vires* points to the capacity or power of the person to do that act. It is not necessary that an act to be *ultra vires* must also be illegal. It may be but it may as well, not be. An act may be illegal because it is prohibited by law or for reasons like fraud, undue influence or because it may be opposed to public policy. These reasons are not occasioned by the absence of any power in the person to do the act. The essence of the doctrine of *ultra vires* is that the act is done in excess of the powers possessed by the person in law.[14] The act done by the directors are valid even the act incidental or ancillary powers those which have a reasonably proximate connection with the objects specified.[15]

A company has power to do (through directors) old that he is reasonably necessary for attaining is objects. The courts have become increasingly ready to imply powers of this nature.

> A trading company has implied power to borrow, give security, to sell or mortgage land, to appoint an act by agents for purposes of its business. Such powers are incidental or properly to be inferred from the powers expressed the memorandum.[16] Any step taken to augment working capital of the company will be incidental to the business of the company and conducive to the attainment of objects.[17]
>
> A non-trading company will exercise only such powers as are necessary to enable it to discharge the duties and fulfill the purposes for which it is constituted.[18] Were company has power to purchase land, it is implied that it has power to let

13 *Charterbridge Corpn. Ltd.* v *Llyods Bank Ltd.* [1969]2 All ER 1185.

14 *Anand Prakash* v *Assistant Registrar, Co-Operative Societies* AIR 1968 All 22.

15 *Lakshmanaswami Mudaliar* v *L.I.C.* (1963)1 Comp LJ 248 (SC); AIR 1963 SC 1185; (1963)33 Comp Cas 420.

16 *Oakbank Oil Co.* v *Crum* [1882]8 App Cas 65.

17 *Turner Morrison & Co Ltd.* v *Hungerford Investment Trust Ltd.* AIR 1972 SC 1311; (1972)42 Comp Cas 512.

18 *Baroness Wenlock* v *River Dee* (1885)10 App Cas 354.

out or sell the land.[19] Negotiation of negotiable instrument is within the ordinary course of business of a company, no special power is necessary.[20] Payment to a retired secretary and a member of a club by way of annuity, pension or gratuity is within the powers of the club although under the memorandum no dividend is to be paid by way of profit to its members.[1] A chemical manufacturer may spend money on research and education likely to lead to direct and substantial advantage to the company.[2] Where the company is formed for walking a patented machine, it is not *ultra vires* to purchase the patent. A company empowered by its memorandum to assist in the formation of other company can buy shares of a railway company.[3] A *bona fide* compromise of my reasonable claim by them in of a sum of money out of the company's capital is not *ultra vires.*[4]

Sections 290-293 provides that the former of the company had to be exercised by the board. The board is to be validly constituted. An individual director has no power to act unless authorized by the board of the power are to be exercised by the board at the general meeting. Again certain powers cannot be advised without prior approval of the general meeting. Any act beyond the powers of the directors for beyond the powers of the company has to be decided on the basis the facts established and not on any abstract rule.[5]

A company acts through directors who or agents for the purposes of transactions entered into on behalf of the company. Their powers are derived from the articles. A director alone has no power except such as is dedicated to him by the board or by the articles. Except for merely ministerial work, he director has no authority to bind the company.[6] If there is authority in the articles for delegation of powers by the board of directors to one of themselves, then an outsider acting

19 *Gujarat Ginning & Manufacturing Co.* v *Motilal H.S. Weaving Co.* AIR 1930 Bom 84.
20 *Choonilal* v *Spence's Hotel Co.* [1868]1 BLR (OS) 14.
1 *Cyclist Touring Club* v *Hopkinson* [1910]1 Ch 179.
2 *Evans* v *Burnerr Mond & Co.* [1921]1 Ch 359.
3 *International Contract Corpn's Case* [1869]20 LT 96.
4 *Irish Provident Assurance Co.* [1913] Ir R 352.
5 *Turner Morrisson & Co Ltd.* v *Hungerford Investment Trust Ltd.* AIR 1972 SC 1311; (1972)42 Comp Cas 512.
6 *Rama Corpn. Ltd.* v *Proved T. & G. Investment Ltd.* [1952]1 All ER 554.

bona fide is entitled to rely on the ostensible authority of a director to fact bind the company. The board and the company may also ratify all act of such a single director provided they are *intra vires* the company. In any event, an outsider has a cause of action against such a director for breach of warranty of authority and for misrepresentation. If the particular act is *intra vires* the company but outside the authority of the directors, is effect will depend upon the fact weather such absence of authority was evident to the other party to the transaction or not. If a person with the notice of the powers of directors cannot hold the company liable for acts *ultra vires* of directors. However, there are certain cases where the absence of authority of the directors is not evident from any public document. Articles may require the directors to obtain the consent of the members by a resolution before exercising their specified borrowing powers or for delegation of power to the managing director by the board resolution is necessary. If a person may transactions the company without any reason of suspicion, things that the director with whom he enters into a contract is authorized to act on behalf of the company, the company will generally be bound by the act of such a director.[7]

A contract or transaction *ultra vires* the company is not binding on the company.[8] However, if a property is acquired by expenditure, the company's right over it may be protected.[9] If the director carry on a trade which is *ultra vires* the company, they cannot recover in respect of the goods supplied. A loan which is *ultra vires* the company cannot be recovered. An *ultra vires* transaction creates no debt, and upon winding up of the company contributories are not liable to pay such debts. A company can retain property and recover money although the transactions through which they were acquired are *ultra vires.*[10] In *Mathura Mohan* v *Ram Kumar,*[11] the Calcutta High Court has taken a different view. In this case it was held that:

1. if the contract is fully executed on both sides it will be effective and neither party will be deprived of what is been acquired under such a contract;

7 *Royal British Bank* v *Turquand* [1856]6 E&B 327.
8 *Re European Society Arbitration Acts* [1878] LR 8 Ch D 679.
9 *National Telephone Co.* v *Constables of St. Peter Port* [1900] AC 317.
10 *Great Eastern Railway* v *Turner* [1872-73] LR 8 Ch App 149.
11 ILR (1915)43 Cal 790.

2. is the contract is executory on both sides, neither party can maintain an action;
3. if the contract the executory on one side and the other party has fully performed the contract the party who has taken the benefit will be required either to perform his part of the contract or to restore the benefit he has taken.

A company cannot ratify anything beyond the powers of the company. Such an act cannot be validated by the general meeting of the shareholders or by obtaining judgments by consent or by *estoppel.*[12] Whether a transaction is *ultra vires* the company has to be decided on the basis of facts of each case and in accordance with provisions of the memorandum and not on the basis of any abstract rule and a company may validly undertake the tax liability of another company in respect of the undistributed dividends kept back for being used as working capital.

Supreme Court in *Matajog Dobey* v *H.C. Bhari,*[13] held that:

> Where a power is conferred or a duty imposed by statute or otherwise, and there is nothing said expressly inhibiting the exercise of the power or the performance of the duty by any limitations or restrictions it is reasonable to hold that it carries with it the power of doing all such acts or employing such means as are reasonably necessary for such execution.

A company cannot by its own shares or advance money to a director to do so or accept or surrender of shares involving reduction of share capital. It is *ultra vires* for the company to issue unauthorized capital or reduce capital and or issue shares at a discount without complying with statutory requirements. Payment out of capital, dividends out of capital, unreasonable remuneration paid for services rendered, making payments for the benefit of a section of shareholders, paying costs talks prosecution for different cases not instituted by the company would be *ultra vires* the company. If the ratification is not possible in all these cases, the directors are individually liable to the company and to the outsiders.

A corporation is liable for tortious and criminal acts. If a corporation expressly authorized agent to commit tort it will be liable for just as

12 *Ashbury Rly. Co.* v *Riche* [1874-75] LR 7 HL 653.
13 AIR 1956 SC 44 (50).

any other tort-feasor. Every act authorized by or on behalf of the corporation by the governing authority of the corporation or any other authority is liable for the court and the corporation is liable for the court committed by any of its agents. A company is held liable for criminal libel and malice, of making his statement intending it to be false.[14]

3.10 Conclusion

The powers of the director board and directors are vast in terms of administration of a company in terms of economic activities, finance, property and finally they are the trustees of the company itself. The entire management of a company is in the hands of the directors. They are managers as well as shareholders of the company. The powers vested in them are in accordance with the articles and memorandum of association or special resolution passed in the general meeting. Their powers include allotment and transfer of shares, issue of debentures and declaration of dividends, dealing with capital and money, borrowing, lending, investment, contract on behalf of the company, make loans, and to make political contributions. The directors cannot delegate these essential responsibilities. It is essential that the directors of a company fully comprehend their duties and responsibilities. The directors must be fully aware of their powers, statutory responsibilities, the extent of their powers and the duty to manage the affairs of the company. The directors will be held liable for misuse of powers. They are responsible for *ultra vires* acts and damages to the company.

14 *Municipal Council, Masulipatanam* v *G. Krishna Rao* AIR 1964 AP 260.

4

Fiduciary Duties of Directors

4.1 Introduction

The fiduciary[1] duties of directors were first elaborated by common-law judges, out of codified company law. It is a relationship in which one person is under a duty to act for the benefit of another on matters within the scope of the relationship. For example, such as trustee-beneficiary, Guardian-ward, principal-agent, require an unusually high degree of care.[2] It is described as an elusive concept in the

1 A fiduciary is someone who has undertaken to act for and on behalf of another in a particular matter in circumstances which give rise to a relationship of trust and confidence, *Breach of Fiduciary Duty Law & Legal Definition, Legal Terms Dictionary.* The Black's *Law Dictionary* defines fiduciary is a person who is required to act for the benefit of another person on all matters within the scope of their relationship; one who owes to another duties of good faith, trust, confidence, and candor; one who must exercise a high standard of care in managing another's money or property. "Fiduciary is a vague term, and it has been pressed into service for a number of ends.... My view is that the term 'fiduciary' is so vague that plaintiffs have been able to claim that fiduciary obligations have been breached when in fact the particular defendant was not a fiduciary *stricto sensu* but simply had withheld property from the plaintiff in an unconscionable manner". D.W.M. Waters, *The Constructive Trust,* 4 (1964).

2 The fiduciary relationship arises in the following situations: (1) when one person places trust in the faithful integrity of another, who as a result gains superiority or influence over the first, (2) when one person assumes control and responsibility over another, (3) when one person has a duty to act for or give advice to another on matters falling within the scope of the relationship, or (4) when there is a specific relationship that has traditionally been recognized as involving fiduciary duties, as with a lawyer and the client or a stockbroker and a customer. Black's *Law Dictionary*, 9th Ed. 2009.

Anglo-American law.[3] The duties of care and loyalty were considered as core characters of the company directors.[4] Most important fiduciary duty is the duty of loyalty.[5] The director's fiduciary duties lie at the heart of the corporate governance.[6] At the same time, the use of large powers within the board and a real risk that the powers will be exercised by the directors other than for the purpose of which it was given was a concern of all stake holders. The company law regulates the potential abuse of powers by directors. The governance rights of the directors of a company are always under controversy. By virtue of their office, directors of corporations are deemed to owe duties as fiduciaries to the corporations and its shareholders.[7] The nature of director's duties are prescribed and to be exercised within the limit of their powers. The duties of directors as a fiduciary in a company may be analyzed in detail.

The directors are trustees of the company's property, money and they stands indisputably in a fiduciary capacity *vis-a-vis* the company. He must act for the paramount interest of the company. He does not have any statutory duty to perform so far as individual shareholders are concerned subject of course to any special arrangement which may be entered into or a special circumstance that may arise in a particular case. Each case, thus, is required to be considered having regard to the fact situation obtaining therein and having regard to the existence of any special arrangement or special circumstance.

Chapter IX of the Indian Trusts Act 1882, provides for certain obligations in the nature of trusts. The Trust Act recognizes various kinds of trusts including resulting trust. An express trust, however, may be created by reason of an agreement between the parties.[8]

3 Deborah A. Demott, *Beyond Metaphor: An Analysis of Fiduciary Obligations*, Duke Law Journal, vol. 1988, No. 5 (Nov. 1988), pp. 879-924.

4 See, for example, William T. Allen & Reinier Kraakman, *Commentary and Cases on Corporate Law* (unpublished Materials, 2001); Melvin A. Eisenberg, *Corporations and Other Business Organizations: Cases and Materials,* 8th Ed. 2000; American Law Institute, *Principles of Corporate Governance: Analysis and Recommendations,* Parts IV-V (1994).

5 Bernard S. Black, *The Core Duties of Outside Directors*, Asia Business Law Review, 2001, pp. 3-16.

6 Sarah Worthington, *Reforming Directors' Duties*, The Modern Law Review, vol. 64, No. 3 (May 2001), pp. 439-458.

7 Harvey Gelb, *Director Due Care Liability: An Assessment of the New Statutes*, vol. 61, Temple Law Review, 1988, pp. 13-14.

8 *Barclays Bank* v *Quistclose Investments* [1970] AC 567.

By reason of s. 88 of the Indian Trusts Act, a person bound in fiduciary character is required to protect the interests of other persons but the heart and soul thereof is that as between two persons one is bound to protect the interests of the other and if the former availing of that relationship makes a pecuniary gain for himself; s. 88 would be attracted. What is sought to be prevented by a person holding such fiduciary benefit is unjust enrichment or unjust benefit derived from another which is against conscience that he should keep. When a person makes a pecuniary gain by reason of a transaction, the *cestui qui trust* created thereunder must be restored back.[9]

As a legal principle, the obligation originated in equity. Equity granted relief and common law courts did not in numerous situations involving one person's abuse of confidence reposed in him by another.[10] The term "fiduciary" itself was adopted to apply to situations falling short of "trusts," but in which one person was nonetheless obliged to act like a trustee.[11] The corporate directors occupy the position of trustees. They are entrusted with powers vested by the company memorandum and article of association to conduct or supervise the corporation's business; the directors are bound by fiduciary principles. The relation of fiduciary obligation insists that the person (fiduciary) must be loyal to the interest of the other person (beneficiary). The fiduciary must avoid activities where there is a conflict of interest with the beneficiary. If the fiduciary benefits through the acts inconsistent with the interest of beneficiary, the beneficiary can recover any benefit so realized. The directors are fiduciaries working for the company and its shareholders.

Directors are subject to various duties both in common law and statutory. In addition to their statutory duties, directors owe their company a number of fiduciary duties similar to those owned by an agent to his principal, and also a duty at common law and in equity to take reasonable care in the management of a company's affairs. These duties can be directed by four well defined objects.

(*i*) To compel directors to act in accordance with the strict terms of their mandate;

9 *Sangramsinh P. Gaekwad* v *Shantadevi P. Gaekwad (Dead Through LRs)* Civil Appeal Nos. 6360 & 6361 of 2001.

10 Sealy, *Fiduciary Relationships*, Cambridge Law Journal, 1962, vol. 69, 69-70.

11 *Ibid*, fn. 1, p. 71-72.

(*ii*) To compel them to exercise care and skill in carrying out their various functions;

(*iii*) To compel them to use their wide discretionary powers in good faith and for proper purposes; and

(*iv*) Finally, to compel them to act loyally in advancing the interest of their company.[12]

It is of vital importance to see the scope and extend of the duties of directors in the exercise of their powers. This is because of the fact that they occupy a key position in the management and administration of the company and they invested with wide powers. It is obvious that those who are placed in high position and are having unlimited powers are tend to abuse their position and power. So it is for the interest of the shareholders and the public at large that the powers of directors and managers are to be regulated. The primary duties and responsibilities of directors include instructing and directing the company and its officers in the realization of its objectives. William C. Doughlas aptly remarked[13] that corporate executives are possessed of immense power which must be regulated not only for the public good, but also for the protection of those whose investments are involved. Directors occupy various positions and under various capacities in a company.

Directorships will always be susceptible of abuse. "Some directors will always be faithless to their trust. They can capitalize their strategic position in the company to serve their own interest."[14] To quote D.N. Hossie,[15] "the law, therefore, continues to struggle against their wills and imposes upon them certain duties which, when properly enforced, will, without driving away from the field competent men, materially reduce the changes of abuse." They are not only agents of the company but also to some extent trustees or in the position of trustees of the company's property and funds in their hands.[16]

12 Susan Worthington, *Corporate Governance: Remedying and Ratifying Director's Breaches* [2003]116 LQR 638.

13 *Directors Who do not Direct*, (1934)47 Harvard Law Review, pp. 1305-1307.

14 *Ibid*, p. 1317.

15 *The Civil Liability of the Directors of a Corporation*, (1952)30 Can BR 908.

16 *Chinnappa Chettiar* v *Official Liquidator Oriental Investment Trust Ltd.* (1944)14 Comp Cas 207.

In *Percival* v *Wright,*[17] the question therein posed was: Assuming that directors are, in a sense, trustees for the company, are they trustees for individual shareholders? The Chancery Division despite holding that the Directors must act *bona fide* and for the best interest of the company did not accept the argument that the relationship between the shareholders *inter se* is the same as that of partners in an unincorporated company holding:

> The contrary view would place directors in a most invidious position, as they could not buy or sell shares without disclosing negotiations, a premature disclosure of which might well be against the best interests of the company. I am of the opinion that directors are not in that position.

The law thus, imposes certain duties upon the directors of corporate enterprises for the benefit of the shareholders and the general public. Director's duties are usually regulated by the articles of the company. Therefore, some statutory obligations along with duties of a general nature are cast on the directors. It is often stated that directors are trustees and that the nature of their duties can be explained on this basis. Moreover most of the powers that are supposed to be exercised by directors are exercised by them according to their personal discretion. This use of discretion also invites certain duties which are attached to trusts. The pertinent question is duties to whom?

4.2 Duty towards company, shareholders and employees

To answer the above question, the answer in British law is clear: the duties of the directors were owed to "the company" which is contained in s. 170(1) of the Companies Act. The British Companies Act 2006 specifically defined the duties of directors. They are:

1. The duty to act within their powers (the duty to adhere to the company's constitution) (s. 171);
2. The duty to promote the success of the company. There are six things a director must consider here, including consideration of the company's employees, the long-term consequences of decisions, fairness to members (shareholders) and the impact of decisions on the community and environment (s. 172);

17 *Percival* v *Wright* [1902]2 Ch 421.

3. The duty to exercise independent judgment. This is not as restrictive as it may seem, but means not being the 'yes man' of the person responsible for his or her appointment. It does not prevent having an interest in transactions nor relying on the opinion of an expert where appropriate (s. 173);
4. The duty to exercise reasonable skill, care and diligence. This duty has particular implications for non-executive directors, who can no longer afford to take a 'hands-off' approach (s. 174);
5. The duty to avoid conflicts of interest. This includes conflicts involving connected persons such as family members (s. 175);
6. The duty not to accept benefits from third parties (s. 176); and
7. the duty to declare an interest in transactions or arrangements (s. 177). This includes the duty to declare interests of persons connected with the director.[18]

However, the director's duties are not specifically mentioned in the Companies Act 1956 of India. Strictly speaking, directors are not the agents or trustees of individual shareholders. In a case dealing with the rights of members of a club, the court confirmed that in general a director does not owe fiduciary duties to members or shareholders as such.[19] The directors owe a duty to the company and not directly to the shareholders. In exercising their powers directors must act primarily in the interests of the shareholders of the company as a whole.[20] They also owe a duty to protect the interest of the company's employees in general. It is same as that of any other fiduciary duty cast upon the directors.[1]

The Companies Bill 2011 enumerates duties of a director in s. 166 as follows:

> (1) A director of a company shall act in accordance with the articles of the company.

18 See words4business.com, visited on 31.07.2009.
19 *Peskin* v *Anderson* [2000]2 BCLC 1; [2000] EWCA Civ 326.
20 *Piercy* v *S. Mills & Co.* [1920]1 Ch 77.
1 Companies Act 1985, section 308(1) (British).

(2) A director of a company shall act in good faith in order to promote the objects of the company for the benefit of its members as a whole, and in the best interests of the company, its employees, the shareholders, the community and for the protection of environment.

(3) A director of a company shall exercise his duties with due and reasonable care, skill and diligence and shall exercise independent judgment.

(4) A director of a company shall not involve in a situation in which he may have a direct or indirect interest that conflicts, or possibly may conflict, with the interest of the company.

(5) A director of a company shall not achieve or attempt to achieve any undue gain or advantage either to himself or to his relatives, partners, or associates and if such director is found guilty of making any undue gain under sub-section (7) he shall be liable to pay an amount equal to that gain to the company.

(6) A director of a company shall not assign his office and any assignment so made shall be void.

(7) If a director of the company contravenes the provisions of this section such director shall be punishable with fine which shall not be less than one lakh rupees but which may extend to five lakh rupees.

The obligations to the company employees should be discharged according to the articles of association. In *Coleman* v *Myers,*[2] the New Zealand Court of Appeal found that a fiduciary duty of disclosure arose, even in the absence of any agency, in the case of a small family company where there was a gross disparity of knowledge between the directors and the shareholders and where the shareholders of the company had traditionally relied on the director for information and advice. When the directors negotiated with the shareholders for the purchase of their shares and, therefore, were clearly not acting on behalf of the shareholders, they were nevertheless held to be subject to a fiduciary duty of full disclosure of relevant facts about the company to the shareholders.

In *Peskin* v *Anderson,*[3] the Royal Automobile Club Ltd. (RACL) owned the Royal Automobile Club (RAC) and a motoring services business RAC Motoring Services (RACMS). The full members of RAC were members of RACL and therefore had an indirect interest in

2 [1977]2 NZLR 225.
3 *Peskin* v *Anderson* [2001]1 BCLC 372.

RACMS. Clause 4 of the memorandum of association of RACL contained a prohibition on distribution to members. Clause 4 of the memorandum of RACMS contained a similar prohibition, but in slightly different terms with a further cl. 5 which prohibited any addition, alteration or amendment to cl. 4. In 1998, RACL was approached with a view to selling RACMS. In order to effect the sale, a special resolution was passed for deletion of cl. 4 of RACL's memorandum, and schemes of arrangement of RACMS and RACL were approved by the court by which the members ceased to be members of RACL on 8th July 1998 and became shareholder members of a new holding company, RACH. After the sale the members received £34,000 each in respect of the sale of their shares in RACH. The claimants were all former members of RAC and RACL whose membership had ceased before the schemes of arrangement took effect, and thus they did not receive any part of the benefits flowing from the sale. They brought an action against the directors of RACL, claiming damages for breach of fiduciary duty in failing to disclose to them the proposals relating to the de-mutualization of the RAC, the de-merger of RACMS in particular the expenditure by them of the assets of RACL on the proposed cancellation of cl. 4 of the memorandum of RACL so as to permit distributions to be made to the members. It was alleged that if those matters had been disclosed to the claimants before they retired, they could have made an informed decision about their membership and would have decided not to retire so as to benefit from the sale. On the application of the defendants the judge dismissed the application under CPR Pt 24, on the ground that it had no real prospect of success. The claimants appealed.

The court held that there was no fiduciary duty owed to the claimants. There was no duty to inform members of negotiations regarding the proposed sale of RACMS. It was not *ultra vires* for the directors to authorize the expenditure of the company's money on investigating proposals to sell RACMS, or on proposals to de-mutualise the company. On its true construction, the prohibition in cl. 4 did not extend to attempts to change the law of the company by altering the clauses or cancelling it from the memorandum, so as to permit what was previously prohibited. In substance, the expenditure complained of was no different to expenditure on changing the objects in the memorandum so as to allow the company to carry on a different business, which was impliedly prohibited until the objects were changed.

In the above case it was clearly distinguished between the fiduciary duties owned by directors to the company which arise out of the relationship between the director and the company, and fiduciary duties owned to shareholders are dependent upon establishing "a special factual relationship between the directors and the shareholders in the particular case". *Percival* v *Wright,*[4] is a leading authority for the proposition that the directors' duties are not owned to the shareholders individually, the directors purchased shares from their members without revealing that negotiations were in progress for the sale of the company's undertaking at a favourable price. They were held not to be in breach of duty through their non-disclosure.

In *Briess* v *Woolley,*[5] the directors with the consent of shareholders assumed the role of their representative for finalizing the sale of their shares. They made misrepresentations to the buyer. The selling shareholders were deemed to have been affected by the misrepresentation as if it was made by their own agent. The principle that directors owe a fiduciary duty to their company and not to individual shareholders, this position has been affirmed in *Allen* v *Hyatt.*[6] When the directors register a proposed transfer, they are under a fiduciary obligation to both the company and the shareholders even if as individuals they hold a majority of the shares.[7]

In *Re a Company (No. 008699 of 1985)*,[8] in this case Hoffmann, J said, "I emphasize that we are dealing with a private company and the board's duty to refrain from conduct, acts or omissions which are unfairly prejudicial to shareholders within the meaning of s. 459. The provisions of the City Code on Take-overs and Mergers applicable to public companies are a helpful guide to the City's views on fairness in similar circumstances and I have borrowed the phrase 'sufficient information and advice to enable the shareholders to reach a properly informed decision' from general principle 4 of the Code. But the detailed provisions of the Code do not necessarily coincide with the requirements of fairness for the purposes of s. 459".[9]

4 [1902]2 Ch 421.
5 [1954]1 All ER 909; [1954]2 WLR 832; [1954] AC 333.
6 [1914]30 TLR 444.
7 *Cope* v *Butcher* [1996]20 ACSR 37 (Aust).
8 [1986] BCLC 382.
9 *Ibid,* p. 389.

In *Re, Sherborne Park Residents Co. Ltd.,*[10] Hoffmann, J held that the directors' fiduciary duty to issue shares for a proper purpose was owned to the shareholders, not the company. It was observed that "although the alleged breach of fiduciary duty by the board is in theory a breach of its duty to the company, the wrong to the company is not the substance of the complaint. ...an abuse of these powers is an infringement of the members' contractual rights under the articles".

In *Murray's Judicial Factor* v *Thomas Murray & Sons (Ice Merchants) Ltd.,*[11] it was observed that "it is not so important that the directors were in breach of any duties imposed upon them by the statute or by the articles, and the question must be whether there is something beyond the articles which imposes upon the directors a duty to make this information available".[12]

In *Dawson International* v *Coats Paton,*[13] Lord Cullen held that a company could have an interest in the identity of its shareholders on a take-over. The directors in general owned no fiduciary duty to shareholders with respect to the disposal of their shares in the most advantageous way. However, when directors were concerned with the shares of shareholders, they owed a fiduciary duty to them.[14] It was also observed that in giving advice to shareholders upon a proposal to acquire their shares, it was recognised that directors had duties towards them, including a duty to be honest and a duty not to mislead.[15]

At the same time Vinelott, J rejected the view that the directors were bound by their undertaking, whether or not they thought that it was in the interests of the company that the resolution be passed. He said:

> I think I should say (and this is, of course, an interlocutory hearing) that I am not persuaded that this is a possible view. The terms of the agreement must clearly be read in the light of the facts known to all parties that directors owe a fiduciary duty to act in

10 [1986]2 BCC 99.

11 [1993] BCLC 1437.

12 *Ebrahimi* v *Westbourne Galleries Ltd.*; *Re Bird Precision Bellows*; *Re RA Noble & Sons (Clothing) Ltd.* [1983] BCLC 273 and *Re a Company* (No. 008699 of 1985) [1986] BCLC 382.

13 1988 SLT 854; 1988 SCLR 371; [1989] BCLC 233.

14 *Ibid.*, p. 243-I.

15 *Gething* v *Kilner,* per Brightman, J, p. 341.

> the interests of their company and to make full and honest disclosure to shareholders before they vote on such a resolution. It seems to me that it must have been understood by all that the undertaking to use reasonable endeavours to procure the passing of the resolution would be necessarily subject to anything which the directors had to do in pursuance of that fiduciary duty. . . . It seems to me plain beyond question that directors are under a duty to disclose the facts to the shareholders. Indeed a resolution passed in ignorance of them would be worthless. If directors must disclose the facts, then it seems to me that they must equally express their honest opinion as to what is in the interests of the company (pp. 6 to 8 of the revised transcript with which I was furnished).

It can summarize and held in this case that:

- that a company could be interested in a change of identity of its shareholders and a company could enter into a contract of the nature alleged;
- that directors did not owe a fiduciary duty to shareholders with respect to the disposal of their shares;
- that it was for the defenders to aver and prove a qualification to the alleged contract to the effect that it was conditional upon the pursuers' bid remaining the best bid for the shareholders;
- that the pursuers had given fair notice of the making of the alleged contract and its breach; and the pursuers' case of breach of contract by the company sent to a proof before answer;
- that reimbursement of expenditure by one party occasioned by the representations of another required reliance on an agreement which fell short of being a binding contract; and
- that the pursuers' averments on representations were irrelevant; and the action against the directors dismissed and the pursuers' averments on representations withheld from probation.

The above decision was followed in *Dawson International* v *Coats Paton.*[16] Lord Ordinary's opinion was that "Thus if a third party made

16 [1990] BCLC 560; [1989] BCC 405.

an unsolicited offer it would be for the directors to consider it in the exercise of their fiduciary duty to the company and their secondary fiduciary duty to the shareholders. If it appeared to be clearly better they would require making an appropriate recommendation. So here it was accepted that the contract was subject to an implied condition that in the event of such a change of circumstances it would not be a breach of contract if the first defenders did not recommend acceptance of the original offer. This would be implied on the principle of what was required to give business efficacy".

It is always the functions of the directors become subordinated to their fiduciary duty to the company and some time to the shareholders.[17] In this case, *Crowther Group Plc.* (Crowther) entered into an agreement to purchase the shares of *Carpets (UK) Ltd.* (UK), a subsidiary of *Carpets International Plc. (International).* As the transaction affected a substantial part of the business of International, it had under Stock Exchange requirements to be made conditional on the approval of the shareholders of International. As part of the agreement, International agreed to recommend the proposal to its shareholders and to propose resolutions of acceptance to its shareholders irrespective of any other offers that might be made for the share capital of UK. The directors of International sent out a circular recommending to shareholders that the Crowther bid be accepted. A rival bidder, *PMA Textiles Ltd.* (PMA) entered in the field. The bid of PMA was on more attractive terms than that of Crowther and the directors of International sent a circular to the shareholders of International recommending that the Crowther bid should not be proceeded with. In the present action Crowther sought, *inter alia*, damages on the ground that the directors of International had breached the agreement to use their best endeavours to obtain the approval of International's shareholders of the sale of UK to Crowther and applied for interlocutory relief.

It was held that the agreement between Crowther and International must be read in the light of the fact that the directors of a company owe a fiduciary duty to act in the interests of their company and to make full and honest disclosure to the shareholders before they vote on any resolution. The undertaking of the directors to International

17 *John Crowther Group plc.* v *Carpets International plc.* [1990] BCLC 460 (Ch D).

to use endeavours to procure the resolutions of International shareholders necessary for the effecting of the sale of UK to Crowther was subject to this fiduciary duty. Accordingly it was observed that the directors had done nothing wrong in putting the higher bid before the shareholders. It is clear that directors must not deliberately mislead the shareholders. Otherwise, they are not liable.[18]

In Palmer's *Company Law*, 23rd Ed., p. 848, it is stated:

> 64-02. Relationship is with company:
>
> > The fiduciary relationship of a director exists with the company: the director is not usually a trustee for individual shareholders. Thus, a director may accept a shareholder's offer to sell shares in the company although he may have information which is not available to that other, and the contract cannot be upset even if the director knew of some fact which made the offer an attractive proposition.

In Pennington's *Company Law*, 6th Ed. at pp. 608-09, it is stated:

> Directors owe no fiduciary or other duties to individual members of their company in directing and managing the company's affairs, acquiring or disposing of assets on the company's behalf, entering into transactions on its behalf, or in recommending the adoption by members of proposals made to them collectively. If directors mis-manage the company's affairs, they incur liability to pay damages or compensation to the company or to make restitution to it, but individual members cannot recover compensation for the loss they have respectively suffered by the consequential fall in value of their shares, and they cannot achieve this indirectly by suing the directors for conspiracy to breach the duties which they owed the company. However, there may be certain situations where directors do owe a fiduciary duty and a duty to exercise reasonable skill and care in advising members in connection with a transaction or situation which involves the company or its business undertaking and also the individual holdings of its members.

In *Dawson International plc.* v *Coats Patons plc.,*[19] Percival was relied upon and held that the Directors are, in general, under no

18 *Guthing* v *Kinley* [1972]1 WLR 337.
19 1988 SLT 854.

fiduciary duty to shareholders and in particular current shareholders with respect to the disposal of their shares in the most advantageous way as directors are not their agents and as such are not normally entrusted with the management of their shares. It was, however, observed that if the directors take it upon themselves to give advice to current shareholders they have a duty to act in good faith and not fraudulently nor can mislead the shareholders whether deliberately or carelessly, in which event, they may have a remedy. A distinction, thus, has been carved out as regards the fiduciary duty of the directors with regard to the property and funds of the company as contra-distinguished from the duty of directors to current shareholders as sellers of their shares. In case of conflict between two interests, the company's interest must be protected. The directors, however, will have a fiduciary relation if they have taken unto themselves the burden of giving advice to current shareholders.

Needle Industries (India) Ltd. v *Needle Industries Newey (India) Holding Ltd.*, held that:

> Where directors of a company seek, by entering into an agreement to issue new shares, to prevent a majority shareholder from exercising control of the company, they will not be held to have failed in fiduciary duty to the company if they act in good faith in what they believe, on reasonable grounds, to be the interests of the company. If the directors' primary purpose is to act in the interests of the company, they are acting in good faith even though they also benefit as a result.[20]

Contrary view were also expressed by courts on *Percival* in many subsequent cases[1] and held that fiduciary duty of the Director's to the company should not be equated with the duty to the shareholders. The court observed that the directors had no fiduciary duty to the shareholders in the facts and circumstances obtaining therein. However, observations were made therein that such duties may arise in special circumstances demonstrating the salient features and well-established categories of fiduciary relationship such as agency which involves duties of trust, confidence and loyalty. Absence of special circumstances or special reasons normally would not bring in the

20 (1981)3 SCC 333; (1981)51 Comp Cas 743 (SC).

1 *Peskin* v *Anderson* [2001]1 BCLC 372; *Brunninghausen* v *Glavnics* [1999]46 NSWLR 538; [1999]17 SCLC 1247.

concept of fiduciary relationship in a director vis-a-vis the current shareholders.

But in *Dale & Carrington Invt. P. Ltd.* v *P.K. Prathapan*, SC held that:

> The fiduciary capacity within which the Directors have to act enjoins upon them a duty to act on behalf of a company with utmost good faith, utmost care and skill and due diligence and in the interest of the company they represent. They have a duty to make full and honest disclosure to the shareholders regarding all important matters relating to the company. It follows that in the matter of issue of additional shares, the directors owe a fiduciary duty to issue shares for a proper purpose. This duty is owed by them to the shareholders of the company. Therefore, even though Section 81 of the Companies Act which contains certain requirements in the matter of issue of further share capital by a company does not apply to private limited companies, the directors in a private limited company are expected to make a disclosure to the shareholders of such a company when further shares are being issued. This requirement flows from their duty to act in good faith and make full disclosure to the shareholders regarding affairs of a company. The acts of directors in a private limited company are required to be tested on a much finer scale in order to rule out any misuse of power for personal gains or ulterior motives.[2]

The above decision was elaborated by the court in *Westfort Hi-Tech Hospital* v *V.S. Krishnan*, and reiterated and confirmed that fiduciary duty is towards the company and not individual shareholders and there is no agency relationship with shareholders and directors.[3] But in *Bajaj Auto Ltd.* v *N.K. Firodia*,[4] SC held that directors are in a fiduciary position, both towards the company and towards every shareholder.

In *M.A. Malik* v *V.S. Thiruvengadaswami Mudaliar*,[5] it has been held that a director of a company occupies a fiduciary position with regard to the members of the company and they can call upon him to

2 [2004]62 CLA 245.
3 Company Appeal No. 14 of 2006(A), High Court of Kerala.
4 AIR 1971 SC 321; (1971)2 SCR 40.
5 (1949)19 Comp Cas 311 (Mad).

account for the property over which he has control on their behalf. In that case in misfeasance proceedings, a director was ordered to pay a certain sum of money which he failed to pay. It was held that he was liable to be arrested in execution of the order under s. 15(*c*) of the Code of Civil Procedure upon the observation that "the director was bound in fiduciary capacity to account." It was also observed that "the relationship between a director and a member of the company is that of trustee and a *cestui que* trust".

The duties towards shareholders are important in the background of multi crore scams like happened in "Satyam" and millennium financial scandals happened like "Enron." Thus the minority shareholders are cheated and exploited in closely held corporations.[6] Since they were both shareholders, a duty of care and loyalty must be shown to the company and fellow shareholders.[7] It can be concluded that the directors, being bound by fiduciary duties, should ensure that the company's interests as well as other shareholders' interests are protected.

4.3 Duties to creditors

A company director owes a fiduciary duty to its creditors to keep its property available for repayment of debts.[8] Other theory is that the directors owe a duty only to the company.[9] The management being vested with the directors, the directors owes a duty to the company and the creditors to ensure that the affairs of the company are properly conducted and that its property is not dissipated or exploited for the benefit of the directors themselves and to the prejudice of the creditors. Creditors are able to obtain protection, when extending credit to companies, pursuant to either self-help strategies or legislative enactment. The duty requires directors, at a time when the company is in some form of financial distress, to take account of the interests of the company's creditors.[10]

6 Paula J. Dalley, *Shareholder (and Director) Fiduciary Duties and Shareholder Activism*, Houston Business and Tax Journal, Vol. VIII, 2008, p. 302.
7 *Demoulas* v *Demoulas Supermarkets Inc.* 424 Mass 501, 528 (1997).
8 *Sutton Mfg. Co.* v *Hutchinson* 63 Fed 496 (503) (7th Circ.).
9 *Taylor* v *Mitchell* 80 Minn 492, 496; 83 NW 418, 420. See case Notes *Corporations, Power of Directors: Whether Directors May Prefer Themselves*, Harvard Law Review, vol. 38, No. 4 (Feb 1925), pp. 521-522.
10 A. Keay, *The Director's Duty to Take into Account the Interests of Company Creditors: When is it Triggered?* (2001)25 MULR 315, 334-338.

The question of whether directors owe fiduciary duties to creditors when the company is insolvent or of doubtful solvency now seems beyond doubt. Dicta supporting such an extension of directors duties now spans some twenty years. For example, in *West Mercia Safetywear Ltd.* v *Dodd*[11] the Court of Appeal, citing with approval the decision of the New South Wales Court of Appeal in *Kinsela* v *Russell Kinsela Pty Ltd.*,[12] held that shareholders cannot absolve directors from a breach of duty to creditors so as to bar the liquidator's claim. It is pertinent to note in Dillon, LJ's view was the following passage from Street, CJ's judgment in *Kinsela*:

> In a solvent company the proprietary interests of the shareholders entitle them as a general body to be regarded as the company when questions of the duty of directors arise ... But where a company is insolvent the interests of the creditors intrude. They become prospectively entitled, through the mechanism of liquidation, to displace the power of the shareholders and directors to deal with the company's assets. It is in a practical sense their assets and not the shareholders' assets that, through the medium of the company, are under the management of the directors pending either liquidation, return to solvency, or the imposition of some alternative administration ...

The House of Lords in *Winkworth* v *Edward Baron Development Co. Ltd.*,[13] Lord Templeman explained that directors owe a fiduciary duty to the company and its creditors, present and future, to ensure that its affairs are properly administered and to keep the company's 'property inviolate and available for the repayment of its debts'. In *Yukong Line Ltd of Korea* v *Rendsburg Investment Corpn of Liberia (No. 2),*[14] it was pointed out that creditors have no standing, individually or collectively to bring an action in respect of any such duty. Toulson, J, held that a director of an insolvent company who, in breach of duty to the company, transferred assets beyond the reach of its creditors owed no corresponding fiduciary duty to an individual creditor of the company. This decision was confirmed in

11 [1988] BCLC 250 (CA).
12 [1986]10 ACLR 395.
13 [1986]1 WLR 1512; [1987]1 All ER 114; *Lonhro Ltd.* v *Shell Petroleum Co. Ltd.* [1980]1 WLR 627 (HL).
14 [1998]2 BCLC 485; [1998]4 All ER 82; [1998]1 WLR 29.

In *Re Pantone 485 Ltd.*[15] It was held in another case that with regard to an insolvent company the directors, when considering the company's interests, must have regard to the interests of the creditors.[16]

In *Walker* v *Wimborne,*[17] High Court of Australia held that the directors of a company had breached their duties in authorizing a loan to a related company. The loan did not produce any benefit or advantage to the lending company, and in fact carried the risk of a substantial loss as the borrower was in financial difficulties and was unlikely to be able to repay the loan. Justice Mason noted that this transaction had seriously prejudiced the company's unsecured creditors. The court held that:

> The directors of a company in discharging their duty to the company must take account of the interests of its shareholders and creditors. Any failure by the directors to take into account the interests of creditors will have adverse consequences for the company as well as for them.

This statement raises the question of what 'the company', to which directors owe their duties,[18] actually consists of the shareholders as a whole;[19] or the business entity itself, which would require consideration of the wider group of stakeholders including creditors?[20]

15 [2002]1 BCLC 266. Richard Reid, QC, sitting as a deputy judge in the High Court held that "In my view, where the company is insolvent, the human equivalent of the company for the purposes of the directors' fiduciary duties is the company's creditors as a whole, *i.e.* its general creditors. It follows that if the directors act consistently with the interests of the general creditors but inconsistently with the interest of a creditor or section of creditors with special rights in a winding-up, they do not act in breach of duty to the company."

16 *Colin Gwyer and Associates Ltd.* v *London Wharf (Limehouse) Ltd.* [2003]2 BCLC 153.

17 [1976] HCA 7; [1976]137 CLR 1.

18 Lord Greene in *Re Smith & Fawcett Ltd.* [1942] Ch 304, 306; [1942]1 All ER 542 (CA) stated that directors must act in 'the interests of the company'; and in *Greenhalgh* v *Arderne Cinemas Ltd.* [1951] Ch 286, 291 it was held that directors must act for the benefit of 'the company as a whole'. David Wishart describes this as 'one of the most tenacious principles in company law': *Models and Theories of Directors' Duties to Creditors*, [1991]14 New Zealand Universities Law Review 323, 326.

19 See John Farrar, Nigel Furey, Brenda Hannigan and Philip Wylie, *Farrar's Company Law*, 3rd Ed. 1991, p. 384.

20 See generally Reginald Barrett, *Directors' Duties to Creditors*, (1977)40 Modern Law Review 226; and Francis Dawson, *Acting in the Best Interests of the Company—For Whom are Directors "Trustees"?* [1984]11 New Zealand Universities Law Review 68.

The recent decision of the High Court of Australia in *Spies* v *The Queen*,[1] however, strongly suggests that the interests of 'the company' should be seen as quite distinct from those of its creditors, whatever the circumstances. The court, in the course of considering whether or not a company director had defrauded the company's creditors, held that directors do not owe an enforceable duty to creditors.

The court in this case noted the existence of other judgments which do suggest that directors have a duty which is owed to and enforceable by creditors,[2] it held that any such suggestions in these cases are 'contrary to principle and later authority and do not correctly state the law'.[3] The court preferred the interpretation of Gummow, J in *Sycotex Pty. Ltd.* v *Baseler*, where his Honour stated:

> The duty to take into account the interests of creditors is merely a restriction on the rights of shareholders to ratify breaches of the duty owed to the company. ... This restriction does not, in the absence of any conferral of such a right by statute, confer upon creditors any general law right against former directors of the company to recover losses suffered by those creditors ... the result is that there is a duty of imperfect obligation owed to creditors, one which the creditors cannot enforce save to the extent that the company acts on its own motion or through a liquidator.[4]

The High Court's decision in *Spies* confirms the traditional view of directors' duties, namely that such duties are owed to the company, and no independent duty is owed by directors to a company's creditors or to individual shareholders.

The American decision in *Trevor* v *Whitworth,*[5] stands as unassailable authority for the proposition that creditors have a right to rely on the capital remaining undiminished by any expenditure outside the limits

1 [2000] HCA 43; [2000]201 CLR 603.
2 See, for example, *Grove* v *Flavel* [1986]43 SASR 410; *Nicholson* v *Permakraft (NZ) Ltd.* [1985]1 NZLR 242.
3 [2000] HCA 43; [2000]201 CLR 603 (637).
4 [1994]13 ACSR 766, 785. See also *Kuwait Asia Bank* v *National Mutual Life Nominees Ltd.* [1990]3 NZLR 513 (529); and *ANZ Executors & Trustee Co. Ltd.* v *Qintex Australia Ltd.* [1990]2 ACSR 676 (682), where it was held that directors have no 'duty in law directly owing to and enforceable by creditors, and sounding in debt or damages'.
5 [1887]12 App Cas 409.

of the authorized objects or by the return of any part of it to the shareholders. English courts have developed their own version of the American 'trust fund' doctrine, but without any clear identification of creditors as the beneficiaries of the trust. The notion of directors as quasi trustees is recognized in a number of cases, but it is the company itself that is the beneficiary.[6]

In *Multinational Gas and Petrochemical Co.* v *Multinational Gas and Petrochemical Services Ltd,* Dillon, LJ said that: The directors indeed stand in a fiduciary relationship to the company, as they are appointed to manage the affairs of the company, and they owe fiduciary duties to the company though not to the creditors, present or future, or to individual shareholders.[7]

In *West Mercia Safetywear Ltd* v *Dodd*[8] the same judge, quoting from the decision of the New South Wales Court of Appeal in *Kinsela* v *Russell Kinsela Pty. Ltd.*,[9] held that where a company is insolvent, the interests of the creditors infringe.

They become prospectively entitled, through the mechanism of liquidation, to displace the power of the directors and shareholders to deal with the company's assets. It is in a practical sense their assets and not the shareholders' assets that, through the medium of the company, are under the management of the directors ...[10] This suggests that directors' duties are owed to creditors when a company is insolvent, on the grounds that it is they who have the ultimate financial interest in the company once its capital has been lost.[11]

In *Australian Growth Resources Corp. Pty. Ltd.* v *Van Reesema*, King, CJ said that the interests of creditors may become the dominant factor in what constitutes the interests of the company 'if a company's

6 *Russell* v *Wakefield Waterworks Co.* [1875]20 Eq. 474 per Jessel, MR. See also Notes of Cases, Reginald Barrett, *Directors' Duties to Creditors*, The Modern Law Review, vol. 40, No. 2 (Mar 1977), pp. 226-31.
7 [1983] Ch 258, 288; [1983]2 All ER 563.
8 [1988] BCLC 250.
9 [1986]4 NSWLR 722, 730.
10 [1988] BCLC 250 (253).
11 Paul Davies, *Gower's Principles of Modern Company Law*, 6th Ed. 1997, p. 603. Davies describes the *West Mercia* case as the 'clearest recognition of (the argument that directors owe duties to creditors) in the English courts'.

financial position is precarious'.[12] In *Brandy* v *Brandy,*[13] a case concerned with the validity of a scheme for the reorganization of a group of companies. The court considered the question of illegal financial assistance in purchase of own shares or whether it was within the permitted exceptions, provided they are done in good faith in the interests of the company. Nourse, LJ stated that "the interests of a company, an artificial person, cannot be distinguished from the interests of the persons who are interested in it. ...admittedly the existing creditors are interested in the assets of the company as the only source of the satisfaction of their debts. If the assets are too much and credit is too low, the interests of the creditors ought not to count for very much. Conversely, where the company is insolvent, or even doubtfully solvent, the interests of the company are in really the interests of existing creditors alone".

The position taken in all these cases was that the duties of directors are owed to the company. On the facts of particular cases this may require the directors to consider *inter alia* the interests of creditors. This suggests that the possibility of direct action by a creditor against a director is limited to situations where a 'particular duty of care arising from ordinary negligence principles' can be established. It means that creditors are not owed an independent and enforceable duty by company directors.[14] It was also observed that "in this respect it should be emphasized that the directors of a company in discharging their duty to the company must take into account of the interests of its shareholders and its creditors. Any failure by the directors to take into account the interests of creditors will have adverse consequences for the company as well as for them".[15] The common position is that if the company is liquidated, the fiduciary duties of the directors will tilt from the company towards creditor's interests.

On the other hand opposite views are also taken in some of the cases like in, *Yukong Lines Ltd.* v *Rends Burg Investments Corporation,*[16]

12 [1988]13 ACLR 261 (268-271). See also *Nicholson* v *Permakraft (NZ) Ltd.* [1985]1 NZLR 242 (discussed below); *Kinsela* v *Russell Kinsela Pty. Ltd.* [1986]4 NSWLR 722; *Chew* v *The Queen* [1991]5 ACSR 473.

13 [1988] BCLC 20 (CA).

14 Matthew Berkahn, *Directors Duties To 'The Company' and to Creditors: Spies* v *The Queen*, 10 Deaking Law Review, 2001.

15 Andrew Keay, *The Duty of Directors to Take Account Interests: Has it any Role to Play*, 2002 JBL 379.

16 *Queen's Bench Division*, The Times, 30th October 1997, Thursday.

in this case Mr. Justice Toulson held that "A director of an insolvent company who acted in breach of his fiduciary duty to the company by transferring the company's assets out of the reach of its creditors owed no direct fiduciary duty towards an individual creditor of the company. No individual creditor was entitled to sue for breach of the fiduciary duty owed by the director to the company". From the above discussion the position is clear that the directors of a company in discharging their duty to the company must take account of the interests of its shareholders and creditors. Any failure by the directors to take into account the interests of creditors will have adverse consequences for the company as well as for them.

The situation in a joint family for payment of debt is different from a juristic person. A property belonging to the joint family is ordinarily managed by the father or a senior member for the time being of the family. The manager of the joint Hindu family is called *karta*. So long as the members of a family remind undivided, a senior member of the family is entitled to manage the family property. Akaka or manager has to offer to contract debts for family purpose and family business. A joint in the family may have no business at all, and yet debts may be contacted at a manager for a joint family purpose. Such debts are binding on other members. Besides the power to contract debts for the family business, the manager has the power of making contracts, giving receipts and compromising or discharging claims ordinarily incidental to the business. It was held that the debts had not been raised by the appellant's father as a karta for his personal benefit and had not been taken for immoral of illegal purposes. The loan and credit facilities were away of by the abundance father as Akaka of the joint Hindu family readiness for legal necessity that is family business. Hence, the contract is not personally liable for the debts incurred during the business.[17]

If the company is solvent, the director's primary duty is towards the shareholders and if a company is under liquidation, then the duty of the directors to the company is principally to consider the creditors' interest, since it is their money which is now at risk, rather than the shareholders.[18] It can also be observed that directors don't have any

17 *Rajat Pangaria* v *State Bank of Bikaner and Jaipur* (2008)141 Comp Cas 323 (DRAT).

18 *Chamundi Chemicals and Fertilisers Ltd. (In Liquidation)* v *M.C. Cherian* (1993)77 Comp Cas 1 (Kar); ILR (1993) Kar 620.

personal liability if he is acting in official capacity as a director of a company at the time of winding up of the company.

An action against a defaulting director may be brought by the company itself or where the breach of duty complained of is a breach of fiduciary duty by a member suing in a derivative action on behalf of himself and all other members of the company, his liability for breach of fiduciary duty by misfeasance proceedings in the company's winding up is well known. But directors owe no fiduciary or contractual duties nor any duty of care to persons who deal with their company unless they deal with the contracting party not on behalf of the company but on their own behalf, a director is therefore not liable to pay the debts incurred by the company. Even during the course of winding up proceeding of a company, the directors may be made personally liable by order of the court only if they are found guilty of fraudulent trading, i.e., an act of misfeasance or the like. Directors are not liable for breach of contracts by the company and the other party to a contract cannot make them directly liable by suing them in tort even for their mismanagement of the company's affairs. The liability of the directors even in common law is confined only where they have been guilty of a tort toward the creditors as well as breach of duty owed to the company. Consequently, directors are personally liable to persons who lend money to the company only if they obtain the loan by fraudulent misrepresentations. It is, therefore, obvious that directors are generally immune from liability to creditors of their company.[19]

This position was confirmed in *Sangramsinh P. Gaekwad* v *Shantadevi P. Gaekwad*,[20] the SC held that a director of a company indisputably stands in a fiduciary capacity vis-a-vis the Company. He must act for the paramount interest of the company. He does not have any statutory duty to perform so far as individual shareholders are concerned subject of course to any special arrangement which may be entered into or a special circumstance that may arise in a particular case.

4.4 Discretionary powers and limitations

Almost all powers of directors are exercised by them in their personal discretion. However, there are certain limitations upon their discretion.

19 *Hrushikesh Panda* v *Indramani Swain* AIR 1987 Ori 79.
20 Civil Appeal No. 6360 and 6361 of 2001 of the SC; (2005)11 SCC 314.

They are not competent to do what the Act, memorandum and articles of association don't permit or by the shareholders in general meeting. The delimitation of power of directors is specifically demarcated in the articles and statutes of company laws. Historically, the *ultra vires* doctrine in company law gave rise to important limitations on director's powers. The powers of board and the directors can be summarized as follows:[1]

1. The rule that the board must act with due formality.[2]
2. Directors vested with discretion must not act on the dictate of someone else.[3]
3. Fiduciary powers vested in board of directors must not be improperly fettered.[4]

According to *Henry G. Manue*[5] the areas of management control and shareholder control are demarcations there will always be a scope, however limited may be, for clash between the two primary organs of the company viz; the shareholders and the directors, as to their respective powers. This problem raises the question of the true nature of the relationship that is to be subsisted between the shareholders and the directors.

Until the end of the nineteenth century it seems to have been generally assumed that the position of directors is subordinate to that of the shareholders in general meeting. The shareholders in general meeting was considered as the company. This principle got recognition in *Isle of Wight Ry.* v *Tahourdin*,[6] where the court refused an application by the directors of a company for an injunction to restrain the holding of a general meeting, one purpose of which was to appoint a committee to reorganize the management of the company. The court observed:

> It is a very strong thing indeed to prevent shareholders from holding a general meeting of the company, when such a meeting is the only way in which they can interfere, if the majority of them

1 Barry A.K. Rider, *The Realm of Company Law*, (Kluwerlaw International: The Netherlands), p. 18.

2 *In Re Bonelli's Telegraph Company (Collie's Claim)* [1871]12 Eq 246, p. 258.

3 *Scottish Co-operative Wholesale Society* v *Meyer* [1959] AC 324; [1958]3 All ER 66 (HL).

4 See *Thorby* v *Goldberg* [1964]112 CLR 597, pp. 605-606.

5 *The Higher Criticism of Modern Corporations* (1962)62 Col LR 399 (408).

6 [1883]25 Ch D 320 (CA).

> think that the course taken by the directors, in a matter *intra-vires* of the directors, is not for the benefit of the company.[7]

However, this position has been changed with the down of the present century in 1906, where the court of Appeal made it clear in *Automatic Self Cleansing Filter Syndicate Co. Ltd.* v *Cunninghame,*[8] that where powers has been vested in the board the general meeting could not interfere with their exercise. In this case the articles of the company vested the general power of management and control of the company in the directors subject to the regulations made by the shareholders by extraordinary resolutions. Again the articles specifically provided that the directors are empowered to sell or otherwise deal with the property of the company on such terms as they think fit. The directors refused to carry out a proposal of the sale of the company's assets by the shareholders passed by a simple resolution. The share holders contended that it is a mere question of principal agent relations and the directors are bound to carry out the sale into effect. But the court held:

> Directors are agents not of a majority of the shareholders, but of the company of the whole entity made up of all the shareholders. And if the whole entity of the shareholders has entrusted the directors with a particular power a simple majority could not interfere in the exercise of it. The articles constitute a contract by which all the members had agreed that the directors and the directors alone shall manage.[9]

This new approach received approval in *Gramophone & Typewriter* v *Stanley,*[10] where the court observed: "Even a resolution of a numerical majority at a general meeting cannot impose its will upon the directors when the articles have confined to them the control of the company's affairs."[11] However, this principle did not secure acceptance in *Marshall's Valvet Gear Co.* v *Manning Wardle & Co.*[12] But in *Quin & Axtens* v *Salmon,*[13] the court held that the general meeting cannot interfere with a decision of the directors unless they are acting contrary to the

7 Per Cotton, D.T. at p. 329.
8 [1906]2 Ch 34.
9 Per Cozens-Hardy, LJ at p. 44.
10 [1908]2 KB 89; 99 Lt 39.
11 *Ibid,* Per Farwell, LT.
12 *Ibid,* Per Farwell, LT.
13 [1909] AC 442; [1909]1 Ch 31.

provisions of the act or the articles. In *John Shaw & Sons Ltd.* v *Peter Shaw & John Shaw,*[14] Gear, LJ expressed the same view.

The modern rule as expressed in *Scott* v *Scott,*[15] held that the members in general meeting cannot give directions to the directors on how the affairs of the company are to be managed, nor can them overrule any decision of the directors in the conduct of its business.

The above said rule has been followed by the courts in India in many cases.[16] Thus the Kerala High Court in *Suburban Bank Ltd.* v *Thariath,*[17] held that the directors were entitled to enforce the payment of a debt as against the resolution of the shareholders where the power of management was vested with the directors by the article of the company.

However, despite the fact that the officers of the company are managed and controlled by the directors, the shareholders can interfere under certain exceptional circumstances. In *L.I.C.* v *Escorts Ltd.,*[18] the Supreme Court of India upheld the rights of shareholders to interfere in the management by replacing the existing management.

Thus under certain exceptional situations the general meeting is competent to interfere with matters delegated to the board. In *Satya Charan* v *Ramaswar Prasad Bajoria,*[19] Supreme Court held[20] that even though the directors are the only persons competent to conduct litigations in the name of the company, the shareholders may take steps for the same when the wrong doors are the directors themselves and have acted *mala fide*. The board of directors of a corporation exercised their discretion and abolished the post of joint managing director. Their exercise of the discretion was not shown to be *mala fide*. The court refused to interfere in the matter.[1]

14 [1935]2 KB 113; [1935] All ER Rep 456 (CA).
15 [1943]1 All ER 582. Reviewed by Plowman, J in *Bamford* v *Bamford* [1970] Ch 212; [1969]2 WLR 1107; [1969]1 All ER 751.
16 *M.P. & Vs. Works* v *M. Murarka* AIR 1961 Cal 251: (1961)31 Comp Cas 301; *A.P. Pothen* v *Hindustan Trading Corpn.* AIR 1968 Ker 149; (1967)37 Comp Cas 268; *Suburban Bank (Pvt.) Ltd.* v *Thariath* AIR 1968 Ker 206; (1968)38 Comp Cas 13.
17 (1968)38 Comp Cas 13; (1967)2 Comp LT 182 (Ker).
18 (1986)1 SCC 264, 340-341.
19 AIR 1950 FC 133; (1950)20 Comp Cas 39; 1949 FCR 673.
20 Per Fazi AL, J.
1 *Taunton* v *Royal Insurance Co.* [1864]2 Hem & M 135; *Bank of Turkey* v *Ottoman Co.* [1866] LR 2 Eq 366.

To sum up, it can be summarized that the true relationship subsisting between the directors and the general meeting is not a superior-subordinate one. It is one of federation and co-operative in nature.

4.5 Discretionary powers and trusteeship

4.5.1 *Trustees and their position*

It is often stated that the directors are trustees and that the nature of their duties can be explained on this basis. This idea is not a new one. Till the middle of the nineteenth century most of the joint stock companies were unincorporated and depend for their validity on a deed of settlement vesting the property of the company in trustees. Often the directors themselves were the trustees. Even where separate persons were appointed as trustees, the directors and managers were regarded as trustees in so far as they dealt with the trust property of the company.

The general view is that the directors of a company are its agents and they stand in a fiduciary relationship to the company. The duties of good faith which are imposed by this fiduciary relationship are virtually identical with those imposed on trustees. The directors are generally expected not to place themselves in a position where their duties towards the company conflict with their personal interests.[2]

This position of the directors as trustees of the properties of the company had been recognized by the courts of equity. Thus in *Griures* v *Harrison*[3] the directors of a building society were held liable for breach of trust, while the actual trustees escaped from liability since they had acted only ministerially under the instructions of the directors.

Even though "trusteeship" was attached only to directors of unincorporated companies, the courts may often did extend it's to incorporated companies also as their duties are the very same whether the company was an incorporated one or not. Moreover, it was for long believed[4] that the property of a corporation was held on trust by the corporation for its members, and since it would be the directors who managed the property, they would be liable as constructive trustees if they misapplied it. Further, the courts of equity always tend to apply

2 *National Worker's Union* v *P.R. Ramkrishnan* AIR 1983 SC 75; (1983)1 SCR 9.

3 [1859]26 Beav 435.

4 *Child* v *Hudson's Bay Co.* [1723]2 Wms 207.

the label "trustee" to anyone in a fiduciary position. The extent to which the courts were prepared to carry this analogy is well illustrated in *Re German Mining Co.,*[5] where the directors were afforded a trustee's right to be indemnified by the shareholders as beneficiaries. The company in this case was an incorporated one. Nevertheless, directors are not trustees in the proper sense of the term. *In Re City Equitable Fire Insurance Co.*, the Court observed:[6]

> "It has sometimes been said that directors are trustees. If this means no more than that directors in the performance of their duties stand in a fiduciary relationship to the company, the statement is true enough. But if the statement is meant to be an indication by way of analogy of what those duties are, it appears to me to be wholly misleading I can see but little resemblance between the duties of a director and the duties of a trustee of a will of a marriage settlement."[7]

Even though directors are considered as trustees, their actual position is that of agents of the company. But they will be treated as trustees of the company's properties which are actually under their control.[8] Again as agents of the company they stand in a fiduciary position towards their principal, the company. Further, it may be noted that whereas the authority of the directors to bind the company as its agents normally depends on their acting collectively as a board, their duties of good faith are owed by each director individually. Thus, a single director is not an agent of the company to bind it with responsibility for his act, but he will be a fiduciary of it. Here, again the directors resemble trustees who must normally act jointly but each of whom severally owes duties of good faith towards the beneficiaries.

In Cairns, LJ in *Ferguson* v *Wilson*,[9] held that:

> What is the position of directors of a public company? They are merely agents of a company. The company itself cannot act in its own person, for it has no person; it can only act through directors, and the case is, as regards those directors, merely the ordinary case of principal and agent. Wherever an agent is liable, those

5 [1853]4 De GM & G 19.
6 [1924] All ER Rep 485 (CA); [1925] Ch 407 (426).
7 Per Romer, J.
8 *In Re Forest of Dean Coal Co.* [1878]10 Ch D 450.
9 [1867]2 Ch App 77 (89).

> directors would be liable; where the liability would attach to the principal, and the principal only, the liability is the liability of the company.

Later on the position was clarified in *Great Eastern Rail Co.* v *Turner*,[10] it was held that:

> The directors are the mere trustees or agents of the company—trustees of the company's money and property—agents in the transactions which they enter into on behalf of the company.

The fiduciary position of directors attaches to their office two major duties which are analogous to the duties of normal trustees, viz., duty of honesty and good faith and the duty of care and skill.[11] They are expected to exercise their powers *bona fide* and are on the best interest of the company. The fiduciary duty within which the directors have to act enjoins upon them a duty to act on behalf the company with utmost care, skill and due diligence and in the interest of the company. Directors are not entitled to use their powers merely for the purpose of maintaining their control over the affairs of the company or merely for their extraneous purposes to benefit themselves. They have a duty to make full and honest disclosure to the shareholders regarding all important matters related to the company. The acts of the directors deprived limited company are required to be tested on a much finer scale in order to rule out any misuse of power for personal gains or ulterior motives. If the petitioner approached the court under ss. 397 and 398 of the Companies Act and the petitioners should come to the court with clean hands.[12] If the petitioners had acted against the interest of the company and also breached their fiduciary duties and failed to prove that siphoning off funds against the respondents due to the alleged mismanagement by the respondents. The petitioner seeking equitable relief must come with clean hands and good conduct, failing which the petitioner would constitute a gross abuse of the process of court, and the petitioner is not entitled for any relief under ss. 397 and 398 of the Act.[13]

10 [1872] LR 8 Ch App 149.

11 *S. Gururaja Rao* v *State of Karnataka* (1979)49 Comp Cas 825 (Kar); (1979)2 Kar LJ 185.

12 *Kultar Sehgal* v *Broad Digital Prints (I) Pvt. Ltd.* (2008)141 Comp Cas 680 (CLB).

13 *Sri Kanta Datta Narasimharaja Wadiyar* v *Sri Venkiteswara Real Estates Enterprises Pvt. Ltd.* (1991)72 Comp Cas 211.

4.5.2 *Duty of good faith and bona fides*

The first and foremost obligation of a person in fiduciary position is to act with honesty. They must act in good faith and *bona fide*. "Greatest good faith is expected in the discharge of their duties."[14] Good faith requires that all their endeavours must be directed to the benefit of the company. Thus a director was held liable to account his profit which he earned as bonus from another company in which he was a member for providing certain business facility of the company, even though the company had lost nothing and also could not have earned bonus from such transaction.[15]

Similarly, a director should not make use of the company's property or undertakings or money for his own advantage. They should not enter into such transactions in which they have a personal interest conflicting with that of the company.[16] They should not make benefit out of the opportunities of the company which they could not have made available to themselves, if they had not been in the position of directors.[17] They are under a fiduciary duty to disclose this personal interest in a particular transaction with the company.[18] Yet another duty of directors having controlling block of shares is not to make money for themselves from selling their controlling block. If they do so they would be liable if they have negligently or fraudulently passed the control to a person who would took the assets of the company.[19] They must defeat all takeover bids which they think honestly are not in the interest of the company with all possible means.

Ordinarily the day-to-day businesses of the companies are carried out by directors and other managerial persons. Shareholders cannot interfere with such matters. However, the majority of members can effectively interfere in the administration of the company in case the directors acted *mala fide*. If their personal interest is in conflict with

14 Per Patel, J in *Bank of Poona Ltd.* v *Narayandas* AIR 1961 Bom 252 (253); (1961)31 Comp Cas 364. Also, *Turner Morrison & Co.* v *Shalimar Tar Products* (1980)50 Comp Cas 296 (Cal).

15 *Boston Deep Sea Fishing & Ice Co.* v *Ansel* [1888]39 Ch D 339; [1886-90] All ER Rep 65.

16 *Aberdeen Railway* v *Blaikie* [1854]1 Macq 461.

17 *Cook* v *Decks* [1916]1 AC 554; [1916-17] All ER Rep 285.

18 Section 299, the objects of this rule has to be explained by Chagla, CJ in *Walchandnagar Industries* v *Ratanchand* AIR 1953 Bom 285.

19 [1955]68 Hari LR 1275; Janning 44 California LR I (1956) Hill sale of controlling shares [1957]70 Hari LR 986.

their duty in such a way that they cannot or will not take steps to safeguard the interest of the company, the majority of shareholders may interfere with the administration of the company. This rule was applied in *Marshall's Valve Geer Co. Ltd.* v *Manning Wardle & Co. Ltd.*, where:

> A and three other persons were the four directors of M.Co. and they held substantially the whole of the subscribed capital of the company. A was the majority shareholder, but held less than three-fourth. Another company known as N.Co., was committing an infringement of M.Co.'s trade mark and the other three directors were interested in the company. With the result that they declined any proceeding against N.Co. A, at a general meeting of the shareholders resolved and, commenced action to restrain the use of the trademark of M.Co. Other directors contended that as the articles had left the powers of management with the board the shareholders could not interfere by a single resolution.[20]

However, the court held that the majority of the shareholders had the right to control the actions of the directors in the matter. The court observed:

> Now it is obvious that in the position in which they (directors) have placed themselves on this question their duty and their interest are in direct conflict. On the one hand, it is their duty as directors to protect the interest of the original patent which is the property of the company; on the other hand their personal interest is clearly to maintain the validity of the patent which belongs to them. And, therefore, the majority shareholders are entitled to decide whether or not an action in the name of the company shall proceed.[1]

The breach of implied contract and good faith were discussed by various courts. The relevant principles on the main issues with regard to the claims for breach of the contract of employment are these. First, there is an implied term that the employee will serve the employer with loyalty and fidelity. Second, acts done while the contract of employment subsists but which are preparatory to competition after

20 [1909]1 Ch 267; 100 LT 65.
1 Per Neville, I., at p. 271.

it terminates, may not in themselves be in breach of the implied term as to loyalty and fidelity.[2]

Third, while the contract of employment subsists the employee cannot use confidential information to the detriment of the employer; after it ceases the employee may compete, and may use know-how acquired in the course of his employment (as distinct from trade secrets–although the distinction is sometimes difficult to apply in practice).[3]

Fourth, the contract of employment (in the absence of an express term) may be determined on reasonable notice. What is reasonable depends on all the circumstances, and may have to reflect the prevailing standards on employment mobility. Fifth, for most purposes (but not for all) neither the employer nor the employee can unilaterally bring the relationship to an end by breach. Sixth, a breach of the terms of the employment contract by the employer (including an attempt to force on the employee a variation against his or her will) may be so serious as to be repudiatory and entitle the employee to treat it as terminating the contract or as a constructive dismissal. Seventh, a failure to pay the agreed remuneration is a breach of contract (unless the employee has waived the right to receive payment or has agreed to a delay in payment), but is not necessarily a fundamental or repudiatory breach. A deliberate, repeated and persistent failure is likely to be repudiatory (*Cantor Fitzgerald International* v *Callaghan)*[4] but whether a failure to pay amounts to a repudiatory breach is a question of degree to be answered in the light of the facts. Eighth, a party who refuses to perform without giving a reason may later justify it on the ground of the other party's repudiation, but not where the breach could have been put right.[5] This position was also recognized in *Glass* v *Atkin.*[6] In India this rule was accepted by the Supreme Court in *Satya Charan* v *Rameswar Prasad Bajbrila.*[7]

2 *Laughton & Hawley* v *Bapp Industrial Supplies Ltd.* [1986] ICR 634; *Tither Barn Ltd* v *Hubbard* EAT, 7th November 1991; contrast *Marshall* v *Industrial Systems and Control Ltd.* [1992] IRLR 295.

3 *Roger Bullivant Ltd.* v *Ellis* [1987] ICR 464, applying *Faccenda Chicken Ltd.* v *Fowler* [1986] ICR 297. In *Symbian Ltd.* v *Christensen*, unreported, 8th May 2000 [without reference to this point (2001) IRLR 77 (CA)].

4 [1999] ICR 639.

5 *Heisler* v *Anglo-Dal Ltd.* [1954]1 WLR 1273.

6 [1967]65 DLR (2d) 501, Ontario High Court.

7 AIR 1950 FC 133; (1950)20 Comp Cas 39.

The Pepsu High Court in *Fateh Chand Kad* v *Hidsons (Patiala) Ltd.*,[8] held that a director stands in a fiduciary position to the company. He is always expected to guard the company's interests, and surely not to utilize the position and knowledge possessed by him in virtue of his office to the detriment of the company's interest and for his personal advantage.

The petitioner, upon starting a separate business of his own similar to the business of the company of which he was one of the directors, forwarded a letter to the company saying: "kindly consider me from today as a sleeping partner." The company considered that letter as resignation of his office as a director and accepted his resignation. The court opined that the language used in the letter admitted of the interpretation placed upon it and the most that could be said was that an honest mistake was committed in interpreting that letter. Similar view was expressed in *T.H. Condon and A. Butterworth* v *The Muir Mills Company, Limited of Cawnpore*.[9] It was held that:

> A fiduciary nature and must be exercised in good faith, i.e., legitimately, for the purpose for which it is conferred. It must not be exercised corruptly or fraudulently or arbitrarily or capriciously or wantonly. It may not be exercised for a collateral purpose. In exercising it the Directors must act in good faith in the interests of the Company, and they must fairly consider the question of the transferee's fitness at a Board Meeting. Then as to the power of the Court to interfere with the Directors' decision, the judgment lays down that the Court will not review the Directors' decision when they have in good faith rejected a transfer on the ground that the transferee is not a fit person to become a member of the Company.

4.5.3 *Duty to promote the interest of the company*

The duty to promote the success of the company is the modern version of the basic loyalty duty of directors. The interest of the company is the sole motive force by which the directors of a company are expected to act. They must act *bona fide* in the interest of the company. Lord Greene M.R. observed in *Re Smith & Faweett*,[10] that "the principle is

8 (1957)27 Comp Cas 340; AIR 1956 Pepsu 89.
9 (1900) ILR 22 All 410.
10 [1942] Ch 304 at 306 (CA).

undoubted that directors must act *bona fide* in what they consider—not what a court may consider. But it is generally accepted that there is always a presumption in favour of the honesty of the acts of the directors". The court will accept that the directors have done what they honestly believed to be right unless satisfied that they have not behaved as honest men of business might be expected to act. However, there is a breach of duty when they act in their own interests without considering the interest of the company even if it is not shown that they have acted with any dishonesty. Thus *in re W & M Roith Ltd.,*[11] a director of a company entered into a service agreement with the company whereby it is provided that after his death his widow has to be entitled to a pension for life. The court held that the transaction is not binding on the company as no thought had been given to the question whether the arrangement was at any rate beneficial to the company. Thus, the court will assume a breach of trust on the part of the directors even in the absence of any conscious dishonesty if they have acted without considering the interest of the company.[12] This principle was accepted in many cases.[13] In *Lingren* v *L.&P. Estates Ltd.,*[14] it was held that there had been no failure to consider the commercial merits.

Thus, the directors of a company must always act honestly in the interest of the company. But in construing the meaning of the saying that they must act in the interest of the company, they are not expected to act for the economic advantage of the corporate entity, disregarding the interest of the members.[15] In many cases a company is equated with its members. Thus, in *Greenhalgh* v *Arderne Cinemas,*[16] in connection with members voting in general meeting, Evershed, MR said the phrase 'the company as a whole' does not mean the company as a commercial entity as distinct from the corporators. Again in *Savoy*

11 [1967]1 WLR 432.
12 Following *Re, Lee, Behrens & Co. Ltd.* [1932]2 Ch 46.
13 *Alexander* v *Automatic Telephone Co.* [1900]2 CLI 56 (CA); *Re Lee Behrens & Co. Ltd.* [1932]2 Ch 46; *Millers (Invercargill) Ltd.* v *Maddams* [1938] NZLR 490 (NZ CA); and *Ngutli Ltd.* v *Mc Cann* [1954]90 CLR 425 (Aust HC).
14 [1968] Ch 572 (CA).
15 *Parke* v *Daily News* [1962] Ch 927 at 963.
16 [1951] Ch 286 (CA) [4.27].

Hotel case,[17] it has been said that "the company does not mean the sectional interest of some or the majority or even all the present members, but of present and future members of the company, on the footing that it would be continued as a going concern, balancing a long-term view against short-term interests of present members."[18]

However, director's personal interest cannot be always disregarded. They are not detached persons. As they themselves are normally shareholders and are entitled to have regard to their own interests such and not to think only of the others. They are "not required by the law to live in an unreal region of detached altruism and to act in a vague mood of ideal abstraction from obvious facts which must be present to the mind of any honest and intelligent man when he exercises his powers as a director".[19] However, they are apparently entitled to have regard only to the interests of the members, present and future and not any other outside interest.

The principle that the directors shall have regard only to the interest of the company virtually renders the interests of the employees, consumers or the nation as a whole is legally irrelevant.[20] This position is not desirable.[1] But the truth is that directors habitually pay regards to these interests and declare their commitment to employees, consumers and the nation as well as to the shareholders.[2] Again for

17 A 'cause celebre' which never reached the courts but in which a board of trade inspector was appointed to report on the legality of the directors action in attempting to remove the Berkeley Hotel from the Company's control so as to take it beyond the reach of a take-over bidder. The Inspectors Report (H.M.S.O. 1954) Com [1955]68 Harv LR 1176.

18 Counsel's advise to the director.

19 Per Lathaur, CJ in *Mills* v *Mills* [1938]60 CLR 150 (Aust HC) at p. 164.

20 *Parke* v *Daily News* [1962] Ch 927; following *Hutton* v *W. Cork Ry* [1883]23 Ch D 654 (CA).

1 In *Brandy* v *Brandy* [1988] BCLC 20, it was suggested that it is not possible to say whether it is in the interests of the company as a separate legal entity distinct from all those involved in its success that, over a given period of time, it is desirable to maximize the company's profitability, size, number of employees or any other business objective, assuming that, as will be the case, these objectives are not all compatible one with the other, at least at the margin. However, identify the company with its shareholders, its managers, its employers or some other group, then the question becomes much easier to answer.

2 The late Henry Ford in *Dodge* v *Ford Motor Co.* [1919]204 Mich 459; 170 NW 668, the Michigan Supreme Court has suggested that the shareholders interest should be totally subordinated to those of the employees, consumers and the public.

gaining business prosperity by completing with other commercial institutions, a company should pay regard to other interests, rebellious employees, hostile trade unions, dissatisfied customers, aggrieved public and government. All these outside forces compel the management to choose the course of action which is most conducive to the interest and future prosperity of the company.

Hence, generosity to employees, charitable donations and even political contributions, all these become inevitable for the larger interest of the company.[3] But the directors must justify these contributions by showing positively that they were made *bona fide* for the benefit of the company.[4]

In *Suresh Arora* v *Grevlon Textile Mills Pvt. Ltd.*, the CLB observed that is well settled proposition of law that the conduct of the parties is a relevant factor to be considered in the equitable proceedings under ss. 397 and 398 of the act. If the respondent and the petitioner had not come with clean hands, the petition deserved to be dismissed.

The CLB categorically held that the directors are required to act on behalf of the company in a fiduciary capacity and their powers have to be exercised for the benefit of the company. The fiduciary capacity within reach the directors have to act enjoins upon them a duty to act on behalf of a company with utmost good faith, care, skill and due diligence and in the interest of the company and stop they have a duty to make full and honest disclosure to the shareholders regarding all important matters relating to the company. It is objectionable to use such power simply or solely for the benefit of directors or merely for extraneous partners likes maintenance or acquisition of control over the affairs of the company. The directors of the company had breached their fiduciary duty and acted against the interest of the company to dupe each other, trying to grab the maximum benefits out of the transaction is of the company for their proprietorship consent is conduct of the parties had been but in some, hash and wrongful. Equity prohibits a trustee from making any profit by his management, directly or indirectly. Directors are required to act on behalf of a company in a

3 *Hutton* v *West Cork Ry.* [1883]23 Ch D 654 at p. 673. Also *Evans* v *Brunner Mond & Co.* [1921]1 Ch 359.

4 *Parke* v *Daily News Ltd.* [1962] Ch 927 (954); *Re W & M Roth Ltd.* [1967]1 WLR 432.

fiduciary capacity and their acts and deeds have to be exercised for the benefit of the company.[5]

However, under certain exceptional circumstances the true interest of the company seems difficult to be contemplated. For example when a company becomes insolvent the directors should have regard to the interests of the creditors. Then the members of the company have little remaining interests to be considered. Same is the position when the company's business is about to cease.

In Halsbury's *Laws of England*, 3rd Edition, Volume 6, it has been stated at page 623 that misfeasance and breach of trust include a breach by a promoter, director etc. of a duty to the company the direct consequence of which has been a misapplication or loss of its assets for which he could be made responsible in an action. Allegations or proof of fraud are not essential and it is immaterial that the offence is one for which the offender may be criminally liable.[6]

Thus it can be said that, the directors as fiduciaries must always act *bona fide* for the interest of the company. It is they who decide what is best for the interest of the company, and not the court. They alone can know the commercial currents and circumstances. Thus they have great discretion in exercising their power of management. But this power is a fiduciary one to be exercised honestly and in good faith.

4.5.4 *Duty to group companies*

There is no provision in the British or Indian Companies Act to impose special duties on directors of the parent company and subsidiaries in the same group of companies. However, under the common law, it is common for directors to take decisions in the interests of the group company as a whole without considering the interests of the particular company to which they have been appointed. The courts have held that it is not proper for directors of a subsidiary to compel the subsidiary to guarantee the parent company's debts or give the subsidiary company's properties a security for such debts in circumstances where the parent company alone is benefited.[7] In

5 (2008)142 Comp Cas 963 (CLB); (2007)80 SCL 228 (CLB).

6 *P.K. Nedungadi* v *Malayalee Bank Ltd. (In Liquidation)* AIR 1971 SC 829; (1972)42 Comp Cas 120 (SC).

7 *Chaterbridge Corporation Ltd.* v *Lloyds Banks Ltd.* [1969]2 All ER 1185; *Rolled Steel Products (Holdings) Ltd.* v *British Steel Corporation* [1985]3 All ER 52; [1986] Ch 246; [1985]2 WLR 908.

Ferruecio Sias v *Jai Manga Ram Mukhi,*[8] it was held that it is fundamental to the functioning of any company that the board of directors of the company owes allegiance only to the company in which they are the directors. It is not permissible for the board of directors to act on the dictates of any other company even if it is the holding company. Directors cannot give up their duty and right of independent action for the purpose of promoting the interests of the company as also the interests of the shareholders as a whole. The court followed the decision in *Bell* v *Lever Brothers.*[9] But in *Charterbridge Corp.* v *Lloyds Bank,*[10] the directors of a company forming part of a group had considered the benefit of the group as a whole without giving separate consideration to that of the company alone when they caused the subsidiary company of which they were directors to give security for a debt owed by the parent company to the bank. It was held that "the proper test ... in the absence of actual separate consideration must be whether an intelligent and honest man in the position of a director of the company could ... have reasonably believed that the transactions were for the benefit of the company." The latest position on this issue is that the core duty of loyalty does not recognize a duty "to the group" or to other companies in the group.[11]

4.5.5 *Duty to Act within powers*

The directors must act within their powers conferred within the mandate of the memorandum and articles of association of the company. Directors must not do any act or enter into any transaction which is illegal or *ultra vires* the company.[12] Without the express sanction of the members in general meeting, directors cannot enter into transactions with others which are beyond the powers conferred on them by the articles of the company. If they exceed the powers and as a consequence the company suffers loss in consequence, the company can recover the amount of its loss from them personally, and it is not

8 (1998)93 Comp Cas 750 (Del).
9 [1932] AC 161 (HL).
10 [1970] Ch 62. A similar approach has been adopted in the area of unfair prejudice. See *Nicholas* v *Soundcraft Electronics Ltd.* [1993]1 BCLC 360 (CA).
11 See *Lindgren* v *L&P Estates Co. Ltd.* [1968] Ch 572.
12 *Selangor United Rubber Estates Ltd.* v *Cradock* (No. 3) [1968]2 All ER 1073; [1968]1 WLR 1555.

necessary for it to show that they acted negligently.[13] The directors are personally liable for any manipulation in the profit and loss account and subsequently paid dividends to shareholders in violation of statutory rules.[14]

Directors who are employed under service contracts may also be sued for damages for breach of these contracts if they engage in illegal acts, or exceed the company's objects or powers or their own powers, but it would appear that they may be absolved from their contractual liability by a special resolution passed by a general meeting.[15] The directors are liable to his company for exceeding his powers only if he causes loss by sanctioning an improper use of its assets, or by exposing it to liability to third persons.[16] The basic principle that the action must meet with some kind of loss to the company as a result of director's *ultra vires* act in question.[17] At common-law, an act or decision of the directors which is outside the company's constitution is void and no effect. On the other hand, if the directors simply exceed an authority which has been conferred on them, the decision is only voidable.[18]

4.5.6 *Duty to exercise reasonable skill and diligence*

The duties of loyalty and care are inseparable as far as a company director is concerned. If the duty of loyalty is based on fiduciary principles, the duty of care and skill is based on the principle of the law of negligence. A director of a company must exercise reasonable care, skill, and diligence. This means that a director should exercise his duties as a reasonably diligent person with the general knowledge, skill and experience that may reasonably expected of a person carried out by the director in relation to a company, and the general knowledge, skill and experience that the director has.[19] Historically, the common

13 *Cullerne* v *London and Suburban General Permanent Building Society* [1890]25 QBD 485.

14 *Allied Carpets Group Plc.* v *Nethercote* [2001] BCC 81.

15 *Besnson* v *Heathorn* [1842]1 Y & C Ch Cas 326.

16 *Bishopsgate Investment Management Ltd.* v *Maxwell* (No. 2) [1993] BCLC 814; [1992]2 All ER 856; [1992]2 WLR 991.

17 *Selangor United Rubber Estates Ltd.* v *Cradock* (No. 3) [1968]2 All ER 1073; [1968]2 All ER 1073; [1968]1 WLR 1555.

18 *Hogg* v *Cramphorn* [1967] Ch 257. In this case a decision to attach multiple voting rights to shares issued to the company's pension fund, in breach of the company's articles, ineffective.

19 Palmer's *Company Law: Annoted Guide to the Companies Act 2006*, (Sweet & Maxwell, 2007), p. 170.

law was based upon a very low standard of care which was subjectively formulated. The general subjective test of reasonable skill and care was laid down in *City Equitable Fire Insurance Co. Ltd., Re,*[20] the minimum standard of objectively expected from a person in the directors' position. The subjective standard can be raised according to the knowledge, experience and special skill of a director. This objective test and subjective test are strictly followed by the courts in different cases. It has been laid down that so long as a director acts honestly he cannot be made responsible in damages unless guilty of gross or culpable negligence in a business sense.

The British Companies Act 2006 incorporated these two tests in the Act and set a standard for reasonable care expected from company directors.[1] However, the Act does not mention whether it is a common law duty or equitable one. This duty is owed to the company and not to the members. Members have no right to expect a reasonable standard of general management from the companies' managing director. Management quality is always a risk of investment.[2] The expression of skill and care can be seen in s. 174 of the Companies Act 2006 Act and also in s. 214 of the Insolvency Act 1986.

It provides that:

> This means the care, skill and diligence that would be exercised by a reasonably diligent person with (*a*) the general knowledge, skill and experience that may reasonably be expected of a person carrying out the same functions carried out by the director in relation to the company, and (*b*) the general knowledge, skill and experience that the director has.

The decisions like, in *Francis* v *United Jersey Bank,*[3] it requires directors to have at 1east a rudimentary, understanding of the business of the corporation to become familiar with the fundamentals of the business in which the corporation is engaged. The beginning of the modern approach, common law can be found in the decision of *Dorchester Finacne Co* v *Stebbubg,*[4] which marked a move towards a fully objective approach.

20 [1925] Ch 407; [1924] All ER Rep 485 (CA).
1 Section 174 of the Companies Act 2006.
2 *Re, Elgindata Ltd.* [1991] BCLC 959.
3 [1981]87 NJ 15 (30); 432 A 2d 814 (821-822).
4 Decided in 1977, but only reported in 1989; [1989] BCLC 498.

Duty of care is a standard that requires a board member to exercise the same care that an ordinary, prudent person would exercise in a like position or under similar circumstances. It means that board members should attend board meetings and be informed about the activities of the organization in order to be able to make informed and make independent decisions when voting. State laws differ on the degree of care required to be taken by board members.[5]

Neville, J in *Re Brazilian Rubber Plantations & Estates Ltd*, held that directors are not 'bound to take part in the conduct of the company's business' and only in so far as they do, they are required to exercise any care in the performance of their duties. However, even though the courts were also careful not to impose too high a duty when there is evidence of inactivity, what is clear from several reported cases is that, in finding directors liable for breach of the duty of care, skill and diligence, the courts were not as reluctant to find directors liable for inactivity or 'neglect of duty', as is generally perceived.[6]

Directors have three principle duties towards their companies:

1. A fiduciary duty to act honestly and in the best interest of the company. A director should not allow personal interests to conflict with those of the company.
2. A duty to exercise due skill and care.
3. A duty to ensure that the company complies with its statutory obligations, which have widened considerably over recent years under UK law, and the European Union's Company Law directives.

It means that the directors must act lawfully, loyally and carefully.[7] The appropriate degree of skill and care required by directors has emerged solely through case law. The relevant passage from the Insolvency Act provides:

> "The facts which a director of a company ought to know or ascertain, the conclusions which he ought to reach and the steps

5 http://www.navref.org/bestpractices/gov_bod_responsibilities_duties.htm, visited on 07.03.2009.

6 Demetra Arsalidou, *To be Active or Inactive: Is this a new Question of Company Directors*, Deakin Law Review, vol. 17, 2003.

7 See Eisenberg, *The Duty of Care of Corporate Directors and Officers* [1990]51 U Pitt L Rev 945.

which he ought to take, are those which would be known, ascertained, reached or taken by a reasonably diligent person having both: the General knowledge skill and experience that may reasonably be expected of a person carrying out the same functions as are carried out by that director in relation to the company; and the general knowledge, skill and experience that director has."

Therefore, directors are required to exercise the skill and care which may reasonably be expected from someone in their position. Any professionally qualified director should act with due diligence expected from their profession. In *Smith* v *Van Gorkom,* the Delaware Supreme Court held that directors breached their duty of care in agreeing, after a two-hour meeting, to sell the company through a merger transaction for $750,000,000. The directors, the court said, lacked sufficient information about the value of the corporation at the point they agreed to the terms of the merger.[8] Authors like Deborah see the standard of duty of care as equal to that of business judgments.[9]

Directors may be held personally liable for business losses stemming from the failure to meet their duty of care. Most states apply the gross negligence standard when evaluating directors' conduct. This standard reflects the statutory and judicial views that corporate goals, and those of the nation's economy, are best served by a degree of risk-taking that may be greater than that of the prudent person. Only where directors' actions are based in self-dealing, fraud or are found to be wholly lacking in good faith will courts find conduct which constitutes gross negligence.[10] It means that directors cannot escape liability for negligence by avoiding activities in their director's role.[11] It has been observed that in relation with that of skill and care to other ways of controlling competence and in rethinking those duties, measures should be sought that allow those with interests in a company effectively to counter directorial incompetence; that encourage higher levels of competence and that avoid the imposition of such onerous

8 *Smith* v *Van Gorkom* [1985] 488 A 2d 858 (Delv.)

9 Deborah A. De Mott, *Directors Duty of Care and the Business Judgment Rule: American Precedents and Australian Choices*, (1992)4 BOND LR, pp. 133-144.

10 http://www.questia.com, visited on 09.03.2009.

11 *Dorchester Finance Co. Ltd.* v *Stebbing* [1989] BCLC 498 (Ch D).

liabilities on directors as would deter competent persons from entering company direction.[12]

4.5.7 *Duty to reveal conflict of interests and profits*

A director, like any other agent, must account to the company for any profit he has made without the company's consent or in consequence of the exercise of his function as a director. The rule of equity has been the bedrock of fiduciary duties for more than 280 years. This was established in *Keech* v *Sandford,*[13] in which it was explained the fiduciary duty of loyalty. In this case a child had inherited the lease on Romford Market in London. Mr. Sandford was entrusted to look after this property until the child matured. But before then, the lease expired. The landlord had told Mr. Sandford that he did not want the child or to have the renewed lease. There was clear evidence of the refusal to renew for the benefit of the infant. Yet the landlord was happy to give Mr. Sandford the opportunity of lease and he took the lease in his name. When Mr. Keech grew up, he sued Mr. Sandford for the profit that he had been making by getting the market's lease. The Lord Chancellor, Lord King ordered Mr. Sandford should disgorge his profits. The judgment concerns the law of trusts and has affected much of the thinking on directors' duties in company law. It holds that a trustee owes a strict duty of loyalty so that there can never be a possibility of *any* conflict of interest.

The common law rule is very clearly held that the trustee not to derive advantage from a purchase of trust property.[14] In *Parker* v *McKenna,* it was held that the directors had to account for all profits made through the sale of the shares. James, LJ made famous comment in this case was that:

> I desire to add but little to what the Lord Chancellor has said. I do not think it is necessary, but it appears to me very important, that we should concur in laying down again and again the general principle that in this Court no agent in the course of his agency, in the matter of his agency, can be allowed to make any profit without the knowledge and consent of his principal; that rule is

12 Vanessa Finch, *Company Directors: Who Cares about Skill and Care?* The Modern Law Review, vol. 55, No. 2 (March 1992), pp. 179-214.

13 [1726]25 ER 223.

14 *Whelpdale* v *Cookson* [1747]1 Ves Sen 9; 27 ER 856.

> an inflexible rule, and must be applied inexorably by this Court, which is not entitled, in my judgment, to receive evidence, or suggestion, or argument as to whether the principal did or did not suffer any injury in fact by reason of the dealing of the agent; for the safety of mankind requires that no agent shall be able to put his principal to the danger of such an inquiry as that.[15]

The position was confirmed in *Regal (Hastings) Ltd.* v *Gulliver,*[16] The House of Lords, reversing the High Court and the Court of Appeal judgments, held that the defendants had made their profits "by reason of the fact that they were directors of Regal and in the course of the execution of that office". They therefore had to account for their profits to the company. The governing principle was succinctly stated by Lord Russell of Killowen:

> The rule of equity which insists on those who by use of a fiduciary position make a profit, being liable to account for that profit, in no way depends on fraud, or absence of *bona fides*; or upon questions or considerations as whether the property would or should otherwise have gone to the plaintiff, or whether he took a risk or acted as he did for the benefit of the plaintiff, or whether the plaintiff has in fact been damaged or benefited by his action. The liability arises from the mere fact of a profit having in the stated circumstances been made.

According to Laskin, J:

> An examination of the case law in this Court and in the Courts of other like jurisdictions on the fiduciary duties of directors and senior officers shows the pervasiveness of a strict ethic in this area of the law. In my opinion, this ethic disqualifies a director or senior officer from usurping for himself or diverting to another person or company with whom or with which he is associated a maturing business opportunity which his company is actively pursuing; he is also precluded from so acting even after his resignation where the resignation may fairly be said to have been prompted or influenced by a wish to acquire for himself the opportunity sought by the company, or where it was his position

15 [1874-75] LR 10 Ch App 96.
16 [1967]2 AC 134.

with the company rather than a fresh initiative that led him to the opportunity which he later acquired.[17]

This rule was followed by the House of Lords in *Boardman* v *Phipps.*[18] The Canadian Court in *Canadian Aero Services* v *O'Malley,*[19] it was held that "Descending from the generality, the fiduciary relationship goes at least this far a director or a senior officer like [the defendants] is precluded from obtaining for himself, either secretly or without the approval of the company (which would have to be properly manifested on full disclosure of the facts), any property or business advantage either belonging to the company or for which it has been negotiating; and especially is this so when the director or officer is a participant in the negotiations on behalf of the company."

In *Industrial Development Consultants Ltd.* v *Cooley*[20] per Roskill, J held that "a director may come under a positive duty to make a business opportunity available to his company if it is in the company's line of business or if the director has been given responsibility to seek out particular opportunities for the company and the opportunity concerned is of such a nature as to fall within the scope of that remit".

In *Mohan Singh Bhullar* v *Indrajit Sight Bhullar,*[1] it was confirmed the position that "the appellants in the instant case had, at the material time, one capacity and one capacity only in which they were carrying on business, namely as directors of the company. In that capacity, they were in a fiduciary relationship with the company". The court held that the defendants breached a fiduciary duty to the company by purchasing personal property. The fiduciary duties are concerned with the concepts of loyalty and honesty and not with competence.[2] In *Plus Group Ltd.* v *Pyke,*[3] it was held that no-conflict rule does not allow a director to "cheerfully go to the brink so long as he does not fall over the edge. The rule renders a fiduciary liable to account for any gain which he obtained as a result of taking advantage of his fiduciary position, whether there was a conflict of interest or not".

17 *Ibid,* p. 382.
18 [1967]2 AC 46; [1966]3 All ER 721 (HL); [1966]3 WLR 1009.
19 [1973]40 DLR (3d) 371 (Can SC).
20 [1972]1 WLR 443 at 451F; [1972]2 All ER 162.
1 [2003] EWCA Civ 424; [2003]2 BCLC 241.
2 *Extrasure Travel Ins. Ltd.* v *Scattergood* [2003]1 BCLC 598 (Ch D).
3 [2002]2 BCLC 201.

Except with the consent of the board of directors, a director of the company or his relative, a firm in which such a director or relative is a partner, any other partner in such a firm, or a private company of which the director is a member or director, shall not enter into any contract with the company like:

- for the sale, purchase or supply of any goods, materials or services;
- for underwriting the subscription of any shares in, or debentures of, the company.

Every director of a company who is in any way, whether directly or indirectly concerned or interested in a contract or arrangement, or proposed contract or arrangement entered into or to be entered into, by or on behalf of the company, shall disclose the nature of his concern or interest at a meeting of the Board of Directors.

In the case of a proposed contract or arrangement, the disclosure required to be made by a director shall be made at the meeting of the board at which the question of entering into the contract or arrangement is first taken into consideration, or if the director was not, at the date of that meeting, concerned or interested in the proposed contract or arrangement, at the first meeting of the board held after he comes so concerned or interested.

In the case of any other contract or arrangement, the required disclosure shall be made at the first meeting of the board held after the director becomes concerned or interested in the contract or arrangement. A general notice given to the board by a director, to the effect that he is a director or a member of a specified body corporate or is a member of a specified firm and is to be regarded as concerned or interested in any contract or arrangement which may, after the date of the notice, be entered into with that body corporate or firm, shall be deemed to be a sufficient disclosure of concern or interest in relation to any contract or arrangement so made.

Any such general notice shall expire at the end of the financial year in which it is given, but may be renewed for further periods of one financial year at a time, by a fresh notice given in the last month of the financial year in which it would otherwise expire (Form 24AA).

No such general notice, and no renewal thereof, shall be of effect unless either it is given at a meeting of the board, or the director concerned takes reasonable steps to secure that it is brought up and read at the first meeting of the board after it is given. Every director who fails to comply with the aforesaid provisions shall be punishable with fine which may extend to five thousand rupees. Nothing in these provisions shall be taken to prejudice or adversely affect the operation of any rule of law restricting a director of a company from having any concern or interest in any contracts or arrangements with the company.

Nothing in these provisions shall apply to any contract or arrangement entered into or to be entered into between two companies where any of the directors of one company or two or more of them together hold not more than 2 per cent of the paid up capital in the other company.

The Allahabad High Court considered the question of fiduciary duty of a managing director and the company who was undertaken to sell some of the shares belonging to one of its shareholders in *Co-operative Company Ltd., Saharanpur* v *Bhagwan Dass & Co.*[4] the position of its managing director in negotiating and completing the sale of shares is clearly one of a fiduciary character. Utmost good faith should be expected and should be insisted upon in transactions of this description. Even any advantage was obtained by the managing director as the fruit of the sale, whether the parties was made in the name of his Sons, the benefit must go to the owner of the shares. If any dividend declared during the transaction has to be disclosed to the owner of the shares.

Ordinarily, and in the absence of a contract to the contrary, the purchaser of shares is entitled to all the dividends, which may have been declared after the date of the purchase. But there is nothing in law to preclude a shareholder from selling the shares only and reserving the dividends to himself. If there is no specific contract on the dividends, it may public sale or a private treaty and it is definitely understood that the shares and not the dividends on the shares are the subject of bargain. The parties cannot deprive the original owner of this right to the dividend of a period prior to the sale, even though the dividend may have been declared subsequent to the date of the purchase. The court ultimately decreed the suit in favour of the original shareholder. It is clear that selling shares on behalf of the shareholder

4 (1931)1 Comp Cas 47.

by the managing director is an act of fiduciary and the managing director has a fiduciary duty to disclose the secret profits to the shareholder.

The courts have been strict in making directors account for money and shares given to them by the company's promoters or the vendors of the property or business which the company was formed to acquire. *Prima facie* he cannot make use of director's powers for his own benefit and accountable, unless the terms of his service contract preclude him from competing. He is also accountable if he uses company's property or trade secrets[5] or his knowledge of company's customers[6] or any other special skill acquired by him while engaged in the company's business.

A director's duty is not ending with his resignation from the company. In *Island Export Finance Ltd.* v *Umunna*, the Queen's Bench Division held that:

> A director's fiduciary duty did not necessarily come to an end when he ceased to be a director. A director was precluded from diverting to himself a maturing business opportunity which his company was actively pursuing even after his resignation where the resignation was prompted or influenced by a desire to acquire that opportunity for himself. Thus the nature of the fiduciary duties is such that even after leaving a company, a director should not act against the interest of the company.[7]

4.6 Fiduciary obligation and abuse of confidence

The courts regard a trusting relationship as most worthy of protection.[8] The first and foremost duty of every person in fiduciary position is to act with honesty. Directors of a company are not permitted to use for their own purposes anything entrusted to them for use on behalf of the company. Greatest good faith is expected in their dealing with the properties and assets of the company.[9] Again they are not supposed to

5 *Bell* v *Lever Bros Ltd.* [1932] AC 161; [1931]1 All ER Rep 1 (HL).

6 *Measures Bros Ltd.* v *Measures* [1910]2 Ch 248.

7 [1986] BCLC 460.

8 Robert Flannigan, *The Fiduciary Obligation*, Oxford Journal of Legal Studies, 1989, 9(3): 285-322.

9 Comment by Patel, J in *Bank of Poona* v *Narayanadas* AIR 1961 Bom 252 (253); (1961)31 Comp Cas 364. Also *Turner Morrison & Co.* v *Shalimar Tar Products* (1980)50 Comp Cas 296 (Cal).

make unjust enrichment with the interest of the company at peril. Thus a director of a company was held liable to account the profit which he earned as bonus from another company for providing some business.[10] A person who is under a fiduciary obligation must account to the person to whom the obligation is owed for any benefit or gain:

(1) Which has been obtained or received in circumstances where a conflict or significant possibility of conflict existed between the fiduciary's duty and the fiduciary's personal interest in the pursuit or possible receipt of such a benefit or gain;

(2) Which was obtained or received by use or by reason of her or his fiduciary position or opportunity or knowledge resulting from it.

It is immaterial that there was absence of good faith or damage to the person to whom the fiduciary obligation was owed.[11] The principle is not restricted to property in the strict sense or money; it also includes trade secrets[12] and confidential information.[13]

4.7 Abuse of corporate opportunities

A director is not expected to exploit his own corporate opportunities. The doctrine of 'Corporate Opportunity' has been described as 'an act of a director or controlling shareholder in diverting from the benefit of the corporation any enterprise or transaction in which reasonable persons would agree that the corporation has some expectancy or interest.'[14] It means "any opportunity to engage in a business activity of which a senior executive becomes aware and knows is closely related to a business in which the corporation is engaged or expects to engage."[15] It is an equitable principle that a director must restore or resale the property or account the profit which he obtained by exploiting the corporate opportunity.

10 *Boston Deep Sea Fishing & Ice Co.* v *Ansell* [1888]39 Ch D 339; [1886-90] All ER Rep 65.

11 *Chan* v *Zacharia* [1984]154 CLR 178; *Philips* v *Boardman* [1967]2 AC 46.

12 *British Industrial Plastics* v *Ferguson* [1940]1 All ER 479 (CA); *Eranleigh Precision Engineering Ltd.* v *Bryant* [1965]1 WLR 1293.

13 *Printers & Finishers Ltd.* v *Holloway* [1965]1 WLR 1; [1964]3 All ER 731.

14 *The American Close Corporation and its Dutch Equivalent*, Jan Houywink, Business Lawyer, 250.

15 American Law Institute's *Principles of Corporate Governance*, Analysis and Recommendations 5.05, 1992.

A director cannot appropriate for his own benefit a commercial opportunity which the company is pursuing or is in a position to pursue and of which the director became aware by reason of his office of director. Where a director misappropriates a corporate opportunity belonging to the company, *prima facie* he is liable to account for any profits that he makes and he holds any property acquired as a result on constructive trust for the company.[16]

Most of the questions regarding the use of corporate opportunities have been answered by the House of Lords in *Regal (Hastings) Ltd.* v *Gulliver.*[17] The facts of the case were as follows:

> The company owned one Cinema in Hastings and the directors decided to acquire two other with a view to selling the whole undertaking as a going concern. For this purpose they formed a subsidiary company to take a lease of the other two Cinemas. But the owner insisted on a personal guarantee from the directors unless the paid-up share capital of the subsidiary was at least £5,000. The company was unable to subscribe in cash for more than 2,000 shares and the directors were not willing to give personal guarantees. Accordingly the original plan was changed; instead of the company subscribing for all the shares, in the subsidiary the company took up 2,000 and the remaining 3,000 were taken by the directors and their friends. Later, instead of selling the undertaking, all the shares in both companies were sold, a profit of 16s-ld being made on each of the shares in the former subsidiary. The new controllers of the company brought an action against the former directors to recover the profits they made.

From these facts it is clear that the directors had not deprived the company of any of its property (unless information can be regarded as property), or robbed it might have exercised for its own advantage. Again, recovery by the company would only benefit the purchasers, who, if the action was successful, would recover an undeserved windfall resulting in a reduction in the price which they had freely agreed to pay. However, the House of Lords held that the directors were liable to account, once it was established "that what the directors did was so related to the affairs of the company that it can properly be said to

16 *Carlton* v *Halestrap* [1988]4 BCC 538.
17 [1942]1 All ER 378.

have been done in the course of their management and in utilization of their opportunities and special knowledge as directors; and that what they did resulted in a profit to themselves".

This ruling of the House of Lords carried the principle to the farthest limit beyond its scope as set out by earlier decisions. Thus, in *Cook* v *Deeks*[18] the directors of a company diverted a contract opportunity of the company to themselves and by their votes as holders of 3/4 majority resolved that the company had no interest in the contract. It was held that the benefits of the contract belonged in equity to the company and the directors could not validly use their voting power to vest it in themselves. Their Lordships observed that, "men who assume complete control of a company's business must remember that they are not at liberty to sacrifice the interests which they are bound to protect, and while ostensibly acting for the company divert it, their own favour business which should properly belong to the company they represent".

Again, where a director is instructed to purchase some property for the company, and he purchases the same for himself and then sells it to the company at a profit, he is clearly liable to account for the profit so made. As he was under an obligation to acquire the property for the company, the same belonged in equity to the company from the moment he purchased it and he could not have made a profit on its resale. However, where he is not under any such direction to purchase for the company, but purchases some property on his own account which is subsequently sold to the company at a profit, the company is not entitled to this profit. In *Borland* v *Earle,*[19] the judicial committee of the Privy Council upheld this view. "It is one thing if a director sells a property to the company which in equity as well as at law his own. It would be quite another thing of the director had originally acquired the property which he sold to the company under circumstances which made it in equity the property of the company." Their Lordships further observed: "It may be that, he had an intention in his own mind to resell it to the company when he was purchasing the property,

18 [1916]1 AC 554; [1916-17] All ER Rep 285. Other illustrative cases on the right of a company to recover such secret to commissions are: *Grant* v *Gold Exploration & Development Syndicate Ltd.* [1900]1 QB 233; *Salford* v *Lever* [1891]1 QB 168; *In Re London and Mashonaland Exploration Co.* v *New Mashonaland Exploration Co.* [1891] WN 165.

19 [1902] AC 83; [1900-3] All ER Rep Extg 1452.

but it was an intention which he was at liberty to carry out or abandon at his own will."

However, a director who acquires property while in office will be liable to account for his profit upon resale if two elements are present. He must have acquired property only by reason of the fact that he was a director and in the course of the exercise of the office of director. This liability of the directors to account seems to be just and clear. But to handover this profit to the purchaser shareholders would be to give them the benefit of an undeserved reduction in price which they had willingly paid up. Therefore, recovery should have been in favour of the old shareholders who had really suffered. This view was preferred in the American case of *Common Wealth Title Insurance & Trust Co.* v *Seltzer.*[20]

The basic principle applied in cases where the directors made advantages from corporate opportunities were that the *Regal (Hastings) Ltd.* v *Gulliver.* However, it cannot be said that its exact scope is altogether clear. If the director's decides not to invest their company's funds in some proposed investments, that is, a director who thereafter embarks his own money therein is accountable for any profits? In *Phipps* v *Boardman*[1] the House of Lords considered this question. In this case, as in Regal, the agents were liable because not only did the knowledge comes to them while acting as fiduciaries but so did the opportunity to acquire the shares and to make the profit. They were also liable because there was a possibility of a conflict of duty and interest since unprejudiced advice could not be given on whether the trustee-principal should apply to the court for permission to acquire the share despite the fact that they were not authorized the investment. Lord Hodson stated the relevant proposition as follows:

> "No person standing in a fiduciary position, when a demand is made upon him by the person to whom he stands in the fiduciary relationship to account for profits acquired by him by reason of his fiduciary position and by reason of the opportunity and knowledge or either, resulting from it is entitled to defeat the claim upon any ground same that he made the profits with the knowledge and assent of the other person".[2]

20 227 Pa 410-76 Art. 77, (1910).
1 [1967]2 AC 46.
2 At p. 105.

However, he himself then qualified this proposition by saying that the knowledge must be 'special information' which included "confidential information". The directors as the agents of the company hold the property they had acquired as constructive trustees for the company and are bound to account for it. But they are not liable to account where there had been no improper use of information which could have been used for the benefit of the company.

Thus, the mere fact that knowledge comes to directors while acting as such does not make them liable to account. But they will be liable if the knowledge is presented to them confidentially as a possible investment for the company even though the company does not avail itself of the opportunity. Thus, in *Phipps* v *Boardman,* the House of Lords reaffirmed its earlier decision *Regal (Hastings) Ltd.* v *Gulliver* in evaluating the standard of honesty expected from directors. But in *Peso Silver Mines* v *Croper,*[3] the Canadian Supreme Court has given a different decision. Court held that where a new venture is offered to a company and its directors *bona fide* come to the conclusion that it is not an investment the company ought to make, the individual directors who subsequently buy the same do not violate any duty to the company even though they have consulted the company's geologist. The court further held that the subsequent decision of the directors to purchase the shares for themselves was not in their capacity as directors but as individual members of the general public.

Thus, if we take these two decisions together we would come to the conclusion that directors may be entitled to take personal advantage of an opportunity originally offered to the company, only the opportunity was rejected by the company and the directors while they were acting in connection with its rejection acted *bona fide* in the interest of the company. Again the information given to them must not be confidential and the subsequent use of the opportunity is not related to their position as directors.

Even though the Canadian Supreme Court has given a liberal interpretation to the standard of honesty expected from directors with regards to the conversion and misuse of corporate opportunities, the English Courts are in no way relax their standards fixed in *Regal (Hastings) Ltd.* v *Gulliver*. Thus in *Industrial Development Consultants*

3 [1966]58 DLR (2d) 1.

Ltd. v *Cooley*[4] they reaffirmed their faith in the 'Regal' standard of honesty. In this case the Managing Director was held to be liable to account for the profit.

In *Queensland Mines Ltd.* v *Hudson*,[5] the managing director of a company entered into negotiations on its behalf for a mining license. The company ran into financial difficulties. Then the managing director took the license in his own name, resigned from the company and made substantial profits out of the transaction. The Privy Council held that the former managing director was not liable to account for those profits as he had fully discussed the situation with the board of the company and they resolved to proceed further in pursuit of the license.

However, there are some cases when a director may profit by a corporate opportunity without incurring the liability to account for it. Thus, where the opportunity is completely outside the scope of the corporate business is *ultra vires* or where the corporation has not shown any interest in the property, an officer may invest his money. Again where the corporation becomes insolvent or defunct, its officers are free to act for themselves.[6]

4.8 Transfer of controlling block of shares

The right to control the management of the company is a valuable asset. The power of general management of the affairs of the company is vested with the directors who hold it as a trust and a mark of confidence. So, it is the fiduciary duty of the directors not to abuse the confidence reposed on them by transferring the right to control the company. Again it is the duty of the controlling shareholders not to make money for themselves from selling their controlling block of shares. The directors or other persons holding the majority of shares could control the company. When majority of shares or the controlling block of shares are transferred the power to control the company is also being transferred. Controlling power itself is an asset which may not be traded or disposed of without regard to the interest of the corporation, or the totality of shareholders.[7]

4 [1972]1 WLR 443; [1972]2 All ER 162.
5 [1978]18 ALR 1; [1978]52 ALJR 399 (Aust).
6 Berle, *Liability of Directors for Taking Corporate Opportunities, Using Corporate Facilities or Engaging in a Competing Business*, [1939]39 Col LR 219.
7 Berle and Means, *The Modern Corporation and Private Property,* 1932, p. 244.

The power to control the company is usually transferred by transferring the controlling block of shares. This kind of transfer is affected by giving excess payment for the shares sold. If the price received by the directors for the controlling block of shares is greater than the prevailing market price of their shares, the real consideration for the inflated price "the power to control" the company which is coupled with the shares transferred. This additional payment for the transfer of the controlling block of shares, being a profit obtained through the breach of a fiduciary duty, is, therefore, has to be shared with the minority shareholders.

Again, besides this duty to account and share the additional payment, the sellers of controlling block would be liable if they have 'negligently' or 'fraudulently' passed the 'control' to a person who would loot the assets of the company.[8] Such purchasers are often tempted by large assets and sound prospectus of the company which they may afterwards misuse in paying off short-term loans taken to finance for the purchase of the shares.[9] In such cases it is not necessary that the seller should have actual knowledge of the purchasers' evil design to loot the company. It will be enough to make him liable that there were circumstances putting him on inquiry, for example, purchaser's previous history, excessive price offered, liquidity of the corporate assets etc.[10] Under such circumstances the transferor has personal liability for the fraudulent conduct of the transferee of shares.

4.9 Take-over bids

The expression take-over bid in its broadest sense includes all circumstances deliberately made or created in which the control of a company may pass. The right to control the management of a company is a valuable asset and it is desirable that if any price is obtained for the sale of this right, the same should be shared by the members in accordance with their rights.

Just as the equitable principle has received statutory recognition in its relation to directors' contracts, so has in its connection with secret profits obtained from take-overs. There are number of circumstances

8 Hill, *Sale of Controlling Shares,* [1957]70 Harv LR 986 and Janning [1956]44 California LR 1.

9 John Boyle, *The Sale of Controlling Shares,* [1964]13 hit Anc Comp LQ 185.

10 *Ibid.,* p. 192.

in which the directors, in connection with a take-over bid, may receive additional payments.

4.10 Transfer of undertakings

Anyone wish to obtain control of a company may buy the company's undertakings. The whole undertaking or property of the company may be sold.[11] In such a case the directors have to retire from office as the purchasers will like to place their nominees on the board. The directors may receive some payment from the company by way of compensation for loss of office or from the transferee as a consideration for retirement. As long as the amount thus received is nothing more than a *bona fide* payment by way of damages for breach of contract or by way of pension in respect of past services, there is hardly anything objectionable in it.

In a sale of the company's undertaking or property what is involved is a sale by the company for whom the directors are acting. Thus they are not entitled to retain any profit or proceeds of the sale. But what may happen is that under the cover of compensation for loss of office, they may manage to make money as an inducement to retire and to facilitate the transfer of control. Indeed they may be getting the money as a price for the right to control or for procuring the transfer of the right to control.

The general equitable principle of disclosure of interests is also applicable in cases where the directors of a company receive any payment from the transferee in connection with the transfer of the company's undertaking on property. This principle is embodied in s. 319 of the Indian Companies Act. Section 319 provides that any money received by the directors of a company from the transferee in connection with the transfer of the company's property or undertaking must be disclosed to the members of the company and approved by the company in general meeting. If this is not done the amount received is to be held by the directors in trust for the company.[12]

11 For a discussion of the various modes of transfer of control and how side payments are obtained by the majority sellers references are made in *Some Theoretical Aspects of Share Voting,* by Henry G. Marine, (1964) Col LR 1427.

12 Section 319(2).

4.11 Purchase of shares

Another method of acquiring the control of a company is by purchasing its shares. What normally occurs of on a take-over bid of this sort is that the bidder requests the directors to forward an offer to their shareholders to purchase their shares at a specified price, the offer being expressed to be conditional on acceptance by holders of certain percent of the shares. Here the directors act as a convenient channel of communication between the bidder and the shareholders and can bargain for additional payments to themselves for procuring the sale. Section 320 of Companies Act is designed to prevent this.

The section applies where there has been a transfer of shares:

(1) by making an offer to the general body of shareholders.

(2) Where the purchaser is a company, by inviting the company to become its subsidiary or a subsidiary of its holding company;

(3) by making an offer on behalf of an individual with a view to obtaining the right to control the exercise of one-third of the total voting powers;

(4) by making any other offer which is conditional on acceptance to a given extent.[13]

In this case also those who acquire control will replace the existing management. The outgoing directors may be induced on payment of money to facilitate the transfer of control, although outwardly the payment may have been made as a compensation for retirement. If the transferee or any other person proposes to pay something to the directors, it shall be the duty of the concerned directors to take all reasonable steps to inform the shareholders of the particulars of such payment along with any notice of the offer made for their shares.[14] If any such director fails to do shall be punishable with fine which may extend to two thousand five hundred rupees.[15] Again where this disclosure is made to selling shareholders, the directors may call a meeting of such shareholders and get the proposed payment approved before any transfer is made.[16] Further, where they do neither, they

13 Clauses (*i*), (*ii*), (*iii*) & (*iv*) of the sub-section (1) of s. 320 of the Companies Act 1956.

14 Section 320(2).

15 Section 320(3).

16 Section 320(4)(*b*).

shall hold the amount in trust for the shareholders who have sold their shares.[17]

In this case also, the Act provides for restoration only to those who have been truly indemnified, and not to company as a whole giving an undeserved reduction of price to the bidder. To this extent, therefore, the Act has recognized an exception to the general rule that directors are trustees of the company as a whole and not of individual shareholders. They become trustees for shareholders, but not for all of them, merely for those who have sold.

Section 321 refers, as do ss. 319 and 320, to payments "by way of compensation for loss of office or consideration for retirement" i.e., to what are known as "golden handshakes" though the gold is no longer of standard carat. The scope of the words "compensation for loss of office" and "consideration for retirement" is considerably widened by s. 321. So that directors may not avoid their obligation to account by apparently separating the transfer of control from payment. This section provides that any payment made by the transferee in pursuance of any arrangement entered into as a part of the agreement for the transfer of shares, shall be deemed to have been received as "compensation for loss of office" or "consideration for retirement" and liable to be accounted for.[18] Similarly, if the price paid to retiring director for his shares in the company is in excess of the price paid to other shareholders or any other valuable consideration has been given to him, it shall also be regarded as "compensation" or "consideration" and must be disclosed to shareholders.[19]

These statutory principles enlarged the scope of the fiduciary obligation of directors. It was once believed that the directors are not trustees of the individual shareholders, but of the company as a whole. But in cases falling within the scope of the above sections directors become trustees, for those individual shareholders who have sold their shares, for any profits made by the directors. Thus, these statutory provisions also modified the result of *Percival* v *Wright*.[20]

17 *Ibid.*
18 Section 321(1).
19 Section 321(2).
20 [1902]2 Ch 421.

It appears to be well recognized that most of the powers that the directors has to exercise are powers in trust and are given to them in confidence that they shall not abuse them. The property, the funds and the whole undertaking of the company are entrusted with them in confidence. The fiduciary duties of directors demand that they shall not abuse this confidence.

4.12 Conclusion

The directors sometimes act as agents and trustees of company. They owe duties to the company and not directly to the shareholders. However, directors owe a fiduciary duty to the shareholders and the company as a whole. As a company director, he owes duties to creditors to pay debts. The director has to perform their duties in accordance with the memorandum and articles of association of the company. They act as trustees of the company's property held on trust by the corporation for its members and they are the managers of the company's properties.

It can summarize that a director must exercise his powers honestly and for their proper purpose, and in accordance with the company's constitution (memorandum and articles of association) and decisions taken lawfully under it or under the general law. Subject to that requirement, the director must exercise his powers in the way he believes in good faith is best calculated in the circumstances, taking into account both the short and the long term consequences of his acts, to promote the success of the company for the benefit of its members as a whole. He has to foster the company's business relationships, including those with its employees and suppliers and the customers for its products and services. He needs to maintain a reputation for high standards of business conduct.

Directors are liable for contract with the company if they are acted within their powers. They must act for the best interest of the company and must disclose personal interest to the company. A director of a company must show reasonable care and skill in the management of the company. He must disclose conflict of his interest to the company and must account for profits. He is not supposed to exploit corporate opportunities for his own advantages. Directors are personally liable for abuse of confidence entrusted with them and the general power of controlling the affairs of the company. In short, they are the "pillars and powerhouse" of the affairs of the company. If the pillars are not properly laid or shaken or abuse the powers by directors, it is severely going to affect the company like recently happened to an IT major "Satyam" in India. If the managing director and the directors make money out of the corporate opportunities and build family business with corporate money, they are accountable for their profit and must be booked under law for breach of fiduciary, breach of trust and "corporate fraud" on creditors, shareholders, investors and the society at large.

5

Fiduciary Duties of Directors and Personal Interests

5.1 Introduction

The directors as fiduciaries must not place themselves in a position in which their duties to the company are likely to conflict with their personal interests. Utmost good faith is required for a person standing in a fiduciary position. The law will not allow a fiduciary to place in a situation in which his judgment is likely to be biased. Directors should not make a profit as a result of their position as directors, without company's consent. The best alternative is not to place themselves in a position which may tend to be biased. Good faith must not only be done but must manifestly and seemed to be done. It is not only for the directors to convince themselves that they have acted in good faith but others also should be convinced. They must be beyond the shadow of doubt.

So directors must not place themselves in a position or engaged in transactions which tend to affect their duties to the company adversely. Certain circumstances are contemplated by the Companies Act and by courts which tend to bias the directors in the discharge of their duties towards the company. The Companies Bill 2008[1] enumerates some of the duties of directors or as follows:

1. A director of a company shall act in good faith in order to promote the objects of the company for the benefit of its members as a whole, and in the best interest of the company.

1 Section 147 of the Companies Bill 2008.

2. A director of a company shall exercise his duties with reasonable care, skill and due diligence.
3. A director of a company shall not involve in a situation in which he may have a direct or indirect interest that conflicts, or possibly may conflict, with the interest of the company.
4. A director of a company shall not achieve or act done to achieve any undue gain or advantage either to himself or to relatives, partners or associates.
5. A director of a company shall not assign his of fees and any assignment so made shall be void.
6. In a director who contravenes the provisions of this section shall be punishable with fine which shall not be less than one lakh rupees but which may extend to 5 lakh rupees.
7. If any director is found guilty of making any undue gain either to himself or to his relatives, partners or associates he shall also be liable to pay an amount equal to that gain to the company.

These principles were inserted in the Companies Bill 2011 in s. 166. The punishment for contravening the provisions (duty of skill, care and due diligence) is ₹ 1 Lakh fine which may extend to ₹ 5 Lakh.

5.2 Contracts with the company

In common law, interested director were prohibited from entering into contract with the company.[2] During the 19th century, contracts between corporations and directors were absolutely voidable at the option of the corporation or the shareholders without regard to the fairness or unfairness of the dealing.[3] Later on this principle were changed and approved the transaction if it is taken and approved by a disinterested majority of directors in the board.[4] The principle of good faith receives its most importance when the directors enter into contracts with the company. It is well accepted that the fiduciary

2 Norwood P. Beveridge, *Interested Director Contracts at Common Law: Validation under the Doctrine of Constructive Fraud*, Loyola of Los Angeles Law Review, vol. 33, 1999, p. 97.

3 Harold Marsh. Jr., *Are Directors Trustees? Conflict of Interest and Corporate Morality*, 22 Bus Law 1966, pp. 35-36.

4 *Ibid*, p. 40.

position of directors is tend to be vitiated by contracts which the board entered into on behalf of the company with one of their member.

This is because of the presumption that those who enter into a contract will always have a personal interest to be suffixed and if a person standing in a position to dominate or control the will of the other contracting party is tend to insert undue influence to get an over privilege over others.[5]

This principle received its first clearest expression in *Aberdeen Ry. Co* v *Blaikie Brothers,*[5] where a contract between the company and a partnership of which one of the directors was a partner was held invalid at the instance of the company notwithstanding that its terms were perfectly fair.

In the above case, the plaintiff needed a large quantity of iron chairs (rail sockets) and contracted for their supply over an 18-month period with Blaikie Brothers, a partnership. Thomas Blaikie was the managing partner of Blaikie Brothers and a director and the Chairman of the Aberdeen Railway Co. The contract was partly performed but, having taken delivery of about two-thirds of the iron chairs, the Aberdeen Railway Company refused to accept any more. The defendant sought to enforce the contract or for damages for breach. At that point of time in England and in Scotland, special statutes which incorporated companies provided that no person interested in a contract with the company would be qualified to be a director. If any director thus enter into such a contract was deemed to have vacated his office immediately. The court observed that:

> This, therefore, brings us to the general question, whether a Director of a Railway Company is or is not precluded from dealing on behalf of the Company with himself, or with a firm in which he is a partner. The Directors are a body to whom is delegated the duty of managing the general affairs of the Company. A corporate body can only act by agents, and it is of course the duty of those agents so to act as best to promote the interests of the corporation whose affairs they are conducting. Such agents have duties to discharge of a fiduciary nature towards their principal. And it is a rule of universal application, that no one, having such duties to discharge, shall be allowed to enter into engagements

5 [1854]1 Macq HL 461 (HL SC).

> in which he has, or can have, a personal interest conflicting, or which possibly may conflict, with the interests of those whom he is bound to protect. So strictly is this principle adhered to, that no question is allowed to be raised as to the fairness or unfairness of a contract so entered into.

While describing the principle the House of Lords held that:

> A corporate body can only act by agents, and it is, of course, the duty of these agents so to act as best to promote the interest of the corporation whose affairs they are conducting. Such agents have duties to discharge of fiduciary nature towards their principal. And it is rule of universal application that no one, having such duties to discharge, shall be allowed to enter into engagements in which he has, or can have, a personal interest conflicting, or which possibly may conflict, with the interests of those whom he is bound to protect.

So strictly is this principle adhered to that no question is allowed to be raised as to the fairness or unfairness of a contract so entered into.[6] The above case greatly influenced the development of the law on director-company contracts.

This decision was followed in a later decision of *The Cumberland Coal and Iron Company* v *Sherman.*[7] In this case Sherman was appointed as a director and a Committee member who actively participated in the management of the company. A resolution was passed to sell some area of mining land of the company by a committee headed by Sherman. With the approval of the board of directors, the land was sold to Sherman. The deal was subsequently approved by the shareholders in a general meeting. It was alleged that the price fixed was comparatively very low and thus the company lost a huge amount. Mr. Sherman resigned from the company in 1858. Thereafter the company brought a suit for nullifying the transactions alleging that the deal was unfair. The court held that at the time of ratification of the deal by the shareholders, they were not properly informed about the facts of the deal. The court therefore enjoined any transfer or use of the properties and contract.

6 Per Lord Cranworth, LC, pp. 471-742.
7 30 Barb 553 (NY Sup Ct 1859).

In India, this principle finds its expression in s. 297 of the Companies Act. The Act provides that board's sanction is required for certain contracts in which particular directors are interested. The Act expressly provides the following categories of contracts require the sanction of the board when particular directors are interested:[8]

(*a*) any contract with the company for the sale, purchase or supply of goods, materials or services; or

(*b*) any contract with the company for underwriting the subscription of any shares in or debentures of, the company.

The consent of the board is required when such contracts are made with the company by any director or his relative, a firm in which such a director or relative is a partner, any other partner in such a firm, or a private company of which the director is a member or director. But in the following cases such consent is not necessary:[9]

(*a*) where the contract for the sale or purchase of goods and materials is for cash at prevailing market price; or

(*b*) where the company or the director, relative, firm, partner or private company, as the case may be, regularly trades to does business in such goods, materials or service; or

(*c*) any transaction in the ordinary course of business by a banking or insurance company.

Again such contracts may be made in any emergency even beyond the value or cost of five thousand rupees, provided approval of the board must be obtained within three months.[10] The act specifically provides that if consent is not accorded to any contracts under this section, such contracts shall be voidable at the option of the board.[11]

The Act, thus, requires the consent of the board of directors for all contracts (other than those exempted under sub-sec. (2) with the company by a director or his relative or a firm in which such a director or relative is a partner or any other partner of such firm or a private company in which such director is a member or director. The object of this provisions that the board of director should have knowledge of the

8 Section 297(1)(*a*) and (*b*).
9 Section 297(2).
10 Section 297(3).
11 Section 297(5).

extent of interest of a director in any contractual dealings with the company, or of any person connected with the director in any of the ways mentioned in sub-sec. (1), and accord their consent to such dealings.

Again the consent of the board must accorded by a resolution passed at a meeting of the board. It is not enough to obtain the consent by means of a resolution by circulation. Further, the consent of the board contemplated is not a general consent but consent referable to each particular or specific contract or contracts. In *Walchand Nagar Industries Ltd.* v *Ratanchand Khimchand Motishaw,*[12] the court held that the consent requires the knowledge of necessary facts and materials which lead to the consent and cannot be given in a general or an abstract manner.

The respondent in the above was a director of the Walchandnagar Industries, Ltd. In June 1951 he entered into a contract with the company for the supply of one tin of ghee, and the question that arises is whether by reason of the respondent entering into this contract he has ceased to be a director of the company. Section 86F imposes a personal disability upon a director of the company and the disability is that a director of the company, or the firm of which he is a partner or any partner of such firm, or the private company of which he is a member or director is precluded from entering into any contracts for the sale, purchase or supply of goods and materials with the company. The disqualification is not absolute, because the section provides that with the consent of the directors, a director can enter into contracts which are prohibited under this section. It is clear that in enacting this provision, which is a novel provision and finds no place in the English Companies Act, the Legislature wanted to suppress a particular mischief had a particular object in mind. A director of a company occupies a responsible position and the Legislature wanted that while occupying that position he should not be placed in a situation where there would be a conflict between his interest and his duty. His duty would be to his company of which he is director. His interest would be to enter into a profitable contract with the company. It is also clear that a director holding the position that he does can obtain undue benefit by entering into profitable contracts with the company, and in order to suppress that mischief and to achieve the object which the Legislature had in mind, s. 86F was enacted.

12 (1953)23 Comp Cas 343; AIR 1953 Bom 285.

However, it may be noted that the only consequences of contravening of the provision of this section is that the contract in question is only voidable at the option of the board of directors and not illegal *per se*. But under the corresponding s. 86-F of the Companies Act of 1913, failure to obtain the consent of the board rendered the contract an illegal one and entailed the vacating of his office by the particular direction. This position led to several absurd results. But under the present Act this position is modified. Thus in *Globe Motors Ltd.* v *Mehta Teja Singh and Co.*[13] the court held that of the consent is not given within three months after the date of contract, but is given at a later date, even then it will be good, so long as the contract has not been avoided by the board. Section 299 of the Companies Act provides that every director of accompany who is in any way, whether directly or indirectly, concerned or interested in a contract or arrangement, or proposed contract or arrangement, entered into or to be entered into, by or on behalf of the company, shall disclose the nature of his concern or interest at a meeting of the board of directors.

The courts have been very jealous in seeing that the fiduciary relationship of the Directors with the Company is not abused. The Directors have been held to be trustees of title assets of the company and courts have directed them to reimburse the loss to the company where it was found that directors had applied title Company's money in payment of an improper commission. Little strictness with which the courts view the responsibility and the sacredness of the trust reposed in the Directors was emphasized long time back in *Imperial Mercantile Credit Assn.* v *Coleman.*[14] The court correctly observed that:

> "It is of the highest importance that it should be distinctly understood that it is the duty of Directors of companies to use their best exertions for the benefit of those whose interests are committed to their charge, and that they are bound to disregard their own private interests whenever a regard to them conflicts with the proper discharge of such duty."

The above position was approved in *Regal* v *Gulliver.*[15] The court held that directors were in a fiduciary position and their liability to

13 (1984)55 Comp Cas 445 (Del); (1983)24 DLT 214.
14 [1873] LR 6 HL 189.
15 [1942]1 All ER 378.

account does not depend upon proof of *male fide intentions*. In holding that the directors were liable to account for title company, the Court observed (p. 383 F) "at all material times they were directors and in a fiduciary position, and they used and acted upon their exclusive knowledge acquired as such directors. They framed resolutions by which they made a profit for themselves. They sought no authority from the company to do so, and by reason of their position and actions they made large profits for which, in my view, they are liable to account to the company."

Gower in *Company Law*, 3rd Ed., p. 526 has noticed that because of the trustee like position of the directors a contract between the company with another firm of partnership of which one of the directors was a partner have been avoided at the instance of the company notwithstanding that its terms were perfectly fair and that in the words of Lord Granworth, LC "so strictly is this principle adhered to and no question is allowed to be raised as to the fairness or unfairness of a contract so entered into......." Thus the contract will be voidable at the instance of a company and any profits made by the Directors personally will be recoverable by the company.

In most of the jurisdictions it was considered that directors as standing in a fiduciary relationship towards their company and, applying to the equitable principle have made them accountable for profits accruing to them in title course and by reason of their directorship. They should not use the company's money or other property or information or other matters in their possession in their capacity of directors, in order to gain any advantage to themselves at the expense of the company, and if they make any profit for themselves or cause any damage to the company, they will liable to make good the same to the company.

From the above decisions the position is clear that whenever a company enters into a contract with the board in which one of the director has interested, unless that interest has been disclosed to the company and ratified by the company in general meeting, the contract may be avoided by the company.

The Calcutta High Court in *Rabindra Nath Mitra* v *Emperor,*[16] it was held that s. 91-A of the Companies Act 1913 which imposes upon

16 (1938)8 Comp Cas 176 (Cal).

directors the duty of disclosing their interest in contracts and arrangements entered into by or on behalf of the company is not confined to contracts entered into at a meeting of the directors. Further, the term 'contract' in the said section includes even petty purchases of articles.

The non-disclosure of personal interest of a director in a contract under s. 299 of the Companies Act 1956 does not render the contract void or unenforceable. This principle was confirmed in *Naini Oxygen & Acetylene Gas Ltd.* v *Bisheshwar Nath.*[17] The director is not prohibited from contracting with the company under this provision nor his contractual rights are not taken away by this provision. The purpose of this provision is to assure fairness in dealing between the company and the directors. The objective of the ss. 297, 299 and 300 of the Companies Act 1956 are founded on the principle that directors are precluded from dealing on behalf of the company or entering into contract in which he has a personal interest conflicting with the interest of the company to whom he have a fiduciary duty. If a director enter into a contract with a company and he does not disclose his interest, he is liable for breach of trust.[18]

The legal position is clear that it is an obligation of the director to disclose his interest in a contract and the obligation is similar to that of a trustee. The directors are in the position of trustees and have a fiduciary relation to the shareholders. They have to account for any secret profits made. Section 283(1)(*i*) of the Companies Act 1956 are therefore bases in common-law principle.[19]

In contravention of the provisions can lead to the following consequences:

1. Liability to be prosecuted under s. 299(4).
2. Cessation of office of directorship under s. 283(1)(*i*).
3. Liability to be prosecuted under s. 283(2A); and

17 (1986)60 Comp Cas 990 (All).

18 *Yashovardhan Saboo* v *Groz-Beckert Saboo Ltd.* (1995)83 Comp Cas 371 (CLB).

19 *Mukkattukara Catholic Co. Ltd.* v *Thomas* (1995)4 Comp LJ 311; (1996)22 CLA 348 (Ker); *Avanti Explosives Pvt. Ltd.* v *Principal Subordinate Sub-Judge* (1987)1 Comp Cas 301 (AP).

4. Liability to refund to the company all remuneration received by the petitioner as director after the cessation of his directorship.[20]

The Companies Bill 2011 stipulates that every director of a company who is directly or indirectly interested in a contract or arrangement, disclose it in the board of meeting. Such enter into contract without the disclosure of interest will be voidable at the option of the company. Contravention of the provisions, such director shall be punishable with imprisonment for a term which may extend to one year or with fine which shall not be less than fifty thousand rupees but which may extend to one lakh rupees.[1]

5.3 Competing business

Another area in which the personal interest of a director is likely to conflict with his duties to the company is where he does any business which is of a competing nature with that of the company. A fiduciary is normally strictly precluded from entering into competition with his *Cestus Que Trust*. But this duty applies only during the subsistence of the fiduciary relationship, not after it has ended. Thus, the fiduciary duty to refrain from competing business does not survive the cessation of the fiduciary relationship.[2]

The mere existence of outside involvement does not automatically render a director in breach of duty. In particular, it has been held that a director of a company is on the whole free to take up a directorship with another company, even though the two companies are competitors in the same field of business.[3] There are various grounds to be taken into consideration such as how his work is of a specialized nature, how far his services for the competitor are likely to cause harm to the company, whether these services are deliberately concealed from the company, and how likely is that confidential information will filter through to the competitor. If such a term is implied and has been broken, the court may grant an injunction restraining further breaches.[4] There are also argument that if his

20 *M.O. Varghese* v *Thomas Stephen & Co. Ltd.* (1970)40 Comp Cas 1131 (Ker).
1 Section 184 of the Companies Bill 2011.
2 *Nordisk Insulin Laboratorium* v *Gorgate Products* [1953] Ch 430 (CA).
3 *London & Masonaland Exploration Co. Ltd.* v *New Mashonaland Exploration Co. Ltd.* [1891] WN 165.
4 *Hivac Ltd.* v *Park Royal Scientific Instruments Ltd.* [1946] Ch 169.

agreement with the first company does not prohibit him from associating with a competing company, he can work for the second company as long as he does not disclose the confidential information obtained by him as a director of the first company.[5]

The restriction finds its clearest expression in partnership law, where a partner is prohibited from entering into a business competing with that of the firm and if does so he must account for the profit.[6] Generally nothing prevents a director from doing a business which is of a competing nature with that of the company. There is also a clear decision to the effect that a director of one company cannot be restrained from acting as a director of a rival company.[7] However, such freedom of trade is available to a director only so long as that it cannot be shown that "be was making to the second company any disclosure of information obtained confidently by him as a director of the first company".[8] Again a company can restrain its directors from breaking their fiduciary duties by entering into private transactions under which liability might be incurred by the company.[9]

A director is breaching his fiduciary duty if the close relatives have incorporated a new company to do competing business. They have not only started a competing business, they have also employed those whose resignations were accepted by the first petitioner from the employment of the company and are also using the intellectual property of the company. In addition, they are also seeking to take away the customers of the company for their own company as is evident from certain orders placed by the new company on the suppliers of the respondent company. Such a person can never seek nor is entitled for any equitable relief from this Board.[10] This position was confirmed in *Gujarat Bottling Company Ltd.* v *Coco Cola Ltd.*[11]

5 Charlesworth and Cain, *Company Law,* 13th Edition, 1987, p. 406.
6 Section 16(*b*), Indian Partnership Act.
7 *London & Mashoualand Exploration Co.* v *New Mashualand Exploration Co.* [1891] WN 165. This ruling was approved by Lord Blanesbargh in *Bell* v *Lever Bros.* [1931] All ER Rep 1 (HL); [1932] AC 161 at 195.
8 *Ibid,* Per Lord Blanesbargh in *Bell* v *Lever Bros.* [1931] UKWL 2; [1932] AC 161.
9 *Ibid.*
10 *Sh. Gurmit Singh, Sh. Digvijay* v *Polymer Papers Ltd.* (2005)123 Comp Cas 489 (CLB); (2003)3 Comp LJ 228 (CLB).
11 (1995)5 SCC 545.

It is doubtful about the position of directors and their fiduciary duties after resigning from a company. A director who has informed the company of his intention to resign his post does not owe any fiduciary duty to the company to tell that he is resigning because he actively intends to set up a competing business on his departure from the company. Actual competitive behavior while still in force is not acceptable. After retirement, use of general expertise acquired while in office as a director is permitted. But attempts to solicit entire customers or employees away would be a wrong towards the company.[12] But in some of the cases it was held that a director's fiduciary duty does not necessarily come to an end when he ceases to be a director, especially if he ceases by resignation with a view to taking advantage of current business opportunities available to the company.[13]

This decision was followed in *CMS Dolphin Ltd.* v *Simonet.*[14] This case questioned the findings in *Regal (Hastings) Ltd.* v *Gulliver,*[15] Supreme Court of Canada in *Canadian Aero Service Ltd.* v *O'Malley*[16] held that a director is disqualified from usurping for himself or diverting to a company with which he is associated a maturing business opportunity of his company not only while he is still a director, but also even after his resignation, when the resignation may fairly be said to have been prompted or influenced by a wish to acquire for himself the opportunity sought by the company.

The underlying principles in *Regal (Hastings) Ltd.,* held that a fiduciary must not place himself in a position where his duty and his interest may conflict, and that a fiduciary may not retain a profit which he makes from the use of property subject to the fiduciary relationship or which he makes by reason of his fiduciary position, go back to the eighteenth century.[17] The directors are liable when they used their fiduciary position and acted upon their knowledge of an opportunity which they had acquired in the course of their management and in utilization of their opportunities and special knowledge as directors.[18] A person in a fiduciary position must account for profits acquired by

12 *Balston* v *Headline Filters* [1990] FSR 385.
13 *Robb* v *Green* [1852]2 QB 315.
14 [2001]2 BCLC 704 (Ch D).
15 [1942]1 All ER 378; [1967]2 AC 134.
16 [1973]40 DLR (3d) 371 at 382.
17 *Keech* v *Sandford* [1726] Sel Cas Ch 61, Ct of Chancery.
18 *Ibid* Per Lord Macmillan, p. 153.

him by reason of his fiduciary position, and by reason of the opportunity and/or knowledge arising from it; or a person occupying a position of trust must not make a profit which he can only acquire by use of his fiduciary position.[19]

In *Industrial Development Consultants Ltd.* v *Cooley,*[20] Mr. Cooley was an architect who was also the managing director of the plaintiff company, which was in a group supplying construction services. One of his duties was to procure new business, particularly in connection with the gas industry and the gas boards, since he had highly relevant experience having been chief architect of the West Midlands Gas Board. The company had unsuccessful negotiations with the Eastern Gas Board for a contract to design and build depots. Subsequently the deputy chairman of the Eastern Gas Board made a tentative approach to Mr. Cooley in his private capacity about the design and construction of new depots. He realized that if he could obtain his release from his position with the company he could acquire a valuable contract from the board. He falsely told the company that he was ill and obtained a release, and was subsequently awarded a contract by the board which was substantially the same business as the company had been attempting to obtain. Roskill, J held him accountable.

The following matters were relevant: (*a*) Mr. Cooley got the work as the result of work which he did while he was still managing director, even though the contract was not concluded until after he had left the company; (*b*) the company would have wanted the work, which was in substance the same work as they had tried to get;[21] (*c*) he possessed knowledge while a director (that the gas board was back in the market) which was not possessed by the company and which they would have wished to possess. The overriding principle was that a person in a fiduciary position is not allowed to enter into engagements in which a personal interest may conflict with the interests of those he is bound to protect.[1]

In the Canadian case of *Canadian Aero* v *O'Malley,*[2] it was held that from the obedient role of servants, it followed that O and Z stood in a fiduciary relationship to C Ltd., which in its generality betokens

19 *Ibid,* Per Lord Porter, p. 158.
20 [1972]1 WLR 443; [1972]2 All ER 162; [1972]116 SJ 255.
21 Although it had a very small chance–put at 10 per cent by Roskill, J of obtaining the contract.
1 Citing, *inter alia, Boardman* v *Phipps* [1967]2 AC 46.
2 (1974) SCR 592.

loyalty, good faith and avoidance of a conflict of duty and self-interest. A director or a senior officer like O or Z is precluded from obtaining for himself, either secretly or without the approval of the company, any property or business advantage either belonging to the company or for which it has been negotiating; and especially is this so where the director or officer is a participant in the negotiations on behalf of the company.

A strict ethic in this area of the law disqualifies a director or senior officer from usurping for himself or diverting to another person or company with whom or with which he is associated a maturing business opportunity which his company is actively pursuing; he is also precluded from so acting even after his resignation where the resignation may fairly be said to have been prompted or influenced by a wish to acquire for himself the opportunity sought by the company, or where it was his position with the company rather than a fresh initiative that led him to the opportunity which he later acquired.

The Canadian Supreme Court observed that their fiduciary duty had survived over their resignations. The general standards of loyalty, good faith and avoidance of a conflict of duty and self-interest to which the conduct of a director or senior officer must conform, must be tested in each case by many factors which it would be reckless to attempt to enumerate exhaustively. Among them are the factor of position or office held, the nature of the corporate opportunity, its ripeness, its specificness and the director's or managerial officer's relation to it, the amount of knowledge possessed, the circumstances in which it was obtained and whether it was special or, indeed, even private, the factor of time in the continuation of fiduciary duty where the alleged breach occurs after termination of the relationship with the company, and the circumstances under which the relationship was terminated, that is whether by retirement or resignation or discharge.[3]

However, in English law a director's power to resign from office is not a fiduciary power. A director is entitled to resign even if his resignation might have a disastrous effect on the business or reputation of the company. So also in English law, at least in general, a fiduciary obligation does not continue after the determination of the relationship which gives rise to it.[4] For the reasons given in *Island Export Finance*

3 *Ibid,* p. 621.

4 *Att. Gen.* v *Blake* [1998] Ch 439 (453), varied on other grounds [2000]3 WLR 625 (HL).

Ltd. v *Umunna,*[5] a director may resign (subject, of course, to compliance with his contract of employment) and he is not thereafter precluded from using his general fund of skill and knowledge, or his personal connections, to compete.

In India, there is no restriction on the conduct of any competing business by director of a company and the court would not interfere unless there is clear proof of gross breach of trust. However, the articles of a company may make provisions restraining the directors from doing a like business. Again a provision in a service contract that the director shall devote his time and attention during the usual office hours to the business of the company would preclude him from working during these hours for himself or anyone else.

5.4 Abuse and misappropriation

Directors owe fiduciary duties to the company with regards to the property of the company which is actually under their control. Trustees are not supposed to make unauthorized use of trust properties. Thus, directors are not permitted to use for their own purposes anything entrusted to them for use on behalf of the company. This restriction exists not only during the period of service, but it goes beyond the termination of service. The principle is not restricted to property in the strict sense. In *British Industrial Plastics* v *Ferguson,*[6] the court held that the directors are not entitled to use trade secrets of the company for their own purpose. Likewise in *Measures Bros.* v *Measures,*[7] court opined that directors have no authority to use confidential information such as customers list and confidential documents for their own personal purposes. The same principle was applied in *Percival* v *Wright*[8] in which the directors have used confidential information regarding an impending dividend declaration to speculate successfully in their company's shares. Again it was held in *Philips* v *Boardman*[9] that the fact that the company itself suffers no damage is irrelevant.

5 [1986] BCLC 460 (QBD).
6 [1938]4 All ER 504 (CA); *Cranheigh Precision Engineering Ltd.* v *Bryant* [1965]1 WLR 1293.
7 [1910]1 Ch 336; [1910]2 Ch 248 (CA); *Printers & Finishers Ltd.* v *Holloway* [1965]1 WLR 1; [1964]3 All ER 731; [1965] RPC 239.
8 [1902]2 Ch 421.
9 [1967]2 AC 46 (HL) following Cf. *Reading* v *Att. GCA* [1951] AC 507 (511).

The directors of a company, holding majority shares, formed a new company to which they proposed to divert the company's distribution rights. This amounts to misappropriation of company's property.[10] Even the ex-directors are liable to account if there is a real loss of business opportunities. Similar view was adopted by the Australian High Court in *Warman* v *Dwyer*.[11] A director had resigned from his company in order to enter into a pre-negotiated joint-venture arrangement with a third party, an Italian gearbox manufacturing company. As a result, the Australian company lost its own established distribution agency agreement with the third party. The Australian company sued its ex-director for breach of his duty of loyalty. The Australian High Court held that the director's profits from the breach did not encompass the entire profit of the new joint-venture arrangement. The Court awarded an account of the profits of the venture for two years, less an allowance for the director's efforts, expenses, skill and expertise.

The Madras High Court in a recent judgment in *Official Liquidator, High Court, Madras* v *Gautham Dhiraj Mal Ranka*[12] and *GDA Security P. Ltd.* v *Mangal Processing Mill Ltd.*,[13] held that "if it is found in the course of the winding up of a company, it appears that any business of the company has been carried on, with intent to defraud creditors of the company or any other person, or for any fraudulent purpose, the court, on the application of the official liquidator, or any creditor or contributory of the company, may, if it thinks it proper so to do, declare that any persons who were knowingly parties to the carrying on of the business in the manner aforesaid shall be personally responsible, without any limitation of liability, for all or any of the debts or other liabilities of the company as the court may direct".[14]

5.5 Procedure where Directors are interested

The law is well settled with regards to the principle that the sanction of the board should be obtained for certain contracts in which directors are personally interested. But this alone is not a guarantee that the

10 *Edney* v *Commodore Computer (NZ) Ltd.* [1985] LRC (Comm) 767 (NZ High Court).
11 [1995]182 CLR 554.
12 C.A. No. 609 of 2005.
13 C.P. No. 365 of 1997.
14 (2008)141 Comp Cas 129 (Mad).

decision of the Board will not be biased. So s. 300 of the Companies Act goes further and saying that the interested director shall not take part in the discussion or vote on any contract which he is personally interested. Section 300(1) says:

> No director of a company shall, as a director, take any part in the discussion of, or vote on, any contract or arrangement entered into, or to be entered into, by or on behalf of the company, if he is in any way, whether directly or indirectly, concerned or interested in the contract or arrangement; nor shall his presence count for the purpose of forming a quorum at the time of any such discussion or vote; and if he does vote, his vote shall be void.

The effect of this section is that it applies not only to contracts directly with the directors, but also to those in which they are in any way concerned or interested, whether they benefit personally or indirectly, or they are subject to a conflicting duty. Again it was held that the term 'interest' contemplated in this section means personal interest and not official or other interest.[15] But it is not limited to financial interest only and may include interest arising out of fiduciary duties or closeness of relationship such as that of father and son or daughter, or husband and wife.[16] Further, it is also immaterial whether the interest belongs to him beneficially or as a trustee for others.[17] However, where a resolution is passed with a view to protect the interest of the company, from the mere fact that the directors also along with other members stand to be benefited thereby, no question of viability will arise.[18] Again, even if the director concerned has disclosed his interest to the board and complied with s. 299 which requires the disclosure of interests by the director to the board, the present section says that he has no fight to vote. If he does vote, his vote shall be void, that is to say, it has to be ignored. But where an interested director vote, the proceeding are not thereby invalidated, but only his vote will not be counted.[19] There are no indication in

15 *Public Prosecutor* v *T.P. Khanan* AIR 1957 Mad 4; (1957)27 Comp Cas 77.

16 For a full discussion and review of case law on the subject, *Firestone & Rubber Co.* v *Synthetic & Chemicals Ltd.* [1970]2 Comp LJ 200 (Bom) may be referred.

17 *T.R. Pratt Ltd.* v *M.T.W.* (1938)8 Comp Cas 137; AIR 1938 PC 159.

18 *Seth Mohanlal* v *Grain Chambers* (1968)1 Comp LT 275; (1968)38 Comp Cas 543 (SC).

19 *C. Sundararaja Pillai* v *Sakthi Talkies Ltd.* (1967)37 Comp Cas 463 (DB) (Mad).

sub-sec. (1) making the contract or arrangements void for the contravention of the sub-section. It is voidable at the instance of the company, other parties to contract cannot avoid it.[20]

Again it is to be noted that not only voting but also participation in the discussion is prohibited to the directors who are concerned or interested. However, in *Mehta Teja Singh & C.* v *Globe Motors Ltd.*[1] the court pointed out that the mere presence of director at the meeting where the matter of interest was being considered would not invalidate the decision of the Board. Again the word arrangement used in the section besides the term contracted is intended to cover transaction in which a director acquires some right or incurs some liability as a result of it.[2]

As regards the quorum, it may be said that, where there is difficulty in having a quorum, the safe course will be to summon and get the approval in general meeting. However, the Madras High Court upheld the decision of the directors allotting shares to themselves, in which all directors were interested.[3] But in *V.S. Ramaswami Iyer* v *Madras Times Printing & Publishing Co.*,[4] the court gave an opposite verdict. In this case the company's articles provided that two directors constitute a quorum for a meeting of the board. Two were present and they appointed one of themselves as managing director and co-editor of the newspaper run by the company. The appointments were held to be invalid as when the vote of the interested director was excluded there was no quorum to make the appointment in each case. In *Venkatachalapathy* v *Guntur Cotton Mills*,[5] a mortgage of ₹ 1,23,354 was created over the mill property of the company. The loan was advanced by the wife of a director. Thus he was interested in the transaction. But he participated and voted in the board meeting. It was contended by the company in an action to set aside the mortgage that his voting on the matter vitiated the contract. The court was, however, of the opinion that mere voting by an interested director could not

20 *Narayandas* v *Sangli Bank Ltd.* AIR 1966 SC 170; (1965)3 SCR 777; (1965)35 Comp Cas 596 (SC).
1 (1983)54 Comp Cas 883 (Del).
2 *Mohanlal* v *Brain Chambers Ltd.* AIR 1958 All 276.
3 *Stec Ayyanar Spinning & Weaving Mills* v *V.V.V. Rajendran* (1973)43 Comp Cas 225 (Mad).
4 AIR 1915 Mad 1179.
5 AIR 1929 Mad 353; 115 IC 486.

render the contract void or voidable, unless in the absence of that vote, there would have been no quorum qualified to contract. The mere fact that voting is an offence punishable does not *ipso facto* render the contract void or voidable.[6]

Thus it is clear, as an equitable principle and a statutory provision, that the directors of a company, being fiduciaries, place themselves in a position in which his personal interest is in, or likely to, conflict with his duty towards the company. He shall not, except with the consent of the board, enter into contract, either directly or indirectly, with the company.[7] He shall not do any business which is competing or is likely to compete with that of the company by violating his fiduciary obligation. He shall not abuse the confidence reposed on him by using or converting anything entrusted to them for his own purpose. It is recognized that directors' duty of fidelity imposes higher obligations and full duty of good faith than that of a mere servant.[8] The CLB in *Sureshkumar Sanghi (DECD)* v *Sanghi Bros. (Indore) Ltd.,* recently held that if the directors are used the company funds to give interest-free loans to other firms and sister concerns of the controlling director, the respondent has been directed to restore the amounts siphoned off from the accounts of the company.[9]

5.6 Secret profits and duty of disclosure

Every person occupying a fiduciary position owes a duty towards his beneficiary to see that his personal interest and his duty towards the beneficiary do not conflict. A fiduciary is not expected to make profits without the knowledge of the beneficiary by using fiduciary position. Secret profits in its wide range and form represent the perpetuation of personal interest conflicting with fiduciary duty. The equitable principle regarding personal interest conflicting with duty does not concern, merely with contracts between the company and its directors, or contracts in which the directors are indirectly interested. The motive for other kinds of secret profits also may tend to bias the directors in their judgment.

6 Sub-section (4) of s. 300 imposes a penalty for the contravention of the section which may extend up to five thousand rupees.
7 Jackson, *The Wisdom of the Supreme Court*, 417-8 (1962).
8 *Bell* v *Lever Bros.* [1932] AC 195.
9 (2008)141 Comp Cas 17 (CLB).

The word 'Secret Profits' applies not only to payments in the nature of bribes made to directors in the hope of influencing their judgment, but also to any benefit which they would not have reaped but for some use of their special position. Most of the questions regarding the subject had been answered in *Regal (Hastings) Ltd.* v *Gulliver.*[10] In this case the plaintiff contented that the Respondents were in a fiduciary capacity in relation to the Appellants and as such accountable in the circumstances for the profits they made on the sale of the shares.

The House of Lords held that the directors are liable to account once it is established that "what the directors did was so related to the affairs of the company that it can properly be said to have been done in the course of their management and in utilization of their opportunities and special knowledge as directors; and iliac what they did resulted in a profit to themselves."

In *Imperial* v *Hampson,*[11] makes no exception to the general rule that a solicitor or director if acting in a fiduciary capacity is liable to account for the profits made by him from knowledge acquired when so acting.

Although the ruling in *Regal (Hastings) Ltd.* v *Gulliver* followed and applied in many subsequent cases,[12] its exact scope does not seem to be clear. It insisted that directors shall not derive secret benefits from their trust. And it is probably well that this should apply whether or not any actual loss is suffered by the company or not.

But does the above said principle go so far as to establish that if directors *bona fide* decision not to invest their company's funds in some proposed investments, a director who thereafter embarks his own money therein is accountable for any profits? The question was considered by the House of Lords in *Philipps* v *Boardman*[13] and answered in the affirmative. However, Lord Cohen said that the mere use of knowledge or opportunity would not lead to accountability, this depends on the

10 [1942]1 All ER 378.

11 *Imperial Hydro-pathic Company* v *Hampson* [1882]23 Ch D 1.

12 *Zwicker* v *Stanbury* [1953]2 SCR 438 (Corn SC); *Canada Safeway Ltd.* v *Thomson* [1951]2 DLR 295; [1952]2 DLR 591 (B Col SC); [1952]30 Can BR 179; *Smith Ltd.* v *Smith* [1952] NZLR 470 (NZSC); *Fine Industrial Commodities* v *Powling* [1954]71 RPC 253.

13 [1967]2 AC 46.

facts of each case. In the instant case the knowledge and opportunity came to them while acting as fiduciaries. They were also liable because there was a possibility of a conflict of duty and interest since a trustee is not supposed to give prejudiced advice to his principal. Lord Hudson stated the relevant proposition of law in the widest terms as follows:[14]

> No person standing in a fiduciary position, when a demand is made upon him by the person to whom he stands in the fiduciary relationship to account for profits acquired by him by reason of his fiduciary position and by reason of the opportunity and knowledge or either, resulting from it, is entitled to defeat the claim upon any ground save that he made the profits with the knowledge and assent of the other person.

However, he then qualified the reasoning by saying that the knowledge must be 'Special information' which included confidential information. Lord Dilhorne, on the other hand, adopted a narrower formula holding that the agents were not liable to account since there had been no improper use of information which could have been used for the benefit of the principal.[15] According to Lord Upjohn, there was "no general rule that information learnt by a trustee during the course of his duties is property of the trust and cannot be used by him.[16] He could so use it unless it is confidential information which is given to him in circumstances which, regardless of his position as a trustee, would make it a breach of confidence for him to communicate to anyone or in a fiduciary capacity, and its use would place him in a position where his duty and his interest might possibly conflict".[17]

It was held in *Cook* v *Deeks,*[18] that both the directors and the company are liable to account for profits. Directors of the Toronto Construction Company formed the Dominion Construction to divert a contract to build a railway line for the Canadian Pacific Railway. They entered into the contract personally and then subsequently "the contract was....taken over by this company, by whom the work was carried out and the profits made."[19] The conclusion was:

14 At pp. 103-104.
15 At pp. 84-94.
16 At p. 128.
17 At p. 129.
18 [1916]1 AC 554 (Privy Council).
19 *Ibid,* p. 561.

.... the defendants T.R. Hinds and G.S. and G.M. Deeks were guilty of a distinct breach of duty in the course they took to secure the contract, and...they cannot retain the benefit of such contract for themselves, but must be regarded as holding it on behalf of the company.... It follows that the defendants must account to the Toronto Company for the profits which they have made out of the transaction...Their Lordships have throughout referred to the claim as one against the defendants G.S. Deeks, G.M. Deeks, and T.R. Hinds. But it was not, and could not be disputed that the Dominion Construction Company acquired the rights of these defendants with full knowledge of the facts, and the account must be directed in form as an account in favour of the Toronto Company against all the other defendants.[20]

Now it is an established principle that the company may be liable to account for profits on the basis of knowing receipt of trust property, including profit deriving from a breach of trust,[1] and the director/ shareholders who set it up will be liable as principal wrongdoers. Whatever the analysis they will be constructive trustees of the profits and liable to account.

But it would appear that they will be so liable if the knowledge is presented to them confidentially as a possible investment for the company even though the company does not avail itself of the opportunity. Now it appears to be settled that the directors may be entitled to take personal advantage of an opportunity originally offered to the company only if:

(*a*) the opportunity was rejected by the company;

(*b*) the directors who acted in connection with its rejection did so *bona fide* in the interest of the company;

(*c*) the information was not given to them confidentially on behalf of the company; and

(*d*) their subsequent use of opportunity was not related to their positions as directors.

In *Imperial Mercantile Credit Assn.* v *Coleman,*[2] Mr. Coleman, a director, was accountable for a profit on a contract with the company

20 *Ibid,* pp. 563, 565.
1 *Lewin on Trusts*, 17th Ed. 2000, para 42-24.
2 [1873] LR 6 HL 189.

in which he had not disclosed an interest. The profit was made on a contract with a firm of stockbrokers, Messrs Knight and Coleman, for the placing of debentures on commission. It was argued that even if Mr. Coleman was liable to the company, it was only his share of the profits which he was bound to restore, and not those attributable to Mr. Knight's share. That argument was rejected by the House of Lords. Lord Chelmsford said (at 202):

> ...the liability of partners who are implicated in a breach of trust (and this is an analogous case) has been held to be joint and several. It would be a strange conclusion that Mr. Coleman, who was the active agent in diverting the money, which belonged to the association, to the partnership funds, should not be answerable for the whole, whether his co-partner, Mr. Knight, was liable or not for any part of it.

Lord Cairns said (at 208):

> The profit on the transaction was obtained by Mr. Coleman, and...was obtained by him as a director of the association. Whether he desired or whether he determined to reserve it all to himself or to share it with his firm appears to be perfectly immaterial. The source from which the profit is derived is Mr. Coleman. It is only through him that his firm can claim. He is liable for the whole of the profits which were obtained; and it is not the course for a Court of Equity to enter into the consideration of what afterwards would have become of these profits.

In *Pacifica Shipping Co. Ltd.* v *Anderson,*[3] the breach of duty was discussed elaborately. In this case, a director took up an opportunity to buy a ship that his company was also interested in buying, but differed the decision until a feasibility study was conducted. The director formed a separate business with the technical consultant employed by Pacifica Shipping and bought the ship.

It was held by Davison, CJ that the route specified for the business of the new company was a specific business opportunity developed by the plaintiff company with the full knowledge and participation of Anderson as one of its directors. It was the duty of the director to refer the new business proposal to Pacifica and not to usurp the opportunity

3 [1986]2 NZLR 328.

for himself. Accordingly it was held that Anderson had breached his fiduciary duty as director.

Property or rights which belong to the directors can be used by them for their own good. A fund managing director employed by a company had the right on leaving the company's employment to take away the funds he managed to his new company. The advantages obtained by him as a part of the consideration for transfer of the funds were held to be not within the range of secret profits which demanded disclosure.[4]

Non-disclosure of an interest will not *per se* render the contract void or voidable at the option of the Company. Voting by an interested Director will not *per se* render the contract either void or voidable. But non-disclosure, or voting, where, but for the vote, the contract would not have been sanctioned, will in all cases render the interested Director liable to account for secret profits.[5]

5.7 Bribes and additional payments

There are number of circumstances under which the directors may receive additional payments without being informed to the company. Receiving additional payments may be opposed on two possible legal grounds. Firstly it may be argued that they have broken some duty to the individual shareholders. But it was believed for a long time that directors normally owe no duty to individual shareholders. Hence, in *Percival* v *Wright*[6] it was held that the directors were not liable to members whose shares they bought without disclosing a take-over bid at a higher price. But *Allen* v *Hyatt,*[7] shows that this must not be taken too far; the Board may by their conduct place themselves in a fiduciary position towards shareholders in the course of negotiating terms with the bidder.[8] Thus the rule that the directors are in a fiduciary relationship to individual shareholders seems to be universalising itself and got repeated recognition in many cases.[9]

4 *Framlington Group Plc.* v *Anderson* [1995]1 BCLC 475 (Ch D).

5 *Rao Bahadur Pydah Venkatachalapathi* v *The Guntur Cotton, Jute And Paper Mills Co. Ltd.* 115 Ind Cas 486.

6 [1902]2 Ch 421.

7 [1914]30 TLR 444 (PC).

8 Closely resembles to the 'special facts' doctrine, widely adopted in U.S.A. flowing from the decision in *Strong* v *Repide* [1909]213 US 419.

9 *Kardon* v *National Gypsum Co.* [1947]73 F Supp 798; *Speed* v *Transamerica Corpn.* [1951]99 F Supp 808.

Again, they may even be expressly appointed by the shareholders to act as their agents. Thus, in *Briess* v *Wooley,*[10] the shareholders were held liable for the fraud practiced by the directors on the bidder. But this happens rarely in the case of public companies whose shares were held valid. Thus, if the directors have become fiduciaries of the shareholders it is clear that normal equitable principles compel them to restore the additional profits they have made in respect of the members shares.[11]

Again, they will have to account if the bidder pays them something to induce them to persuade the shareholders to accept the offer; for the fact that this would be nothing less than a bribe and the directors would be liable accordingly.[12]

The second legal ground on which the acceptance of additional payments may be opposed is the allegation of a breach of the directors' fiduciary duties towards the company. Wherever the additional payments have been made to the directors because, and only because, they were directors there is a strong argument for saying that the principle exemplified in *Regal (Hastings)* v *Gulliver*[13] applies, and that they must account the secret profit to the company. This rule is extensive so as to cover the case where the payment is made to secure their resignations to effect the sale of the undertaking or shares. In United States the courts have many often taken a narrower view that their offices are corporate property.[14]

Another mode of obtaining secret profit is trafficking in shares, The facts in *Percival* v *Wright,*[15] present the well known example of this kind of transaction. Such profits are recoverable by the company even in the absence of confidential information received by the directors. However, the position is somewhat more difficult where the payment received is simply to secure their favourable recommendation to the

10 [1954] AC 333 (HL); [1954]1 All ER 909; [1954]2 WLR 832.

11 *Ibid, Allen* v *Hyatt.*

12 *Safford Corporation* v *Lever* [1891] QB 168 (CA); *Grant* v *Gold Exploration & Development Co.* [1900]1 QB 233.

13 [1942]1 All ER 378.

14 *Gerdes* v *Reyholds* [1941]28 NVS 2d 622, where the directors were held liable not only to account for the sums paid for their resignations but also to restore the loss suffered by the company from the looting of its assets by the new board that they had negligently installed.

15 [1902]2 Ch 421.

shareholders. This hardly seems to be a bribe. However, a payment to secure their acceptance of a transfer of shares was held to be recoverable.[16]

In *Lister* v *Stubbs,*[17] the Court of Appeal held that the principal has no proprietary claim; the relationship between the agent and his principal is that of debtor and creditor not that of trustee and beneficiary. This decision was highly controversial and not followed by courts and there is little academic support for this judgment. An agent who receives a bribe or secret commission in breach of fiduciary duty is accountable in equity to his employer. In case of directors, they are agents of the company and trustees of trust property. They are accountable to the company.[18]

There is complete prohibition for taking bribe or commission by the directors of a company for awarding a contract.[19] The company can recover from its director any money received by him by way of a bribe in fraud of the company. But the company cannot follow the profit or bribe as trust property.[20]

In *Sumitonia Bank Ltd.* v *Kartika Ratna Thahir,*[1] also allowed the person received the bribe to keep any benefit in the accretion in value of his bribe or property in which it has been invested. It has been taken as explaining the attitude of the courts to issues such as ratification of breaches of duty against a company. It is probable that the courts would take the view that it covers secret profits as well as bribes. If that is so the profit obtained by a fiduciary through insider dealing might well be considered traceable. Confidential information is a property for the purposes of the law of constructive trusts.

In *Hannibal (E) & Co.* v *Frost,*[2] the managing director of a company withdrew a sum of money from the company's account and used it to pay bribes to a contract awarding authority. The company sued him and he contended that the company had benefited by having substantial contracts awarded to it. The court held that as a director of a company,

16 *Clark* v *Workman* [1920]1 R 107 (Irish).
17 [1890]45 Ch D 1.
18 *Attorney-General for Hong Kong* v *Reid* [1994]1 AC 324.
19 *Boston Deep Sea Fishing & Ice Co. Ltd.* v *Ansell* [1888]39 Ch D 339.
20 *Salford Corpn.* v *Lever* [1891]1 QB 168 (CA). See Halsbury's *Laws of England*, 4th Ed., vol. 7(1), para 623.
1 (1993)1 SLR 735.
2 [1988]4 BCC 3 (CA).

he had no authority to use the company's money to pay bribes and the fact that the company may have benefited from the payment of the bribes did not provide the director with any defence.

5.8 Disclosure of interests and profits–equitable principles

The equitable principles regarding the normal fiduciary duties of directors prescribe that interacted director shall disclose his interest and profit and if this is not complied with,[3] the contract or other transaction shall not be liable to account for any profits made. Again if the duty of disclosure is not performed *bona fide* the contract is voidable by the company and any profits made by the interested director are recoverable.[4] But failure to disclose the interests and profits does not make the contract void, it merely becomes voidable under the general equitable principles and if it is too late to rescind it in fully enforceable against the company.[5]

Again it is not sufficient to disclose merely that one is interested. The equitable principle demands that the nature of the interest must also be disclosed. This normally involves the disclosure of the exact amount which the director will make as a result of the contract.[6] However, it is only the nature of the interest and not all material facts that has to be disclosed, the director may freely contract with, without disclosing any material facts other than his interest. However, if there is an 'interest' it has to be disclosed even if it is too small to be material. Again it should be noted that even under the basic equitable principle the obligation to make full disclosure only arises when a contract is to be entered into with the company. Thus a director is not under a general duty to disclose his own breach of other duties.[7] On the other hand he may be under a duty to disclose the misdeeds of other directors and officers. 'It is, apparently, more blessed to denounce the Sins of others than to confess one's own'.[8]

3 The onus of proving this is on the director: *Gray* v *New Augarita Porcupine Mines* [1952] DLR 1 PC.

4 *Rely Hutchinson* v *Brayhead Ltd.* [1968]1 QB 54 (CA). (Lord Denning, MR, Wilberforce and Pearson). See also *Imperial Mercantile Credit Association* v *Coleman* [1873] LR 6 HL 189.

5 *Ibid.*

6 *Imperial Mercantile Credit Association* v *Coleman* (supra); *Gray* v *New Augarita Porcupine Mines* [1952]3 DLR 1 PC.

7 *Healey* v *S.A. Francaise Rubastic* [1917]1 KB 946, approved in *Bell* v *Lever Bros* [1932] AC 161 (HL).

8 The observation in *Bell* v *Lever Bros.*, ibid.

The managing director was arranged the sale of second-hand and refurbished equipment of the company through his own private company. He was held to be under a strict liability to the company for an account of the benefit or gain obtained or received by using the business opportunity that would otherwise have been available to the company. It was irrelevant that the company could not or would not have taken up the business opportunity or that the profit accrued because of the director's own skill or property. A director can only escape from potential accountability by obtaining prior approval of the company's shareholders after full disclosure of all the facts and circumstances. Thus the director and his company were accountable for the profit made on the sale of new or second hand asphalt plant.[9]

Finally the meaning of the word 'interested' must be looked into. It has been held that an interest as trustee is sufficient to bring the basic equitable principle into operation since the resulting conflict of duties is as serious as a conflict of pecuniary interests.[10] However, it has been held that a director of another company remunerated only by salary is not deemed to be 'interested' in a contract with that other company.[11] Thus the interest does not have to be immediate, however, it appears to be generally recognized that holding of an office in another company is a sufficient 'interest' in a contract with that company to require to be disclosed.

Account of profits will be a more advantageous remedy than equitable compensation in breach of duty, since the actual profits obtained by the director may be higher than the damages for the loss of opportunity suffered by the company. The fiduciary is liable for the whole of the profit. There are no firm rules for determining which the relevant profit is.[12] According to Mason, J, "where, as here, the business (to use a neutral term, not distinguishing between Mr. Simonet and Blue) is not restricted exclusively to the performance of contracts which were obtained from CMSD, the fiduciary should be accountable for the profits properly attributable to the breach of fiduciary duty, taking into account the expenses connected with those profits and a

9 *Gencor ACP Ltd.* v *Dalby* [2000]2 BCLC 734 (Ch D).

10 *Transvaal Lands Co.* v *New Belgium (Transvaal) Land & Development Co.* [1914]2 Ch 488 (CA).

11 *Wilson* v *L.M.S. Ry.* [1930]1 KB 41; *Ch AK Lumpish* v *Branwaite* [1926] AC 275 (HL).

12 *Hospital Products Ltd.* v *United States Surgical Corp.* [1984]156 CLR 41, p. 110.

reasonable allowance for overheads (but not necessarily salary for the wrongdoer), together with a sum to take account of other benefits derived from those contracts. For example, other contracts might not have been won, or profits made on them, without (e.g.) the opportunity or cash flow benefit which flowed from contracts unlawfully obtained. There must, however, be some reasonable connection between the breach of duty and the profits for which the fiduciary is accountable."

5.9 The statutory duty of disclosure

Every agent occupying a fiduciary position has the duty to see that his personal interests and his duties to his principle do not conflict each other. Thus, for the proper exercise of the functions of a director he must be free from any interest conflicting with that of the company. The Companies Act lays down a special procedure to be followed where a director is personally interested in a transaction of the company.

Section 299 of the Companies Act 1956 provides that every director of a company who is in any way, whether directly or indirectly concerned or interested in a contract or arrangement, entered into or to be entered into, by or on behalf of the company, shall disclose the nature of his concern or interest at a meeting of the Board of Directors. Again it is provided that the disclosure must be made at the first meeting of the board held after he has become so interested.[13] Further if he is a member of a company or of a firm with which the company has to deal he may give a general notice to the board of his interest in that concern. Such notice must be renewed after every year.[14] Again sub-sec. (4) says that every director who fails to comply with these provisions shall be punishable with fine which may extent to fifty thousand rupees. However, this procedure has not to be followed where the contract is between two companies and a director does not hold more than 2 per cent of the paid up share capital of the company.[15]

The above said provisions are based upon the sound principle that the company is entitled to get unbiased advice of every director upon matters which are brought before the board.[16] "It is possible, of course,

13 Section 299(2)(*a*) and (*b*).
14 Section 299(3).
15 Section 299(6).
16 The objects of these provisions are explained by Chagla, CJ In *Walchand Nagar Industries* v *Ratawnchand* AIR 1953 Bom 285.

that a person may be altruistic and in coming to arrangements in which he is concerned he will give better terms to the other contracting party than if lie had no interest at all but persons of such dispositions are not usually found among directors of a company and it must be assumed that in the making of an arrangement a man will consider his own interest rather than the interest of the other contracting party."[17]

Section 299 has a wider scope than s. 297 and covers all kinds of contracts and arrangements and proposed contracts and arrangements. However, the s. 299 deals only with contracts and arrangements of the company in which the directors only and not their relatives or partners also are interested.

The contract or arrangement hit by this section is one in which the director has a personal interest conflicting with his duties towards the company and does not cover any case where there is no personal interest involved.[18] But the interest need not be direct. Where a company issued certain debentures to a bank to secure an overdraft and the overdraft has previously been guaranteed by some directors, this was held to be an interest which ought to be disclosed.[19]

The word 'interest' which comes within the mischief rule is not personal interest only, nor is it confined to pecuniary interest on1y.[20] The interest to be disclosed in a business sense might be regarded as 'influencing judgment', the essence of the matter being that any kind of personal interest which is material in the sense of not being insignificant must be revealed.[1] In short, the interest must be conflicts with the director's duties towards the company. Thus, where the directors took part in and voted at a meeting of the board which granted debentures to two of them by a resolution was held to be bad.[2] However, where a resolution allotting shares to a defaulting director at a meeting

17 *In re Alexander Timber Co.* [1901]70 LJ Ch 767. Also *V. Ramaswamy Iyer* v *Madras Time Printing & Publishing Co.* AIR 1915 Mad 1179.

18 *Public Prosecutor* v *T.P. Khaitan* AIR 1957 Mad 4; (1957)27 Comp Cas 77; (1956)2 MLJ 590.

19 *Victor Ltd.* v *Lingard* [1927]1 Ch 323.

20 The Principle underlying this section is discussed in *Fateh Chand* v *Hinsons (Patiala) Ltd.* (1957)27 Comp Cas 140; AIR 1956 Pepsu 89.

1 *In re Coltness Iron Co.* [1951] SC 476 (Scotland); [1951] SLT 344.

2 *In re North Eastern Insurance Co. Ltd.* [1919]1 Ch 198.

where he was present and voted was held not void.[3] As noted above, all 'Personal Interests' do not come within the purview of the mischief of the rule. Only such interest has to be disclosed which is 'personal' in the 'business sense' of the word. Thus the appointment of a director as Chairman or as a managing director is not such an interest and the appointment will, therefore, be valid even if the director to be appointed was present at the board meeting and voted.[4] In *Public Prosecutor* v *T.P. Khaitan,*[5] it was held that a resolution which a director was authorized to draw cheques on the company's bankers was not bad simply because the director so authorized had acted in the meeting of the board.

Again, the words used in the section "in any way, whether directly or indirectly concerned or interested" are given the widest meaning so as to bring within their application all manner of relationships. The concern or interest may arise out of blood relationship such as that of husband and wife or father and son, or fiduciary relationship such as that of principal and agent or trustee and beneficiary. The word 'concerned' is of quite general importance, clearly it cannot be limited to 'concerned' in the sense of 'financial interests' only. Thus, where a director who was for long time a Solicitor of some other directors in their private business was held to be concerned or interested in those so as to be bound to disclose at the meeting of the board his concern or interest is those other directors.[6] But in *Needle Industries Newey (India) Holding Ltd.,*[7] it was held that the interest or concern spoken of by this section cannot be merely sentimental or ideological concern. A relationship of friendliness with directors interested in a contract or even a mere lawyer-client relationship will not qualify a director as an interested director.

Again it may be noted the s. 299 does not prohibit altogether a contract in which a director is interested; only that it should be disclosed, *bona fide* and fair.[8] Even where the interest is not disclosed the

3 *Bank of Poona* v *Narayandas* AIR 1961 Bom 252; (1961) Comp Cas 364; 63 Bom LR 122. Also *Public Prosecutor* v *T.P. Khaitan*; supra.

4 *Foster* v *Foster* [1916]1 Ch 532; [1916-17] All ER Rep 856 and *N.W. Transportation Co.* v *Beatty* [1887]12 AC 589; 57 LT 426.

5 (1957)27 Comp Cas 77; AIR 1957 Mad 4.

6 *Firestone Tyre & Rubber Co. Ltd.* v *Synthetics & Chemicals Ltd.* (1970)2 Comp LJ 200; (1971)41 Comp Cas 377 (Bom).

7 (1981)51 Comp Cas 743, p. 815 (SC).

8 *P. Leslie & Co.* v *V.O. Wapshare* AIR 1969 SC 843; (1969)2 Comp LJ 113; (1969)39 Comp Cas 808.

transaction is only voidable against the interested director and not void.[9] If the company waives the irregularity and affirms the transaction he becomes bound by it. He cannot insist on irregularity.[10] Again a formal disclosure is not necessary where the whole body of directors is already aware of the facts. Thus, in *Venkatachalapathy* v *Guntur Cotton, etc Mills.*[11] A mortgage was created over the mill property of a company. The loan was advanced by the wife of a director. But the director did not disclose this fact. In an action by the company to set aside the mortgage, it was held that as the facts were already known to the directors there was no necessity for a formal disclosure.

Finally, failure to comply with this section invites certain consequences. Sub-section (4) of s. 299 provides that every director who fails to disclose his interest to the board shall be punishable with fine which may extend to fifty thousand rupees. According to Kerala High Court[12] the consequences of default under the section are: (1) Liability to be prosecuted under s. 299(4), (2) cessation of the office of directorship;[13] (3) Liability to be prosecuted for acting as director after incurring a disqualification;[14] and (4) Liability to refund remuneration.[15]

5.10 Conclusion

A "conflict of interest" may exist whenever the interests of a director conflict in any way with the interests of the company. While the directors should be free to make personal investments in accordance with the insider trading rules of the SEBI. They must not have any interests that adversely influence the performance of their responsibilities as directors. Conflicts of interest also may arise when a director, or a member of his or her family, receives improper personal benefits as a

9 *Narayandas* v *Sangli Bank* AIR 1966 SC 170; (1965)35 Comp Cas 596; (1965)2 Comp LJ 99.

10 *Ibid*, also *Yuill* v *Greymouth, etc. Ry. Co* [1904]1 Ch 32 where a director was not allowed to an allotment on the ground that he took part in it.

11 AIR 1929 Mad 353; 115 IC 486.

12 Peter Issac, J, in *M.O. Varghese* v *Thomas Stephen & Co. Ltd.* (1970)40 Comp Cas 1131.

13 Under s. 283(1)(*i*): Punishment by way of fine which may extend to five thousand rupees. Also *Globe Motors Ltd.* v *Mehta Teja Singh & Co.* (1984)55 Comp Cas 445 (Del).

14 Section 283(2-A).

15 Also *Costa Rica Rail Co. Ltd.* v *Forwood* [1901]1 Ch 746.

result of his or her relation with any business entity whether received from that entity or a third party. Usually the directors are prohibited from (*a*) taking personal benefits by depriving any opportunities that belong to the company or (*b*) competing with the company business (*c*) using corporate property, information, or position for personal gain. A code of conduct for directors in each and every company with the backup of SEBI rules can give a correct direction to the directors of Indian companies.

6

Liabilities of Directors

6.1 Who is Liable?

Liability or responsibility is an elusive term. It has many equally plausible definitions and the values it expresses differ from time to time, place to place. Indeed, it has been described so integral part of human relationships that it, in its various meanings and shadings, serves as a synonym for every important political word.[1] Directors of a company are holding a key position in the eye of company law and they have to comply with the provisions of the Memorandum and articles of the company. They have to take a reasonable care and act honestly in discharging their duties. Any interest in the company has to be disclosed by a director. Directors are personally liable to outsiders in entering into contracts on behalf of the company. They are also liable to the company where they acted *ultra vires* the company, for negligence, fraud, breach of trust and misfeasance. Directors are also criminally liable for extreme breach of duties and can impose penalties in a series of cases. The present chapter discusses the civil and criminal liabilities of company directors in detail and the jurisprudence emerged through a series of decisions from various courts all over the world.

Directors are agents of the company in transactions they enter into on behalf of the company, though they are not agents for individual shareholders or members. A director may be an employee, a servant or even a 'worker' of the company. He occupies the position of a trustee, though he is not a trustee in the strict sense in respect of the company's

1 A. Widavsky, *Responsibilities are Allocated by Cultures* (1986), p. 1.

properties and funds. Director's liability arises because of their position as agents or officers of the company as being in the position of trustees or having fiduciary relation with the company or its shareholders. The directors are statutorily liable under the companies and other similar legislations. They are liable for breach of contract, torts and all other illegal acts. Fixing of liability is important in the context that the 'company' does not have any mind or soul. In the context of corporate liability, an oft-cited opinion is the 18th century expression of Baron Edward Thurlow, LC that *corporations have no soul to be damned and no body to be kicked.*[2] Hence, somebody should bear the liability of the company for its civil and criminal activities. But director and company are separate legal entities and there is no personal liability for the director on behalf of the company.[3]

The Madras High Court in *Sivandhi Adityan* v *Additional Registrar of Companies*,[4] held that the combined effect of sub-sec. (30) of s. 2 and s. 5 of the Companies Act 1956 is that all the Directors of a company cannot at all be construed as "officers in default",[5] unless each of the Directors is an "officer in default" within the meaning of s. 5. The High Court also held that service of notice is a crucial factor for determining the question as to whether an accused could be construed as an "officer in default". Also the Supreme Court of India in *Raymond Synthetics Limited* v *Union of India*[6] has held that a director of a company who is an officer in default appearing in the Companies Act must be understood with reference to the definition of an "officer who is in default" contained in s. 2(31) read with s. 5 of the Companies Act 1956. The definition of "officer" in s. 2(30) includes a Managing Director or

2 The expression has become commonly associated with the intricacies of corporate accountability following the discussion in J.C. Coffee, *No Soul to Damn, No Body to Kick-An Un-scandalised Inquiry into the Problem of Corporate Punishment* (1981).

3 http://www.narasappa.com, visited on 11.05.2012.

4 (1995)83 Comp Cas 616 (Mad); 1994 Cr LJ 1149.

5 Section 5, meaning of 'officer who is in default'. For the purpose of any provision in this Act which enacts that an officer of the company who is in default shall be liable to any punishment, or penalty, whether by way of imprisonment, fine or otherwise, the expression 'officer who is in default' means any officer of the company who is knowingly guilty of the default, non-compliance, failure, refusal or contravention mentioned in that provision or who knowingly and wilfully authorises or permits such default, non-compliance, failure, refusal or contravention.

6 (1992)73 Comp Cas 762 (SC); AIR 1992 SC 847; (1992)1 SCR 481.

a Whole-time Director of a company. The liability imposed under sub-sec. (2A) on a director of the company falls only upon a director who is 'an officer in default'. as defined under s. 2(31) read with s. 5(*a*) & (*b*), and not upon any other director.

Clause 2(60) of the 2011 Companies Bill provides whom are the officers in default. They are:

(*i*) whole-time director or directors;

(*ii*) other key managerial personnel;

(*iii*) where there is no key managerial personnel such director or directors as specified by the Board in this behalf and who has or have given his or their consent in writing to the Board to such specification, or all the directors, if no director is so specified;

(*iv*) any person who, under the immediate authority of the Board or any key managerial personnel, is charged with any responsibility including maintenance, filing or distribution of accounts or records, authorises, actively participates in, knowingly permits, or knowingly fails to take active steps to prevent, any default;

(*v*) any person in accordance with whose advice, directions or instructions the Board of Directors of the company is accustomed to act other than a person who gives advice to the Board in a professional capacity;

(*vi*) every director, in respect of a contravention of any of the provisions of this Act, who is aware of such contravention by virtue of the receipt by him of any proceedings of the Board or participation in such proceedings without objecting to the same, or where such contravention had taken place with his consent or connivance;

(*vii*) in respect of the issue or transfer of any shares of a company, the share transfer agents, registrars and merchant bankers to the issue or transfer.

The decision of the Supreme Court of India in *N.K. Wahi* v *Sekhar Singh*[7] is also relevant as it analyzed, *inter alia*, the vicarious liability

7 (2007)2 CLJ 10 (SC); (2007)9 SCC 481.

of company directors and held that if any offence is committed by a company, then every person who is a director of the company is not liable, but only such person would be held liable if at the time when the offence is committed, he was in-charge of and was responsible to the company for the conduct of the day-to-day business of the company. Merely being a director of the company by itself would not make him liable and that the prosecution will have to show and prove as to how the accused was in-charge of and responsible for the day-to-day management of the affairs of the company and was responsible for the commission of the alleged offence/violations and that the Complainant/ Prosecution will have to sufficiently aver in this regard in the complaint itself to enable the Court to proceed against the accused persons.

So understood, the liability imposed under the provisions of the Act on a director of the company falls only upon a director who is an "officer in default", as defined under s. 2(31) read with s. 5 of the Companies Act 1956 and not upon any other Director and that the Nominees of the Government or Financial Institutions on the Board of Directors of the company, but not directly in-charge of its administration as full time directors, are exempted from personal liability.

6.2 Liability for illegal Acts

Directors' powers are given to them to be used for the benefit of the company, that is, for the benefit of the shareholders of the company as a whole and not for the benefit of the directors themselves. A public company or a subsidiary of a public company is prohibited from advancing loans to purchase its own shares. If the directors have used their powers to part with moneys of their company in a manner or for a purpose which the law forbids, it is not a defence to proceedings to make them liable for their act to plead merely that they acted in ignorance of the law.[8] Similarly an allotment of shares made for any improper motive is bad and can be struck down.[9] But knowledge of such illegal act is a necessary ground for prosecuting a person. In *R* v *Boal,*[10] a book shop was owned by a company. A person designated as assistant manager had in charge of day-to-day responsibility of running the shop. He was giving no input into policy matters lime

8 *Louis Steen* v *Charles Allen Law* (1964)34 Comp Cas 195 (PC).
9 *Unit Trust of India* v *Om Prakash Berlia* (1983)54 Comp Cas 723 (Bom).
10 [1992] BCLC 872 (CA).

implementation of proper health and safety procedure as required by a statute. He was held to be not a manager for the purpose of being prosecuted when the company was found to be guilty of breaching the statute.

In *Alim Ahuja* v *Registrar of Companies,*[11] the Rajasthan High Court has held that persons having voluntarily accepted directorship of a company and having not established that they were not concerned with day-to-day management of company and business thereof, cannot be relieved under s. 633(2) of the Companies Act 1956 from having to comply with the provisions and procedures of the Companies Act and other relevant Acts.

Legal heirs are liable for the acts of directors those who misused the funds of the company as trustees.[12] If a director also used their powers to part with their money of their company for the purpose which the law forbids, ignorance cannot be pleaded.[13]

6.3 Liability for negligence

A director, like any other agent, owes a duty at common law and in equity to his company to exercise reasonable care in the management and conduct of its affairs, and he is liable to the company in damages if he fails to do so. There is no hard and fast rule or standards of skill and care which help in determining whether a director has been negligent. However, the courts are developed standards and reasonable skill that expect from directors. It can be said that a director is expected to display the same standard of care in his company's affairs as a reasonable man would in his own affairs. One of the earliest cases of *Charitable Corporation* v *Sutton,*[14] where Lord Hardwicke said:

> Directors may be guilty of acts of commission or omission, of malfeasance or non-feasance … . By accepting a trust of this sort, a person is obliged to execute it with fidelity and reasonable diligence; and it is no excuse to say that they had no benefit from it, but that it was merely honorary; and therefore, they are within the case of common trustees.

11 (2005)62 SCL 110 (Raj); (2006)129 Comp Cas 104 (Raj).
12 *Ramasamy Iyer* v *Brahmayya & Co.* (1996)1 Comp LJ 107 (Mad).; *Ekambaram* v *Venkata Chalapathi Mills Ltd.* (1967)37 Comp Cas 693 (AP).
13 *Louis Steen* v *Charles Allen Law* [1963]3 All ER 770.
14 [1742]2 Atk 400, 405, 406.

A director has to use only such "skill as may reasonably be expected from a person of his knowledge and experience." Traditionally, only gross negligence the directors used to be made liable. But the current trend is towards objectivity.[15]

The Court in *Kavanaugh* v *Commonwealth Trust Company,*[16] case it was held that "If in the performance of his duties, with the care and attention an ordinarily prudent man, actuated by self interest, would have given to his own business affairs, he would have learned of the wrongful acts in time to have prevented them or lessened the loss, then he was negligent in failing to know them".[17] It means that the directors are held to be "the same degree of care that men of common prudence exercise in their own affairs".[18]

The view of Lord Hatherley, LC in *Turquand* v *Marshall,*[19] is probably the law point. There, in relation to a loan made by the board to one of their member who died insolvent and never repaid the loan, held that:[20]

> It was within the powers of the deed to lend to a brother director, and however foolish the loan might have been, so long as it was within the powers of the directors, the Court could not interfere and make them liable . . . Whatever may have been the amount lent to anybody, however ridiculous and absurd their conduct might seem, it was the misfortune of the company that they chose such unwise directors; but as long as they kept within the powers of their deed, the Court could not interfere with the discretion exercised by them.[1]

15 M.J. Trebilock, *Liability of Directors for Negligence,* (1969)32 Modern Law Review 499.

16 *Supreme Court of Saratoga County,* New York, in September, 1909.

17 See Notes and Comments, *Michigan Law Review,* vol. 8(2), 1909, pp. 137-140.

18 See *Hun* v *Cary* [1880]82 NY 65; 37 Am R 546; *Bosworth* v *Allen* [1901]168 NY 157; 61 NE 163; *Marshall* v *Farmers Bank* [1889]85 Va 676; 17 Am St R 84; *Union National Bank* v *Hill* [1899]148 Mo 380; 71 Am St R 615; *Warren* v *Robison* [1899]19 Utah 289; 75 Am St R 734; *Commercial Bank* v *Chatfield* [1899]121 Mich 245; *Fisher* v *Parr* [1900]92 Md 245.

19 [1869] LR 4 Ch App 376.

20 *Ibid,* p. 386.

1 See *Re New Mashonal and Exploration Company* [1892]3 Ch D 577 (585) per Vaughan Williams, J; *Re Forest of Dean Coal Mining Company* [1878]10 Ch D 450 (453), per Jessel, MR; *Re Faure Electric Accumulator Company* [1888]40 Ch D 141 (152), per Kay, J; *Grimwade* v *Mutual Society* [1885]52 LT 409 (416) per Chitty, J.

In *Lagunas Nitrate Co.* v *Lagunas Syndicate,*[2] it was held that if the directors acted honestly for the benefit of the company and within the powers, they are not liable. The directors are not bound to bring any special qualifications into their office. Mere omission to take every possible care will not amount to negligence.[3] In the *Brazilian Rubber Plantations* case Neville, J described the director's position thus:

> The directors of the company, Sir Arthur Aylmer Bart., Henry William Tugwell, Edward Barber and Edward Henry Hancock were all induced to become directors by Harboard or persons acting with him in the promotion of the company. Sir Arthur Aylmer was absolutely ignorant of business. He only consented to act because he was told the office would give him a little pleasant employment without his incurring any responsibility. H.W. Tugwell was partner in a firm of bankers in a good position in Bath; he was seventy-five years of age and very deaf; he was induced to join the board by representations made to him in January, 1906. Barber was a rubber broker and was told that all he would have to do would be to give an opinion as to the value of rubber when it arrived in England. Hancock was a man of business who said he was induced to join by seeing the names of Tugwell and Barber, whom he considered good men.[4]

A director has to perform his functions with reasonable care. He has to attend with due diligence and caution the work assigned to him.[5] An example is *Overend Gurney & Co* v *Gibb,*[6] where a company was formed to take over a private bank. Without investigating the value of the bank's assets and the extent of its liabilities and with knowledge that the bank was in a state of insolvency, the directors paid £50,000 for goodwill. Still holding them not liable, the House of Lords laid down that there should be violation of either the Act or the memorandum

2 [1899]2 Ch 392.

3 *Brazilian Rubber Plantations & Estates Ltd., Re* [1911]1 Ch 425 (CA).

4 *Ibid,* p. 437.

5 The Nigerian Act set provisions on this aspect of directors duties: "A Director shall act at all times in what he believes to be the best interests of the company as a whole so as to preserve the assets, further its business and promote the purposes for which it is formed and in such manner as a faithful, diligent, careful and ordinarily skilful director would act in the circumstances." Section 279(1) of the Companies and Allied Matters Act 1990.

6 [1872] LR 5 HL 480.

or the transaction was such that no man of ordinary prudence would have entered into. Lord Hatherley, LC said that directors would be liable only if:

> ....they were cognizant of circumstances of such a character, so plain, so manifest, and so simple of appreciation, that no men with any degree of prudence, acting on their own behalf, would have entered into such a transaction as they entered into.

Directors may not know the nature of the company's trade, because all that the law expects from them is that if they know they must use the knowledge for the benefit of the company.[7] Accordingly the directors were held guilty of negligence when they participated in a transaction without trying to know whether the transaction was really for the purposes of the company or they were authorized by the Board in that respect, and it was no defence for any director to show that he believed that he was bound to sign because the other directors wanted it or that he joined under protest or that even without his joining, the other directors were determined to carry out the transaction.[8]

In *Lagunas Nitrate Co* v *Lagunas Syndicate,*[9] Lindley, MR said:

> If directors act within their powers, if they act with such care as is reasonably to be expected of them, having regard to their knowledge and experience, and if they act honestly for the benefit of the company they represent, they discharge both their equitable as well as their legal duty to the company. ... the amount of care to be taken is difficult to define; but it is plain that directors are not liable for all the mistakes they may make, although it they had taken more care they might have avoided them .... Their negligence must not be the omission to take all possible care; it must be much more blamable than that; it must be in a business sense culpable or gross.

Liability for negligence also followed where without any board resolution being properly passed a single member was allowed

7 *Brazilian Rubber Plantations and Estates Ltd, Re* [1911]1 Ch 425; 103 LT 697.

8 *Land Credit Co of Ireland* v *Lord Fermay* [1869] LR 3 Eq 7; [1850]5 Ch App 763.

9 [1899]2 Ch 392.

to manage a part of the company's business and he misconduct himself.[10]

Directors are not liable for delegating their power to manage the company to a properly appointed managing director whose periodic reports and accounts they accepted without checking, with the result that the managing director was able to dispose of the company's investments for his own purposes.[11] In *Public Prosecutor* v *T.P. Khaitan,*[12] it was held that though the directors as a body are responsible to the shareholders for the conduct of the company's business, it is undoubted law that they can delegate their powers to one or more of themselves for the purpose of carrying it on more conveniently. In *City Fire Insurance Co. Ltd., Re,*[13] it was held that a director of a company is not bound to take any definite part in the conduct of the company's business, but so far as he does undertake it he must take reasonable care in its dispatch.[14] In this case it was held that:

> His duties will depend upon the nature of the company's business and the manner in which the work of the company is distributed between the directors and other officials of the company. In discharging these duties a director must exercise some degree of skill and diligence. But he does not owe to his company the duty to take all possible care to act with best care. Indeed, he need not exhibit in the performance of his duties a greater degree of skill than may reasonably be expected from a person of his knowledge and experience, or in other words, directors are not liable for mere errors of judgment.[15]

In the above case, one *B* was the director of City Equitable Fire Insurance Co. the company was ordered to be wound up. *A* searching investigation of the affairs of the company was then made and this investigation showed a shortage of funds which the company should have been possessed of over £12,00,000. The collapse of the company was due to bad investments, bad debts and misappropriation. All the

10 *City Equitable Ins. Co., Re* [1925] Ch 407; [1924] All ER Rep 485 (CA).
11 *Dovery* v *Cory* [1901] AC 477.
12 (1957)27 Comp Cas 77 (83); AIR 1957 Mad 4.
13 [1925] Ch 407.
14 Followed in *Brazilian Rubber Plantations and Estates Ltd., Re* [1911] Ch 425.
15 Directors are not liable for ignorance of trade practices.

losses were due to *B*'s instrumentality. He was accordingly convicted for his frauds.

But the question of whether during the period covered by *B*'s nefarious activities the other directors was properly discharging their duties to the company. But there was exemption clause in the articles to which the directors were liable only for gross negligence. The facts of the case did not disclose that the degree of negligence and, therefore, the case of the official receiver against B's co-director failed.

While therefore appointment to the office of director does not of itself imply any obligations as to the time and attention which will be devoted to company activities, it has been suggested that there is a minimum requirement that a director attend most board meetings. Romer, J said in *Re City Equitable Fire Insurance Company Ltd.*:

> A director is not bound to give continuous attention to the affairs of his company. His duties are of an intermittent nature to be perforated at periodical board meetings, and at meetings of any committee upon which he happens to be placed. He is not, however, bound to attend all such meetings, though he ought to attend whenever in the circumstances he is reasonably able to do so.[16]

It was held in *Norman* v *Theodore Goddard,*[17] that the test of a director's duty of care permits him to trust persons in positions of responsibility until there is reason to distrust them. On the facts it was found that the information received by the director concerned from a senior partner in an eminent firm of city solicitors was the basis of the investment authorised by the director without making further inquiries. Thus the director had not abdicated his responsibility in relying upon information worthy of being trusted.

If the director has special knowledge about the nature of the company's business, then he is bound to give the company the advantage of his knowledge when transacting the company's business. The director of a property development company is not expected to be an expert in tax planning.[18]

Directors were also held liable where they released the company's funds for paying the debt without trying to know whether anything

16 [1925] Ch 407 (429).
17 [1992] BCLC 1028 (Ch D); [1992] BCC 14.
18 In *D' Jan of London Ltd., Re* [1994]1 BCLC 561 (CA).

was really due and for purchasing the assets without knowing whether there was any real transfer of those assets.[19]

The Supreme Court of New South Wales explained the law governing the duty of care of company directors and their liability for negligence in *Daniels* v *Anderson.*[20] The court observed that a person who accepts the office of director of a particular company undertakes the responsibility of ensuring that he or she understands the nature of the duty a director is called upon to perform. The duty will vary according to the size and business of the particular company and the experience or skills that the director held himself or herself out to have in support of appointment to the office. None of this is novel. The duty includes that of acting collectively to manage the company.[1] However, a director who knowingly makes a false representation whilst acting as a director can be personally held liable not only in deceit, but also for negligent misrepresentation.[2]

In the words of Justice Cardozo, "The diligent director is the one who exhibits in the performance of his trust the same degree of care and prudence that men prompted by self-interest generally exercise on their own affairs".[3] In *New Fleming Spinning & Weaving Company Limited* v *Kessowji Naik,*[4] the court held that it is an established rule that trustees cannot delegate their office, and, if they do thus divest themselves of their trust, they are held liable for any breach of trust committed by the person to whom the office has been entrusted.

Directors would be liable for omitting to do what they could have done in the circumstances. Where the president of an investment company improvidently invested in companies in which he was interested and caused loss, his fellow directors were held liable because they had left the investment of the company's funds to the president's unfettered discretion and exercised no supervision over him.[5] Mere absence from a meeting is not alone sufficient to establish negligence.[6]

19 *Selangor United Rubber Estates* v *Cradock (No. 3)* [1968]2 All ER 1073; [1968]1 WLR 1555.

20 [1995]16 ACSR 607 (Australia).

1 This decision was followed in *Barings Plc.* (No. 5), *Re* [1999] BCLC 433 (Ch D).

2 *Thomas Saunders Partnership* v *Harvey* The Independent, 5th May 1989; 1989 CLY 304.

3 *People* v *Mancuso 255* GY 463, 469.

4 (1885) ILR 9 Bom 373.

5 *Kavanangh* v *Common Wealth Trust Co* [1918] 233 NY 103 USA.

6 *Warner* v *Penoyer* [1898] GI Fed R 587; 44 LRA 761; *Murphy* v *Penniman* [1907]I05 Md 452; 121 Am St R 583.

In a pre-independence case, the Madras High Court considered the question of liability of the directors for misfeasance under s. 235 of the Companies Act 1913 in *Rao Sahib V Subbaiah* v *C.T. Machayya.*[7] The court held that to become a director of a company by accepting a gift of shares without paying for them is a misfeasance. Section 235 of the Companies Act 1913 does not *prima facie* exclude nonfeasance. It would apply to every act of a director, whether of commission or omission, is a breach of duty to the company in consequence whereof loss results to the company. A director signed the prospectus without in least caring to know what the antecedents of the other directors were more how the company was going to be what and who the partners of the firm or managing agents were. The court held that if any pecuniary clause was sustained by the company, in such circumstances, it could not be said that the director was guilty of any misfeasance or breach of trust. It was further held that where a director of a company not only did not exercise that amount of reasonable care which was expected of him as a director in ascertaining the true state of affairs of the company but also wilfully shut his eyes to it until a very late stage, he was guilty of gross negligence which would be misfeasance within the meaning of s. 235.[8]

The Madras High Court in *Madhavan Nambiar* v *Registrar of Companies,*[9] it was held that in the matter of proceedings for negligence, default, breach of duty, misfeasance or breach of trust or violation of the statutory provisions of the Act and the Rules, there is no difference or distinction between the whole time or part time director or nominated or co-opted director and the liability for such acts, commission or omission is equal. So also the treatment for such violations as stipulated in the Companies Act 1956. In *Kenji Tamiya, in re,*[10] the Bombay High Court relieved the Japanese directors who were not connected with the day-to-day affairs of the company and they were directors by virtue of share holding of their parent company. It is clear that the director must be in-charge of the affairs of the company at the time of committing the breach of duty.

7 (1942)12 Comp Cas 102 (Mad).
8 See also *Official Liquidator, Navarashtra Publishing Co. Ltd. (In Liquidation)* v *Ashok Kumar* (1976)46 Comp Cas 572 (Pat).
9 (2002)108 Comp Cas 1 (Mad).
10 (1990)68 Comp Cas 142 (Bom).

If a director cause his company to lend money without ensuring that the lending was at commercial rate of interest it constitute a breach of duty. It is not a *bona fide* exercise of fiduciary duty.[11]

Again, the Delhi High Court in *In Re, Beejay Engineers Private Limited,* and *In Re Satinder Sandhu,*[12]has held that the circumstances of a person being on board of directors on account of his special skill and expertise is a relevant factor in deciding whether he has acted honestly and reasonably, but it is *per-se* no ground for exonerating him from liability on account of negligence, breach of duty, misfeasance or breach of trust etc. s. 201 renders void any provision in the company's articles or in any agreement which excludes liability for negligence, default, misfeasance, breach of duty or breach of trust. One must look to see whether there are reasons of policy for saying that a director does not owe a duty of care to the company. The concept of negligence which depends ultimately upon a general public sentiment of moral wrongdoing for which the offender must pay can be adopted to measure appropriately in the given case whether the acts or omission of an entrepreneur are negligent.

6.4 Liability for breach of warranty of authority

A director is not personally liable for his company's failure to perform a contract which he has made on its behalf. But he is liable in damages to a person with whom he purports to make a contract which is not binding on his company at all. When a director is negotiating or contracting with a company, he impliedly represents to the other party that he has the authority to bind the company as its agent. If he lacks his authority, he is guilty of a breach of warranty of authority when the contract is *ultra vires* the company.[13]

In order to make the director liable, the representation must be one of fact, and not of law. A director was held liable where he negotiated a loan to his company which resulted in exceeding the limits of his borrowing powers fixed by company's memorandum. The effect of the transaction was that the director impliedly represented to the lender as a matter of fact that the company was not exceeding its borrowing powers by borrowing from him.[14] Directors are liable if they induce

11 *Knight* v *Frost* [1999]1 BCLC 364 (Ch D).
12 (1983)53 Comp Cas 918 (Del).
13 *Weeks* v *Propert* [1873] LR 8 CD 427.
14 *Firbank's Executors* v *Humphrey* [1886]18 QBD 54 (CA).

the company's bank to honour cheques signed by one of them when no resolution has been passed by the board authorizing the signatory to issue cheques. The directors impliedly represent to the bank that such a resolution has been passed.[15] If the directors misrepresent the powers of their company or of its board of directors to a person who deals with the company, they will be liable for breach of warranty of authority. The directors were held personally liable for accepting a bill of exchange in the company's name when the company itself had no power to do so by its memorandum.[16]

The court in *Iron and Hardware (India) Co.* v *Sham Lal and Bros.,*[17] held that to succeed a claim for compensation for an alleged breach of a warranty of the contract if the petitioner-contractor disputes it the respondent-purchaser has to prove (*i*) that there was in law a breach of contract on the part of the contractor and (*ii*) that as a result of that breach, the particular amount claimed was suffered by the purchaser by way of damages. Until these two conditions are fulfilled the claim for damages remains only a right to sue for damages and not a claim in the sense of being a debt recoverable from the contractor. Such a right is an indeterminate claim and not a chose in action assignable in law. Chagla, CJ (as he then was) said:

> It is well settled that when there is a breach of contract the only right that accrues to the person who complains of the breach is the right to file a suit for recovering damages. The breach of contract does not give rise to any debt and therefore it has been held that a right to recover damages is not assignable because it is not a chose in action. An actionable claim can be assigned, but in order that there should be an actionable claim there must be a debt in the sense of an existing obligation. But inasmuch as a breach of contract does not result in any existing obligation on the Part of the person who commits the breach, the right to recover damages is not an actionable claim and cannot be assigned.[18]

15 *Cherry and M'Dougall* v *Colonial Nank of Australia* [1896]38 LIPC 49.
16 *West London Commercial Bank* v *Kitson* [1884]13 QBD 360.
17 AIR 1954 Bom 423.
18 See also *Marwar Tent Factory* v *Union of India* AIR 1975 Del 27; 1974 RLR 218.

6.5 Liability in contracts

Directors' civil liability stems from the violation of a legal or contractual duty to protect the interests of the company, the shareholders, the company's creditors and third parties. Directors are bound to use fair and reasonable diligence in discharging the duties and to act honestly, and act with such care as is reasonably expected from him, having regard to his knowledge and experience. It includes entering into contracts and other transactions the directors will be personally liable if they contract in their own names without disclosing that they are acting on behalf of the company. If the directors' acted beyond their powers, they will be personally liable in damages, where their acts do not bind or are not ratified by the company.[19] Directors are liable to a third person for breach of warranty of authority if they contract with him outside their powers. A director is liable if he negotiates a loan to his company which results in it exceeding the limits of its borrowing powers as fixed by memorandum of association.[20] They are also liable if they induce company's bank to honour cheques signed by one of the director where no resolution has been passed by the board to authorize him to issue cheques.[1]

A director is personally not liable under a contract which is lawful and which made with proper authority. In *Elkington & Co* v *Hurter*,[2] where an accountant was appointed for the company by its director cum majority shareholder and he subsequently acting as a director removed the accountant. It was held that the director was not liable to compensate the accountant because he had acted only as an officer of the company.[3]

While negotiating a contract for his company, a director should make it clear to the other party that the contract will be entered into by the company and not by the director personally. If he does not do this and the other party believes that he is contracting with the director

19 *Sealand of the Pacific* v *Robert C. McHaffie Ltd.* [1974]51 DLR (3d) 702; *Trevor Ivory Ltd* v *Anderson* [1992]2 NZLR 517; *Banfield* v *Johnson* [1994] 7 NZCLC 260, 496; *King* v *Milpurrurru* [1996]136 ALR 327; *Microsoft Corporation* v *Auschina Polaris Pty. Ltd.* [1996-7]142 ALR 111.

20 *Weeks* v *Property* [1873] LR 8 CP 427.

1 Pennington's *Company Law*, 6th Ed. 1990, p. 611.

2 [1892]2 Ch 452.

3 *Schouls* v *Canadian Meat Processing Corporation* [1980-84] LRC (Comm) 778.

or agent and not the company, the contract they conclude will be a personal one and he will be personally liable for the fulfillment of the promises made.[4]

A director of a company is not necessarily an agent of the company or its shareholders. If he acts as an agent he must specifically say so. So where in his written statement a director did not raise such a plea, he is deemed to have acted on his personal capacity. So a suit against him alone is not barred by ss. 230 and 235 of the Contract Act.[5]

It is well established that the onus of showing that a director has not acted honestly in the exercise of his or her powers and the discharge of his or her office is upon the aggrieved party. The point is well established in *Hindle* v *John Cotton Ltd.*[6] where the House of Lords were asked to declare a resolution of the board void. Although the articles gave literal power to do what had been done, the House of Lords nonetheless granted the order sought. In doing so, Viscount Finlay outlined the nature of the task that the court must undertake as the following passage from his celebrated speech to the House of Lords demonstrates:

> Where the question is one of abuse of powers, the state of mind of those who acted, and the motive on which they acted, are all important and you may go into the question of what their intention was, collecting from the surrounding circumstances all the material which genuinely throw light upon that question of the state of mind of directors so as to show whether they were honestly acting in discharge of their powers in the interests of the company or were acting from some bye-motive, possibly of personal advantage, or for any other reason.[7]

In *R.K. Dalmia* v *The Delhi Administration,*[8] it was held that "A director will be personally liable on a company contract when he has accepted personal liability either expressly or impliedly. Directors are the agents or the trustees of a company".

Express liability will usually arise only when a director has personally guaranteed the performance of a contract. Implied liability

4 *Bridges & Salmon Ltd.* v *The Swan (Owners)* [1968]1 Lloyds Rep 5.
5 *Raja Ram Jaiswal* v *Ganesh Parshad* AIR 1959 All 29.
6 (1919)56 SC LR 625.
7 (1919)56 SC LR 625 at 630-631.
8 AIR 1962 SC 1821; (1963)1 SCR 253.

will arise when a director signs a contract for the Company or mentioning the name but failing to add the vital word 'limited' or its abbreviation. This rule rests on the ordinary principle of agency that where an agent enters into a contract without disclosing that he is acting as agent he accepts personal liability. In the case of *Penrose* v *Martyr,*[9] case a company secretary accepted a bill of exchange drawn on a limited company. The name of the company was as written but the company secretary omitted the words 'limited', held to be personally liable by the Court of Exchequer Chamber.

An agreement between directors of one company for sale of shares to the directors of another company in their individual capacity was held to be not enforceable by one company against the other.[10] In *Nadgerhill Properties Ltd.* v *Cottrel,*[11] it was held that while all the contracts for services were made in the name of the companies trading under their trade names and the director sought to be made liable merely appended his name to authenticate the contracts on behalf of the companies, he could not be held personally liable. There will be no liability if there is a clause in the contract imposing personal liability on the director. Such a clause will not bind unless his attention was drawn by the other party to the contract to such an onerous and unusual clause.[12] Even an informal undertaking to pay the company's debts may make the director liable.[13] It was held in *Davis* v *Temco* that the extent of contractual liability will depend upon the wording of the contract.[14]

If, having requisite authority, directors make a contract professedly for and on behalf of the company, then the company only is liable for it; if they have no authority to make the contract on behalf of the company, they are still not personally liable on the contract, although they may be liable for damages for breach of an implied warranty of authority. The directors who have duly acted on behalf of the company are not personally liable to the contracting party even if the company's failure to carry out the contract is due to the fault of the directors. Only in the case of a fraud, can the directors be held personally liable.

9 [1858] EB & E 499.
10 *Raj Cylinders & Containers* v *Hindustan General Industries P. Ltd.* (1999)33 CLA 327.
11 [1991] BCLC 805 (CA).
12 *Montgomery Litho Ltd.* v *Maxwell* 2000 Scot Cases 56 (HL Scot).
13 *Paulger* v *Butland Industries Ltd.* [1989]3 NZLR 549.
14 1992 CLY 2064.

Whatever the extent to which either the company's memorandum and articles of association or resolutions of the shareholders may seek to impose limitations on a director's powers, the directors can bind the company, or authorize others to do so, by entering into a contract with a *bona fide* third party.

The contract will be binding on the company. To balance this, the directors may be held personally liable for any loss caused to the company as a result of the unauthorized transaction. The directors' actions can be ratified by a separate, special resolution of the shareholders, which will relieve the directors from liability.

If a director is actually a party or associated with a party to a contract with the company, and the directors have exceeded their powers, the company can avoid the contract, and require the director to account for his gain or indemnify the company for any loss it has suffered. Any director who authorized the transaction (whether or not a party to the contract) will be so liable.

The civil liability of directors can be summarized as follows:

(1) The directors' liability implies the violation of legal or contractual duties, above all the duty of care.

(2) Where an unlawful fact exists, the director is assumed to be guilty of improper conduct; accordingly it is up to the director to prove that his action has not been improper.

(3) Liability to creditors exists only in case of violation of a legal or contractual provision intended to protect the creditors' interests.

(4) The directors are liable for others actions and the liability are joint and several.

6.6 Liability in torts

If a company commits any wrongful act, injury or damage to somebody, a director of a company is personally liable in damages for a tortious[15]

15 Tort means harm or wrong. This French word derives from Latin *tortus*, meaning twisted or crooked. Tort is a wrongful act for which damages can be obtained in a civil court by the person wronged. The law of tort is mainly concerned with providing compensation for personal injury and property damage caused by negligence. It also protects other interests, however, such as reputation, personal freedom, title to property, enjoyment of property, and commercial interests.

act committed by the company. A tort is a civil wrong recognized by courts even though it may not be contemplated under statute, and for which the injured party may seek damages. Directors are not personally liable for torts committed in a corporate context unless their conduct itself is tortious.[16]

It is difficult to distinguish between the tort of the corporation and the tort of the director because directors control a corporation's managerial policy and public activities, and director's intentions and state of mind are attributed to the corporation. While the essence of corporate personality is that a director's acts are the corporation's acts, rendering the corporation primarily liable, both English and Italian law recognize that each person should be responsible for his own torts. Thus, whether and to what extent a director is jointly liable with the corporation when his actions cause a tortious injury to a third party depends on whether there has been an actual assumption of personal responsibility.[17]

In Winfield and Jolowicz on *Tort*,[18] the general principle is summarized thus: "Because the company is a separate legal person, its directors are not, apart from statute personally liable on contracts made by the company, nor for torts of company servants for which the company is vicariously liable. To identify the director with the company would be too great a brake on commercial enterprise and adventure, however, small the company and however powerful the control of the director. Nevertheless, where directors order an act by the company which amounts to a tort, they may be liable as joint tort feasors on the ground that they have procured the wrong to be done."

The last sentence in the above paragraph is an exception to the principle stated in the earlier part of the paragraph. Accordingly, where a director orders or instructs a particular act to be done by the company, and in obedience of the order or instructions a servant of the company does it and such an act causes loss, injury or damage, it will be tort for which the concerned director will be personally liable.

16 *ADGA Systems International Ltd.* v *Valcom Ltd., et al.* [1999]43 OR (3rd) 101 (CA). See also *ScotiaMcLeod et al.* v *Peoples Jewelers Limited et al.* [1996]26 OR (3d) 481 (CA), p. 491.

17 Sabrina Bruno, *Personal Liability of Corporate Directorsunder English Common Law and Italian Civil Law*, 2 UC Davis, J Int'l L & Policy 37.

18 13th Ed., p. 676.

English case law generally reflects an inductive method of reasoning to impose personal liability on directors, emphasizing that each decision depends upon specific relevant facts and involves policy considerations. English courts rarely impose tortious liability on directors toward third parties and typically limit liability to cases of 'physical damage' to persons or property. The basic principle is that "a director as such is not personally liable for the tortious acts of the corporation; he is only liable if he has acted in such a way to take upon himself the dealing which had constituted the wrongful act".[19] The court in *White Horse Distillers Ltd.* v *Gregson Assoc. Ltd.*, termed personal liability for directors "irrational" when imposed merely on the basis of express or implied direction or procurement of the tortious conduct.[20]

The decision of the Court of Appeal in *Williams* v *Natural Life Health Foods Ltd.,*[1] suggests that the balance may be now having shifted against individual liability. The case arose out of a franchise agreement under which the plaintiffs set up a health food shop in Rugby. The franchiser was the first defendant company formed by one Mr. Mistlin who successfully runs a similar shop in Salisbury. He prepared the business projections and the plaintiff proceeded on the good income projections. The projections found to be inaccurate and the shop wound up within 18 months with substantial loss to the plaintiff.

The plaintiff alleged that the projections were made inaccurately and negligently and sought damages from the company. A personal claim was brought against Mr. Mistlin, alleging that he owed a personal duty of care in respect of the projections. In the High Court Langley, J accepted that the projections had been prepared negligently and held the company to be in breach of duty to the plaintiffs.[2] The court held that even though Mr. Mistlin, had not prepared the projections directly, was to be taken to have assumed personal responsibility. But

19 *Singer & Co. Ltd.* v *D.E. Foulkes & Co. Ltd.* (1931) 75 (2) Solic, J 603. In that case the plaintiffs, motor-car manufacturers, claimed damages for the wrongful conversion of a car against two directors and the corporation, a motor-car dealer. The Court held that one of the directors was liable because he knew exactly the situation, having signed the agreement with the plaintiffs and authorized the salesman to carry out the sale.

20 1984 Rep Privy Council 61. See also *Hoover P.L.C.* v *George Hulme (Stockport) Ltd.* [1982]8 Fort Solic Rep 565.

1 [1997]1 BCLC 131.

2 [1996]1 BCLC 288.

the court clearly said that the mistake is of personal liability to be incurred.[3]

Lord Steyn held that he had not first, contrary to the majority view in the Court of Appeal, the mere fact that the relevant experience upon which the company gave advice was acquired by Mistlin in his personal capacity did not lead to the inference that Mistlin as director had personally assumed responsibility.[4] The assumption of personal responsibility and under what circumstances is crucial of fixing the liability. The defendant must have been relied upon the advice for fixing personal liability. The mere fact that the defendant is the managing director of the company is not sufficient to fix the personal liability.

However, a director is not automatically liable for torts of the company irrespective of the size of the company or of the degree of his control over its affairs. There is no general requirement that a director would be liable for torts committed by a company only if he has acted recklessly or with the knowledge that the acts are tortious. If the directors order amounts to a trespass, he would be personally liable regardless of whether or not he was aware that his order would give rise to a trespass.[5] Directors are liable in tort for negligently causing loss to a person with whom the company has entered into a contract, if the circumstance imposes a personal duty on the directors toward that person to act with proper skill or care.[6] In *Hale* v *Guildarch,* it was held that an employee or director would be personally liable for activities carried out on behalf of the company if there was proof of assumption of personal responsibility.[7] In the *PLG Research Ltd.* v *Ardon International Ltd.,* in a patent infringement case, where it was held that a director would not be liable unless his involvement would be such as to render him liable as a joint tortfeasor.[8]

Some cases establish that if a director of a company gives instructions for the commission of a tort by the company, the director may be

3 [1997]1 BCLC 131 (153), per Hirst, LJ.
4 In Lord Steyn's view, the Court of Appeal's point that, because Mistlin's experience was derived personally he must have assumed responsibility, "will simply not bear the weight put upon it". *Ibid.,* 838.
5 *Evans (C) Ltd.* v *Spritebrand Ltd. and Sullivan* [1985] BCLC 105.
6 *Fairline Shipping Corpn.* v *Adamson* [1974]2 All ER 967.
7 [1999] PNLR 44 (UK).
8 [1993] FSR 197.

personally liable in damages to the injured party for the tort although the tort was the act of the company. If a director authorizes an employee of the company to do something which is a tortious act, the directors will be liable for the consequences. A director may be held personally liable for damage caused by the tortious act of the company, if he had given instructions for the act to be done by an employee of the company or any other...[9]

While company law places the liability exclusively on the artificial corporate entity, the law of torts imposes liability on the director as the actual tortfeasor. In order to make the director is to be personally liable, some additional factor beyond the bare commission of the tortious act.[10] While more recently the courts have relied upon a notion of an assumption of personal responsibility.[11]

In *Cameron* v *Kenyon Connell, etc. Co.* (Mont.), a corporation stored in its warehouse a large quantity of explosives, contrary to a State statute. By an explosion of such material, plaintiff's intestate was killed. In an action against the corporation and its directors, it was held, that the directors, though ignorant of the excessive amount of explosives on storage, were personally liable, if in the exercise of ordinary diligence as directors they could have known the true situation.[12]

Directors as such are not liable for the torts or civil wrongs of their company. To make a person liable for a tort, e.g. for negligence, trespass, nuisance or defamation it must be shown that he was himself the wrongdoer or that he was the employer or principal of the wrongdoer in relation to the act complained of, or that the tort was committed on his instructions.[13] The effective control or owner of the company

9 The Financial Express, 16th April 2006.

10 Generally, see F.M.B. Reynolds, *Bowstead and Reynolds on Agency,* 16th Ed., (London: Sweet & Maxwell 1996), para 9-114.

11 *Trevor Ivory Ltd* v *Anderson* [1992]2 NZLR 517. The Court of Appeal in Williams adopted this approach, and it is arguable that this was the approach taken by Kerr, J in *Fairline Shipping Corporation* v *Adamson* [1975] QB 180.

12 56 Pac 358. See also Notes and Cases, "*Corporations Torts. Liability of Directors*", The Virginia Law Register, Vol. 5, No. 1 (May, 1899), p. 53.

13 In *Trevor Ivory Ltd.* v *Anderson.* In his Honour's view, a director is not personally liable for torts committed on behalf of the company because of the combined effect of the company's separate existence and the doctrinal process by which the company acts. While directors may act as the agents of the company, in appropriate circumstances the directors' actions, knowledge and intention will be directly attributed to the company and treated as if

is insufficient rather directly involved in the committal of tort.[14] The test for personal liability was whether the director had himself assumed a duty of care to the third party, actual or imputed, and that depended on the particular facts.[15] But in the case of deceit, it does not require the existence of a special relationship between the claimant and the alleged tortfeasor. An agent making a statement knowingly that it was false is a tort on the part of the agent.[16] The directors are liable under civil and criminal law for any mis-statement in the prospectus, and also shall be liable to pay compensation to every person who subscribes for any securities on the faith of the prospectus for any loss or damage he may have sustained by reason of any untrue statement.[17] If a director of a company is fraudulently inducing anybody to invest money based on any deceptive, misleading or dishonest concealment of material facts, he shall be punishable under the Act.

The Madras High Court's judgment in *In re Peerdan Juharmal Bank Ltd. (In liquidation),*[18] it has been held that the proceedings taken under s. 235 of the Companies Act 1913, against a director of a banking company, ordered to be wound up, cannot be continued after his death, and the liability if any of such a director cannot be enforced against his legal representative in those proceedings.

But other courts are of the view that the cause of action against the legal representatives of the directors survived as being laid not on tort but on a breach of trust. The directors of a company are trustees for the company and not for the individual shareholders thereof, and with reference to their powers of employing the funds of the company and for misuse of the power they could be rendered liable as trustees and, on their death, the cause of action survived against their legal

they were the acts, knowledge and intention of the company itself. The special treatment of directors thus arises because the tortious act is not that of the director, but of the company itself. [1992]2 NZLR 517 (526-527). J. Farrar, *The Personal Liability of Directors for Corporate Torts'* [1997]9 Bond LR 102 (108); R. Grantham, *Company Directors and Tortious Liability* [1997] CLJ 259 (262).

14 *Thomas Saunders Partnership* v *Harvey* [1990]30 Con Lr 103.
15 *Treveor Ivory Ltd.* v *Anderson* [1992]2 NZLR 517.
16 *Williams* v *Natural Life Health Foods Ltd.* [1998]1 BCLC 689.
17 Sections 62 and 63 of the Companies Act 1956.
18 (1958)28 Comp Cas 546; AIR 1958 Mad 583.

representatives. The maxim *actio personalis moritur cum persona* does not apply to a liquidator's claim against the legal representatives of a deceased director of a banking company where the foundation of the liability is not laid on tort but laid on a breach of a fiduciary relationship, the failure to perform duties undertaken by a director who is in the position of a trustee.[19]

If a director unfairly diverts the funds of the company for extraneous purposes, the court can order for repayment of the amount to the company not only against the directors, former directors and third parties those who have involved in the unlawful diversion.[20]

In Palmer's *Company Law*, 23rd Ed., in the Chapter dealing with the 'Liability of Directors to Outsiders', it is expressed:

> Any director who is a party to a fraud or to the commission of any other tort is personally liable to the injured party. This is on the principle that whoever commits a wrong is liable for it himself, and nonetheless so that he was acting as an agent or servant on behalf, and for the benefit, of another; for the contract of agency or service cannot impose any obligation on the agent or servant to commit, or assist in the committing of, fraud or any other wrong. The company may also be liable, but that does not exonerate the director. So, too, if, by the order of the directors, a trespass is committed, a patent infringed, or another wrongful act committed, the directors who are parties to it are personally liable. If more than one person is concerned in the commission of a wrong, the person wronged has his remedy against all, or any one or more of them, at this choice; for every wrong-doer is jointly and severally liable for the whole damage, and it does not matter whether they acted as between themselves as equals, or one of them as agent or servant of another.

In *Santanu Ray* v *Union of India*,[1] the court held that after the veil of the corporate entity is lifted, the adjudicating authorities will determine as to which of the Directors is concerned with the evasion of the excise duty by reason of fraud, collusion or wilful mis-statement or suppression of facts, or contravention of the provisions of the Act

19 *Official Liquidator* v *Dr. Sailendra Nath Sinha* (1973)43 Comp Cas 107 (Cal).

20 *Lowe* v *Fahey* [1996]1 BCLC 262 (Ch D).

1 (1988)18 ECC 51; (1988)19 ECR 257 (Del); (1988)3 Comp LJ 259.

and the Rules made there under. So far as individual liability of a Director to the payment of excise duty and penalty is concerned, no liability can be fastened on him unless the department is able to show as to how and to what extent a particular Director is liable.

The court discussed the personal liability of the director in action for tort in *Hrushikesh Panda* v *Indramani Swain*,[2] it was held that:

> Under the Company Law, in addition to their statutory duties, the directors owe to their company fiduciary duties similar to those owed by an agent to his principal. These duties are owed exclusively to the company of which the defendant is a director.
>
> An action against a defaulting director may be brought by the company itself or where the breach of duty complained of is a breach of fiduciary duty by a member suing in a derivative action on behalf of himself and all other members of the company, his liability for breach of fiduciary duty by misfeasance proceedings in the company's winding up is well known. But directors owe no fiduciary or contractual duties nor any duty of care to persons who deal with their company unless they deal with the contracting party not on behalf of the company but on their own behalf. A director is therefore not liable to pay the debts incurred by the company. Even during the course of winding up proceeding of a company, the directors may be made personally liable by order of the court only if they are found guilty of fraudulent trading, i.e. an act of misfeasance or the like. Directors are not liable for breach of contracts by the company and the other party to a contract cannot make them directly liable by suing them in tort even for their mismanagement of the company's affairs. The liability of the directors even in common law is confined only where they have been guilty of a tort toward the creditors as well as breach of duty owed to the company. Consequently, directors are personally liable to persons who lend money to the company only if they obtain the loan by fraudulent misrepresentations. It is, therefore, obvious that directors are generally immune from liability to creditors of their company.

Finally the court held that no personal liability is attached to the appellant in his individual capacity, and the executing court was,

2 AIR 1987 Ori 79; 1987 Ori LR 62.

therefore, right in holding that the personal properties of the appellant could not be attached.

6.7 Liability in company's debts

Are company directors personally liable for their company's debts and loans? This is vexed question that often bothers directors, especially non-executive directors. Limited liability is the most cardinal attribute and privilege of a company. It is this celebrated principle that limits the liability of a shareholder of a company towards his company and also towards its creditors. There is no provision in the Companies Act making the managing director of a company personally liable for the company's debts. Such liability will turn upon the application of agency principle to the transaction in question.[3] The court affirmed an earlier judgment in *Surinder Nath Khosla* v *Excise and Taxation Commissioner Punjab.*[4] It was held that unless the statute in question made the managing director of a company personally liable for the dues recoverable from the company, he could not be held personally responsible. The court also observed that neither in the company law nor in the Industrial Disputes Act 1947 does any provision making the managing director personally liable for recovery of dues against the limited company exist. This position was upheld in *Tikam Chand Jain* v *State Government of Haryana.*[5]

The Punjab & Haryana High Court in *H.S. Sidana* v *Rajesh Enterprises,*[6] held that where a decree was obtained against the managing director and the company, the managing director was not to be proceeded against unless there was proof that he was to be personally liable under the circumstances relating to the debt. The court observed that the discharge of amount, arrears of rent was that of the company and not of its managing director. The attachment of his property for this purpose was held to be not permissible.[7]

On incorporation, a company acquires its own independent personality distinct from the members constituting it and becomes a legal person in the eyes of law. The members of the company are not joint or part owners of the company or its property unlike in the case

3 *Kundan Singh* v *Moga Transport Co. P. Ltd.* (1987)62 Comp Cas 600 (P&H).
4 (1964)15 STC 838 (P&H).
5 (1987)62 Comp Cas 601 (P&H); (1987)67 STC 388 (P &H).
6 (1993)77 Comp Cas 251.
7 *Kuriakose* v *P.K.V Group Industries* (2002)111 Comp Cas 826.

of partnership which does not acquire a separate legal entity distinct from its partners. Hence, the shareholders of a company are not personally liable for the company's debts either. The debts of the company are its own independent debts like the property and assets of the company, which are its own.

Section 322 of the Act provides that in a limited company, the liability of the directors or of any director or manager may, if so provided by the memorandum, be unlimited. The expression 'limited company' is defined in s. 2(23) of the Act as a company limited by shares or limited by guarantee. Section 12 of the Act, which lays down the mode of forming an incorporated company, provides for the incorporation of, among other things, two types of companies, namely, (1) a company limited by shares, and (2) a company limited by guarantee. That section also, explains those two types, the common factor being limited liability. It is thus clear that liability referred to in s. 322 is the liability contemplated by s. 12, i.e. liability of a member of a limited company for the company's debt, as explained above. The only difference is that while liability referred to in section is the liability of members of a company towards the company's debts, liability contemplated by s. 322 is the liability of directors of a company for the company's debts.

Limited liability means the status of being legally responsible only to a limited amount for debts of a trading company. Unlike proprietorships and partnerships, in a limited company the liability of the members in respect of the company's debts is limited. In other words, the liability of the members of a company is limited to the extent of the face value of shares taken up by them. The liability may be limited by shares, in which case the liability of the members on a winding-up is limited to the amount (if any) unpaid on their shares, or alternatively by guarantee. In the latter case, the liability of members if limited by the memorandum to a certain amount, which the members undertake to contribute on winding-up. These are usually societies, clubs, or trade associations. An exception to this rule is when the members of the company voluntarily agree to take unlimited liability. This proposition of law applies to directors of a company. Directors, being agents of the company are, therefore, not personally liable for contracts purporting to bind their company, provided, of course, contracts are made by them for and on behalf of the company.

The managing director of a company who executed the documents for obtaining cash credit facility form a bank on behalf of the company would not incur any personal liability for the loan obtained by the company. He may not be a necessary party to a suit by the bank against the company.[8] However, directors are personally liable to persons who lend money to the company if they obtain the loan through fraudulent means.[9]

In a loan transaction of the company, it was held in *Indian Overseas Bank* v *R.M. Marketing & Services P. Ltd.,*[10] that the directors who had not given any personal guarantee for the loan could not be made liable merely because they were directors. The company is as much a separate entity from shareholders as from directors. Where a director guaranteed his company's debts, it was held that the director's guarantee would cover that debt also. The terms of the guarantee also covered the contingent liability for the holding company for the debts of its subsidiary as these liabilities crystallized.[11]

The position is clear that in such circumstances the director is liable. "Even where a director consciously enters into a guarantee there is room for him being confused as to the degree of his exposure. The case indicates a potential trap for directors of subsidiary companies. Here such a director knowingly guaranteed the debts of the company of which he was a director, but unfortunately, because of a failure to appreciate the complexities of the guarantee document, he did not realize that he was guaranteeing the obligations of the whole group". The guaranteeing directors cannot say that the creditor should first proceed against the borrowing company. The borrower and guarantor are equally liable by virtue of the provisions in ss. 126 and 128 of the Contract Act 1872.[12]

In *Indian Overseas Bank* v *A.B. Senan,*[13] the bank granted a temporary overdraft to a company for the purpose of meeting its working capital requirements. The advance was granted on the strength

8 *Bank of Maharashtra* v *Racmann Auto Pvt. Ltd.* (1992)74 Comp Cas 752 (755) (Del).

9 *Hrushikesh Panda* v *Indramani Swain* (1998)63 Comp Cas 368 (372) (Ori).

10 (2001)107 Comp Cas 696 (Del).

11 *Bank of Scotland* v *Wright* [1991] BCLC 224 (QBD).

12 *Tripati Plywood Products P. Ltd.* v *Pradeshik Industrial Investment Corpn. of U.P. Ltd.* (1998)29 CLA 67 (All).

13 (1999)96 Comp Cas 839 (Ker).

of a specific undertaking or promise made by the managing director and a director, to liquidate within one month the entire outstanding in the account including costs and expenses. A decree passed against the director and the managing director personally was held to be justified.

If a bank guarantee is made by directors and retire after some time and the new directors are also signed the guarantee bond and there was no agreement to show that the earlier guarantee had ceased to be operative it was held that all directors including retired directors were liable jointly and severally under the guarantee.[14]

Supreme Court in the matter of *A.K. Kripak* v *Union of India,*[15] and in the context of project oriented financing, taking of any personal guarantee and or collateral or any such security is lacking authority of any statute on the part of Banks/FIs. The banks and public financial institutions have unilaterally and arbitrarily developed a practice, without the authority of law, to execute personal guarantee agreements with the directors of a company to secure the debts of the company. The court held that the banks have developed the practice to execute personal guarantee agreements with the directors of a company to secure the debts of the company without the authority of law. This practice is against the principle of limited liability of the shareholders as well as directors of the company as provided in the Companies Act 1956.[16]

Can a company's monetary liability be fastened to the directors and they called upon to discharge the company's liability, e.g., liability towards tax arrears or to its creditors, if the company fails to discharge such liability? The plain answer is no. Where a company fails to discharge its liability, be it by way of taxes or other statutory liabilities, or other dues, can the directors be made personally liable for such dues and accordingly proceeded with, is indeed an important question which often times arises with increasing instances of corporate enterprises failing to discharge such liabilities.

Under the Income Tax Act 1961, where any tax due from a private company in respect of any income of any previous year cannot be

14 *Bank of Baroda* v *Official Liquidator* (1992)73 Comp Cas 688 (MP).
15 AIR 1970 SC 150.
16 *Karnataka State Financial Corporation* v *N. Narasimahaiah* 2008 AIOL 348 Civil Appeal No. 610-612 of 2004 decided on 13/03/2008.

recovered from such private company, then, every person who was a Director of such private company at any time during the relevant previous year is liable, jointly and severally, for the payment of such tax. But they can escape the liability if he can prove that there is no such negligence, misfeasance or breach of duty from his part.

As a corollary of the doctrine of corporate personality having an independent entity, neither the shareholders nor the directors of a company can be called upon to discharge the company's tax liability nor can tax arrears due from the company be recovered from the directors personally. Criminal liability of directors for company's failure to pay taxes is one thing, but recovery of the company's tax dues from them is quite another thing.[17] The retired director cannot escape from such liability of guarantees of his company's overdraft.[18]

The Delhi High Court considered the question of liability of directors in recovery of money by lifting the corporate veil in *Saurabh Exports* v *Blaze Fin Lease and Credits (P) Ltd.,*[19] the plaintiff had filed a suit for recovery of ₹ 21,00,650 against the defendant company and its directors jointly and severally. The defendant Nos. 2 and 3 stated that the company is almost defunct and they denied the liability on the ground that there is no personal liability on their part as the deposit was received in the name of the defendant No. 1, the company. The liability of the company was not disputed. Defendant No. 4 has denied the liability on the ground that it had nothing to do with the transaction in question as he was neither a director nor a shareholder of defendant No. 1 company. The court held that D4 was not a director of the company at the time of transaction,[20] even though he had signed a document on behalf of the company when accepting loan or deposit. Hence, D4 was not liable for the transaction. The court also observed that D3 is only a housewife and no standing or say in the affairs of the company.

The defendant counsel argues that the corporate veil is liable to be lifted as a view to the contrary would amount to a premium on the fraud which has been played by the defendants on the plaintiff.[1] Lifting

17 *The Financial Express*, 27th November 2005.
18 *M.R. Lakshmi Narayanan* v *Syndicate Bank* (2000)99 Comp Cas 87 (Mad).
19 (2006)133 Comp Cas 495 (Del).
20 The court found that he is the husband of defendant No. 3.
1 *Singer India Ltd.* v *Chander Mohan Chadha* (2004)122 Comp Cas 468 (SC); (2004)7 SCC 1.

the corporate veil is necessary when the existence of dualism between the corporation and company on the one hand and its members or shareholders on the other.[2] The counsel argued that the present company is a family company and the directors cannot escape personal liability at the guise of corporate liability. The court referred to Gower, *Principles of Modern Company Law*[3] and Pennington's *Company Law*, 5th Ed. 1985, p. 53, which states that "where the protection of public interests is of paramount importance or where the company has been formed to evade obligations imposed by the law", the court will disregard the corporate veil.....

> "The concept of corporate entity was evolved to encourage and promote trade and commerce but not to commit illegalities or to defraud people. Where, therefore, the corporate character is employed for the purpose of committing illegality or for defrauding others, the court would ignore the corporate character and will look at the reality behind the corporate veil so as to enable it to pass appropriate orders to do justice between the parties concerned..."[4]

The court held that in the present case, the corporate veil must be lifted especially taking into consideration that D1 is a family arrangement of the defendants. The test of lifting the corporate veil cited in *Aron Salomon* v *Salomon and Co. Ltd.*[5] case was satisfied in this case. The court observed that the concept of corporate entity was evolved to encourage and promote trade and commerce, but not to defraud people. In the present case the plaintiff is sought to be defrauded of an amount of ₹ 15 Lakhs under the cloak of a corporate entity of D1, the company, the corporate veil must be lifted to fix the liability on family members. The court thus passed a judgment fixing the liability on D1 and D2, jointly and severally.

The Madras High Court considered the question of criminal liability of directors under ss. 138[6] and 142 of the Negotiable Instruments Act

2 *Tata Engg. and Locomotive Co. Ltd* v *State of Bihar* (1964)34 Comp Cas 458 (SC).

3 4th Ed. 1979, p. 137.

4 See *Delhi Development Authority* v *Skipper Construction Co (P) Ltd.* (1997)89 Comp Cas 362 (SC).

5 [1897] AC 22.

6 Section 138 of the Negotiable Instruments Act 1881 provides that dishonour of cheque for insufficiency, etc., of funds in the account. Where any cheque drawn by a person on an account maintained by him with a banker for

1881 and its synchronization with s. 446 of the Companies Act[7] in *Counter Point Advertising (P) Ltd.* v *Haritha Finance Ltd. & TVS Finance and Services Ltd.*[8] In this case the cheques were returned with the endorsement "account freezed." The defendants were argues that they could not be prosecuted as the entire administration of the company was taken up by the official liquidator on winding up of the company and the cheques were returned with the endorsement "account freezed," it would not amount to return of the cheque for insufficiency of funds in the accounts of the petitioner.

The court held that the company has issued shares for the existing liability was bound to see that the cheques were honoured at any cost. The negotiable instruments act is a special legislation which overrides the provisions of the Companies Act, the legal liability contemplated under s. 446 of the Companies Act does not synchronize with the criminal proceedings under the Negotiable Instruments Act and the personal criminal liability and not the civil liability of the company is

---

payment of any amount of money to another person from out of that account for the discharge, in whole or in part, of any debt or other liability, is returned by the bank unpaid, either because of the amount of money standing to the credit of that account is insufficient to honour the cheque or that it exceeds the amount arranged to be paid from that account by an agreement made with that bank, such person shall be deemed to have committed an offence and shall, without prejudice, to any other provision of this Act, be punished with imprisonment for a term which may extended to two years, or with fine which may extend to twice the amount of the cheque, or with both:

Provided that nothing contained in this section shall apply unless—

(*a*) the cheque has been presented to the bank within a period of six months from the date on which it is drawn or within the period of its validity, whichever is earlier;

(*b*) the payee or the holder in due course of the cheque as the case may be, makes a demand for the payment of the said amount of money by giving a notice, in writing, to the drawer of the cheque, within thirty days of the receipt of information by him from the bank regarding the return of the cheque as unpaid; and

(*c*) the drawer of such cheque fails to make the payment of the said amount of money to the payee or, as the case may be, to the holder in due course of the cheque, within fifteen days of the receipt of the said notice.

Explanation. For the purposes of this section, "debt or other liability" means a legally enforceable debt or other liability.

7 The expression "other legal proceedings" in s. 446 of the Companies Act 1956.

8 (2006)133 Comp Cas 435 (Mad); 2006 Cr LJ 2289.

enforced under s. 138 read with s. 142 of the Negotiable Instruments Act. The company and its directors cannot shrink their criminal liability on the ground that the company was already wound up and the official liquidator had taken charge of the affairs of the company. Proceedings under s. 138 of the Negotiable Instruments Act 1881, can end only in the conviction or at acquittal of the accused in the case and no recovery of any amount covered by the dishonoured cheques can be made in the criminal proceedings under s. 138 of the Negotiable Instruments Act or not in respect of the assets of the company, the proceedings pending in the criminal courts cannot be quashed under s. 446 of the Companies Act.

In *Nitin Kumar* v *NCT of Delhi,* the court held that penal statute attracting vicarious criminal liability must be construed strictly and there must be strict compliance with the statutory provisions before such attracts criminal liability under s. 141 of Negotiable Instruments Act.[9] Hence, the officer who is in charge of the affairs of the company cannot escape liability at the time of commission of the offence.

6.8 Liability for negligent advice

In *William* v *Natural Life Health Foods Ltd. & Mistlin,*[10] the principal question on this appeal was whether a director of a franchisor company

9 Section 141 of the NI Act provides that: *Offences by companies.* (1) If the person committing an offence under section 138 is a company, every person who, at the time the offence was committed, was in charge of, and was responsible to the company for the conduct of the business of the company, as well as the company, shall be deemed to be guilty of the offence and shall be liable to be proceeded against and punished accordingly:

Provided that nothing contained in this sub-section shall render any person liable to punishment if he proves that the offence Was committed without his knowledge, or that he had exercised all due diligence to prevent the commission of such offence.

(2) Notwithstanding anything contained in sub-section (1), where any offence under this Act has been committed by a company and it is proved that the offence has been committed with the consent or connivance of, or is attributable to, any neglect on the part of, any director, manager, secretary or other officer of the company, such director, manager, secretary or other officer shall also be deemed to be guilty of that offence and shall be liable to be proceeded against and punished accordingly.

Explanation. For the purposes of this section—

(*a*) "company" means any body corporate and includes a firm or other association of individuals; and

(*b*) "director", in relation to a firm, means a partner in the firm.

10 [1998]2 All ER 577; [1998]1 WLR 830.

is personally liable to franchisees for loss which they suffered as a result of negligent advice given to them by the franchisor company. The mere statement in the brochure of the company stating that the managing director is responsible for running of the company is not sufficient for personal liability of a company with limited liability.

The House of Lords observed with regard to skill and care of a company director: "great emphasis was placed on the fact that it was made clear to the franchisees that Mr. Mistlin's expertise derived from his experience in running the Salisbury shop for his own account ... Postulate a food expert who over ten years gains experience in advising customers on his own account. Then he incorporates his business as a company and he so advises his customers. Surely, it cannot be right to say that in the new situation his earlier experience on his own account is indicative of an assumption of personal responsibility towards his customers."

The Court held that "... in the present case, liability of the company is dependent on a special relationship with the respondents giving rise to an assumption of responsibility. Mr. Mistlin was a stranger to that particular relationship. He cannot therefore be liable as a joint tortfeasor with the company. If he is to be held liable to the respondents, it could only be on the basis of a special relationship between him and the respondents". Whether there was such an assumption of responsibility was to be determined objectively, so that the primary focus had to be on exchanges or conduct between the director and the franchisees. The test of reliance is not simply reliance in fact, but whether the plaintiffs can reasonably rely on the assumption of responsibility.

The above position was confirmed by the High Court of England in *MGB Printing and Design Ltd* v *Kall Kwik U.K. Ltd.*[11] court held that the franchisor was liable for negligent advice and subsequent loss even if there was disclaimer clause in the cash flow agreement. It highlights that a franchisor may owe its franchisee a duty of care that exists separately from its contractual obligations under the franchise agreement.

In a *New Zealand* case,[12] it was held that "it is no doubt that, in relation to an obligation to give careful and skilful advice, the owner

11 [2010] All ER (D) 18 (Apr).
12 *Trevor Ivory* v *Anderson* [1992]2 NZLR 517 (524).

of a one-man company may assume personal responsibility. Fairline is an analogy. But it seems that something special is required to justify putting a cause in that class". In Fairline case the director was made personally liable for the negligent storage of perishable goods by his company, which was the actual contracting party.[13]

Where a director is deliberately provided wrong information the liability would be in the tort of deceit and where it is done negligently, the liability would be under the principle laid down in *Heldey Byrne & Co. Ltd.* v *Heller & Partners Ltd.*[14]

6.9 Liability for frauds

The more important offences of dishonesty that apply to corporate officers include the offence of dishonesty in the exercise of a power or the discharge of a duty. Fraud is a more serious offence committed by company directors which requires a deliberate disregard of a conscious awareness that what was being done was not in the interests of the company.[15]

The term 'fraud' is generally defined in the law as an intentional misrepresentation of material existing fact made by one person to another with knowledge of its falsity and for the purpose of inducing the other person to act, and upon which the other person relies with resulting injury or damage.[16] The Court of Appeal in *Standard Chartered Bank* v *Pakistan National Shipping Corporation,*[17] held that in an action for deceit against a company officer, it is necessary to show that the officer in question made the statements and the plaintiff relied upon them. There must also be an assumption of responsibility so as to create a special relationship between the plaintiff and defendant director. If the director is used fraudulent misrepresentation for obtaining payment under a letter of credit, the court found that the director was not liable for the deceits, only the company was. The

13 See also, Paul L. Davies and John P. Lowery, *Personal Liability of Directors,* (1998) JBL 573 (UK).

14 [1963]2 All ER 575 (HL).

15 http://www.aic.gov.au/en/publications, visited on 11.05.2012.

16 http://www.lectlaw.com/def/f079.htm, visited on 25.02.2009. Thus, to constitute fraud, a misrepresentation must be false (or an omission must make other statements misleading), and it must be 'material' in the sense that it relates to a matter of some importance or significance rather than a minor or trivial detail.

17 [2000]1 Lloyd's Reports 218; [2000]1 All ER (Comm) 1 (CA).

director assumes no personal liability.[18] In *Leslie Treadwell* v *David Edward Dawkins, Lawtel,*[19] it was held that the directors are liable only in three circumstances. First, where the directors commit the tort themselves, the second is where they assume personal liability and the third is where they do not carry out the tortious act themselves nor they assume liability for it, but they procure and induce the company to commit the tort. Court finally followed the decision in *Standard Chartered Bank* and held that a director who makes a false representation deliberately or recklessly could be personally liable in tort jointly with the company. The court held that the director in question had falsely represented to the victim that funds were in place, and relying on the statement, the latter entered into the building contract and suffered loss.

In *Standard Chartered Bank* v *Pakistan National Shipping Corp. (No. 2)*[20] the House of Lords considered the question, can a person (such as a company director) escape liability for deceit, where he commits a fraud while acting on behalf of another person (such as the company) who is also liable for the fraud?

The company Oakprime Ltd., was the beneficiary of a letter of credit, issued by Incombank and confirmed by Standard Chartered Bank (SCB). The credit was issued in connection with a sale of Iranian bitumen by Oakprime to a Vietnamese organization. Pakistan National Shipping Corporation (PNSC) was the shipping agents and ship owners. A condition of the credit was that shipment would take place by 25th October 1993.

Oakprime were unable to ship the goods by 25th October, but Mr. Mehra, Oakprime's managing director, persuaded PNSC to issue bills of lading before the goods had been shipped. On 9th November Oakprime presented the false bill of lading and other documents to SCB under cover of a letter signed by Mr. Mehra. That letter fraudulently stated that the documents were as required by the credit. SCB, which would not have paid if it had known that the bill of lading had been falsely dated, authorized payment of US$ 1,155,772, even though the documents had been presented late. SCB sought reimbursement from

18 *Williams* v *Natural Life Health Foods Ltd.* [1998]1 WLR 830; [1998]2 All ER 577.

19 3rd July 2000.

20 [2003]1 All ER 173.

Incombank. Although it was unaware of the false dating of the bill of lading, Incombank rejected the documents on account of other discrepancies which SCB had not noticed, and SCB was unable to obtain reimbursement.

SCB then sued PNSC, Oakprime and Mr. Mehra for deceit. The House of Lords held that Mr. Mehra was personally liable for his deceit. While his representation was made on behalf of Oakprime, and relied upon as a representation of Oakprime, it was nevertheless his representation which he knew to be false. It was also relied upon by SCB as being his representation, because otherwise there could have been no representation and no attribution of it to Oakprime. Mr. Mehra was liable for the tort which he had committed.

Different considerations applied to a claim for negligent misstatement. As the House of Lords made clear in *Williams* v *Natural Life Health Foods Ltd*,[1] liability in such a case depends on an assumption of responsibility by the defendant. As with contractual liability, an agent (such as a company director) can assume responsibility on behalf of another person (such as the company) without assuming personal responsibility. This reasoning cannot apply to fraud. Mr. Mehra was not liable by virtue of his position as a director, but because he had himself carried out the acts of deceit. As with the criminal law,[2] a director cannot escape liability simply because his own acts are also sufficient to fix the company with liability.

The House of Lords also held, affirming the judgment of Mummery, J in *Alliance & Leicester Building Society* v *Edgestop Ltd*,[3] that contributory negligence is not a defence to a claim in deceit. While SCB had been negligent in making payment on the documents (because it should not have paid even if the bills of lading had been correct), its damages would not be reduced. There was, however, no trace in the authorities that the negligence of the claimant was a defence to an action for deceit at common law.[4]

1 [1998]2 All ER 577; [1998]1 WLR 830.

2 See *Meridian Global Funds Management Asia Ltd* v *Securities Commission* [1995]3 All ER 918; [1995]2 AC 500; [1995]3 WLR 413.

3 [1994]2 All ER 38.

4 See *Reeves* v *Commissioner of Police of the Metropolis* [2000]3 All ER 897 (915).

As Lord Hoffmann pointed out, a defendant will be liable for misrepresentation (of any kind), even if the claimant could with reasonable diligence have discovered that the representation was false.[5] Indeed, the authorities supported a wider rule. In *Edgington* v *Fitzmaurice*,[6] the directors of a company were liable for fraudulent misrepresentations in a prospectus for the issue of debentures. That the claimant would not have made any investment, if he had not negligently believed that the debentures were secured upon the company's land, did not affect the directors' liability. Lord Hoffmann noted that 'The law simply ignores the other reasons why he paid'. Similarly, while SCB would not have paid under the credit, if it had not negligently believed that it could obtain reimbursement; this was not a defense to its claim in deceit. It is made clear that an individual director cannot escape liability for personal dishonesty by claiming that he or she is acting on behalf of the company. The correctness of the decision was still under academic discussions.

It was held to be a fraud on the part of a director have told an investor as to who was to be a major partner in the project when in fact this was not to be so. Those representations were made dishonestly with the intention of inducing the victims to invest and they suffered loss because but for such representations they would not have gone in for investment. That was no defense to the claim for deceit that the claimants would have discovered the falsity of the representation but failed to do so.[7]

The Indian Companies Act as regards the liability of the directors for misfeasance is s. 235(1), which is in the following terms:

> Where in the course of winding up of a company it appears that any person who has taken part in the formation or promotion of the company, or any past or present director, manager or liquidator, or any officer of the company has misapplied, or retained or become liable or accountable for any money or property of the company, or been guilty of any misfeasance or breach of trust in relation to the company, the Court may, on the application of the liquidator, or of any creditor or contributory made within three years from

5 See, for example, *Redgrave* v *Hurd* [1881-5] All ER Rep 77.

6 [1881-5] All ER Rep 856.

7 *DEG – Deutschc Investigations–und Entwicklungsgeselschaft mbH* v *Koshy* [2002]1 BCLC 478 (Ch D).

the date of the first appointment of a liquidator in the winding up or of the mis-application, retainer, misfeasance or breach of trust, as the case may be, whichever is longer, examine into the conduct of the promoter, director, manager, liquidator, or officer, and compel him to repay or restore the money or property or any part thereof respectively with interest at such rate as the Court thinks just, or to contribute such sum to the assets of the company by way of compensation in respect of the misapplication, retainer, misfeasance or breach of trust as the Court thinks just.

The Indian Courts uniformly hold that misfeasance must be such as would amount to breach of trust in relation to the company and must result in loss to the company. It is necessary that in all cases, loss to the company must be established.[8] Under the 2009 corporate governance code, even the non-executive directors are held liable and can be punished for failure on the part of the company. This includes independent directors as well. But one section of the industry argues for total immunity for the independent directors from criminal action and they view that "vicarious criminal liability" cannot be applied to independent directors.[9] But the Companies Act never defined the liability of independent directors and their responsibility in fraudulent activities of the company and fellow directors. This means that sometime lack of information or ignorance is almost connivance to fraud.[10]

6.10 Liability for insider trading

Insider trading is trading of a corporation's stock or other securities by individuals with potential knowledge or access to non-public information about the company. If any insider of a company like directors, employees, managing director or any other officer who have the non-public access to the information, not taking any advantage of such information is not liable. If such officials are using non-public information for advantage then it is considered as breach of fiduciary

8 *Gopalaswami* v *Krishnaswami* ILR 1941 Mad 120; *National Bank of Upper India, Lucknow* v *Dinanath Sapru* 1 Luck 334; *Connell* v *The Himalaya Bank Ltd.* 18 All 12 and *Bhim Singh* v *Union Bank of India* 8 Lah 167. See also *The Karnataka Films Ltd.* v *The Official Receiver, Madras* AIR 1952 Mad 481; (1951)21 Comp Cas 138 (Mad).

9 http://www.outlookindia.com/printarticle.aspx?266149, visited on 11.02.2012.

10 http://articles.economictimes.indiatimes.com/2011-08-01/news/29838722_1_independent-directors-boards-sebi, visited on 11.02.2012.

duty. Taking advantage of inside information as regards circumstances favourable (such as proposed mergers, and schemes of arrangement, expansion schemes, new contracts acquisitions etc. or such as bad working results or losses. Anyone who misappropriates (steals) information from their employer and trades on that information in any stock (not just the employer's stock) is guilty of insider trading. In simple terms the term 'insider trading' means selling or buying in securities on the basis of price sensitive unpublished information of a listed corporate which if published could to a fall or rise in the prices of shares of the corporate.

In *SEC* v *Texas Gulf Sulphur Co.* (1966), a US Federal Circuit Court stated that anyone in possession of inside information must either disclose the information or refrain from trading.[11] In *Dirks* v *SEC,*[12] the Supreme Court of US considered insider trading.

In this case the petitioner, serving as an officer of a broker-dealer, who specialized in providing investment analysis of insurance company securities to institutional investors, received information from a former officer of an insurance company that its assets were vastly overstated as the result of fraudulent corporate practices, and that various regulatory agencies had failed to act on similar charges made by company employees. Upon petitioner's investigation of the allegations, certain company employees corroborated the fraud charges, but senior management denied any wrongdoing. Neither petitioner nor his firm owned or traded any of the company's stock, but, throughout his investigation, he openly discussed the information he had obtained with a number of clients and investors, some of whom sold their holdings in the company. The Wall Street Journal declined to publish a story on the fraud allegations, as urged by petitioner. After the price of the insurance company's stock fell during petitioner's investigation, the New York Stock Exchange halted trading in the stock. State insurance authorities then impounded the company's records and uncovered evidence of fraud. Only then did the Securities and Exchange Commission (SEC) file a complaint against the company, and only then did the Wall Street Journal publish a story based largely on information assembled by petitioner. After a hearing concerning petitioner's role in the exposure of the fraud, the SEC found that he had aided and abetted violations of the antifraud provisions of the federal securities laws,

11 446 F 2d 1301.
12 463 US 646 (1983).

including § 10(b) of the Securities Exchange Act of 1934 and SEC Rule 10b-5, by repeating the allegations of fraud to members of the investment community who later sold their stock in the insurance company. Because of petitioner's role in bringing the fraud to light, however, the SEC only censured him. On review, the Court of Appeals entered judgment against petitioner.

The court held that receivers of second hand information (tippees) are liable if they had reason to believe that the tipper had breached a fiduciary duty in disclosing confidential information and the tipper received any personal benefit from the disclosure. 'Constructive insiders' who are lawyers, investment bankers and others who receive confidential information form a corporation while providing services to the corporation. They are also liable for insider trading violations of corporations.

Where the directors had committed a breach of their judiciary duties by wrongful use of confidential information and their speculation in the company's shares, it was held that this was a breach of trust and not a breach of contract and therefore there was no limitation period for proceedings against them.[13]

Directors are liable for profits they made on buying or selling the company's share by making use of the confidential information available with them as directors.[14] The question of what is inside information is always under controversy. Any information about the context in which a company operates is to be regarded as inside information. It is further necessary that the information must not have been made public already. The information must also be such that it must be likely to have a significant effect on the price of any securities. The information must potentially have a major impact on the price. If confidential information is used for a takeover bid with the help of directors of the company, it amount to insider trading.[15]

6.11 SEBI (Insider Trading) Regulations 1992 amended in 2000, 2002, 2003, 2007, 2008, 2010 and 2011

The (SEBI) has formulated regulations for preventing and punishing the use of price sensitive unpublished inside information in dealing

13 *Carrian Investments Ltd.* v *Wong* [1987] LRC (Comm) 794.

14 *Diamond* v *Oreamuo* [1969]24 NY 2 & 494 (USA).

15 *Dunford & Elliot Ltd.* v *Johnson & Firth Brown Ltd.* [1976]121 Sol Jo 53.

with the company's securities. Where the directors sold their shares before publishing half-yearly statements and the market went down after the publication because the accounts were not according to expectations, they were held liable to hand over profits to the directors dealing with their own company's shares is not illegal. It is considered desirable that the directors of listed companies should hold the shares of their companies.

The principal regulation was subsequently amended by

(*a*) SEBI (Appeal to Securities Appellate Tribunal) (Amendment) Regulations 2000 vide SO No. 278(E) published in the Gazette of India on 28th March 2000.

(*b*) SEBI (Prohibition of Insider Trading) (Amendment) (Regulation) 2002 vide SO 221/(E) published in the Gazette of India on 20th February 2002.

(*c*) SEBI (Prohibition of Insider Trading) (Second Amendment) Regulation 2002 vide SO 1245(E) published in the Gazette of India on 29th November 2002.

Clause (*e*) of Regulation 2 of the Chapter II defines 'insider' as follows:

> "insider" means any person who is or was connected with the company or is deemed to have been connected with the company, and who is reasonably expected to have access to unpublished price sensitive information in respect of securities of a company, or who has received or has access to such unpublished price sensitive information.

The prohibition on dealing on matters relating to insider trading as contained in Regulations 3 is as follows:

No insider shall:

(*i*) Either on his own behalf of any other person deal in securities of a company listed on any stock exchange when in possession of any unpublished price sensitive information.

(*ii*) Communicate, counsel or procure, directly or indirectly, any unpublished price sensitive information to any person who while in possession of such unpublished price sensitive information shall not deal in securities.

Provided that nothing contained above shall be applicable to any communication required in the ordinary course of business or under any law.

In 1998, SEBI has advised all stock exchanges that all listed companies are required to publish unaudited financial results on a quarterly basis.[16] Also, the companies are required to inform immediately to the stock exchanges of all events which will have bearing on the performance/operations of the company as well as price sensitive information.[17]

What is price sensitive information is a moot question. A transaction of sale between the undisclosed director and the buying company was brought into effect as a direct result of the director's illegal acts and the court would not help the director in enforcing such a transaction. As the transfer of the shares had not been effected, there was no difficulty about unscrambling the transaction. The court ordered that the transaction was unenforceable against the buyer.[18]

Directors are always an important functionary in a company and an important source of insider information as well. As apart the remuneration package, directors are often given share options which enable them to acquire shares in their company, which they may afterwards sell. When director decide to sell their shares however acquired or to buy more shares, their trading comes to be governed by the legislation on insider trading. "If the director has access to unpublished price sensitive information, such as information on future earnings, figures, security issues, assets disposal and purchases, etc., which if it were made public would have a significant effect on the share prices, it is illegal for them to trade on such information."[19]

However, these rules are framed in 1992 by the market regulator, the SEBI, has been found to be ineffective. These regulations suffered from the following major drawbacks:

(*i*) The fine that can be imposed under s. 15G of the SEBI Act 1992 for insider trading is ₹ 25 crore or three times the

16 Vide Circular No. SMD/POLICY/CIR-12/98, dated 7th April 1998.

17 SEBI Circular dated 07.04.1998.

18 *Chase Manhattan Equities Ltd.* v *Goodman* [1991] BCLC 897 (Ch D); [1991] BCC 308.

19 David Heller and Andrew Marshall, *The Timings of Directors' Trade in the United Kingdom and the Model Code,* 1998 JBL 454.

amount of profits made out of such failure, whichever is higher. Further, even criminal prosecution under s. 24 of the SEBI Act can attract a maximum punishment with imprisonment up to ten year or with fine which may extend to twenty-five crore rupees or with both;

(*ii*) The regulations were ambiguous in respect of terms like 'connected persons', 'insider', 'unpublished price sensitive information' etc;

(*iii*) Lack of power of SEBI to seize documents and detain suspected offenders/violators.

To tackle the menace of insider trading more effectively, SEBI has vide notified the SEBI (Insider Trading) (Amendment) Regulations 2002 which have come into force from 20th February 2002.

(*i*) The definition of 'connected person' has been expanded to include a person who is an officer or an employee of a company or holds a position involving a professional or business relationship whether temporary or permanent with a listed company and has access to price sensitive unpublished information. The term 'connected person' shall also mean any person who is a connected person six months prior to the act of insider trading.

(*ii*) The definition of connected person did not specify temporary or permanent relationship with a listed company nor did it include such a person who is a connected person 6 months prior to the act of insider trading.

(*iii*) The term dealing in securities has been expanded to include subscription or agreeing to subscribe to securities. The term dealings in securities included only selling and buying or agreeing to sell or buy securities. Thus subscribing to securities being offered through public offerings or rights issue or through private placement was not covered.

(*iv*) The definition of 'unpublished price sensitive information' is now split into two separate parts *viz.*, price sensitive information and unpublished, and both parts have now been defined distinctively. The scope of price sensitive information is now more stringent and includes only such information which if published is likely to materially affect the price of securities of a company.

(*v*) A new regulation 4A has been added to empower SEBI to conduct a preliminary inquiry in cases where it suspects that insider trading has taken place to form a *prima facie* opinion that there has been insider trading. It was mandatory for SEBI to have written information regarding suspected insider trading for initiating a full-fledged investigation.

(*vi*) The scope of issuing directions by SEBI under s. 11 of the SEBI Act has been expanded so as to include the following additional directions in the interests of the investors:

(*i*) The power to declare transactions in securities in violation of the insider trading regulations as null and void;

(*ii*) Directing the persons who had acquired the securities in violation of the regulations to deliver the securities back to the seller and where it is not possible to deliver the securities to pay the market price of the securities to the seller.

(*iii*) Directing the person who has dealt in securities in violation of the regulations to transfer an amount or proceeds equivalent to the cost price or the market price of the securities whichever is higher to the investor protection fund of a recognized stock exchange.[20]

SEBI in 2008 proposed to put derivative trading under the insider trading rules by amending SEBI (Prohibition of Insider Trading) Regulations 1992. According to the proposal an insider will be punished if he/she takes exposure in the cash market, but he was not liable to any action if he/she used the same information to make many times more profit by taking leveraged positions in the F&O market.[1]

In *Hindustan Lever Ltd.* v *SEBI,*[2] the SEBI Appellate Authority pointed out that a prosecution should be based upon conclusive determination of all aspects of insider trading and on specific justification

20 The Financial Express, 8th April 2002.

1 http://sify.com/finance/fixedincome/fullstory, 5th March 2008, visited on 23.04.2009.

2 (1998)3 Comp LJ 473 (AA).

in terms of the gravity of the offence. There was no finding in this case showing any serious violation of the duty of not using inside knowledge or trading by using such knowledge. The information in question must be shown to be unpublished or not known generally and also that it is price sensitive.

The Securities Appellate Tribunal in *SEBI* v *Dsq Biotech Ltd. (Earlier Known as Ushta Te Biotech Industries Ltd.,*[3] observed that Regulation 3 merely aims to prohibit the insider from breaching duty to the company. The breach of this duty necessarily involves an element of "manipulation" or "deceit", and the making of some secret profits or personal gain/benefit by the insider. Accordingly, it is only when the insider has dealt in shares of a company on the basis of unpublished price sensitive information, and made secret profits/personal gains that the insider can be held liable for the violation of the regulation under Regulation 4. Any other interpretation of Regulation 3 and Regulation 4 would render the same absurd for *inter alia* the following reasons:

(*i*) All corporate activities on the basis of unpublished price sensitive information would stand prohibited.

(*ii*) Corporate insiders would be subject to a form of strict liability against dealing in securities even if they act in furtherance of their duty to the Company.

(*iii*) A corporate insider would be liable although he has committed no breach of his fiduciary duties to the Company.

(*iv*) Promoters cannot consolidate their holdings in their company subject to limit prescribed by the SEBI (Substantial Acquisition of Shares and Take Over) Regulations 1997, on the basis of unpublished price sensitive information.

The Tribunal also observed that insider trading is always treated as serious irregularity in the capital market all over the world as they impinge on the basic tenets of transparency, fair play, investor confidence, orderly development of the markets, it would be a fit case for invoking the provisions of s. 11 of the SEBI Act to restore the same and debarred the respondent from dealing in securities market for a period of five years.

3 Order dated 27th February 2003.

In *Rakesh Agrawal* v *Securities Exchange Board of India*,[4] the Appellate Tribunal held that insiders receive unpublished price sensitive information by virtue of their connection with the company and for corporate purposes only, such insiders owe a fiduciary duty (or a duty akin to a fiduciary duty) to the company not to misuse or misappropriate such information for an unlawful purpose i.e. to make secret profits or personal gains for themselves. Such insiders are therefore either required to disclose the said unpublished price sensitive information to other transacting parties or to abstain from acting on the said information/dealing in such securities altogether. This requirement has come to be known as the "disclosure or abstain" rule.[5]

A person with whom shares are traded by using price sensitive inside information and undisclosed knowledge suffers loss because he is made to part with his shares or to buy shares at a manipulated price. Those who indulge in such practice are liable to compensate their victims for his losses.

6.12 Civil liability for insider trading

The person with whom he is a traitor by using price since the team inside information and undisclosed knowledge suppose laws because he is in such practice or liable to compensate their victim for their losses. An attempt was made by SEBI to improve such liability of the board of directors of the Hindustan Lever in connection with the takeover of their own subsidiary, Brook Bond. The Appellate Authority found that while the prosecution was for violations of insider trading regulations, civil liability was imposed under an omnibus provision contained in SEBI Act 1992. The Appellate Authority observed that it is necessary for imposing a pecuniary burden that there must be some specific legal provision and also a provision for giving the affected person an opportunity to explain his position and when only a civil liability can be imposed by an authority like SEBI. An omnibus power cannot be used for causing such a serious deprivation. SEBI decision lacked jurisdiction.[6]

4 Order dated 1st November 2003.
5 *Chiarella* v *US* 455 US 222.
6 *Hindustan Lever Ltd.* v *SEBI* (1998)3 Comp LJ 473 (AA).

It has been suggested that even without being held for statutory provisions the courts would have no difficulty in striking down contracts which resulted from the committing of an insider trading offence. This much is clear from the comments of Knox. In *Chase Manhattan Equities* v *Goodman,*[7] it is arguable that the abuse of privileged information should be regarded our objectionable, whether it falls within the statutory provisions or not. Indeed, it could be argued that there is a broad rule of public policy that such transactions should not be enforced.

In *Coleman* v *Myers*,[8] a majority of the Court of Appeal took it for granted that damages or monetary compensation could be awarded for breach of fiduciary duty. In the case of small closely held companies or quasi partnerships, the courts may apply partnership principles good faith and how nasty in mutual relations in temps of the decisions like that in *Law* v *Law*.[9]

6.13 Liability for breach of trust

Traditionally, the duties of directors fashioned out of common law as developed through the cases.[10] Good faith requires that all their endeavors must be directed to the benefit of the company. Thus where a director of a company, being also the member of another company, earned business from the other company by providing some business facility of his company, he was held liable to account for such profits, although the company had itself not lost anything and also could not have earned the bonus.[11] Where a director was aware of the fact that the company's property was being sold for £350,000 when its real value stood at £650,000, this was a breach of the fiduciary duty.

A director who assisted his company to commit a breach of trust, or procured it to do so, was held liable for any loss caused to the beneficiaries of the trust as a result of his actions. It was necessary for this liability to arise that those actions could be characterized as

7 [1991] BCLC 897.
8 [1977]2 NZ LR 225.
9 [1905]1 Ch 140.
10 The Nigerian Act contains the following provisions on the point: "A Director of a company stands in a fiduciary relationship with the company and shall observe the utmost good faith towards the company in any transaction with it or on in itself".
11 *Bostan Deep Sea Fishing & Ice Co.* v *Ansell* [1888]39 Ch D 339.

dishonest rather than negligent. It was not necessary that the company as trustee be acting dishonestly.[12] In this case Mr. Tan, who brought about the misappropriation of the airline's money, was the managing director and principal shareholder of a company called Borneo Leisure Travel. That company was, under a formal written agreement, an express trustee of the money which it collected as agent for the airline. The Court of Appeal of Brunei held (allowing the defendant's appeal) that dishonesty on the part of Borneo Leisure Travel had not been established. Lord Nicholls stated the issue as, whether the breach of trust which is a prerequisite to accessory liability must itself be a dishonest and fraudulent breach of trust by the trustee.[13]

Long ago Lord Hardwicke said of directors and executive committees, "If some persons are guilty of gross non-attendance, and leave the management entirely to others, they may be guilty by this means of the breaches of trust that are committed by others."[14]

In *Barness* v *Addy,*[15] the court discussed the necessary conditions for a third party to be liable as constructive trustee. "stranger are not to be made constructive trustees merely because they act as the agents of trustees in transactions within their legal powers, transactions perhaps of which a court of equity may disapprove, unless those agents receive and become chargeable with some part of the trust property, or unless they assist with knowledge in a dishonest and fraudulent design on the part of the trustees." In this case solicitors acting for Mr. Addy and Mr. Barnes knew perfectly well what a breach of trust was. A company director may have (or may plausibly claim to have) a much less clear understanding of what is a breach of fiduciary duty, and the same may be true of bank officials and even, regrettably, accountants and lawyers.

In 1975 *Selangor* and *Karak Rubber* were considered, among many other authorities, by the High Court of Australia on appeal from the

12 *Royal Brunei Airlines Sdn Bhd* v *Tan* [1995]3 All ER 97.

13 *Ibid,* p. 384.

14 The *Charitable Corporation* v *Sutton* [I742]2 Atk Ch 400. This is considered almost the universal rule: *Mutual Building Fund* v *Bossieux* [1880]3 Fed R 817; *Williams* v *McKay* [1885]40 NJ Eq 189; *Marshall* v *Farmers Bank* [1889]85 Va 676; 17 Am St R 84; *Warren* v *Robison* [1899]19 Utah 289; 75 Am St R 734; *Fisher* v *Parr* [1900]92 Md 245; 48 Atl 621; *Fletcher* v *Eagle* [1905]74 Ark 585; 109 Am St R 100.

15 [1874] LR 9 Ch App 244.

Court of Appeal of New South Wales[16] in *Consul Development* v *DPC Estates*.[17] The facts in barest outline are; Mr. Walton, a solicitor, carried out property development through his company, DPC. Mr. Grey was a director and manager of DPC. Mr. Clowes, Mr. Walton's articled clerk, also engaged in property development through a family company, Consul. Mr. Grey made redevelopment opportunities available to Consul, telling Mr. Clowes that DPC had insufficient resources to take them up itself. Mr. Grey was rewarded with a share of Consul's development profits. DPC's claim against Consul failed at first instance but the Court of Appeal allowed its appeal, Jacobs, P dissenting. In the High Court the principal issue was whether Consul's constructive knowledge, if established, was a sufficient basis for liability. McTiernan, J dissenting, held that it was; Gibbs, J did not, on his view of the facts, find it necessary to express a concluded view; but Barwick, CJ (who concurred in the views of Stephen, J) and Stephen, J held that it was not enough to establish what he called 'that species of constructive notice which serves to expose a party to liability because of negligence in failing to make enquiry'.[18] Earlier he had quoted from the dissenting judgment of Jacobs P below[19] that where the defendant has not received trust property:

> ...something more is required, and that something more appears to me to be the actual knowledge of the fraudulent or dishonest design, so that the person concerned can truly be described as a participant in that fraudulent dishonest activity.[20]

Stephens, J was prepared to go a bit farther:

> If a defendant knows of facts which themselves would, to a reasonable man, tell of fraud or breach of trust the case may well be different, as it clearly will be if the defendant has consciously refrained from enquiry for fear lest he learn of fraud.[1]

In *City Equitable Fire Insurance Co., In re,*[2] it was held that, in discharging his duties, a director must act honestly, and must exercise

16 *DPC Estates Pty. Ltd.* v *Greyand Consul Development Pty. Ltd.* [1974]1 NSWLR 443.
17 *Consul Development Pty. Ltd.* v *DPC Estates Pty. Ltd.* (1975) HCA 8; (1975) 132 CLR 373.
18 *Ibid,* p. 412.
19 DPC, p. 459.
20 *Ibid,* p. 410.
1 *Consul Development*, p. 412.
2 [1925]1 Ch 407; [1924] All ER Rep 485 (CA).

such degree of skill and diligence, as would amount to the reasonable care which an ordinary man might be expected to take, in the circumstances, on his own behalf; and that his duties are of an intermittent nature to be performed at periodical board meetings, and at meetings of any committee to which he is appointed, and though not bound to attend all such meetings he ought to attend them when reasonably able to do so.

With regard to wilful neglect or default, it was held that an act, or an omission to do an act, is wilful where the person who acts, or omits to act, knows what he is doing and intends to do what he is doing, but if that act or omission amounts to a breach of that person's duty, and therefore to negligence, he is not guilty of wilful neglect or default unless he knows that he is committing, and intends to commit, a breach of his duty, or is recklessly careless whether his act or omission is or is not a breach of his duty. The liability of the defendant is based not on a breach of contract but on a breach of duty amounting to a breach of trust. Misfeasance includes a breach by an officer of his duty to the company, the direct consequence of which has been a misapplication or loss of its assets for which he could be made responsible in an action.

It was held in the *New Fleming Spinning and Weaving Company Limited* v *Kessowji Naik*,[3] Scott, J held that:

Misfeasance of a director constitutes a breach of trust. It is more than mere negligence, which consists in the omission to do something which, a reasonable man would do, or the doing something which a reasonable man would not do. Negligence depends upon the public duty which is incumbent upon everyone to exercise due care in his daily life; but a breach of trust depends upon the neglect of some special duty undertaken in regard to some specified person or body of persons.[4]

6.14 Breach of fiduciary duty

Where a director acts dishonestly to the interest of the company, he will be held liable for breach of fiduciary duty. Most of the powers of directors are 'powers in trust' and therefore, should be exercised in the

3 ILR (1885)9 Bom 373 at 398.

4 See *Govind Narayan Kakade* v *Rangnath Gopal Rajopadhye* (1930)32 Bom LR 232.

interest of the company and not in the interest of the directors or any section of members. Thus, where the directors, in order to forestall a take-over bid, transferred the unissued shares of the company to trustees to be held for the benefit of the employees, and an interest-free loan from the company was advanced to the trustees to enable them to pay for the shares, it was held to be a wrongful exercise of the fiduciary powers of the directors.[5]

The director's powers are limited within the provisions of memorandum and articles of association. These lay down the limited activities of the company and subsequently to the board of directors. The directors shall be personally liable for acts beyond the powers of articles of association, being *ultra vires* the company or the directors. As long as the director's act within their powers with reasonable skill and care as expected of them as prudent businessman, they discharge their duties to the company.

The directors are trustees of the moneys and property of the company. If they dishonestly or in a *mala fide* manner, exercise their powers and perform their duties, they will be liable for breach of trust and may be required to make compensation for the losses or damage suffered by the company due to such *mala fide* acts. Directors are also held liable for misconduct or wilful misuse of powers. Directors are also entitled to relief against liability for breach of trust or misfeasance under s. 633. It was held that in *P.K. Nedungadi* v *Malayali Bank Ltd.*[6] Where the director misapplies or misappropriates money or properties of the company or has been guilty of breach of trust or misfeasance, the Court may order him to repay the money or restore the property or to pay compensation.

By taking away the main business of the company, by starting a new company, a director has breached his fiduciary duties to the company as a director. In *Boulting* v *Association of Cinematograph Television*,[7] the Court has held that the rule of equity demands that a person having fiduciary duties will not be allowed to enter into engagements in which he can have an interest conflicting with his fiduciary duties. In case of profit arising from diversion of business by a fiduciary, he

5 *Hogg* v *Cramphorm Ltd.* [1967] Ch 254; [1966]3 All ER 420; [1966]3 WLR 995.

6 AIR 1971 SC 829; [1972]42 Comp Cas 120.

7 [1963]1 All ER 716.

is liable to account for any benefit derived from diversion of business in breach of his fiduciary duties.

In *Industrial Development Consultants Limited* v *Cooley,*[8] the Court observed that a director holds fiduciary position towards the company and if he makes any profit when he is acting for the company, he must account the company. Section 88 of the Indian Trusts Act also stipulates that any advantage gained by a fiduciary should be held in trust for the beneficiary.

The decisions of Indian Courts on the fiduciary responsibilities of a director or a partner are entirely different. Indian Courts have not applied strict fiduciary doctrine on the part of directors as in England. In *Deva Sharma* v *Lakshmi Naralu Gadeodia,*[9] while considering the application of s. 88 of the Indian Trusts Act, the court held that in applying fiduciary responsibilities of a partner in a partnership firm, it must be established that he has acquired financial benefits for himself by representing that he was acting for the partnership and the party dealing with him should also have been under the belief that the partner was dealing on behalf of the partnership.

In *Descin Private Limited* v *Elektrim India Limited,*[10] this Board has held that to substantiate an allegation of diversion of business it should be established that the company had lost a business opportunity to the newly incorporated company. Since in that case, the particular respondent against whom the complaint had been made had already gone out of business and without the assistance of that respondent the company itself could not carry on the business, the Board held that there was no breach of fiduciary duties. If a partnership itself had come to an end, the question of breach of fiduciary duties did not arise.

In *Industrial Development Consultant's* case,[11] In an action by the plaintiffs for an account for breach of fiduciary duty, the defendant denied that there was any fiduciary duty or any breach of such duty, contending that the contract was offered to him in his personal capacity because of his expertise and even otherwise the plaintiffs had suffered no damage since they would not have obtained the work for themselves

8 [1972]2 All ER 162; [1972]1 WLR 443.
9 AIR 1956 Punj 49.
10 (2003)116 Comp Cas 341.
11 [1972]1 WLR 443.

in any case. This defence was rejected by the Court on the ground that while the defendant was managing director of the plaintiff, a fiduciary relationship existed between him and the plaintiff. Accordingly, information which came to him while he was managing director and was of concern to the plaintiffs, it was his duty to disclose this information to the plaintiffs and therefore, such non-disclosure was a breach of his fiduciary duties. It further held that because of his breach of duty, the defendant was liable to account to the plaintiffs for all the benefits he had received or would receive under the contract with Gas Board. The question whether the benefits of the contract would have been obtained for the plaintiffs but for the defendant's breach of fiduciary duties was irrelevant.

It is the accepted principle of law is that in case of any benefit derived by a fiduciary who is in fact a trustee, by breach of his fiduciary duties, is that the benefit so derived has to be held by him as a constructive trustee of the beneficiary is liable to be accountable.[12] This position was confirmed in *Liz Investment Private Ltd.* v *Far Pavilions Tours & Travels Private Ltd.*[13]

The Madras High Court in *Farouk Irani* v *BIFR,*[14] held that where violation of statutory provisions including mandatory provisions take place, the discretionary powers of the court under s. 633 cannot be exercised in favour of the defaulters. However, if the directors are not in-charge of day-to-day affairs of the company or were knowledge of the default, they should be relieved from the prosecution under s. 633.[15]

A director is an agent of the company, not of the other members of the board. It means that anything done by the board without the knowledge of director cannot impose liability on him. To incur liability he must either be a party to the wrongful act or legal acquiescence to it. The absence of a director from meeting of the board does not make him liable for the fraudulent act of a co-director on the ground that he ought to have discovered the fraud.[16] Where a director is made

12 *Shri Kishore Kundan Sippy and Shri Kundan Hashmatrai Sippy* v *Samrat Shipping and Transport Systems Pvt. Ltd.* (2004)118 Comp Cas 472 (CLB); (2004)50 SCL 493 (CLB).
13 (2006)130 Comp Cas 449 (CLB); (2005)64 SCL 439 (CLB).
14 (2002)38 SCL 95; (2002)110 Comp Cas 64 (Mad).
15 *T.K. Seshadri* v *ROC* (2004)54 SCL 118 (Mad).
16 *Dovey* v *Cory* [1901] AC 477.

liable for the acts of a co-director, he is entitled to contribution from the other directors or co-directors who were a party to the wrongful act.[17]

6.15 Conclusion

The liability of a director arises because of their position as an agent of the company, a trustee, and that of a fiduciary. The powers given to the directors should be used for benefit of the company and the director should be restrained from using the powers capriciously. They are bound to use fair and reasonable diligence in dealing with outsiders on behalf of the company. The breach of trust or failed in their duties would visit with liability. The directors are liable in contract on behalf of the company. The directors are as such not liable for the torts or civil wrongs committed by the company personally. If the directors are themselves the wrongdoer in relation to an act complained, or the wrong was committed in accordance with his direction or knowledge, then he is personally liable for the tort committed by the company. Civil liability to the company arises where the directors are guilty of negligence, breach of trust, misfeasance and the directors acted *ultra vires* and the funds of the company have been utilised for the illegal activities. The directors are supposed to act honestly and prudently. The standard of care expected from a director is well explained by many case laws. The directors are liable for holding activities of the company if they have the knowledge of such spending and business activities.

The directors are bound by the articles of association and memorandum of the company. They cannot delegate their powers to managers. The directors are liable for criminal activities of the company along with the company in a criminal case. The tax liabilities are evaded by neither the directors nor the company. They are liable for misleading statements in the prospectus and thus induce people to invest in the company. If the directors are done anything on behalf of the company in good faith is exempted from liability. Always the directors must act in good faith and to the best interest of the company. They must not use their discretion of the manager arbitrarily against the interest of the company.

17 *Ramskill* v *Edwards* [1886]31 Ch D 100.

7

Corporate Criminal Liability of Directors

7.1 Criminal liability

Large multinational corporations have come to dominate the national and global economic scene and their scale of their operations is enormous. The largest ones have grown into enterprises of astonishing magnitude in such a way that their economic activities and dimensions are fully comparable to states. Imposing adequate controls over multinational conduct and achieving accountability by multinational companies for their conduct both at home and abroad should be a major objective of every industrialized power. It is necessary and required to prevent committing economic fraud in such a magnitude like happened in India like Enron and Indian IT company, Satyam.

Historically, the criminal law has been used as the vehicle of deterrence against law breakers. Corporations are increasingly significant actors in our economy and, to the extent their actions can victimize society that too should be deterred. Considering the fact that companies do a large number of economic and financial activities, the liability on directors, the administrators of the company, the directors have a fiduciary duty to the company and shareholders. It is necessary for the directors to act with due diligence, care and caution while dealing with various activities and taking corporate decisions and compliances with various legislations applicable on them.

Some scholars argue that the premise of corporate criminal liability is faulty in two counts: (1) The current standards of corporate criminal liability, which are based on principles of vicarious liability, are incompatible with the criminal law's requirement that an actor be held responsible only for its own action and intent. Since fictional entities like companies have no intent, they are not suitable for criminal prosecution, and the deception of imputing another actor's act and intent to the corporation (even that of a corporate agent) cannot substitute for this deficiency in proof; (2) Imprisonment as a defining characteristic of the criminal law and argues that since fictional entities cannot be imprisoned, corporate criminal liability is inappropriate. These scholars also argue that prosecutors are given unlimited powers to prosecute corporate executives without understanding business environment and proper guidelines.[1]

In the early 15th century discussion on the corporate criminal liability was evident from the findings of Frederic William Maitland which may be found in his book "*A History of English Law*" in 1898. His finding is still valid and gives insights into the jurisprudence of criminal liability and the famous passage is as follows:

> The corporation is invisible, incorporeal, immortal; it cannot be assaulted, or beaten or imprisoned; it cannot commit treason; a doubt has occurred as to whether it can commit a trespass, but this doubt has been rejected by practice, if not removed by any consistent theory. We even find it said that the corporation is but a name. On the other hand, it is a person. It is at once a person and yet but a name; in short it is a *persona ficta*.[2]

These arguments have to be discussed in the background of the company law in India. Corporate criminal liability is an important item for the academicians and practitioners for quite some time in India, even though there is no specific law to deal with it. The Delhi High Court in 2008 considered this question in the new era of information technology developments in *Avnish Bajaj* v *State*,[3] on deemed criminal liability of directors in violation of Information Technology Act 2000 (IT Act) and under s. 292 of the Indian Penal

1 See http://law.jrank.org/pages/745/Corporate-Criminal-Responsibility-Critique-corporate-criminal-liability.html, visited on 27.08.2010.

2 Frederick Pollock & Frederic William Maitland, *A History of English Law*, vol. 1, p. 491 (2nd Ed., Cambridge 1898).

3 (2005)3 Comp LJ 364 (Del); 116(2005) DLT 427. See also the judgment dated 29th May 2008.

Code (IPC).[4] The court held that a *prima facie* case for the offence under s. 67 read with s. 85 of IT Act was made out against the petitioner since the law as explained by the decisions of the Supreme Court recognises the deemed criminal liability of the directors even though the company is not accused. But the court recognised that IPC does not recognise the concept of an automatic criminal liability attaching to the director where the company is an accused, not even a *prima facie* case for the offence under s. 292, IPC is made out even when the charge sheet is read as a whole; it only seeks to implicate him in his designation as MD of the company and not in his individual capacity. This case shows an increased burden on the directors of a company in criminal liability.[5]

The question of punishing a corporation came up in the Supreme Court in a criminal case filed by *Motorola Incorporated.*[6] The allegations were cheating and criminal conspiracy.

The Bombay High Court quashed the proceedings giving several reasons, one of them being that a corporation was incapable of committing the offence of cheating as it has no mind. According to the High Court, although a company can be a victim of deception, it cannot be the perpetrator of deception. Only a natural person is capable of having a guilty mind to commit an offence.

On appeal, the Supreme Court set aside the High Court's finding and asserted that a corporate body can be prosecuted for cheating and conspiracy under the Indian Penal Code. The offences for which companies can be criminally prosecuted are not limited only to the specific provisions made in the Income Tax Act, the Essential Commodities Act, and the Prevention of Food Adulteration Act.

The court decision is against the argument of the group that argues a company cannot commit an offence. The court also opined that companies cannot escape by making the plea that they are incapable of possessing the necessary *mens rea* for the commission of criminal

4 See Priti Suri and Rohan Jhusiwala, *Corporate Criminal Liability: The Case of Bazee.com*, India Business Law Journal, November 2009.

5 This is one of the first cases were the managing director of a company were held liable for an online sale of a video clip in baazee.com (as and then) by a third party, shot on a mobile phone, of two children of a school in Delhi indulging in an explicitly sexual act.

6 *Iridium India Telecom Ltd.* v *Motorola Inc.* 20th October 2010.

offences. In this case the Supreme Court reiterated the principles laid down in the previous case of *Standard Chartered Bank* v *Directorate of Enforcement*.[7]

The major law relating to corporations in India is codified in the Companies Act 1956 and the definition of "Corporation" as given in the Act under s. 2(7) includes a company. Hence, under Indian law the liability of the corporation is essentially liability of the company only. Further, under Indian law as well as under the English law, a company is a creation and of the law. It is not a human being but is an artificial person. On incorporation, the company acquires a separate legal entity distinct from and independent of its members. When a company is incorporated, all dealings are with the company and all persons behind the company are disregarded, whatever important they may be. Thus, a distinction is drawn between the company and its members. Normally, the principle of corporate personality of a company is respected in most of the cases. The separate personality of the company is, however, a statutory privilege; but it must be used for legal and legitimate business purposes only.

Where a fraudulent, dishonest or improper use is made of the legal entity, the concerned individual will not be allowed to take shelter behind the corporate personality. The courts will break through the corporate shell and apply the principle of "Lifting of the corporate veil". The courts will look behind the corporate entity and take action as though no entity separate from the members existed. In other words, the benefit of separate legal entity will not be available and the court will presume the absence of such separate existence.[8] In the landmark judgment of *Kapila Hingorani* v *State of Bihar*,[9] the Apex Court analyzed the rights and liabilities of a company vis-a-vis the Fundamental Rights and Human Rights of the individuals. The Court observed:

> A company incorporated under the Companies Act is a juristic person and has a distinct and separate entity *vis-a-vis* its shareholders. The corporate veil, however, can in certain situations be pierced or lifted. Whenever a corporate entity is abused for an

7 (2005)4 SCC 405.

8 Dalal Praveen, *Corporate Entity in Existing Legal System—Its Rights and Liabilities under the Constitution and other Enactments*, (2004)61 CLA 96 (Mag).

9 2003(4) SCALE 712.

> unjust and inequitable purpose, the court would not hesitate to lift the veil and look into the realities so as to identify the persons who are guilty and liable thereof. The veil can indisputably be lifted when the corporate personality is found to be opposed to justice, convenience and interest of the revenue or workman or against public interest.

It has also been observed that a corporation deemed to be a "State" within the meaning of Art. 12 of the Constitution when acting as an agency of the Government. In that case it would be subject to the same limitations in the field of Constitutional or administrative law as the Government itself, though in the eyes of law they would be distinct and independent legal entities.[10]

Whether a company can be held liable under the criminal law, it is always a contentious question. Because a company doesn't have a soul or mind, these are the directors of a company. The Divisional Court considered the same question in *Director of Public Prosecutions* v *Kent and Sussex Contractors Ltd.*[11] It was alleged that the respondent company violated the Motor Fuel Rationing Order 1941 and r. 82(1)(c) of the Defence (General) Regulations 1939. The company contented that a company registered under the Companies Act cannot be held guilty, as the offence charged involved an act of will or a state of mind implicit in the commission of the offences. The court considered the question whether the offence was committed with the knowledge of agents or officers of the company. The court found that a company cannot be prosecuted for criminal offences like treason or other offences for which it is provided that death or imprisonment is the only punishment based on earlier judgments in *R* v *Cory Brothers & Co.*[12] in which it was held that a company can be convicted for a number of criminal offences. It was observed that:

> What the nature of the offence was to which the observation was intended to apply does not appear; and as a general proposition it is opposed to a number of cases, which show that a corporation may be indicted for breach of a duty imposed upon it by law,

10 See also *R.D. Shetty* v *International Airport Authority* AIR 1979 SC 1628; (1979)3 SCC 489.

11 (1944)14 Comp Cas 133.

12 [1927]96 LJKB 764; [1927]1 KB 816. See also *R* v *Birmingham and Gloucester Railway* 11 LJMC 136.

though not for a felony, or for crimes involving personal violence, as for riots or assaults.

In *Ranger* v *Great Western Railway,*[13] it was held that "strictly speaking a corporation cannot of itself be guilty of a fraud. But where a corporation is formed for the purpose of carrying on a trading or other speculation for profit, such as forming a railway, these objects can only be accomplished by the agency of individuals; and there can be no doubt that if the agents employed conduct themselves fraudulently, so that if they had been acting for private employers the persons for whom they were acting would have been affected by their fraud, the same principles must prevail where the principal under whom the agent acts is a corporation". Finally the court concluded that a corporation through its servants or agents may be guilty of malice so as to render itself liable to be indicted for criminal liability.

The above position was confirmed by the Court of Appeal in *R.* v *I.C.R. Haulage, Ltd.*[14] It was held that relying on an earlier judgment in *Pearks V. Gunston and Tee, Ltd.* v *Ward,*[15] by the principle of general criminal law, a criminal offence imports something in the nature of *mens rea.* Therefore, in ordinary cases a corporation cannot be guilty of a criminal offence, nor can a master be liable criminally for an offence committed by his servants". On the other hand, in *Mousell Brothers* v *London and North Western Railway,*[16] it was held that a company can be convicted for an offence under s. 99 of the Railway Clauses Consolidation Act 1845. The court ultimately held that a limited company is capable of committing the offence of conspiracy to defraud notwithstanding that it can only form an intention through its human agents.

In *A.K. Khosla* v *T.S. Venkatesan,*[17] two companies along with other accused were charged of having committed offences under ss. 420, 467, 471, 477A and 120B of the Indian Penal Code and the Magistrate issued processes against all the accused. In the Calcutta High Court it was contended, *inter alia* that the said companies being juristic persons and they cannot be prosecuted for offences under the

13 5 HLC 86.
14 (1945)15 Comp Cas 47.
15 [1902]71 LJKB 656.
16 [1917]2 KB 836.
17 1992 Cr LJ 1448; Cal LT (1992)1 HC 77; (1991)2 CHN 321

Indian Penal Code where *mens rea* is an essential ingredient. The High Court upheld the contention and pointed out that there are two tests in respect of the prosecution of corporate bodies. The first being the test of *mens rea* and the other is the mandatory sentence of imprisonment. It was held that a company being a corporate body cannot be said to have the necessary *mens rea,* nor can it be sentenced to imprisonment, as it has no physical body. But we can see that the Indian Supreme Court has taken an opposite view in many cases including *Motorola* case.

In *Kalpanath Rai* v *State*[18] one of the questions was whether a company, which was arraigned as, accused No. 12 in a case under the Terrorists and Disruptive Activities (Prevention) Act 1987 was alleged to have harboured one of the terrorists. The Supreme Court observed that:

> We are aware that in many recent penal statutes, companies or corporations are deemed to be offenders on the strength of the acts committed by persons responsible for the management or affairs of such company or corporations e.g. Essential Commodities Act, Prevention of Food Adulteration Act, etc. But there is no such provision in TADA which makes the Company liable for the acts of its officers. Hence, there is no scope whatsoever to prosecute a company for the offence under section 3(4) of TADA.

But that stand was changed during a period of time and in *Standard Chartered Bank* v *Directorate of Enforcement,*[19] the company was being prosecuted for offence under s. 56 of the FERA 1973.[20] In most of the

18 (1997)8 SCC 732; 1997(2) ALD Cri 805; (1998) Cr LJ 369; JT 1997(9) SC 18.

19 (2005)4 CLJ 464; AIR 2005 SC 2622.

20 Section 56: *Provided as Offences and prosecutions.* (1) Without prejudice to any award of penalty by the adjudicating officer under this Act, if any person contravenes any of the provisions of this Act (other than section 13, clause (*a*) of sub-section (1) of section 18, section 18A, clause (*a*) of sub-section (1) of section 19, sub-section (2) of section 44 and sections 57 and 58, or of any rule, direction or order made thereunder, he shall, upon conviction by a court, be punishable,

(*i*) in the case of an offence the amount or value involved in which exceeds one lakh of rupees, with imprisonment for a term which shall not be less than six months, but which may extend to seven years and with fine:

Provided that the court may, for any adequate and special reasons to be mentioned in the judgment, impose a sentence of imprisonment for a term of less than six months.

cases the courts taken a view that whenever a term of imprisonment was awarded by the court, the companies are held not liable but fines were imposed.

A Full Bench of the Delhi High Court in a food adulteration case *Delhi Municipality* v *J.B. Bottling Company,*[1] considered a similar question. The respondent-company was found guilty under s. 7 read with s. 16 of the Prevention of Food Adulteration Act 1954 (PFA) and was fined ₹ 5000. The respondent-company filed an appeal and contended that for the offence under s. 16 of the PFA, the minimum period of imprisonment is six months and the company is immune from prosecution as the sentence contemplated under law cannot be imposed on it. The Court held that:

> The office of the judges is always to make construction as shall suppress the mischief and advance the remedy and therefore it will stay its hand in passing the sentence which will be impossible to execute but pass only such sentence which can be executed, namely, fine. The proviso to section 16 applies only to the three classes of offences mentioned therein and as compared to the rest of the offences contemplated by the Act are of less serious nature and if indictment of the company is confined to only those offences which are covered by the proviso, then not only the intention of the legislature is defeated, but the provisions of section 16(1-D) and section 18 are also to that extent rendered nugatory, insofar as the offences are committed by the companies.

Under the Companies Act and under the common law, directors of a company may also incur criminal liability. Some of the provisions of the Companies Act which make directors criminally liable are:

1. Clause 33 of the Companies Bill 2011. If a company issues application and offering purchase of securities without issuing prospectus, shall be liable to a penalty of fifty thousand rupees for each default.

2. Section 44(4). Circulating prospects with any misleading or untrue statement is punishable.

• *Punishment*: Any person who authorised the filing of such prospectus or statement shall be punishable with imprisonment for a

1 *Delhi Municipality* v *J.B. Bottling Company* 1975 Cr LJ 1148 (Del); 1975 FAC 321.

term which may extend to two years, or with fine which may extend to [fifty thousand rupees], or with both, unless he proves either that the statement was immaterial or that they had reasonable ground to believe, and did up to the time of the filing of the prospectus or statement believe, that the statement was true.[2] The omission from a prospectus or a statement in lieu of prospectus of any matter is calculated to mislead, the prospectus or statement in lieu of prospectus shall be deemed, in respect of such omission, to be a prospectus or a statement in lieu of prospectus in which an untrue statement is included. The Companies Bill 2008 provides for if any person knowingly or recklessly makes any statement, forecast any false, deceptive or misleading statement to induce any person to invest money will be punishable with imprisonment for a term which may extend to three years and with fine which shall not be less than one lakh rupees but which may extend to fifty lakh rupees.[3] The activity will be considered as fraud under cl. 447 of the Companies Bill 2011. Clause 34 also follows the provision of Bill of 2008 and provides for severe punishment for fraud. The provision imposes an imprisonment for a term which shall not be less than six months but which may extend to ten years and shall also be liable to fine which shall not be less than the amount involved in the fraud which may extend to three times the amount involved in the fraud.[4] If any person fraudulently induces anybody to invest in a company by making misstatement, false promise or forecast, deceptive or misleading facts presented shall be liable under Cl. 447 of the Companies Bill 2011 for fraud.

3. Clause 39 of the Companies Bill 2011. If a company is failed to achieve the minimum subscription mentioned in the prospectus within 30 days, such amount must be returned according to the manner prescribed by the SEBI. Returns also to be filed with SEBI on all share capital issues.

- *Punishment for contravention*: In case of any default of the provision, the company and the officer in default shall be liable to a

2 The Companies Bill 2008 increased the punishment to three year of imprisonment and the fine to not less than ₹ 1 lakh which may extend to 25 lakh rupees. Section 29.

3 *Ibid*, section 31.

4 Clause 35 of the Companies Bill 2011 provides for filing a civil case against persons those who make misstatement in the prospectus and consequent damage.

penalty, for each default, one thousand rupees for each day of default or one Lakh rupees.

4. Clause 40 of Companies Bill 2011. Every company making public offer should make an application to the concerned stock exchange and get prior permission for the securities to be dealt.

• *Punishment for contravention*: on default of this provision, the company shall be punishable with a fine which shall not be less than five lakh rupees but which may extend to 50 lakh rupees and every officer of the company who is in default shall be punishable with an imprisonment for a term which may extend to one year or with fine which shall not be less than 50 thousand rupees but which may extend to three lakh rupees or with both.[5]

5. Clause 46(5) of Companies Bill 2011. If a company with an intent to defraud, issues a duplicate certificate of shares, the company shall be punishable with fine which shall not be less than five times of the face value of the shares, which may extend to ten times the face value of the shares or rupees ten crore whichever is higher and every officer of the company in default shall be liable for action under s. 447, punishment for fraud. Section 45 of the Companies Act provides that—If at any time the number of members of a company is reduced, in the case of a public company, below seven, or in the case of private company, below two, and the company carries on business for more than six months while the number is so reduced, every person who is a member of the company during the time that it so carries on business after those six months and is cognizant of the fact that it is carrying on business with fewer than seven members or two members, as the case may be, shall be jointly and severally liable for the payment of the whole debts of the company contracted during that time, and may be severally sued therefore.

6. Clause 48(5) of Companies Bill 2011. The share capital can be divided into various classes of shares with the consent of shareholders of not less than three-fourth of the shares if such variation is permitted under the memorandum or articles of association. Punishment for default: The company shall be punishable with fine which shall not be less than twenty five thousand rupees but which may extend to five lakh rupees and every officer of the company who is in default shall

5 Clause 40(5) of Companies Bill 2011.

be punishable with imprisonment for a term which may extend to six months or with fine which shall not be less than twenty five thousand rupees but which may extend to five lakh rupees or both.

7. Clause 53(3) of Companies Bill 2011. If a company issues shares at a discounted price shall be punishable with fine which shall not be less than one lakh rupees but which may extend to five lakh rupees and every officer who is in default shall be punishable with imprisonment for a term which may extend to six months or with fine which shall not be less than one lakh rupees but which may extend to five lakh rupees or with both.

8. Clause 56 of Companies Bill 2011. Transfer of shares: If any default is made in complying with the provisions of this section shall be punishable with fine which shall not be less than twenty five thousand rupees but which may extend to five lakh rupees and every officer of the company who is in default shall be punishable with an imprisonment for a term which may extend to six months or with fine which shall not be less than ten thousand rupees but which may extend to one lakh rupees or with both.

9. Clause 57 of Companies Bill 2011. Punishment for impersonation as a shareholder. If any person impersonates as an owner of the share and attempts to obtain any share or interest or receive any money, he shall be punishable with an imprisonment for a term not less than one year but which may extend to three years and fine which shall not be less than one lakh rupees but which may extend to five lakh rupees.

10. Section 58A(5). Where a company omits or fails to make repayment of a deposit in accordance with the provisions of cl. (c) of sub-sec. (3), or in the case of a deposit referred to in sub-sec. (4).

- *Penalty (1).* The company shall be punishable with fine which shall not be less than *twice the amount* in relation to which the repayment of the deposit has not been made, and out of the fine, if realised, an amount equal to the amount in relation to which the repayment of deposit has not been made, shall be paid by the Court, trying the offence, to the person to whom repayment of the deposit was to be made, and on such payment, the liability of the company to make repayment of the deposit shall, to the extent of the amount paid by the Court, stand discharged.

(2) Every officer of the company who is in default shall be punishable with imprisonment for a term which may extend to *five years* and shall also be liable to fine.

11. Section 58A(6). Where a company accepts or invites, or allows or causes any other person to accept or invite on its behalf, any deposit in excess of the limits prescribed.

• *Punishment.* (1) Where such contravention relates to the acceptance of any deposit, with fine which shall not be *less than an amount equal to* the amount of the deposit so accepted.

(2) Where such contravention relates to the invitation of any deposit, with fine which may extend to *ten lakh rupees* but shall not be less than fifty thousand rupees.

(3) Every officer of the company who is in default shall be punishable with imprisonment for a term which may extend to *five years* and shall also be liable to fine.

(4) If a company fails to comply with the order of a tribunal to repay any deposits will be punishable with imprisonment which may extend to three years and shall also be liable to a fine of not less than rupees five hundred for every day during which such non-compliance continues.[6]

12. Section 63. Issuing a prospectus with any untrue statement.

• *Punishment.* Imprisonment for a term which may extend to *two years, or with fine which may extend to fifty thousand rupees,* or with both, unless he proves either that the statement was immaterial or that he had reasonable ground to believe, and did up to the time of the issue of the prospectus believe, that the statement was true.

13. Section 68. Any person who, either by knowingly or recklessly making any statement, promise or forecast which is false, deceptive or misleading, or by any dishonest concealment of material facts, induces or attempts to induce another person to enter into, or to offer to enter into:

(*a*) any agreement for, or with a view to, acquiring, disposing of, subscribing for, or underwriting shares or debentures; or

(*b*) any agreement the purpose or pretended purpose of which is to secure a profit to any of the parties from the yield of shares

6 Section 58A(10) of the Companies Act 1956.

or debentures, or by reference to fluctuations in the value of shares or debentures;

• *Punishment.* Imprisonment for a term which may extend to *five years,* or with fine which may extend to *one lakh rupees,* or with both.

14. Section 69. The application money of those applicants to whom no shares has been allotted is not repaid within 130 days of the date of issue of the prospectus, then the Directors shall be jointly and severally liable to repay that money with the prescribed interest from the expiry of 130 days

15. Section 73. Failure to repay excess application money.

• *Punishment.* Default in repayment of application money and interest, the company and every officer of the company who is an default shall be punishable with fine which may extend to *fifty thousand rupees,* and where repayment is not made within six months from the expiry of the eighth day, also with imprisonment for a term which may extend to *one year.*

16. Section 84(3). If a company with intent to defraud, renews a certificate or issues a duplicate share certificate.

• *Punishment.* Fine which may extend to *ten thousand rupees* and every officer of the company who is in default shall be punishable with imprisonment for a term which may extend to *six months*, or with fine which may extend to *one lakh rupees*, or with both.[7]

17. Section 105. Concealing name of a creditor or misrepresenting the nature or amount of the debt or claim of any creditor.

• *Punishment.* Imprisonment for a term which may extend to *one year,* or with *fine,* or with both.[8]

7 The 2008 Bill provides that any person deceitfully personates the owner of any share or interest and thereby obtains or attempts to obtain or receive any money due to any such owner, shall be punishable with imprisonment for a term which shall not be less than one lakh rupees but which may extend to five lakh rupees.

8 Under Clause 77 of the Companies Bill 2011, every company creating a charge on its property or assets or any of its undertakings whether tangible or intangible shall be registered with the Registrar of Companies. Any contravention of the provision shall be punishable with a fine which shall not be less than one lakh rupees and it can be extend to ten lakh rupees and any officer of the company who is in default shall be punishable with imprisonment for a term which may extend to six months or with fine which shall not be less than ten thousand rupees which can be extend to six months or with fine.

18. Clause 127 of the Companies Bill 2011. If the dividend has been declared by a company and has not been paid, every director of the company who is in default shall be punishable with imprisonment for a term of two years and with fine which may not be less than ₹ 1000 per day during such default continues and also the company is liable to pay an interest at the rate of eighteen per cent per annum.

19. Clause 134 of the Companies Bill 2011. Any company contravene the provisions of the financial statements submissions, shall be punishable with fine which shall not be less than fifty thousand rupees but which may extend to twenty five lakh rupees and every officer of the company who is in default shall be punishable with a term of imprisonment which may extended to three years or with fine which shall not be less than fifty thousand rupees but may extend to five lakh rupees or with both.[9]

20. Section 137(3). If a company fails to file financial statements with Registrar, the company shall be punishable with fine of one thousand rupees per day during which the failure continues, but which shall not be more than 10 lakh rupees. The managing director, Chief Financial Officer and any director who is in charge of the financial activities shall be punishable with imprisonment for a term which may extend to six months or fine which shall not be less than one lakh rupees but can be extend to five lakh rupees or with both.

21. Section 147(4). (*a*) If an officer of a company or any person on its behalf uses, or authorizes the use of, any seal purporting to be a seal of the company whereon its name is not engraven in the manner aforesaid;

(*b*) Issues or authorizes the issue of, any business letter, bill head, letter paper, notice or other official publication of the company wherein its name and the address of its registered office are not mentioned in the manner aforesaid;

(*c*) Signs or authorizes to be signed, on behalf of the company, any bill of exchange, hundi, promissory note, endorsement, cheque or order for money or goods wherein its name is not mentioned in the manner aforesaid; or

9 Clause 134(8) of the Companies Bill 2011.

(*d*) Issues, or authorizes the issue of, any bill of parcels, invoice, receipt or letter of credit of the company, wherein its name is not mentioned in the manner aforesaid;

Such officer or person shall be punishable with fine which may extend to five thousand rupees, and shall further be personally liable to the holder of the bill of exchange, hundi, promissory note, cheque or order for money or goods, for the amount thereof, unless it is duly paid by the company.

22. Clause 157(2) of the Companies Bill 2011. If the company fails to furnish DIN within the stipulated period, the company shall be punishable with fine which shall not be less than twenty-five thousand rupees but which may extend to one lakh rupees. Every officer who is in default shall be punishable with imprisonment for a term which may extend to six months or with fine which shall not be less than twenty five thousand rupees, but which may extend to one lakh rupees or with both.[10]

23. Clause 172 of Companies Bill 2011. If any company contravenes the provisions of chapter XI of the Bill regarding the appointment and functioning of company directors and there is no specific provision for punishment is provided in the Bill, the company and every officer of the company who is in default shall be punishable with fine which shall not be less than fifty thousand rupees but which may extend to five lakhs rupees.

24. Section 202(1). Un-discharged insolvent acting as director.

• *Punishment.* Imprisonment for a term which may extend *to two years*, or with fine which may extend to *fifty thousand rupees*, or with both.

25. Section 207. Default in distributing dividends within 30 days from the date of declaration.

• *Penalty:* Simple imprisonment up to *three years* and fine of one thousand rupees for every day during which such default continues.[11]

10 Clause 159 of the Companies Bill 2011.

11 In the case of default of the distribution of dividend, every director who is knowingly part of the default, of the company shall be punishable with imprisonment which may extend to two years and with fine which shall not be less than one thousand rupees for every day during which such default continues and the company shall be liable to pay simple interest at

26. Section 294A. Failure to produce account books before the Registrar or any officer so authorized by Central Government on inspection time.

• *Punishment.* Company who is in default shall be punishable with fine which shall not be less than *fifty thousand rupees*, and also with imprisonment for a term not exceeding *one year.*

27. Section 209(5). No compliance with the requirement of maintenance of proper books of account.

• *Punishment.* Imprisonment that may extend up to 6 months or with fine up to ₹ 10,000 or both.

28. Section 210(5). Failure to lay balance sheet, profit & loss account, etc. at the annual general meeting.

• *Punishment.* Imprisonment for a term which may extend to *six months*, or with fine which may extend to *ten thousand rupees*, or with both for each offence.[12]

29. Section 211(8). Failure to comply with s. 211 regarding form of balance sheet and matters to be stated therein and the content and disclosures to be made in the profit and loss account.

• *Punishment.* Imprisonment for a term which may extend to *six months* or with fine which may extend to *ten thousand rupees*, or with both.

30. Sections 212 and 214. The court refuses to treat the subsidiary company as a separate entity and instead treat it as only a branch of the holding company.

31. Section 217(5). Failure to attach to balance sheet a report of the board of directors.

• *Punishment.* Imprisonment for a term which may extend to *six months,* or with fine which may extend to *twenty thousand rupees*, or with both for each offence.

the rate of eighteen per cent annum during the period for which such default continues.

12 In the 2008 Bill, the punishment increased to one lakh rupees and in the case of a continuing default, further fine of five thousand rupees for every day during which the default continues of section 88.

32. Section 221(4). Failure to supply information to auditors.

• *Punishment.* Imprisonment which may extend to *six months*, or with fine which may extend to *fifty thousand rupees,* or with both.

33. Section 233B(11). Default in complying with the requirements of the section.

• *Punishment.* Company shall be liable to be punished with fine which may extend to *five thousand rupees*, and every officer of the company who is in default, shall be liable to be punished with imprisonment for a term which may extend to *three years*, or with fine which may extend to *fifty thousand rupees,* or with both.[13]

34. Section 242(1). If, from any report made under s. 241, it appears to the Central Government that any person has, in relation to the company or in relation to any other body corporate, whose affairs have been investigated by virtue of s. 239, been guilty of any offence for which he is criminally liable, the Central Government may, after taking such legal advice as it thinks fit, prosecute such person for the offence and it shall be the duty of all officers and other employees and agents of the company, or body corporate, as the case may be other than the accused in the proceedings, to give the Central Government all assistance in connection with the prosecution which they are reasonably able to give.

35. Section 250(9). Failure to honour restrictions upon shares and debentures imposed by the Company Law Board.

• *Punishment. Imprisonment* for a term which may extend to *six months*, or with fine which may extend to *fifty thousand rupees,* or with both.

36. Section 293A(5). Contribution to political parties or for political purposes in contravention of s. 293A.

• *Punishment. The* company shall be punishable with fine which may extend to *three times* the amount so contributed; and every officer

13 *Ibid,* section 130 provides for higher punishment in case of violation of any provisions related to the appointment of auditors. Contravention of provisions from ss. 123 to 129 shall be punishable with a fine which may not be less than twenty-five thousand rupees but which may extend to five lakh rupees and any officer who is in default shall be punishable with imprisonment for a term which may extend to one year or with fine which shall not be less than ten thousand rupees which can extend to one lakh rupees.

of the company who is in default shall be punishable with imprisonment for a term which may extend to *three years* and shall also be liable to fine.

37. Section 295(4). Grant of loan to directors without obtaining the previous approval of the Central Government.

• *Punishment.* Simple imprisonment up to six months or fine up to Rupees *fifty thousand.*

38. Section 299(4). Failure to disclose interest.

• *Punishment.* Fine which may extend to ₹ 50,000.

39. Section 308(3). Failure to disclose shareholdings.

• *Punishment.* Imprisonment up to two years or/and fine up to rupees fifty thousand.

40. Section 407(2). Any person who knowingly acts as a managing or other director or manager of a company.

• *Punishment.* Imprisonment for a term which may extent to one year, or with fine which may extend to fifty thousand rupees or with both.

41. Section 488(3). False declaration of company's solvency.

• *Punishment.* Imprisonment for a term which may extend to six months, or with fine which may extend to fifty thousand rupees, or with both.

42. Section 542. In the course of winding up of the company, it appears that the business of the company has been carried on with intent to defraud the creditors of the company or any other person or for any fraudulent purpose, all those who were aware of such fraud shall be personally liable without any limitation of liability.

43. Section 140 of the Companies Bill 2008 provides for punishment for not getting the Director Identification Number (DIN) to appoint any person without the DIN number shall be punishable with imprisonment for a term which may extend to 6 months or with fine which may extend to 5000 rupees that where the contravention is a continuing one, with a further fine which may extent to 500 rupees for every day during which the contravention continues.

44. Clause 336 of the Companies Bill 2011 (corresponding to s. 538 of the Companies Act 1956). If any person, be a past or present officer

of the company, at the time of the commission of the alleged offence, is being wound up, not delivering such part of the movable or immovable property of the company in his custody at the time of wound up of company to the liquidator within 12 months immediately before the commencement of the winding up shall be punishable with imprisonment for a term which shall not be less than three years but which may extend to 5 years and with fine which shall not be less than one lakh rupees but which may extend to 3 lakh rupees. This liability will be on the director or any other officer only either he had knowledge or intention to defraud or to conceal the true state of affairs of the company or to defeat the law.[14]

45. Clause 338 of the Companies Bill 2011. Where a company is being wound up and if it is found that proper books of account were not kept by the company bought the period of two years immediately preceding the commencement of winding up, and every officer of the company who is in default shall, unless he shows that he acted honestly and that in the circumstances in which the business of the company was carried on, every such officer who is at fault shall be punishable with imprisonment for a term which shall not be less than one year but which may extend to 3 years and with fine which shall not be less than one lakh rupees but which may extend to 3 lakh rupees.

46. Clause 340 of the Companies Bill 2011. In the course of winding up of a company, it appears that any business of the company has been carried out with the intent to defraud creditors of the company or any other person for any fraudulent purpose, the liquidator, creditor, contributory of the company can sue the past director, manager, officer of the company or any person who had knowingly parties to the carrying on of the business shall be personally responsible, without limitation of liability, for all or any of the debts or liabilities of the company.

47. In the course of winding up of a company, it appears that any person who has first taken part in the promotion or formation of the company, past or present director, manager, company liquidator or officer of the company has misapplied, retained, or become liable or accountable for any money or property of the company, has been guilty of any misfeasance or breach of trust in relation to the company, the tribunal can order such person to repay or restore the money or property

14 Section 311 of the Companies Bill 2008.

or any part thereof prospectively, with interest at such rate of the tribunal considers just as a compensation to the company.

48. Chapter 22 of the Companies Bill 2011 provides for permission of foreign companies, incorporated outside India, they are not less than 50 per cent of the paid up share capital, but the equity or preference of partly equity and partly preference, of a foreign company is held by one or more city sense of India or by any company is or body corporate in India, one or more citizens of India or Indian companies should comply with all the provisions of this particular chapter. If any foreign company fails to comply with any of the provisions of this chapter, the company shall be punishable with fine which shall not be less than one lakh rupees but which may extend to 3 lakh rupees and in the case of a continuing offence an additional fine which may extend to 50,000 rupees for every day during which the default continues and every officer who is in default shall be punishable with imprisonment for a term which may extend to 6 months or with fine which shall not be less than 35,000 rupees but which may extend to 1 lakh rupees or with both.[15]

49. If a person makes a false statement with regard to annual returns, report, balance sheet, prospectus, statement or other documents required by or for the purpose of any of the provisions of the company law, he shall be punishable with imprisonment for a term which may extend to 3 years and with fine which may extend to 5 lakh rupees. If any person intentionally gives false evidence upon any examination on oath or solemn affirmation, or in any affidavit, any deposition shall be punishable with imprisonment which shall not be less than three years but which may extend to 7 years and with fine which may extend to 10 lakh rupees.[16]

50. In the case of a company or any officer who is in default repeating the default, he shall be punishable with imprisonment which was provided, but in case of defaults for which fine is provided either along with of exclusive of imprisonment, with fine which shall be twice the amount of fine for such default.[17]

51. If any officer or employee of a company wrongfully obtains possession of any property, including cash of the company shall, on the

15 Clause 379 of the Companies Bill 2011.
16 *Ibid.*, Clause 448 and 449 of the Companies Bill 2011.
17 *Ibid.*, Clause 451.

compliant of the company or of any creditor or any contributory, be punishable with fine which shall be not less than one lakh rupees but which may extend to 5 lakh rupees.[18]

52. If any person carry on business under any name or title of the word "Limited" or the words "Private Limited" or the letters and word "OPC Limited" of any contradiction of limitation of the words, other than under the Act shall be punishable for using that name or title with fine which shall not be less than one lakh rupees but which may extend to 5 lakh rupees.[19]

53. Clause 450 of the Companies Bill 2011. If the new Bill does not specifically provide anywhere in the Bill, any punishment for any offences or defaults, such offences and defaults and such officer of the company shall be punishable with fine which may extent to ten thousand rupees and such contravention is a continuing one, one thousand rupees every day of such contravention.

54. Clause 451 of Companies Bill 2011. Any company or officer of a company commits the same offence second time within a period of three years, then that company and every officer of the company shall be punishable with double the amount of fine for such offence in addition to any imprisonment provided for that offence.

55. Clause 452 of Companies Bill 2011. Any officer or employee of the company wrongfully obtains possession of the company's property including cash of the company, shall be punishable with a fine which may not be less than one lakh rupees but which may extend to five lakh rupees.

7.2 Prosecution of Directors

Directors of a company are susceptible to prosecution of the illegal activities of the company. Penal actions for defaults committed under the Companies Act 1956 are either to be taken against an "officer in default" or a "director(s)" or "persons" as provided in the relevant penal provisions of the Act. Section 5 of the Companies Act 1956, defines officer in default and the Directors are also liable for compliance of

18 *Ibid.,* Clause 452.
19 *Ibid.,* Clause 412. Clause 453 of the Companies Bill 2011 corresponding to s. 631 of the Companies Act 1956.

various provisions of the Act.[20] But this criminal liability is applicable only to company directors or officers those who are in "default." In a circular issued by the Ministry of Corporate Affairs on March 25th 2011 clarified the position of independent directors and nominee directors. The circular states that:

No such Directors as indicated above shall be held liable for any act of omission or commission by the company or by any officers of the company which constitute a breach or violation of any provision of the Companies Act, 1956, and which occurred without his knowledge attributable through Board process and without his consent or connivance or where he has acted diligently in the Board process. The Board process includes meeting of any committee of the Board and any information which the Director was authorised to receive as Director of the Board as per the decision of the Board.

This circular was issued to clarify the position of innocent directors who never participate in the day-to-day affairs of the company.

The Delhi High Court in *In re, Sushila Devi* v *Securities and Exchange Board of India,*[1] elaborately discussed the prosecution of company directors. In the above case relating to prosecution of company directors by SEBI for violations of the provisions of the Securities and Exchange Board of India Act 1992 ("SEBI Act"). The SEBI filed a complaint against the petitioners under s. 200 of the Code of Criminal Procedure 1973 read with ss. 24(1) and 27 of the SEBI Act, stating, *inter alia*, that s. 11 of the SEBI Act casts upon the SEBI the duty to protect the interest of investors in securities and that the SEBI was enjoined upon to promote the development and to regulate the securities market through appropriate measures. A limited submission was made on behalf of SEBI that the averment that petitioners were the directors and persons-in-charge and responsible for the day-to-day affairs of the company was insufficient to proceed against the petitioners. The question that arose for decision was as to what constitutes sufficient averments in a complaint to make it actionable *vis-a-vis* the directors of a company.

The Delhi High Court held that officers responsible for the conduct of the affairs of a company are generally referred to as directors,

20 http://trustman.org/blog/2011/prosecution-of-directors-of-company-india/, visited on 29.05.2012.

1 (2008)1 Cr LJ 155 (Del).

managers, secretaries etc. With reference to ss. 291 to 293 of the Companies Act 1956, it would be evident that what the board of directors of a company is empowered to do would depend upon the roles and functions assigned to the directors as per the Memorandum and Articles of Association of a company. It would be sufficient to state that the question as to what is the role of a Director in a company is a question of fact. The Delhi High Court also rejected the submissions of the petitioners that some of the accused directors were mere investors and that they merely signed the proposal form of directorship and that they never attended any Board Meeting and that they had ceased to be directors of the company.

However, the Court held that since criminal liability is foisted upon a director not merely on account of his or her being a director, but on account of a conduct, act or omission, there must be an averment in a complaint relatable to the said act or omission. By relying the decision of the Supreme Court of India in the case of *SMS Pharmaceuticals Limited* v *Neeta Bhalla*,[2] the Delhi High Court also held that by its very nomenclature, a person who holds the post of managing director would be presumed to be managing and controlling the affairs of the company and since the complaint filed by SEBI makes material averments sufficient to attract cognizance of the complaint and issuance of the summons to answer the charge, issue of summons against the accused directors was upheld.

In deciding the above case, the Delhi High Court also relied on and quoted the observations of the Supreme Court of India in the case of *N. Rangachari* v *Bharat Sanchar Nigam Limited*,[3] which is reproduced below. The decision in *S.M.S Pharmaceuticals Ltd's* case[4] has been a subject-matter of consideration by the Supreme Court in the latest pronouncement reported as *N. Rangachari* v *Bharat Sanchar Nigam Ltd.*[5] in following was observed by the Supreme Court:

> Therefore, a person in the commercial world having a transaction with a company is entitled to presume that the directors of the

2 (2005)6 CLJ 144 (SC); AIR 2005 SC 3512; 2005 Supp (3) SCR 371; (2005)8 SCC 89; 2005(7) SCALE 397; JT 2005(8) SC 450.

3 (2008)1 CLJ 124 (SC); AIR2007 SC 1682; JT 2007(6) SC 292; 2007(5) SCALE 82; (2007)5 SCC 108.

4 (2005)6 Comp LJ 144 (SC).

5 (2008)1 Comp LJ 124 (SC); AIR 2007 SC 1682; JT 2007(6) SC 292; 2007(5) SCALE 821; (2007)5 SCC 108.

company are in charge of the affairs of the company. If any restrictions on their powers are placed by the memorandum or articles of the company, it is for the directors to establish it at the trial. It is in that context that section 141 of the Negotiable Instruments Act provides that when the offender is a company, every person, who at the time when the offence was committed was in charge of and was responsible to the company for the conduct of the business of the company, shall also be deemed to be guilty of the offence along with the company. It appears to us that an allegation in the complaint that the named accused are directors of the company itself would usher in the element of the erecting for and on behalf of the company and of their being in charge of the company.

In Gower and Davies, *Principles of Modern Company Law,* 7th Ed., the theory behind the idea of identification is traced as follows:

> "It is possible to find in the cases varying formulations of the under lying principle and the most recent definitions suggest that the courts are prepared today to give the rule of attribution based on identification a somewhat broader scope. In the original formulation in the *Lennard's Carrying Co.* v *Asiatic Petroleum Co. Ltd.*,[6] Lord Haldane based identification on a person 'who is really the directing mind and will of the corporation, the very ego and center of the personality of the corporation'. Recently, however, such an approach has been castigated by the Privy Council through Lord Hoffman in the *Meridian Global Funds Management Asia Ltd.* v *Securities Commission*,[7] as misleading 'general metaphysic of companies'. The true question, or presumably other rule of law, is to be regarded as the controller of the company for the purpose of the identification rule"...

A person normally having business or commercial dealings with a company, would satisfy himself about its creditworthiness and reliability by looking at its promoters and board of directors and the nature and extent of its business and its memorandum or articles of association. Other than that, he may not be aware of the arrangements within the company in regard to its management, daily routine, etc.

6 [1915] AC 705 (HL).
7 [1995]3 WLR 413.

Therefore, when a cheque issued to him by the company is dishonoured, he is expected only to be aware generally of who are in charge of the affairs of the company. It is not reasonable to expect him to know whether he has been deprived of his authority to do so when he actually signed the cheque. Those are matters peculiarly within the knowledge of the company and those in charge of it. So, all that a payee of a cheque that is dishonoured can be expected to allege is that the persons named in the compliant are in charge of its affairs. The directors are *prima facie* in that position.

In the light of the ratio in *S.M.S. Pharmaceuticals Ltd.'s* case,[8] what is to be looked into is whether in the complaint, in addition to asserting that the appellant and another are the directors of the company, it is further alleged that they are in charge of and responsible to the company for the conduct of the business of the company. We find that such an allegation is clearly made in the complaint which we have quoted above. Learned senior counsel for the appellant argued that in *Saroj Kumar Poddar* v *State (NCT of Delhi)*,[9] this court had found the complaint unsustainable only for the reason that there was no specific averments that at the time of the issuance of the cheque that was dishonoured, the persons named in the complaint were in charge of the affairs of the company. With great respect, we see no warrant for assuming such a position in the context of the binding ratio in *S.M.S. Pharmaceuticals Ltd's* case, and in view of the position of the directors of the company as explained above.

In this regard, it is pertinent to note that the general powers exercised by the Board of Directors of a company are enumerated in s. 291 of the Companies Act and as such whether a person joins the board of a company as a whole-time director or a non-whole time Director, he/she exercises the same powers enumerated in s. 291 of the Companies Act 1956 and it is wrong to assume that such because a person is not in whole-time employment as a Director in a company or fulfills the role of an "Independent Director", he/she can automatically claim immunity from prosecutions for violations committed by the company while such a person occupies the position of a Director.

8 (2005)6 Comp LJ 144 (SC).

9 (2007)1 Comp LJ 302 (SC); (2007)3 SCC 693; 2007(2) SCALE 36; 2007(1) TNLR 87 (SC).

Inserting misleading statement in the annual report of a company, the concerned directors can be prosecuted under ss. 628 and 633 of the Companies Act. The Calcutta High Court in *Deba Prasad* v *Regional Director, Department of Company Affairs,*[10] considered this question. The primary question considered in this case was that s. 633(2) of the Companies Act 1956, whether the petitioners actively concealed material facts from the annual report of SBI Home Finance Ltd. the registrar of companies are required the petitioners to show cause why legal action should not be initiated against them under s. 628 read with s. 211. The company was promoted by the State Bank of India and prominent banking institutions in India. In this case the annual report states that "due to non-infusion of capital, the net worth of the company continues to remain fully eroded." However, the Registrar of companies found that the company has suffered heavy losses and due to that, the net worth of the company has eroded. The directors defended the case by stating that what material facts had been disclosed in the balance sheet of the company and composite papers of which the director's report was only a part of it. Ultimately the directors argued that there was no *mens rea* on the part of the directors and, no laws were suffered by reason of such courage omission of a material fact of an alleged mistreatment in the annual report.

In an early case, decided by the Sind Judicial Commissioner's Court in Official Liquidators of the *Karachi Bank Limited* v *Directors, Manager and Auditors of the Karachi Bank Ltd.,*[11] throws light on the question of liability on false statement in the balance sheet. In this case the official liquidator of the Karachi Bank Ltd. filed an obligation under s. 237 of the Indian Companies Act 1913, for a direction that the prosecute the directors, auditors and manager of the said bank for offences under s. 282 of the Companies Act. It was alleged that there are a false statement in the bank's balance sheet, the assets of the bank were overvalued, the bad or doubtful debts under estimated, and it was falsely shown that the bank made a huge profit in the year 1927.

The court held that where a person signs a balance sheet containing false statements as manager, he renders himself liable to prosecution under s. 282 of the Companies Act, even though it was not necessary for him to sign the balance sheet and he signed merely because the

10 (2008)141 Comp Cas 140 (Cal); 2007(4) CHN 238.
11 (1932)2 Comp Cas 42.

directors wished him to do so. Where a balance sheet contains for statements, auditors who signed the report or not to the balance sheet to the effect that the balance sheet is drawn up in conformity with the law and exhibits a true and correct view of the companies of sales power guilty of making a false statement in their report and render themselves liable for prosecution under s.282 of the Companies Act. If a person join in the board of directors and allow their names to be used as a bait to induce the public to deal with the concern of which they are directors, they must take the consequences if they do not exercise due care and attention in signing a false balance sheet. So it is clear that the officers of the company are criminally liable for making misrepresentation in the balance sheet.

The Madras High Court considered the question of liability of a resigned director for non-filing of the balance sheet in an annual returns. The court observed that there is no provision in the Companies Act 1956, regarding vacancy of the office of a director by resignation. If there is any provision in the articles of Association of a company giving the right to a director to resign at any time, the resignation will take effect without any need for its acceptance by the board on the company in general meeting. The absence of any such provision in the articles, a resignation once made will take effect immediately when the intention to resign is made clear. Accordingly in such cases the resignation tendered by a director or a managing director unequivocally in writing will take effect from the time when such resignation is tendered. Hence, the conviction passed on the managing director for non-filing of the balance sheet and annual returns of the company, was held to be not valid.[12]

The Madras High Court in an old case of *D. Doss* v *C.P. Connel,*[13] considered the question of liability of directors for acts of co-directors. The court observed that in discharging the duties of his position as a director, he must act honestly and must also exercise some degree of both skill and diligence. He need not however exhibit in the performance of his duties a greater degree of skill than may reasonably be expected from a person of his knowledge and experience. If he is held responsible, he is committing a breach of duty recklessly careless in the matter. If the security deposit taken from the employees were

12 *T. Murari* v *State* (1976)46 Comp Cas 613 (Mad).
13 (1937)7 Comp Cas 429; ILR (1938) Mad 292.

misappropriated by the advisory director without the knowledge of others, and the other directors had no reason to suspect the honesty of the chairman or the advisory director, other directors were justified in trusting the chairman and the advisory director, and that they were not guilty of willful negligence and could not be made liable for the sums misappropriated by the advisory director.

The Madhya Pradesh High Court in *S. Chatterjee* v *Dr. K.L. Bhave,*[14] held that if any director of a company publishes any statement willfully giving a false statement about the financial position of the company and a person is induced by these false statements to take shares in the company, it is open to such person to maintain a suit for damages against the director of the company who issue the statement and the other directors even though the statement purports on the face of it to be addressed to the shareholders.

Even though the statement about the financial position of a company may be verbally accurate, it would be a fold statement if its effect is to mislead third persons, by suppressing material facts which would show that the financial position of the company is unsound. To a suit for damages against the officers of a company for floral and statement about the financial position of the company in a pamphlet issued by them, the company is not a necessary party.

The directors would also be liable on the principal's vicarious liability for the tort of his agent. Where an agent makes a false statement in the course of his employment, the principal will be liable under the normal rules of vicarious responsibility for the torts of his agent.[15] If the representations were false both to the knowledge of the principal, viz., the directors and agent, viz., and they have made in the course of employment as agent and consequently, the directors and the agent all are libellous joint tortfeasors. The remedies available to a person who has been the victim of fraud, deceit or other unconscionable conduct are rescission, restitution, damages or constructive trust are some of the usual remedies for fraudulent misrepresentation.

The Madras High Court considered the liability of managing director and other directors of a company in failure to submit first annual

14 (1962)32 Comp Cas 830.
15 *Lloyd* v *Grace Smith & Co.* [1912] AC 716.

balance sheet before the general meeting within 18 months of incorporation of company in *In re Gangipati Appayya.*[16] In this case the managing directors and other directors were convicted under ss. 131(1) and 133(3) of the Indian Companies Act 1913. The managing director contented that in as much as a general meeting was not held within the time prescribed no question of lying the balance sheet arose. Other directors argues that there was no willful default on their part, especially because it was the managing director who was to call the meeting and lay the balance sheet before it, and that the balance sheet could not be placed before the general meeting owing to circumstances beyond their control.

The court relied on an earlier judgment in *Bhagirath Chandra Das* v *Emperor,*[17] the court meant the following observations:

> "If directors, who are responsible for the management of a company and who presumably know the duties imposed upon them by law, make no attempt to see that those duties are carried out there is justification for holding, in my opinion, that they have wilfully and knowingly permitted the company to fail to carry out those duties. The suggestion that these various directors were mere figure heads not taking any active part in the control of the company is in my opinion not worthy of serious consideration. They were directors, they attended meetings throughout the period with which we are concerned and they were responsible for the management of the company.
>
> But these provisions of the Companies Act have been deliberately enacted to protect shareholders and in some cases to protect the general public and impose a definite duty upon directors. It is necessary that those duties should be properly carried out and it is necessary, in my opinion, that's when directors fail to do so, the penalties provided for in the act should be imposed and the directors should be substantially penalised."

Accordingly, the court held that the managing director could not rely upon his own default, viz., failure to call the meeting, and that therefore he was rightly convicted; and that the other directors were also individually responsible and that therefore they were also rightly convicted.

16 (1952)21 Comp Cas 78; (1952)1 MLJ 507 (Mad).
17 (1947)17 Comp Cas 93; AIR 1948 Cal 42.

The Madras High Court confirmed this position in the *Assistant Registrar of Companies, Madras, Tamil Nadu* v *Southern Machinery Works.*[18] The Court held that whether a director could be proceeded against under s. 162 of the Companies Act 1956 must be determined according to the availability of evidence in each case. Whole directors to be deemed to be knowingly guilty of default in the absence of reply to notice issued by registrar of companies.

The Madras High Court in the *Amara Picture (P) Ltd., in re,*[19] held that criminal intention is irrelevant in the context of the trust that is to be applied under s. 633(1) of the Act. What is irrelevant is whether the accused acted honestly, in good faith, and whether he got any justifiable reason to escape from the liability. It was held that the provisions could not be equated with the provision of discharge or acquittal under the Code of Criminal Procedure. It is to be kept in mind that whether the petition is half acted with *mala fide* intention of luring the public for subscribed and fisheries of the company under a false representation. In this case the court allowed the petition and held that the petitioners are not held liable according to the notice issued by the Registrar.

Further, if one analyzes the definition of "officer who is in default" as given in s. 5 read with s. 633 of the Companies Act 1956, it becomes clear that only when certain responsible officials of the company give "consent" and only when the accused Director can satisfactorily show that he/she exercised due diligence and care and caution in performing his/her function as a company director, then the rigors of liability fastened on such Director can be minimized and relief can be granted by the Court. However, in most of the cases, in order to get this relief, the concerned accused Director has to first face the trial and his/her plea for exclusion from the array of accused Director is normally not given serious consideration and relief does not come forthwith. The above mentioned decisions point out that the escape routes for accused Directors have been curbed and relief is not automatic and definitely just not on mere asking.

The Federal Court in India considered the question of the *mala fide* acts of directors and the remedy available to shareholders in

18 (1986)1 MLJ 189 (Mad); (1986)59 Comp Cas 670 (Mad).
19 (1970)40 Comp Cas 130.

Dr. Satya Charan Law v *Rameshwar Prosad Bajoria.*[20] Ordinarily the directors of a company are the only persons who can conduct litigations in the name of the company, but when they are themselves the wrongdoers against the company and have acted *mala fide* court beyond their powers and their personal interest is in conflict with their duty in such a way that they cannot or will not take steps to seek redress for the wrong done to the company, the majority of shareholders or entitled to take steps to redress the wrong. If there is no provision in the articles of association to meet the contingency the majority of shareholders can sue in the name of the company. This rule is applicable even if the articles of Association vest the management of the office of the company in the directors and empowered them to conduct litigation on its behalf and use its name as plaintiff. Misconduct on the part of the director he is an exception to the general rule that only directors are the persons who can conduct litigation in the name of the company.[1]

In *Dantuluri Ranga Devi* v *Registrar of Companies,*[2] on a complaint filed by the registrar of companies for the offence is under s. 162 of the Companies Act 1956, for failure to file the annual returns as required under ss. 159 and 161 of the Act. The petitioners filed a petition under s. 482 of the Code of Criminal Procedure 1973. In this case the accused No. 1, is a public limited company and A2 to A11, or directors/officer-in-charge of the company at the time of offence committed. The directors and officers mentioned in the compliant failed to file the annual returns and therefore they are liable to be punished under s. 162 read with ss. 159 and 161 of the Act. The complainant, registrar of companies issued a notice to the company to show cause why action should not be initiated for contravention of the provisions of the Act. The company has not able to furnish a proper reply in this case. The petitioner argues that there was no specific allegation against the whole time director or managing director, therefore in the absence of any specific allegation it cannot be said that the petitioner is also the officer in default of the company under s. 5 of the Act and had resigned from the company at the time of alleged offence.

20 (1950)20 Comp Cas 39; (1950) SCR 394.

1 *Automatic Self-cleansing Filter Syndicate Company Ltd.* v *Cunninghame* [1906]2 Ch 34.

2 (2007)135 Comp Cas 599 (AP); (2008)83 SCL 376 (AP).

The court found that the offence committed had been prior to the alleged resignation and therefore the petitioners cannot escape from the liability of a director of the company at the time of commissioning of the offence. Hence, the court refused to quash the proceedings against A2 to A11.[3]

In *Thummala Pradeep Reddy* v *Registrar of Companies, A.P.*,[4] the Andhra Pradesh High Court held that no investigation into a criminal proceeding can be quashed unless the allegations combined therein, even on their face value take into the correct, makes out no case. One of the grounds on which a company may be quashed is there are the proceedings or found to be maliciously instituted with the ulterior motive for wreaking vengeance on the accused and the debt due to spite him into private and personal grudge. In this case the petitioner was one of the directors of the company, however, he resigned as a director and the same was accepted by the board of directors on 25th March 1999. The petitioner argues that even though he resigned well before the incident, the depositors who never withdrawn their moneys from the company after the fixed deposits were matured filed a criminal complaint against the director. The petitioner filed a petition under Art. 226 of the Constitution of India to quash the proceedings against him.

The court observed that the petitioners were responsible at the time of committing the offence could be decided only after investigation into the allegations and it could not be decided by exercising jurisdiction under Art. 226 of the Constitution of India and refuse to quash the criminal proceedings against the accused.

A director may be held criminally liable for any offence committed by the company, where he has aided, abetted, counseled, or procured the commission of the offence. Just as individuals owe a duty not to harm or injure others in society without justification, so do companies owe a duty not to poison our water and food, not to pollute our rivers,

3 A reference was made to the case decided by the Supreme Court in *K.P.G Nair* v *Jindal Menthol India Ltd.* (2001)104 Comp Cas 290 (SC); 2000(4) CTC 432, wherein it was held that the absence of any specific allegation in the complaint about the director who is in charge and responsible to the accused company for the conduct of the business, otherwise the compliant is not maintainable. This particular case was filed under s. 141 of the Negotiable Instruments Act.

4 2005(2) ALD Cri 41; (2007)135 Comp Cas 586 (AP).

beaches and air, not to allow their workplaces to endanger the lives and safety of their employees and the public, and not to sell commodities, or provide transport, that will kill or injure people.

In many of the Acts relating to economic offences, imprisonment is mandatory. Where the convicted person is a corporation, this provision becomes unworkable, and it is desirable to provide that in such cases, it shall be competent to the court to impose a fine. This difficulty can arise under the Penal Code also, but it is likely to arise more frequently in the case of economic laws.

If a body corporate is found guilty of offence committed, the court, though bound to impose the sentence prescribed under law, has the discretion to impose the sentence of imprisonment or fine as in the case of a company. In the case of a corporate body, the sentence of imprisonment cannot be imposed on it and as the law never compels to do anything which is impossible, the court has to follow the alternative and impose the sentence of fine. This discretion could be exercised only in respect of juristic persons and not in respect of natural persons. There is no blanket immunity for any company from any prosecution for serious offences merely because the prosecution would ultimately entail a sentence of mandatory imprisonment. The corporate bodies, such as a firm or company undertake series of activities that affect the life, liberty and property of the citizens. Large scale financial irregularities are done by various corporations. The corporate vehicle now occupies such a large portion of the industrial, commercial and sociological sectors that amenability of the corporation to a criminal law is essential to have a peaceful society with stable.

7.3 Criminal breach of trust

Section 405 of the Indian Penal Code (IPC) defines criminal breach of trust. It provides that:

> Whoever, being in any manner entrusted with property, or with any dominion over property, dishonestly misappropriates or converts to his own use that property, or dishonestly uses or disposes of that property in violation of any direction of law prescribing the mode in which such trust is to be discharged, or of any legal contract, express or implied, which he has made touching the discharge of such trust, or willfully suffers any other person so to do, commits criminal breach of trust.

The offence of criminal breach of trust, as defined under this section, is similar to the offence of embezzlement under the English law. A reading of the section suggests that the gist of the offence of criminal breach of trust is 'dishonest misappropriation' or 'conversion to own use' another's property, which is nothing but the offence of criminal misappropriation defined under s. 403. The only difference between the two is that in respect of criminal breach of trust, the accused is entrusted with property or with dominion or control over the property. As the title to the offence itself suggests, entrustment of property is an essential requirement before any offence under this section takes place. It extends to entrustments of all kinds, whether to clerks, servants, business partners or other persons, provided they are holding a position of trust. The term 'entrusted' found in a s. 405, IPC governs not only the words 'with the property' immediately following it but also the words 'or with any dominion over the property.'

The Allahabad High Court in *Life Insurance Corporation of India* v *Hari Das Mundhra,*[5] observed that a director of a company is in the position of an agent of the company, charged with the obligation of carrying on its business. The nature of his duties is determined partly by statute and partly by the law of agency. As agent, he owes two duties to the company: the duty of loyalty and the duty of care. Breach of these duties amounts to breach of trust and misfeasance. The director must be loyal to the company in fact and in appearance. There must never be a clash between his interests and the interests of the company. A director would not be liable for mere errors of judgment or imprudent action.

A director would not be liable for the misconduct of another director unless he has joined with him in the perpetration of a wrong or has omitted to thwart a wrong due to his negligence. The test of negligence is not the post-event detached mind but the mind of the reasonable businessman in the heat of the moment. Willful misconduct of a director may amount to misfeasance.[6] Any fraud or underhand dealing by a director will render him liable to the company for any loss suffered by the company as a result.[7]

5 (1966)36 Comp Cas 371.
6 *In re Central Calcutta Bank Ltd.* (1959)29 Comp Cas 437; AIR 1959 Cal 625.
7 Palmer's *Company Law,* 20th Ed., p. 564.

The allegation of insufficient supervision by directors on the affairs of the company and subsequent loss to the company; the directors cannot be held liable for misfeasance. The directors were liable to make good the loss sustained by means of making fictitious entries in the accounts to cover up withdrawals from other banks. The directors were also liable to compensate the bank for loss incurred by the filing of the false balance-sheet and for sanction of loan to one of the directors.[8]

The allegation of misfeasance in the case of equity companies are a regular phenomenon. The Patna High Court considered the question of misfeasance, misappropriation of company's funds and various acts of the nonfeasance and breach of trust and claiming to recover certain amounts in *Official Liquidator, Navarashtra Publishing Co. Ltd.* v *Ashok,*[9] the court held that allegations of misfeasance, misapplication and breach of trust must be specific and the application by the official liquidator should contain a detailed narration of the specific acts of commission and omission on the part of each director, quantifying the laws to the company arising out of such acts more omission and the burden of proving the same rests on the official liquidator.

If there is only a vague allegation, had not made any specific case, the directors were not responsible for various acts of misfeasance or nonfeasance. However, if there are any lapses from the director which is inexcusable and would amount to gross negligence and nonfeasance for breach he was equally guilty and liable to the company.

The Supreme Court in *Sushil Kumar Gupta* v *Joy Shankar Bhattacharya,*[10] held that the appellant's manner of dealing with the money entrusted to his custody constituted criminal breach of trust. The Directors had no authority under the bye-laws to give any directions contrary to the bye-laws and so, could not ratify the violation of the bye-laws. Any resolution ratifying the use of trust money contrary to the directions contained in the bye-laws would not validate the breach of the bye-laws. The offence of criminal breach of trust is committed when a person, who is entrusted in any manner with property or

8 *K. Madhava Nayak* v *Popular Bank Ltd.* (1969)39 Comp Cas 711 (Ker); AIR 1970 Ker 131.

9 (1976)46 Comp Cas 572 (Pat).

10 AIR 1971 SC 1543; (1970)3 SCR 770.

with dominion over it, dishonestly misappropriates it, or converts it to his own use, or dishonestly uses it or disposes it of in violation.

The Supreme Court in *P.K. Nedungadi* v *Malayalee Bank Ltd. (In Liquidation),*[11] held that, while confirming the finding of the High Court, that it was the appellant (Mr. P.K. Nedungadi) who enabled other person to perpetrate the fraud which resulted in loss to the banking company, he also derived a certain benefit there from and therefore he was liable to repay or restore to the banking company the amount in respect of which there was misapplication, misfeasance and breach of trust resulting in loss to the banking company. The court observed that misfeasance and breach of trust include a breach by a promoter, director etc., of a duty to the company the direct consequence of which has been a misappropriation or loss of its assets for which he could be made responsible in an action. Allegations or proof of fraud are not essential and it is immaterial that the offence is one for which the offender may be criminally liable.

In *State of Gujarat* v *Jaswantlal Nathalal,*[12] the prosecution case was that the Government sold 100 bags of cement to the accused only on the condition that it will be used for construction of a building for the Government litho-printing press. However, 40 bags of cement were diverted to another godown. The accused was sought to be prosecuted for criminal breach of trust. The court observed that it is difficult to accept the contention of the appellant that after the sale of the cement in question the Government had any proprietary right over the same. Nor can it be said that the transaction in question resulted in any fiduciary relationship either between the Government and BSS or between the Government and the respondent. The term 'entrusted' found in s. 405, IPC governs not only the words 'with the property' immediately following it but also the words 'or with any dominion over the property' occurring thereafter. A mere transaction of sale cannot amount to an entrustment. The court held that a property is sold once there is no right any more over the property. If the purchases violated any other statute he must be prosecuted under that Act and not for criminal breach of trust.

11 (1972)42 Comp Cas 120; AIR 1971 SC 829.

12 AIR 1968 SC 700; (1968)2 SCR 408.

In *SESA Goa Ltd.* v *State of Maharashtra,*[13] the Bombay High Court held that the element of entrustment being absent, no offence could be said to have been committed under s. 403/406 of the IPC and, therefore, complaint must be quashed on that ground. In the instant case, the question of misappropriation of the amount which was paid towards the purchase of shares of 'SIL' did not arise as once shares were allotted to the respondent the monies became the property of the company over which she had no right. As already observed, there was no entrustment of the property nor was there entrustment of any dominion over the property. Once the shares are allotted, the money paid for the purchase of the shares becomes part of the assets/property of the company. The only interest that a shareholder could have is to the dividend in respect of his shareholding, the right to attend meetings of the shareholders and to vote at such meetings.[14]

The Supreme Court in *S.K. Alagh* v *State of UP,* it was held that any money received by the managing director of a company on behalf of the company, he could not be said to have committed an offence under s. 406 of the Indian Penal Code. The court observed that if and when a statute contemplates creation of such a legal fiction, it provides specifically therefore. The Indian Penal Code 1860 does not contemplate any vicarious liability on the part of a party lease not short directly for commission of an offence. In the case falling under s. 476 of the Indian Penal Code vicarious liability is not extendable to the directors or officers of the company or an employee cannot be held to be vicariously liable for any offence committed by the company itself.[15]

The Supreme Court in *R.K. Dalmia* v *Delhi Administration,*[16] held that there is no good reason to restrict the meaning of the word 'property' to movable property only when it is used without any qualification in s. 405 or in other sections of the Indian Penal Code. The court observed that what s. 409, IPC requires is that the person alleged to have committed criminal breach of trust with respect to any property be entrusted with that property or with dominion over that property in the way of his business as an agent. The expression 'in the

13 Writ Petition Nos. 2739 of 2006 and 254 of 2008.

14 *Ibid.,* para 26. The Court followed the decision in *Jaswant Rai Manilal Akhaney* v *State of Bombay* AIR 1956 SC 575; (1956) SCR 483.

15 (2008)142 Comp Cas 228 (SC).

16 AIR 1962 SC 1821 (5th April 1962).

way of his business' means that property is entrusted to him 'in the ordinary course of his duty or habitual occupation or profession or trade'. He should get the entrustment or dominion in his capacity as agent. In other words, the requirements of this section would be satisfied if the person be an agent of another and that other person entrusts him with property or with any dominion over that property in the course of his duties as an agent. A person may be an agent of another for some purpose and if he is entrusted with property not in connection with that purpose but for another purpose, that entrustment will not be entrustment for the purposes of s. 409, IPC, if any breach of trust is committed by that person.

In *Employees State Insurance Corporation* v *S.K. Aggarwal,*[17] the Supreme Court held that the definition of principal employer under the Employees State Insurance Act means the owner or occupier. In this case the respondents were, at the material time, directors of a company M/s. Indo Japan Steel Ltd. The company has a factory and having its head office at Calcutta. Under the provisions of s. 40 of the Employees State Insurance Act 1948, the 'principal employer' is required to pay, in respect of every employee, whether directly employed by him or by or through an immediate employer, both the employer's contribution and the employee's contribution. Under sub-sec. (2) of s. 40 the principal employer, in the case of an employee directly employed by him, is entitled to recover from the employee the employee's contribution by deduction from his wages. Under sub-sec. (4) any sum deducted by the principal employer from wages under this Act shall be deemed to have been entrusted to him by the employee for the purpose of paying the contribution in respect of which it was deducted. The complainant who is the appellant before us inspected the head office of the company and found that the company had deducted a sum of ₹ 2,223.50 as employee's share of contribution from their wages during the period February 1981 to September 1981. The employer, however, had failed to deposit the said amount in the Employees' State Insurance Fund within the specified time. Thereupon the appellant lodged a complaint against the respondents of criminal breach of trust under s. 405, Explanation 2 of the Indian Penal Code read with s. 406 of the Indian Penal Code.

17 1998 LLR 806; 1998(80) FLR 199.

The court held that even if we read the definition of 'principal employer' under the Employees' State Insurance Act 1948 in Explanation 2 to s. 405 of the Indian Penal Code, the directors of the company, in the present case, would not be covered by the definition of 'principal employer' when the company itself owns the factory and is also the employer of its employees at the head office.Consequently, the order of the High Court quashing the criminal proceedings initiated under ss. 405 and 406, IPC was upheld by the Supreme Court.

It was at one time thought that a company cannot be made criminally liable for its acts. They clearly have long been given up and it is settled law that 'where a duty is imposed upon a company in such a rate that a breach of the duty amounts to a disobedience of the law, then, if there is nothing in the statute either expressly or impliedly to the contrary a breach of the statute is an offence which can be visited upon the company by means of an indictment'.[18]

The scope of whether a limited company can be punished for offences was discussed by the Calcutta High Court in *Anath Bandhu Samantha* v *Corporation of Calcutta.*[19] In this case the appellant argues that the limited company under the Indian law cannot be proceeded against criminally for abetment of an offence. The court disagreed with the argument of the appellant and referred to s. 11 of the Indian Penal Code, and observed that "I have not been able to find out any Indian decision on the point. It is quite clear that if there is anything in the definition of context of a particular section on the statute which will prevent the application of the s. 2 a limited company, certainly a limited company cannot be proceeded against offence is like rape, is cannot be committed by a limited company". The general principle is that a limited company cannot be tried where *mens rea* is essential. Again it cannot be tried and held that when the only punishment for the offence is imprisonment because it is not possible to send a limited company to prison by way of a sentence. The court found that under the General Clauses Act, "person" includes a limited liability company also. Hence, the court come to the conclusion that the company can be

18 *Reg.* v *Tyler and International Commercial Company* [1891]20 QB 589. It was also noted that only 84 companies were registered in India in 1933 with an authorized capital of ₹ 311 lakhs. See also Comp Cas *Notes and Commentaries,* (1933), 3, p. 52.

19 (1952)22 Comp Cas 175 (Cal); AIR 1952 Cal 759; 56 CWN 594.

proceeded against instead of its officers when fine is the only sentence provided for in the present case. Thus a company can be proceeded against for offence committed under Calcutta Municipal Corporation Act 1951 [s. 407(*i*)(*v*)].

Where the statute provides that if the person contravening an order is a company, every person who is at the time of the contravention was in charge of and was responsible to the company for the conduct of the business of the company, as well as the company, shall be deemed to be guilty of the contravention. *Mens rea* is an essential element of the offence and it would be necessary for the prosecution to allege and establish in order to secure conviction of the member of the board of directors of a company that they were not only in charge of or responsible for the conduct of business of the company but also that they had necessary *mens rea* for the commission of the offence. Where it is found that many of the directors live away from the place of businessof the company and that the company has a whole-time director and manager, the latter must be taken to be the persons in charge of and responsible to the company for the conduct of business of the company and the burden will be on them to establish the absence of *mens rea*. In respect of the directors who stay away from the place of business the burden will be on the prosecution to establish complicity in the commission of the offence by consent or connivance.[20]

The question of criminal prosecution of a company for breach of trust was discussed by the Madras High Court in *Fidelity Industries Ltd.* v *State.*[1] In this case the respondent filed chargesheet for the offences punishable under s. 120B read with ss. 409, 420, 467, 468 and 471 of the Indian Penal Code read with s. 13(2) & s. 13(1)(*d*) of the Prevention of Corruption Act against the company and others. The company filed a petition before the court, on the ground that the traditional company is the company duly incorporated as per the Companies Act, has been also charged under s. 420 of the Indian Penal Codeis punishable with imprisonment compulsory and further the said offence further requires *mens rea* and therefore the company cannot be prosecuted for the offence under s. 420 of the Indian Penal Code.

20 *Smt. Peelamedu Rajewary Ramkrishna* (1972)42 Comp Cas 489.
1 (2006)129 Comp Cas 561 (Mad); 2006(1) CTC 374.

The trial court dismissed the petition to discharge the company from the above provisions. Aggrieved by the judgment, this revision has been filed. The petitioner argues that the company being a juristic person cannot have a mind to be charged with an offence which requires *mens rea,* and therefore, the company should be discharged from the offence under s. 420 of the Indian Penal Code. For the offence under s. 420 of the Indian Penal Code, the punishment shall be imprisonment which may extend up to 7 years and in the end carried added recovered in my head and other in the tower and it is our and also fine. Under s. 11 of the Indian Penal Code, a company can be treated as a person.

The Supreme Court in *M.V. Javali* v *Mahajan Borewell and Co.,*[2] held that if mandatory sentence cannot be enforced on the company but fine alone will be the only punishment. In this case the court observed that this is an offence under the Income Tax Act and is committed by a company, the persons who are liable to be proceeded against and punished are:

(1) the company (which includes a firm);

(2) every person, who at the time the offence was committed, was in charge of, and was responsible to the company for the conduct of the business; and

(3) any director, manager, secretary or other officer of the company with whose consent or connivance or because of neglect attributable to whom, the offence has been committed.

The court come to the conclusion that even in the case where criminal *mens rea* is involved and punishment of imprisonment is mandatory, still a company can be prosecuted and on conviction, the company can be fined. When an offence is committed by a company, whether the company is a natural person or a juristic person need not be gone into, in view of the fact that a company is also a person as defined under s. 11 of the Indian Penal Code. In such a case if it is convicted, the petitioner cannot be imprisoned, but fine can be imposed on the company.

The court referred to Law Commission Reports on the subject and observed that:

2 (1997)6 SCALE 343; 230 ITR 1 (SC); (1997)8 SCC 72.

> An important type of white-collar crime is that committed by Corporations. Since a Corporation has no physical body on which the pain of punishment could be inflicted, not a mind which can be guilty of a criminal intent, traditional punishments prove ineffective, and new and different punishments have to be devised. The real penalty of a corporation is the diminution of respectability, that is, the stigma. It is now usual to insert provisions to the effect that the Director or Manager who has acted for the corporation should be punished. But it is appropriate that the corporation itself, should be punished. In the public mind, the offence should be linked with the name of the corporation, and not merely with the name of the Director or Manger, who may be a non-entity. Punishment of fine in substitution of imprisonment in the case of a corporation could solve the problem in one aspect; but, at the same, it is necessary that there should be some procedure, like a judgment of condemnation, available in the case of an anti-social or economic offence committed by a Corporation. This will be analogous to the punishment of public censure proposed for individuals.

Similar views were taken in *P.V. Pai* v *R.L. Rinawma*,[3] *Kusum Products Ltd.* v *S.K. Sinha*[4] and *Modi Industries Ltd.* v *B.C. Goel*.[5] In 2003, the Supreme Court in *Assistant Commissioner* v *Velliappa Textiles Ltd.*,[6] held that since an artificial person like a Company could not be physically punished to a term of imprisonment, such a section, which makes it mandatory to impose minimum term of imprisonment, cannot apply to the case of artificial person. The Supreme Court, per majority (2:1) held that in such a situation the Company being incapable of suffering corporal punishment may not be prosecuted and held guilty. The Court opined that corporate criminal liability cannot be imposed without making corresponding legislative changes, i.e. the imposition of fine in lieu of imprisonment.

However, the Supreme Court in *Standard Chartered Bank* v *Directorate of Enforcement*,[7] in majority decision of 3:2 expressly overruled the *Velliappa Textiles* case. The question for consideration

3 ILR (1993) Kar 709; (1993)77 Comp Cas 179.
4 (1980)126 ITR 804 (Cal).
5 (1983)144 ITR 496 (All).
6 (2003)11 SCC 405; AIR 2004 SC 86.
7 (2005)4 SCC 530; 2005 SCC (Cri) 961; 2005 AIR SCW 2829.

before the Constitutional Bench was: Whether a company or a corporation being a juristic person, can be prosecuted for an offence for which mandatory punishment prescribed is imprisonment and fine.

The majority in the Constitution Bench, held that there could be no objection to a company being prosecuted for penal offences under the FERA and the fact that a sentence of imprisonment and fine has to be imposed and no imprisonment can be imposed on a company or an incorporated body, would not make s. 56 of the FERA inapplicable and that a company did not enjoy any immunity from prosecution in respect of offences for which a mandatory punishment of imprisonment is prescribed.

K.G. Balakrishnan, J (as he then was) in majority opinion held: (SCC p. 550, para 32):

> We hold that there is no immunity to the companies from prosecution merely because the prosecution is in respect of offences for which the punishment prescribed is mandatory imprisonment (*sic* and fine). We overrule the views expressed by the majority in Velliappa Textiles on this point....

K.G. Balakrishnan, J talking the majority view said that, it could not be said that there is blanket immunity for any Company from any prosecution for serious offences merely because the prosecution would ultimately entail a sentence of mandatory imprisonment. The intention of the legislature is not to give complete immunity from prosecution to the corporate bodies for these grave offences. Consequently, even for offences under s. 56(1)(*i*), FERA, the Company can be prosecuted. The court can ignore the provision that the defaulter should be punished with imprisonment as it is impossible to send the Company to prison.

B.N. Srikrishna, J who delivered the minority view for himself and on behalf of N. Santosh Hegde, J, said that it is not open to the Court to read the words "imprisonment and fine" as "imprisonment or fine"; such a construction is impermissible. Firstly, it virtually amounts to rewriting s. 56 of FERA. The Court would be reading the section as applicable to different situations with different meanings. Whatever the interpretation, it must be uniformly applied to all situations. If the conjunction "and" is read disjunctively as "or" then the intention of Parliament would definitely be defeated as the mandatory term would not be available even in case of natural person. It is trite that punishment must follow conviction. Therefore where a statute imposes mandatory imprisonment plus fine, such a provision would not enable the punishment of a corporate offender.

It is evident that there is lot of confusion on criminal liability of the corporation as such. There are conflicting decisions but in general, it is accepted that mandatory imprisonment cannot be imposed on a company where there is no "soul or body" to be jailed. But the officers in charge of the affairs of the company responsible for the act can be imprisoned. As the Law Commission of India in its 41st (para 24-7) and 47th (para 8-3) Report took cognizance of the legal anomaly and recommended suitable changes in the existing provisions of law by providing that, whenever a Company is guilty of commission of an offence which is punishable with imprisonment, the court instead of sentencing the Company to imprisonment, it may sentence fine only. Law Commission in its 41st Report suggested amendment to s. 62 of the Indian Penal Code by adding the following lines: "In every case in which the offence is only punishable with imprisonment or imprisonment and fine and the offender is the Company or other body corporate or an association of individuals, it shall be competent to the court to sentence such offender to fine only". On the basis of these recommendations, a bill to amend the Indian Penal Code (the Amendment Bill 1972) was also mooted but it lapsed. Therefore, as on today, there is no provision in the penal law of India to resolve this anomaly. There is urgent need to end the legal non-clarity of criminal liability of corporations and the amendment to be passed urgently in the background of several multi-crore corporate frauds are taking place in India.

7.4 Prosecution under Negotiable Instruments Act 1881

The personal liability under ss. 132 to 141 of the Negotiable Instruments Act 1882 has made a drastic change in the form of the Banking Public Financial Institutions and Negotiable Instrument Laws (Amendment) Act 1988. This amendment brought about a major change in the law relating to dishonour of cheques in India. The Supreme Court in *Shri Ishar Ally Steels Ltd.* v *Jayaswals NECO Ltd.*,[8] held that there is a

8 (2001)3 SCC 609; 2001(3) Civil Court Cases 238 (SC); 2001(2) Apex Court Journal 270 (SC); 2001 ISJ (Banking): 0307MANU/SC/0121/2001 at para 5.

high degree of importance attached to the law relating to negotiable instruments and hence there is the need to enforce them strictly.

Section 141 of the Negotiable Instruments Act 1881 provides for offences by companies under s. 138. It includes:

- Every person who was in charge of and was responsible to the company for the conduct of the business of the company at the time of commission of an offence, shall be deemed to be guilty of the offence and liable to be prosecuted.[9]
- If a person is proceeded against, he shall not be liable to punishment if he proves that the offence was committed without his knowledge, or that he has exercised due diligence to prevent the commission of such offence.[10]
- Any director, manager, secretary or other officer of the company shall also be deemed to guilty if it is proved that the offence has been committed with the consent, or negligence of such person.[11]

The Hon'ble Supreme Court in *Anil Hada* v *Indian Acrylic Ltd.*[12] explained the scope of this provision. It observed that:

> Three categories of persons can be discerned from the said provision who are brought within the purview of the penal liability through the legal fiction envisaged in the section. They are: (1) the company which committed the offence, (2) everyone who was in charge of and was responsible for the business of the company, (3) any other person who is a director or manager or a secretary or officer of the company, with whose convenience or due to whose neglect the company has committed the offence. If it is a natural person, such offence can be tried according to the procedure established by law. If the offence is committed by a juristic person like a body corporate it can be prosecuted for an offence under section 138 of the Act.

The question arises is that if a body corporate is committed an offence under s. 138, and under s. 141, whether a company is liable to be prosecuted or director also can be held liable. This question has been upheld by the Supreme Court in the case of *Aneeta Hadav* v

9 Section 141(1) of NI Act.
10 Proviso to s. 141(1) of NI Act.
11 Section 141(2) of NI Act.
12 AIR 2000 SC 145; 1998(2) ALD Cri 736; (2000)1 SCC 1; MANU/SC/0736/1999.

Godfather Travels and Tours Pvt. Ltd.,[13] the court held that... prosecution of the company is a *sine qua non* for prosecution of the other person who fall within the second unpaid categories of the candidates, everyone who was in charge and was responsible for the business of the company and any other person who was a director or managing director or secretary of officer of the company with whose convenience due to whose neglect the company had committed the offence.

In a complaint against a company it has to be alleged that the offence was committed by its directors/managers with their consent or connivance of consent on their part.[14] In many cases the Supreme Court categorically held that there is no requirement that the company must be prosecuted, made a party to the case for prosecuting the directors.[15] This is basically on the notion of law that directors are agents of the company and vicariously liable for activities of the principal, consequently the agent can also be held liable.

In *SMS Pharmaceuticals* v *Neeta Bhalla,*[16] raised the issue of vicarious liability of directors of companies in cases of alleged violations of s.138 of the Negotiable Instruments Act. The respondent, in this case, was director of a company who had issued cheques those were dishonoured on the ground of insufficient funds. The dishonoured cheques were issued by the managing director of the erring company. The respondent was arrayed as 'Accused No. 4' in the proceeding that followed. The issue that was raised before the Supreme Court was whether in order to prove liability under s. 141 (cases in which the offence under s. 138 was committed by a company). It was necessary to aver that the person accused was in charge of and responsible for the conduct of business of the company.

This was answered in the affirmative by the Supreme Court. The Court, then went on to hold that there is no deemed liability of any director unless it is shown that the director was in charge of and responsible for the conduct of business of the company at relevant time. The Court stated that s. 141 of the Act does not say "a director

13 (2008)3 SCC 703; MANU/SC/2118/2008, para. 32.

14 *Harbajan Singh Kalra, Director Orion Auto & Steel Industries (Pvt.) Ltd.* v *State of Haryana* 1992 Bank J 692.

15 *Sheoratan Agarwal* v *State of Madhya Pradesh* AIR 1984 SC 1824; (1984)4 SCC 352.

16 AIR 2005 SC 3512; 2005 Cr LJ 4140; (2005)123 DLT 275 (SC); 2005(7) SCALE 397; (2005)8 SCC 89.

of a company shall automatically be vicariously liable for commission of an offence on behalf of the company. What is necessary is that sufficient averments should be made to show that the person who is sought to be proceeded against on the premise of his being vicariously liable for the commission of an offence by the company must be in charge and shall also be responsible to the company for the conduct of its business."

Hence, the liability of a director must be determined on the date on which the offence is committed. The fact of the transaction (that resulted in the issuance of the dishonoured cheques) does not lead to the inference that she was actively associated with the management of the day to day affairs of the company. The Court further went on to state that managing directors or joint managing directors of a company are in charge of the company and responsible to company for the conduct of its business by virtue of the positions they held. The signatory of a cheque, which is dishonoured, is also clearly responsible for the incriminating act and is covered under s. 141.

In *Dilip S. Dahanukar* v *Kotak Mahindra Co. Ltd.,*[17] the court considered the question of imposition of unreasonable amount of fine or grand of compensation to the complainant, must be reasonable and not arbitrarily. The present case the company and its chairman, the appellant, were convicted of an offence under s. 138 of the Negotiable Instruments Act 1881, the company being sentenced to pay a fine of ₹ 25,000 and the appellant to one month's simple imprisonment. The appellant was also directed to pay compensation of ₹15 lakhs under s. 357(3) of the Code of Criminal Procedure.

The court held that trial court sentenced the accused to imprisonment had been unreasonable. Only fine had been imposed on the company. The liability under s. 141 of the Negotiable Instruments Act was a vicarious one in terms of the Act. The trial judge imposed a fine of ₹ 25,000 upon the company and the appellant to one month's simple imprisonment. The court observed that the High Court should not have been directed to pay a compensation of ₹ 15 lakhs by the chairman of the company. The court must have regard to call relevant factors before fixing the amount of compensation and it must be reasonable. No unreasonable amount of compensation can be directed

17 (2007)137 Comp Cas 1 (SC); (2007)4 SCR 1122; (2007)6 SCC 528; 2007(5) SCALE 452; JT 2007(6) SC 204.

to be paid. The court observed that the Negotiable Instruments Act should be given a purposive interpretation, where two views are possible the construction which favours the accused to be adopted.

An analysis of decided cases reveals that the High Courts normally do not interfere with the issue of process against the accused directors and proceeds with the view that normally a complaint has to be examined by the Magistrate in the first instance on the basis of averments contained therein. If the Magistrate is satisfied that there are averments which bring the case within s. 141, he would issue the process. The Courts have held that merely describing in a complaint that a person is a "Director" in a company, will not be sufficient to satisfy the requirement of s. 138 read with s. 141 of the Negotiable Instruments Act and that with proper averment in the complaint, even a person who is not a director can be alleged to be liable for offences committed under s. 138 read with s. 141 of the Negotiable Instruments Act. Since the charging sections in almost all the economic legislations are clothed in the same language, it can be assumed that the principles enunciated by the Courts relating to offences under the Negotiable Instruments Act and SEBI Act will also be relied upon for prosecutions in respect of violations under other Acts too.

In *Anil Hada* v *Indian Acrylic Ltd.*,[18] the Supreme Court considered the question of whether the director of a company is liable when the company is convicted under s. 138 of the Negotiable Instruments Act 1881. Appellant was one of the directors of the company and the company was under the winding up process. In this case the trial magistrate held that prosecution against the directors of the company, who were in charge of the business of the company, could be maintained even without prosecuting the company itself. A revision petitions filed by the appellant in challenge of the aforesaid orders of the magistrate were dismissed by the learned single judge of the High Court which was challenged before the Supreme Court. The petitioner contended that under s. 141 of the Act,[19] the company could be the principal offender and

18 2000(1) Apex Court Journal 01 (SC); 2000(1) All India Criminal LR (SC) 0229; AIR 2000 SC 195; 1998(2) ALD Cr 736.

19 Section 141 of the N.I. Act provides that—141. *Offences by companies.* (1) If the person committing an offence under section 138 is a company, every person who, at the time the offence was committed, was in charge of, and was responsible to the company for the conduct of the business of the company, as well as the company, shall be deemed to be guilty of the offence and shall be liable to be proceeded against and punished accordingly:

the directors are merely deemed offenders and hence a finding that the company is guilty of the offence is a *sine qua non* for operation of the deeming provision to the prejudice of the directors.

Three categories of persons can be discerned from the said provisions that are brought within the purview of the penal liability through the legal fiction envisaged in the section. They are: (1) the company which committed the offence, (2) everyone who was in charge of and was responsible for the business of the company, and (3) any other person who is a director or a manager or a secretary or officer of the company, with whose connivance or due to whose negligence the company has committed the offence. In *State of Madras* v *C.V. Parekh,*[20] it was held that "The liability of the persons in charge of the company only arises when the contravention is by the company itself. Since, in this case, there is no evidence and no finding that the company contravened cl. (5) of the Iron and Steel Control Order, the two respondents could not be held responsible". In this case the Supreme Court made it clear that if the company is not prosecuted under the NI Act, then the director cannot be convicted for the offence.

In *Sheoratan Agarwal* v *State of Madhya Pradesh,*[1] the Supreme Court held that "Any one or more or all of them may be prosecuted and

---

Provided that nothing contained in this sub-section shall render any person liable to punishment if he proves that the offence was committed without his knowledge, or that he had exercised all due diligence to prevent the commission of such offence:

Provided further that where a person is nominated as a Director of a company by virtue of his holding any office or employment in the Central Government or State Government or a financial corporation owned or controlled by the Central Government or the State Government, as the case may be, he shall not be liable for prosecution under this Chapter (Chapter 17).

(2) Notwithstanding anything contained in sub-section (1), where any offence under this Act has been committed by a company and it is proved that the offence has been committed with the consent or connivance of, or is attributable to, any neglect on the part of, any director, manager, secretary or other officer of the company, such director, manager, secretary or other officer shall also be deemed to be guilty of that offence and shall be liable to be proceeded against and punished accordingly.

Explanation. For the purposes of this section,—

(a) "company" means any body corporate and includes a firm or other association of individuals; and

(b) "director", in relation to a firm, means a partner in the firm.

20 (1970)3 SCC 491; AIR 1971 SC 447.

1 AIR 1984 SC 1824 (1825); (1984)4 SCC 352.

punished. The company alone may be prosecuted. The person-in-charge only may be prosecuted. The conniving officer may individually be prosecuted. One, some or all may be prosecuted. There is no statutory compulsion that the person-in-charge or an officer of the company may not be prosecuted unless the company itself made as a party. Section 10 indicates the persons who may be prosecuted where the contravention is made by the company. It does not lay down any condition that the person-in-charge or an officer of the company may not be separately prosecuted if the company itself is not prosecuted. Each or any of them may be separately prosecuted or along with the company".

The Court agreed with the above view and hold that even if the prosecution proceedings against the company were not taken or could not be continued, it is no bar for proceeding against the other persons falling within the purview of sub-secs. (1) and (2) of s. 141 of the Act.

The question was whether a sick company can escape liability from payment of a cheque and whether a director can escape liability from prosecution if the company is referred under the BIFR. This decision in *BSI Ltd.* v *Gift Holdings Pvt. Ltd.*[2] discussed this issue. It is now a common practice for a creditor to take a cheque well in advance from the debtor so that the creditor then need only to deposit the cheque on the due date and realise his dues and if the cheque does not realise, he can prosecute the debtor. The Supreme Court laid down the important decision that merely because proceedings were pending before the BIFR, prosecution proceedings against the company and its directors for cheques returned unpaid cannot be stopped. This decision is one more nail in the coffin of those attempts to escape liability by persons who negligently or deliberately issued cheques which are not honoured or which were not meant to be honoured.[3]

The Supreme Court in *Lalit Kumar Sharma* v *State of U.P.*,[4] held that in a dishonour of cheque case, the petitioner cannot file two complaints against the respondents on the same course of action under s. 138 of the Negotiable Instruments Act 1881. The Kerala High Court

2 2000 SOL case No. 842.

3 Jayant M Thakur, *Indian Express Newspaper*, 30th October 2000.

4 (2008)143 Comp Cas 593 (SC); 2008(3) Civil Court Cases 171 (SC); 2008(2) Criminal Court Cases 839 (SC); 2008(2) Apex Court Judgments 273 (SC).

considered the question of multiple notices on the same amount of cheque bounced. In this case, the course of transaction between the petitioner and the first respondent, the cheque issued by the petitioner was dishonoured on the ground of insufficiency of funds. The notice was issued and in the reply the petitioner claimed that no such cheque was issued at all. If the same cheque was presented again and upon its dishonour issued another notice of demand may be issued. The court held that the prosecution launched on the basis of second notice was valid.

The Delhi High Court considered the question of non-payment of the deposit on maturity and dishonour of cheques by the company and liability of directors in *Ashok Sikka* v *State.*[5] The petitions were filed under s. 482 of the Code of Criminal Procedure 1973, for quashing of criminal proceedings initiated against the petitioners in their capacity as directors of the company, KMCL. The petitioners took the ground that they had ceased to be directors even before the cheques were dishonoured. The question of vicarious liability attaching to a director of the company did not arise as there was no provision in the Indian Penal Code 1860, to attach liability to the person in charge of the affairs of the company, unlike similar to s. 141 of the Negotiable Instruments Act 1881, where the company was the principal accused. This position was confirmed by the Supreme Court in *Maksud Saiyed* v *State of Gujarat.*[6]

In the above case Supreme Court held that:

> The Indian Penal Code does not confine any provision for attaching vicarious liability on the part of the managing director or the directors of the company when the accused is the company... A Bank is a body corporate. Vicarious liability of the managing director and director arise provided any provision exists in that behalf in the statute. Statutes indisputably must contain provision fixing such vicarious liabilities.

The Supreme Court observed that signature of directors in the prospectus is not sufficient to hold personal responsibility of directors. In the absence of personal allegation against the respondents on failure of statutory or official duty, no criminal liability would be attached in such circumstances.

5 (2008)143 Comp Cas 573; (2008)II AD (Cr) DHC 143.
6 (2007)140 Comp Cas 590; (2006)5 SCC 668.

The Supreme Court in *Presh P. Rajda* v *State of Maharashtra,*[7] held that in an allegation in the complaint under s. 138 of the Negotiable Instruments Act 1881, alleging that the accused had issued two cheques which had been dishonour with the remarks "exceeds arrangements" cannot be quashed before actual trial. If the company is the first accused and other accused were the managing director and other directors, the chairman was responsible for day-to-day activities of the company and therefore he is liable to repay the amount of dishonoured cheques. The accused persons were officers responsible for the affairs of the company. Hence, it is immature to decide the case before trial.

The Madras High Court in *Rajendra Kumar Gupta* v *State of Tamil Nadu,*[8] held that a director cannot abuse the process of the court suppressing the memorandum of understanding and articles of the company. The petitioner alleged that to the directors of the company forged and created false documents and produced the same before the public authorities and also before the company law board as if the *de facto* complainant had resigned from the directorship of Picknic Hotels (P) Ltd. when actually he had been enjoying equal share in Indian business. The petitioner alleged that this amounts to cheating. He lodged a complaint under ss. 465, 468 and 471 read with s. 120B of the Indian Penal Code. The complainant already filed a civil suit before a civil court. The Supreme Court in analogous case in *Inder Mohan Goswami* v *State of Uttaranchal,*[9] held that if a civil suit was already filed before the civil forum and the dispute is also civil in nature, prosecuting a person for offence under ss. 420 and 467 of the Indian Penal Code is liable to be quashed in as much as the criminal prosecution cannot be used as an instrument of harassment for seeking private vendetta or to exert pressure on the accused and ulterior motive. Hence, the criminal complaint, completely suppressing the memorandum of understanding entered into between the parties just to wreak vengeance on the petitioners' abusing the process of law, quashed by the court.

The Madras High Court considered the question of liability of every director under s. 138 of the Negotiable Instruments Act

7 (2008)144 Comp Cas 27 (SC); (2008)7 SCC 442.
8 (2008)144 Comp Cas 319 (Mad).
9 AIR 2008 SC 251; (2007)5 CTC 614.

1881.[10] In this case the cheque issued by the company was bounced and the respondent filed a private complaint under s.138 of the Negotiable Instruments Act. The petitioners are A4 and A5, approached the court for discharging them on the ground that both of them had resigned from the company two years before the transaction and therefore, there is no liability on the part of these petitioners. The persons who are not directors of the company or who were not in charge of the day-to-day affairs of the company could not be charged for a criminal offence. The court allowed the petition on the ground that the second petitioner was not the director who was in-charge of and was responsible for the affairs of the company during the relevant period and therefore the petitioners were liable to be discharged.[11]

In an earlier judgement of the Supreme Court in *S.M.S. Pharmaceuticals Ltd.* v *Neeta Bhalla,*[12] held that:

> The officers responsible for conducting the affairs of companies are generally referred to as directors, managers, secretaries, managing directors, etc. What is required to be considered is: is it sufficient to simply state in a complaint that a particular person was a director of the company at the time the offence was committed and nothing more is required to be said? For this, it may be worthwhile to notice the role of a director in a company. The word director includes any person occupying the position of director, by whatever name called, defined in section 2(13) of the Companies Act 1956.

The Supreme Court in *DCM Financial Services Ltd.* v *J.N. Sareen,*[13] considered the question of the liability of a resigned director under s. 141 of the Negotiable Instruments Act 1881. In this case, the director of a company purchased agricultural equipments on 3rd April 1995, against post-dated cheques in favour of the appellant. One of the directors resigned from the directorship in 1996. The post-dated cheques were issued in 1995 towards the payment dated in 1998, when presented to the bank it was dishonoured. The first respondent was the company and other respondents were directors of the company. Nowhere in the

10 *Parthasarathy* v *Lachman* (2007)137 Comp Cas 780 (Mad).
11 *Ibid*, p. 784.
12 AIR 2005 SC 3512; 2005 Cr LJ 4140; (2005)123 DLT 275 (SC); 2005(7) SCALE 397; (2005)8 SCC 89.
13 (2008)144 Comp Cas 55 (SC).

petition was it stated that the respondent was a signatory to the cheque.

The Supreme Court found that there is no reference in the petition that the respondent is signed the cheque or involvement in the commission of the offence as a signatory. The respondent informed the complainant about his resignation from the company. The liability attached to him was not a personal liability. It was a constructive liability. The court observed that the appellant had taken undue advantage of the post-dated cheques given on behalf of the company. The statute does not envisage misuse of a privilege conferred upon a party to the contract. The Supreme Court's findings are relevant in interpreting the liability of a resigned director from a company.

The Supreme Court confirmed this position in *Everest Advertising Pvt. Ltd.* v *State Government of NCT of Delhi.*[14] The court held that the necessary ingredient of s. 141 of the Negotiable Instruments Act 1881 had been stated in the compliant petition at more than one place. The High Court in this case concerned the position that they should be specific averment as to how respondents were actually involved in the conduct of the business of the company relating to the transaction in question. A chairman of a large company may or may not be aware of the actual transaction. The cheque is of issue in the ordinary course of business, the managing director or a deputy managing director would be deemed to be aware thereof. A chairman or the director of a company need not be. In this case the High Court, while confirming the trial court judgment, ordered for withdrawing the process against the respondents Nos. 2 and 3 on the ground that they don't have any knowledge about the transaction. However, Supreme Court held that active participation in the discretion on the issue is sufficient to comply with the provisions of the Act. The director of a company would be deemed it to be in charge of, and responsible to, the company for conduct of the business of the company and, therefore deemed to be guilty of the offence unless he proves to the contrary. The court relied on its cavalier judgement in *S.M.S. Pharmaceuticals Ltd.* v *Neeta Bhalla*[15] and set aside the High Court order withdrawing the process against accused Nos. 2 and 3.

14 (2007)137 Comp Cas 32 (SC); (2007)5 SCC 54.
15 *Ibid*, (2005)8 SCC 89; (2005)127 Comp Cas 563 (SC).

The Rajasthan High Court in *Devendra Kumar Kedawat* v *Apple Ceremics Ltd.*[16] conceded the question of director's liability as a guarantor of a loan taken by the company. The petitioner was a director of the respondent company and stood guarantee for the loan taken by it from the bank. As the loan was not repaid the bank filed an application before the debt recovery tribunal and it was decreed against the company. The petitioner under s. 633 of the Companies Act 1956 sought to be relieved him from the liability.

The court dismissing the petition, held that the petition was not *bona fide* as it had been filed to escape his liability as a guarantor. The petitioner could raise the objection that the decree was not executable against him before the consent authority in the execution proceedings. The objections raised did not fall under the scope of s. 633 of the Act.

In *Krishnam Raju Finances* v *Abida Sultana,*[17]the Andhra Pradesh High Court considered the question of legally enforceable liability under the Negotiable Instruments Act 1881. In this case the applicant was a money lender from whom the respondent had obtained a loan. On demand, the respondent issued cheques to the appellant. The cheques were bounced when it was presented. The appellant sent a notice demanding the amount but the respondent denied the liability totally. The complaint was filed under s.138 of the Negotiable Instruments Act, upon which the lower court acquitted the respondent on the ground that there was no legally enforceable debt or liability because the appellant claimed to be a money lender but failed to produce any licence.

The High Court held that the appellant had not produced any licence as required under Andhra Pradesh (Telengana Area) Money Lenders Act. Once an Act declared that a particular transaction is illegal, it cannot be made legal for the purpose of any other Act. Only a legally enforceable liability can be enforced under s. 138 of the Act. Therefore, there was no legally enforceable liability against the respondent and no irregularity or illegality in the judgement of the lower court and the High Court confirmed the order of the lower court.

16 (2006)129 Comp Cas 816 (Raj).
17 (2006)129 Comp Cas 33 (AP); 2004(1) ALD Cri 546; IV (2004) BC 146.

7.5 Payment and Settlement Systems Act 2007

This Act specifically provides for the regulation and supervision of payment systems in India and designated the Reserve Bank of India as the authority for that purpose. Section 27 of the Act specifically provides for penalties for contravention of the provisions of the Act.

Section 27(1) provides that:

> Where a person committing a contravention of any of the provisions of this Act or any regulation, direction or order made thereunder is a company, every person who, at the time of the contravention, was in-charge of, and was responsible to, the company for the conduct of business of the company, as well as the company, shall be guilty of the contravention and shall be liable to be proceeded against and punished accordingly.

It has to be proved that the contravention happened with the permission and knowledge of the person without due diligence to prevent such contravention. If the connivance is attributable to any neglect on the part of any director, manager, secretary or other officer of the company, such director, manager, secretary or other officer shall also be deemed to be guilty of the contravention and shall be liable to be proceed against and punished.

7.6 Pollution laws

Indian environment laws provides for the protection and improvement of environment and lays down specific guidelines with respect to handling of hazardous substances and emission norms for industrial undertakings operations and process and any violation of the provisions amounts to an offence thereunder. Making every person directly in charge of, for the conduct of the operations and having control liable. It is possible to delegate this responsibility, however, if it can be established that any omission has been committed with the consent or connivance of, or is attributable to any neglect on the part of any director, he will be liable to be proceeded against and punished accordingly.

Bhopal gas disaster case was one of such incidents in which the directors were held liable under various provisions of the laws under environment and other legislations. On 19th July 2005 the Supreme Court of India ordered the Government to pay a remaining $325.5 million (₹ 15.03 billion) due to Bhopal gas tragedy victims. The U.S.

based Union Carbide Company, now owned by Dow Chemical Co., paid $470 million in compensation to victims in 1989. But distribution of most of that money was held up by bureaucratic disputes over the categorization of victims. At last on 19th July 2005 the victims or their representatives got justice 20 years after the tragedy took place.

The story goes back to the 1984, Union Carbide accident in Bhopal, India, which released a cloud of methyl isocyanate (MIC), hydrogen cyanide, and other toxins. Somewhere between 4,000 and 8,000 people died at the time, and victims' advocates estimate that in total over 20,000 have died as a result of this largest industrial accident ever, with 1,50,000 suffering continuing injuries and medical problems.

In *U.P. Pollution Board* v *Modi Distellery,*[18] the Supreme Court held that the managing director and the members of the board of directors can be prosecuted under the Water (Prevention and Control of Pollutions) Act 1974 and it is not necessary that the company should also be prosecuted along with them. But if the chairman and vice-chairman have been held to be not directly in charge of and responsible for the conduct of the company's business, no liability can be cast on them under the Air (Prevention and Control of Pollution) Act 1981.[19] A site manager cannot be held liable under the pollution laws, because he is not to be equated with a person of managing or governing the company.

7.7 Labour laws

Indian industrial laws provides a general rule in case an offence is committed by a company, then, every director, manager, secretary, agent or other officer or person in the management is liable for the offence, unless he proves that he had no knowledge. However certain laws make a director primarily liable in case of any breach or default, as under the Factories Act 1948, an occupier (the person who has ultimate control over the affairs of the factory and in the case of a company, any one of the directors is deemed to be the occupier) of a factory is responsible for the provision and maintenance of common facilities and services, such as approach roads, drainage, water supply, lighting and sanitation, as he has ultimate control over the factory. Courts of

18 (1987)2 Comp LJ 298 (SC); (1987)3 SCC 684.
19 *N.A. Palkhiwala* v *M.P. Pradushan Niwaran Mandal, Bhopal* 1990 Cr LJ 1856 (MP).

India have view that only a director can be the occupier of the factory and responsible for the conduct of business of the establishment.

The Madhya Pradesh High Court in *Hindustan Steel Works Construction Ltd.* v *Commissioner of Labour,*[20] held that director of a company is liable for non-payment of wages under the Payment of Wages Act 1936. But the Supreme Court held that in order to hold the directors held liable two things need to be established:

(*a*) He was the employer, or

(*b*) He was a person who had been named as Manager of the factory.

But the court in the present case didn't find compliance of these two conditions and held that directors were not held liable.

If a company is defaulted in payment of PF contribution, every person who at the time of offence was committed was in-charge of, and was responsible to the company for the conduct of the business of the company, as well as the company, shall be deemed to be guilty of the offence and shall be liable to be proceeded against and punished accordingly.[1]

Director cannot be made vicariously liable for any and every contravention made by the company unless he is in charge of the day to day conduct of the affairs of the company. Further, all directors have overall responsibility in the conduct of the business of the company.[2]

For the purpose of the Act, s. 14A(1)(*b*) of the EPF Act defines director as "director" in relation to a firm, means a partner in the firm. The question as to whether a director of the company has ultimate control over the affairs of the factory of the company is always a question of fact.[3]

20 (1997)1 LLJ 656 (SC); 1996 VIAD SC 747; JT 1996(7) SC 592; 1996 Lab lC 2520.

1 Section 14A(1) of the EPF Act 1952.

2 *Bhuban Mohan Bose* v *The State* (1991)1 LLJ 11 (Cal); *Orr Cee Electronics Ltd.* v *Judicial Magistrate* (2000)1 Lab LJ 483 (Kar). But he can escape from liability by showing that the offence was committed without his knowledge or that he had exercised due diligence to prevent its commission.

3 *Nathani H.P.* v *ESI Corporation* (1998)1 LLJ 922 (Cal).

In the event of prosecution of offences under ESI Act 1948, all the directors as well as the manager in-charge of the company's affairs and the affairs of the factory, would become liable.[4] In *Rohtas Industries Ltd. (In Liquidation), In re,*[5] the Patna High Court considered the question of whether the official liquidator of a company under winding up process by the court is liable under the Provident Fund and ESI Act. The Calcutta High Court in *Mahalaxmi Cotton Mills Ltd., In re,*[6] held that the official liquidator possesses the ultimate control over the affairs of the company and as such is an employer within the meaning of the Act and rejected the contention of the official liquidator. The court held that where the liquidator has been asked to carry on the factory engaged in the industry and sell it as a going concern, he is liable as an "employer" and occupier within the meaning of the Provident Funds Act, but where the liquidator is asked to wind up a factory and not to carry on the business of the company, he will not be liable for contribution under the Provident Funds Act. The Calcutta High Court judgment was confirmed in this case as well and held that the Provident Funds Act is not applicable and the official liquidator is not liable for contribution under that Act.

The Bombay High Court in *Universal Pollution Control (I) Pvt. Ltd.* v *Regional Provident Fund Commissioner,*[7] it was held that under the Companies Act 1956 each company is a legal entity and abuse of one company cannot be recovered from another company. The Provident Fund Commissioner cannot seize the goods of the sister company for non-payment of provident fund contribution of the holding company. There is no provision in the Employees' Provident Funds and Miscellaneous Provisions Act 1952, permitting the liability of one company to be fastened on the other company even by lifting the corporate veil.

In *J.B. Exports Ltd.* v *BSES Rajadhani Power Ltd.,*[8] the Delhi High Court considered the question of misuse of electricity by the subsidiary company and the liability of the parent company in case filed by the electricity supplier. The court held that the purpose of the principle of

4 *ESI Corporation* v *Veerappan A.L.* (1998)2 LLJ 247 (Mad).
5 C.P. No. 3 of 1984, decided on 23rd December 1998.
6 (1960)30 Comp Cas 107.
7 (2007)137 Comp Cas 319 (Bom); (2007)77 SCL 192 (Bom).
8 (2006)134 Comp Cas 106 (Del); AIR 2006 Del 317.

separate corporate personality is to encourage and facilitate industrialization, not to obstruct it. Hence, the mechanical interpretation of corporate personality is to be avoided, as it may frustrate the very purpose for which it was made. The exception to the principle, the doctrine of piercing the veil of corporate personality should be adopted not merely in cases of fraud or evasion of legal obligations but also in a large number of cases where it would promote the growth of industry. The court opined that in this way, both the principle of corporate personality as well as its exception, the doctrine of piercing the veil of corporate personality will serve a common complimentary purpose, namely, to promote the industrialization. Consequently, the court applied the principle in this case and held that the defendant number one and two are one and the same and there is no question of subletting of electricity by appellant No. 2 to appellant No. 1 both are one and the same company, hence it is not violated any law.

The Calcutta High Court in *Nudea Mills Co. Ltd* v *State of West Bengal,*[9] held that once s. 22 of the Sick Industrial Companies (Special Provisions) Act 1985 is operational and if the court gave a stay on all further proceedings to recover contribution to the Employees' Provident Funds and Miscellaneous Provisions Act 1952, and criminal proceedings initiated by the Provident Fund Authorities would remain stayed.

7.8 Tax laws

Indian Income Tax and Sales Tax laws provides, if a private company is wound up and the tax assessed cannot be recovered, then directors of a private company can be held liable for the payment of such tax, if the non-recovery is attributable to any gross neglect, misfeasance, or breach of duty on his part. Similarly, under the Central Excise and the Customs Laws, if any contravention has taken place with the consent or connivance of, or is attributable to any neglect on the part of any director, he shall be liable to be proceeded against and punished accordingly.

Section 35A of the Indian Gift Tax Act 1958 provides for provisions of offences by companies. It provides that:

> **35A.** (1) Where an offence under this Act has been committed by a company, every person who, at the time the offence was committed, was in charge

9 (2008)142 Comp Cas 394 (Cal).

of and was responsible to, the company for the conduct of the business of the company, as well as the company, shall be deemed to be guilty of the offence and shall be liable to be proceeded against and punished accordingly:

Provided that nothing contained in this sub-section shall render any such person liable to any punishment if he proves that the offence was committed without his knowledge or that he had exercised all due diligence to prevent the commission of such offence.

Section 278B of the Income Tax Act 1961 (IT Act) provides that:

278B. (1) Where an offence under this Act has been committed by a company, every person who, at the time the offence was committed, was in charge of, and was responsible to, the company for the conduct of the business of the company as well as the company shall be deemed to be guilty of the offence and shall be liable to be proceeded against and punished accordingly:

Provided that nothing contained in this sub-section shall render any such person liable to any punishment if he proves that the offence was committed without his knowledge or that he had exercised all due diligence to prevent the commission of such offence.

(2) Notwithstanding anything contained in sub-section (1), where an offence under this Act has been committed by a company and it is proved that the offence has been committed with the consent or connivance of, or is attributable to any neglect on the part of, any director, manager, secretary or other officer of the company, such director, manager, secretary or other officer shall also be deemed to be guilty of that offence and shall be liable to be proceeded against and punished accordingly.

(3) Where an offence under this Act has been committed by a person, being a company, and the punishment for such offence is imprisonment and fine, then, without prejudice to the provisions contained in sub-section (1) or sub-section (2), such company shall be punished with fine and every person, referred to in sub-section (1), or the director, manager, secretary or other officer of the company referred to in sub-section (2), shall be liable to be proceeded against and punished in accordance with the provisions of this Act.

Explanation. For the purposes of this section,

(*a*) company means a body corporate, and includes:

(*i*) a firm; and

(*ii*) an association of persons or a body of individuals whether incorporated or not; and

(*b*) director, in relation to:

(*i*) a firm, means a partner in the firm;

(*ii*) any association of persons or a body of individuals, means any member controlling the affairs thereof.

Similar provision will be applied to the private companies as well. Sub-section (1) of s. 179 of the IT Act 1961 provides that:

> **179.** (1) Notwithstanding anything contained in the Companies Act, 1956 (1 of 1956), where any tax due from a private company in respect of any income of any previous year or from any other company in respect of any income of any previous year during which such other company was a private company cannot be recovered, then, every person who was a director of the private company at any time during the relevant previous year shall be jointly and severally liable for the payment of such tax unless he proves that the non-recovery cannot be attributed to any gross neglect, misfeasance or breach of duty on his part in relation to the affairs of the company.
>
> (2) Where a private company is converted into a public company and the tax assessed in respect of any income of any previous year during which such company was a private company cannot be recovered, then, nothing contained in sub-section (1) shall apply to any person who was a director of such private company in relation to any tax due in respect of any income of such private company assessable for any assessment year commencing before the 1st day of April, 1962.

Applying the provision in *Khaders International Construction Ltd.* v *CIT*,[10] the court did not hold the directors liable. In this case the directors were doing their best in the circumstance of the case. The company was ordered to pay a heavy amount. The directors struggled against the order and it was reduced by about ten times. It could not be said that the directors were neglecting the affairs of the company.

The liability of directors is joint and several as between themselves and not as between themselves and company.[11] There are corresponding provisions in the Sales Tax Act also. The Act of different States provide that the directors of a private company which is being wound up are liable for the sales tax dues of the company if the same cannot be recovered from the company itself.[12]

The Supreme Court in *Velliappa Textiles Ltd.* v *The Assistant Commissioner, Assessment-II, Bangalore,*[13] considered the question of

10 (1989)91 Comp Cas 432 (Ker).

11 *K.V. Reddy* v *Asst. CIT.* (1998)93 Comp Cas 287 (AP); *Bhagwandas J. Patel* v *Deputy CIT* (1999)97 Comp Cas 213 (Guj).

12 *P. C. Chokalingam* v *Deputy Commercial Tax Officer* (1990)68 Comp Cas 673 (AP).

13 2003(4) RCR (Cri) 695 (SC); 2004 Cr LJ 1221; AIR 2004 SC 86.

criminal liability of corporations in India. In this case the first respondent was a limited company which, along with its Managing Director, was sought to be prosecuted under ss. 276C, 277 and 278 read with s. 278B of the Income Tax Act.

The court observed that "The question of criminal liability of a juristic person has troubled Legislatures and Judges for long. Though, initially, it was supposed that a Corporation could not be held liable criminally for offences where *mens rea* was requisite, the current judicial thinking appears to be that the *mens rea* of the person in-charge of the affairs of the Corporation, the *alter ego*, is liable to be extrapolated to the Corporation, enabling even an artificial person to be prosecuted for such an offence."

The court laid down the following dictum in this case:

(1) A company is a juristic person and cannot be prosecuted.

(2) Existing laws do not permit replacing imprisonment with fine.

(3) The law says so and the court can't usurp the legislative function.

(4) Directors and employees of a company not to be affected by the decision.

(5) The dissenting judge said courts would be unfair in holding that a company could not be prosecuted.

In the majority judgment the court held that the first respondent company cannot be prosecuted for offences under ss. 276C, 277 and 278 read with s. 278 since each one of these sections requires the imposition of a mandatory term of imprisonment coupled with a fine and leaves no choice to the Court to impose only a fine. In this case, only the corporation was exonerated from criminal liability and not its employees. It means that directors cannot escape liability when there is a mandatory imprisonment in the statute.

In *Om Prakash Walecha* v *State of Haryana,*[14] the petitioners challenged the notice served on the directors of a private company to recover central sales tax arrears due from the company. The question considered by the court is that whether a director of a company can

14 (2008)145 Comp Cas 799 (P&H); (2008)16 VST 530 (P&H).

be made personally liable for the amount due from the company for the arrears of State and Central Sales Tax. Notices were served on the company and the directors separately to pay the above taxes. The petitioners argue that there is no personal liability under Central sales tax or the Haryana General Sales Tax 1973 which authorizes recovery of ideas due from the company by proceeding against directors. The petitioners submitted that the company is still not wound up or formally liquidated. The petitioners cited an earlier decision of *Lalita Shivram Ubhaykar* v *Commercial Tax Officer,*[15] it has been settled that no recovery either of the Haryana General Sales Tax or Central Sales Tax could be effected personally from the director in respect of the liability of the company.

The Andhra Pradesh High Court considered the question of the personal liability of directors and shareholders for non-payment of sale tax due by the company in *In Re, Desiraju Venkatakrishna Sarma.*[16] In this case the petitioner, the managing director of a company questioned his conviction under s. 15(*b*) of the Madras General Sales Tax Act. The court observed that a company is a body corporate and can be made liable for payment of taxes in respect of taxes payable by it. There is no personal obligation on the shareholders or the directors of a limited company in respect of the debts or the taxes, revenue, etc., due from the company.

The managing director or other directors of a limited liability company cannot be proceeded against as regards recovery of arrears of sale tax payable by the company. The taxing authorities could proceed against the assets of the company. If the tax has been collected from the petitioner personally it will be refunded to him.

7.9 Liability of Directors of a company in liquidation

Section 179(1) of the Income Tax Act 1961 provides that: Notwithstanding anything contained in the Companies Act 1956, where any tax due from a private company in respect of any income of any previous year or from any other company in respect of any income of any previous year during which such other company was a private company cannot be recovered, then, every person who was a director

15 (1975)35 STC 267 (Kar) and *Ramachandran* v *State of Kerala* (1984)55 STC 209 (Ker).

16 (1955)25 Comp Cas 32 (Andh); (1954)5 STC 448; (1954)2 MLJ 184 (AP).

of the private company at any time during the relevant previous year shall be jointly and severally liable for the payment of such tax unless he proves that the non-recovery cannot be attributed to any gross neglect, misfeasance or breach of duty on his part in relation to the affairs of the company.

Where a private company is converted into a public company and the tax assessed in respect of any income of any previous year during which such company was a private company cannot be recovered, then, nothing contained in sub-sec. (1) shall apply to any person who was a director of such private company in relation to any tax due in respect of any income of such private company assessable for any assessment year commencing before the 1st day of April 1962.

The Mysore High Court in *In re, Supreme Bank of India Ltd.,* and *P.A. Tendolkar* v *Official Liquidator,*[17] held that it is intended to allege a breach of duty, fraud or deceit in misfeasance proceedings, those allegations should be clearly, satisfactorily and unequivocally made in the summons so that those against whom they are made should have their attention directed to them and should have an opportunity of meeting them. The act or omission complained must be one resulting in actual loss to the company. Section 235 of the Companies Act applies where a director, officer, etc., has misapplied or retained or become liable or accountable for any money or property of the company or has been guilty of misfeasance or breach of trust in relation to the company; and under the section the court may compel a delinquent director, officer, etc., to repay or restore any money or property which he has misapplied or retained or become liable or accountable to the company or to contribute to the company's assets an appropriate sum by way of compensation. The section does not give the court power to fine a director for misconduct. To sustain a claim under this section, the applicant must show, (*i*) breach of trust or duty or misfeasance, (*ii*) loss arising there from, and (*iii*) an interest in the result of the application. Allegations or proof of fraud are not essential and it is immaterial that the act or omission constitutes an offence for which the director or the officer may be criminally liable.

The directors cannot totally abdicate their powers and functions and divest themselves of responsibility for proper management of the

17 (1967)37 Comp Cas 392.

company. When there is a managing director, they are entitled to rely on the honesty and integrity of the managing director, but they are bound to keep watch and vigilance over the conduct of business of the company by the managing director and other officers of the bank if they come to know of circumstances for suspecting their honesty or diligence.

Until there is such ground for suspicion, the directors are not liable for losses due to the mistake, negligence or dishonesty of the managing director and other officers of the company, although such losses could have been averted if the directors had taken care.

In *O.L. of Ilaxi Modi Export (P) Ltd.* v *Ilaxi D. Modi,*[18] official liquidator filed a complaint under s. 454(4) of the Companies Act 1956. According to the inspection report, the company was a paper company having no assets except an unregistered firm as debtor for ₹ 50,00,000 which was not reflected in the books of account for the statement of affairs of the company and the ex-directors were jointly and severally liable for the liabilities of the company including the amount of ₹ 50,00,000 borrowed by them from somebody in the name of the company. The statement of affairs had been submitted by the ex-directors of the company, it failed to furnish any information other than the transaction of ₹ 50,00,000 received by the company and paid to a firm. The official liquidator issued parties to the directors to show cause while proceedings for misappropriation and diversion of company funds should not be initiated under s. 543 of the Companies Act 1956.

Most importantly the court found that the investigation report reveals the existence of paper companies are support of conspiracy to borrow money on the faith of genuine company but the route for siphoning off money was simultaneously masterminded by creating a bogus unregistered firm in the name of Modi Exports and to create legal hurdles and legal complications to avoid suit for the recovery and other legal proceedings directly against the directors. The court observed that this effect case where corporate veil requires is to be lifted and the directors to be held jointly and severally personally liable and fully accountable for the liabilities of the company including the amount borrowed from outside people.

18 (2008)144 Comp Cas 277 (Guj).

The court found that the criminal proceedings were already pending before the trial court for mismanagement and siphoning off company funds. The court held that the ex-directors were guilty of an offence under s. 454(5) of the Companies Act 1956, for their failure to file correct statement of affairs.

The Delhi High Court considered the question, as to whether a complaint under s. 138 of the Negotiable Instruments Act can be filed against the company/managing director/director after the winding up of the company in *M.L. Gupta* v *CEAT Financial Services Ltd.*[19] The company issued postdated cheques in 1995 against future lease rentals. The cheques were dishonoured with the remark "no account/account closed". The court held that when the complaint is filed against a company prior to the winding up of the company and during the pendency of such a complaint under s. 138 of the Act and the company is ordered to be wound up, the complaint against the company cannot proceed without the permission of the company judge of the High Court which ordered the winding up. After winding up and appointment of official liquidator, it is the official liquidator only who could represent the company. The proceedings were clearly not maintainable against the company as the money payable to the company was initiated after the winding up of the company, which could be recovered by the complainant only in accordance with the provisions of the Companies Act. This position was settled by the Supreme Court in the case of *Anil Hada* v *Indian Acrylic Ltd.*[20]

7.10 Conclusion

The prosecution of directors for criminal offence is always a point of controversy. The main question is whether the company and directors are liable for criminal activities. This is important in the background that a company itself is a juristic personality different from its directors. The jurisprudence emerged in the last five decades shows that a company can be prosecuted for any criminal offence where "*meńs rea*" is not an essential ingredient. Directors can be prosecuted for violation of the SEBI Act, Companies Act 1956, Indian Penal Code, Negotiable Instruments Act 1881, pollution laws, labour laws and tax laws. It

19 (2008)145 Comp Cas 837 (Del); (2007)136 DLT 308.

20 (1999)35 CLA 427; (2000)1 SCC 1; (2000)1 Comp LJ 7 (SC); (1999)7 SCALE 209.

means that a director cannot escape criminal liability of the company when he has the knowledge of such an activity of the company. The courts have reiterated this position through a number of cases and the responsibility and the liability of the directors are proportionate and going to be at high level of fiduciary relationship. The controversy on whether the company as a juristic person have criminal liability to be settled by legislative intervention as proposed by the 41st Law Commission Report.

8

Fiduciary Duties and Remedies for Breach of Trust

8.1 Introduction

Although the directors may be acting within the powers conferred upon them by the company they nevertheless owe certain duties of good faith in the exercise of their powers. These fiduciary duties also make them liable for breach of trust when these duties are violated or disregarded. The rules applicable to the effect of the breach of duty by directors are nothing other than the general principles of common law and equity applicable to agency and trust. However, the term "breach" has a special meaning peculiar to company law as it includes not only a failure to observe the duties of honesty and good faith but also an exceeding the authority conferred upon the director, or one *ultra vires* the board as a whole, or the company itself. So the remedies available depend on the nature of breach.The statutes provide various civil remedies according to the nature of the breach.

The transaction is voidable at the instance of the company unless restitution of the subject matter of the transaction is no longer available. If the third party rights have been intervened, an indemnity has been paid. It is important to discuss the wide ranging remedial scheme under various statutes. The remedies can be categorized as remedies *in personam*, obligation to restore the trust fund and compensation.[1]

1 *Target Holdings* v *Redferns*[1996]1 AC 421; [1995]3 All ER 785 (HL). As per Lord Browne Wilkinson –"Courts of Equity did not award damages but, acting *in personam*, ordered the defaulting trustee to restore the trust estate. If specific restitution of the trust property is not possible, the liability of the trustee is to pay sufficient compensation to the trust estate to put it back to

8.2 Constructive trust or account of profits

Constructive trust has been used as an effective remedy against company directors for accounting their profits as a fiduciary of the company. The conflict between personal interests and company interests is one of the reason for liable to be account for their profits. The unfaithful transactions by using his corporate position have to be accounted. Fiduciary must account for unauthorised profit 'confers the windfall constituted by the fiduciary's profit, not on the community, but on his principal', with the result that the principal is entitled to claim it in preference to the fiduciary's creditors.[2] In *AG for Hong Kong* v *Reid*,[3] the Privy Council held that whenever a fiduciary receives property of his principal in breach of his fiduciary duty, he is a constructive trustee of it, and of any traceable profit from and proceeds of it. The unauthorized profits in the hands of the fiduciary are regarded as a trust fund. The principal of the trust can claim the benefit of the constructive trust. But the liability of deceased director's heirs' liability is under dispute.

The Palmer's *Company Law*, 21st Ed., p. 77. The observations are as follows:

> "It has been held that misfeasance proceedings under section 333 will not lie against the personal representatives of a deceased director, and that the estate of a deceased director was not liable for his tort, except to the extent that he had appropriated funds or property of the company and his estate had benefited."

Section 543(1) of the Companies Act 1956, which provides that:

> "*Power of Tribunal to assess damages against delinquent directors, etc.* (1) If in the course of winding up a company, it appears that any person who has taken part in the promotion or formation of the company, or any past or present director, manager, liquidator or officer of the company—

---

what it would have been had the breach not been committed. Even if the immediate cause of the loss is the dishonesty or failure of a third party, the trustee is liable to make good that loss to the trust estate if, but for the breach, such loss would not have occurred. Thus the common law rules of remoteness of damage and causation do not apply. However, there does have to be some causal connection between the breach of trust and the loss to the trust estate for which compensation is recoverable, viz the fact that the loss would not have occurred but for the breach."

2 J.W. Harris, *Property and Justice* (Clarendon Press, Oxford, 1996).

3 [1994]1 All ER 1.

(a) has misapplied, or retained, or become liable or accountable for, any money or property of the company; or

(b) has been guilty of any misfeasance or breach of trust in relation to the company;

the Tribunal may, on the application of the Official Liquidator, of the liquidator, or of any creditor or contributory, made within the time specified in that behalf in sub-sec. (2), examine into the conduct of the person, director, manager, liquidator or officer aforesaid, and compel him to repay or restore the money or property or any part thereof respectively, with interest at such rate as the Tribunal thinks just, or to contribute such sum to the assets of the company by way of compensation in respect of the misapplication, retainer, misfeasance or breach of trust, as the Tribunal thinks just."

This section is a statutory remedy against delinquent directors for misfeasance. The two ingredients of misfeasance are, (1) an act in the nature of breach of trust, and (2) an act which results in actual loss to the company. According to the common law rules, however, did not bar equitable remedies against the director's estate where he had committed a breach of trust.

In Buckley on *the Companies Act*, 12th Ed., p. 676, it is stated that:

> This section applies where the person attacked has misapplied or retained or become liable or accountable for any money or property of the company, or has been guilty of any misfeasance or breach of trust in relation to the company. By 'misfeasance' is meant 'misfeasance in the nature of a breach of trust': It must be an act resulting in actual loss to the company. The section does not give the court power to fine a director for misconduct. It is not, moreover, applicable to a mere money claim against an officer, when there has been nothing in the nature of breach of duty by him.

A director of a company is always in the position of a trustee. He is proceeded against for offences in the nature of a breach of trust and the losses occasioned, if any, by such breach ought to be restored to the company (in liquidation) from the assets in the hands of his legal representatives.[4] The foundation of liability in misfeasance proceedings is breach of fiduciary relationship or failure to perform duties prescribed by law. Misfeasance in the nature of breach of trust

4 *Maharaja Srish Chandra Nandy* v *Supravat Chandra* AIR 1940 Cal 337.

resulting loss to the company must be restored by the director. Misfeasance action against the directors is a serious charge. It is a charge of misconduct or misappropriation or breach of trust. The gravity of the act is explained by the Supreme Court in *Official Liquidator, Supreme Bank Ltd.* v *P.A. Tendolkar.*[5] The court held that:

> Whether a director, alleged to be liable for misfeasance, had acted reasonably as well as honestly and with due diligence, so that he could not be held liable for conniving at fraud and misappropriation which takes place. A director may be shown to be so placed and to have been so closely and so long associated personally with the management of the company that he will be deemed to be not merely cognizant of but liable for fraud in the conduct of the business of a company even though no specific act of dishonesty is proved against him personally. He cannot shut his eyes to what must be obvious to everyone who examines the affairs of the company even superficially. If he does so he could be held liable for dereliction of duties undertaken by him and compelled to make good the losses incurred by the company due to his neglect even if he is not shown to be guilty of participating in the commission of fraud. It is enough if his negligence is of such a character as to enable frauds to be committed and losses thereby incurred by the company.[6]

The extent of liability is clearly laid down by the court in the above case. At the same time Courts also interpreted s. 543 in a strict sense. Court observed that:

> Under section 543 of the Act the court is vested with jurisdiction to examine the conduct of the past or present director, manager, liquidator or any other officer of the company to find out whether he has misapplied or retained or become liable or accountable for any money or property of the company, or he has been guilty of any misfeasance or breach of trust in relation to the company. In order to enable the court examine the conduct of an individual director or officer and to pass an effective order to make him personally liable for misapplication, etc. of the money or the property of the company, there has to be positive and specific

5 AIR 1973 SC 1104; (1973)3 SCR 364.

6 *Official Liquidator of Shield* v *Fateh Chand Pahwa* (2007)135 Comp Cas 467 (Raj); 2007(2) RLW 1505.

> evidence and pleadings in respect of the individual director of an act of the nature contemplated by the section. In the absence of any specific allegation or positive evidence it is not possible or proper for this Court to indulge in a fishing or roving enquiry so as to compel an individual director to reimburse or compensate the company apart from the mere allegation that the security deposit has been retained by the directors there is no allegation as to who has retained it, who has misapplied the money and if so in what manner.[7]

The position is clear that mere vague allegation is not sufficient to prove misfeasance or breach of trust, the parties has to place positive evidence against a director to take action under this provision.

8.3 Equitable compensation

Compensation is the equitable remedy granted against a trustee or other fiduciary to complete restitution of the loss suffered by his breach of fiduciary duty. The directors who participate in the breach are jointly and severally liable with the usual rights of contribution *inter se*. The participation may be either active or by subsequent acquiescence in it.[8]

Mere protesting will not disprove acquiescence.[9] Further, as regards the breach of fiduciary duties, the right of contribution *inter se* always exists in equity. Apart from the directors' joint liability for breach of trust, third persons who knowingly participate in a breach of directors fiduciary duties are similarly liable.[10] They need not actually know that what is being done in a breach of duty; it suffices if they assist in a transaction with knowledge of circumstances which would put a reasonable man on inquiry whether a morally reprehensible design is being carried out. But clearly if they know that it is a breach of duty it is irrelevant whether they regard it as morally reprehensible.[11]

7 *Sajida Book Shop* v *Kaumudi Exporters (P) Ltd.* (2007)135 Comp Cas 273 (Ker); 2006(4) KLT 763.

8 *Re Land Allotment Co.* [1894]1 Ch 616 (CA).

9 *Joint Stock Discount Co. Brown* [1869] LR 8 Eq 381.

10 *Selangor United Rubber Estates Ltd.* v *Cradock (No. 3)* [1968]1 WLR 1555; *Gray* v *Lewis*[1869] LR 8 Eq 526; *Canada Safe Way* v *Thompson* [1951]3 DLR 295; [1952]2 DLR 591; *Morrison* v *Coast Finance Ltd.* [1966]55 DLR (2d) 710.

11 *Selanger United Rubber Estates Ltd.* v *Cradock,* ibid.

Their liability is clearer still if they knowingly induce a breach of such a duty.[12] However, if the director has a contract with the company, this liability will merge into the tort of knowingly inducing breach of contract.[13] But where third persons are guilty of participating in breach of trust or the company can sue for it, not the director.[14] However, where the third party is innocent and does not know of the facts which constitute the breach of trust, he cannot normally be made liable.[15] However, where the third party is not a purchaser for value and the property concerned is under his custody or is enjoying the benefit thereof he may be asked to account for it.[16]

The director, managing agent, secretaries and treasures or manager, or any officer of the company to compel repayment or restore the money or property of the company or to contribute any sum by way of damages in case of breach of trust by courts. The exercise of the powers is made dependent upon an application being made to the court by a creditor or member of the concerned company. The persons against whom the order can be made are not merely the present director, managing agent, secretary and treasurer or manager or officer of the company, but even against the past director, managing agent, secretary and treasurer or manager, or officer of the company. The section further provides that misapplication, retention, misfeasance or breach of trust, for which repayment, restoration or compensation can be ordered, must appear in the course of proceedings under s. 397 or s. 398 of the Act. In other words, the section provides for an application for recovery of damages to be made if it appears, in the course of proceeding under s. 397 or s. 398 of the Act, that misfeasance etc. has taken place in relation to a company.[17]

12 *Boulting* v *A.C.T. A.T.* [1963]2 QB 606 (CA), where the majority found that no breach was proved on the facts.
13 *Jasperson* v *Dominion Tobacco Co.* [1923] AC 709 (PC).
14 *Boniting* case, Ibid; *Canada Safeway* v *Thompson,* ibid.
15 *Selangor United Rubber Estates Ltd. Cradock,* ibid, where the claim against the *Bank of Nova Scotia* failed on this ground; *Lindgren* v *L&P Estates Co. Ltd.* [1968] Ch 572 (CA); *Cf. McKay* v *Proprietary Mines Ltd.* [1939]3 DLR 215, where the wrong doing director was made to account for proceeds of shares sold to innocent purchasers.
16 *G.L. Baker* v *Medway Building & Supplies Ltd.* [1958]1 WLR 1216 (CA); *Nelson* v *Larholt* [1948]1 KB 339; *Ministry of Health* v *Simpsonm* [1951] AC 251 (HL).
17 *Colaba Land and Mill Co. Ltd.* v *Vasant Investment Corporation* AIR 1964 Guj 107; (1963) GLR 911.

Section 543 of the Indian Companies Act gives power to the court to assess damages in the case of delinquent directors. If in the course of winding up of a company it appears that any director has misapplied or retained or has become liable or accountable, *i.e.,* he cannot properly account for any money or property of the company and appears to be guilty of misfeasance or breach of trust in relation to the company, the court may examine into the conduct of such a director and compel him to re-pay or restore the money or property or any part thereof with interest as the court thinks fit and to contribute such sum of money to the company by way of compensation in respect of such misapplication, retainer, misfeasance, breach of trust as the court thinks fit and proper.[18]

The Madras High Court in *Official Liquidator, High Court, Madras* v *Gautham Dhiraj Mal Ranka,*[19] held that the report of the official liquidator showed that allegations of misfeasance and non-feasance where general in nature without pinpointing specific act of dishonestly and misappropriation on the part of the individual ex-directors, therefore, proceedings intends under ss. 542 and 543 against the ex-directors could not be proceeded without evidence. In this case the liquidator found that the ex-directors acted against the interest of the company, and that the business contrary to the provisions of the Companies Act and failed to account to the liquidator. Official liquidator argued that the ex-directors were jointly and severally liable to contribute to the assets of the company in liquidation by way of compensation for the loss caused by them to the company liquidation in the future claims from the creditors with future interest.

In an earlier judgment the Supreme Court in *Official Liquidator* v *Raghava Desikachar,*[20] it was held that a misfeasance obligation against the directors being a serious charge of misconduct or breach of duty. The application by the official liquidator should contain detailed narration of commission and omissions can the burden of proving misfeasance or nonfeasance rest on the official liquidator. The Delhi High Court also held that an application under ss. 542 and 543 of the Act, if there are no specific allegations against any specific director,

18 *National Sugar Mills Ltd.* v *Unknown* (1978)48 Comp Cas 339 (Cal).
19 (2008)141 Comp Cas 129 (Mad).
20 AIR 1974 SC 2069; (1975)45 Comp Cas 136.

the obligation to be dismissed in so far as a particular director is concerned.[1]

Under s. 542 of the Companies Act, fixed liability for fraudulent conduct of business. If the official liquidator in the course of the winding up of a company, found that any business of the company has been carried on with intent to defraud creditors of the company or any other person, declared any person who had knowingly parties to be business shall be personally responsible, without any limitation of liability for all the debts or liabilities of the company are the court deems fit.

However, the absence of specific allegations and posted dividends, it is not possible or proper for the court to indulge in fishing or roving inquiry source to compel the individual director to reimburse or compensate the company. The Calcutta High Court held in *Central Calcutta Bank Ltd., in re,* that the general principle of liability of joint tort-feasor cannot apply to misfeasance proceedings and, in order that the person may be a joint tort-feasor, there must be a common design and a concerted action.

From the above judgments it is clear that an alleged misfeasance and nonfeasance general in nature without pinpointing a specific fact of dishonestly and misappropriation on the part of the individual ex-director is not sufficient to prosecute directors under ss. 542 and 543 of the Companies Act.

8.4 Injunction

Injunction or declaration is a remedy preventive in character. It is primarily employed where a breach of misfeasance is threatened but has not yet occurred. This is obviously the most satisfactory course of action if it can be taken in appropriate time, *i.e.*, before the breach is began to be effected. Injunctions, permanent or temporary can be extensively employed in a wide range of occasions. Thus, if the board is proposing to take some action which, or is alleged to be, beyond their powers, they can be restrained by an injunction. A declaration of invalidity will also fulfill the same purpose and is generally asked for as an alternative to an injunction.

Again injunction can be employed before the completion of the breach where it is of a continuing nature. Thus an injunction may be

1 *Security and Finance (P) Ltd.* v *B.K. Bedi* (1991)71 Comp Cas 101 (Del).

appropriate where the breach has already occurred but is likely to continue as in the case of the use of Trade Secret[2] and confidential information.[3] Further, injunction can be resorted where the breach has been completed but some of its adverse consequences can thereby be avoided.[4] Thus injunction is a preventive and regressive remedy available against a breach of fiduciary obligation.

8.5 Restoration of property

The property and funds of the company are entrusted with the directors and are under their control. They hold the properties of the company in trust. Since the company is the real owner and the beneficiary of the property which is or should have come under the control of the directors, it may be recovered by the company *in rem* from them and from third persons, who are not purchasers for value, in so far as it is traceable.[5]

The property which is to be restored to the company includes not only property reduced into the company's possession but also property which it was the directors' duty to acquire for the company[6] or to give the company an opportunity of acquiring.[7] It may even include property which the company has no present power to acquire, for it may be the directors' duty to cause the object clause to be amended so that it can do so.[8] Thus, a prime duty is imposed on directors with regard to restoration of properties. But apparently it does not include all profit made by a director for which the company has a right to call upon him to account.[9] These profits and the investments made with them will

2 *British Industrial Plastics* v *Ferguson* [1938]4 All ER 504 (CA); *Cranicigh Precision Engineering Ltd.* v *Bryant* [1965] WLR 1293.

3 Such as List of customers or copies of confidential documents etc.; *Measures Bros.* v *Measures* [1910]1 Ch 336; [1910]2 Ch 248 (CA); *Printers & Finishers Ltd.* v *Halloway* [1965]1 WLR 1.

4 For e.g.; to enjoin the delivery up of confidential documents improperly taken away by a former director: *Measures Bros.* v *Measures Ltd.* [1910]2 Ch 248; *Craneleigh Precision Engineering Ltd.* v *Bryant* [1964]3 All ER 289.

5 *Re Diplock* [1948] Ch 465 (CA). Also Goff & Jones, *The Law of Restitution*, pp. 49-52, reveals the ambit of the equitable rule of tracing.

6 As in *Cook* v *Decks* [1916]1 AC 554 (PC).

7 As in *Canada Safeway Ltd.* v *Thompson* (supra).

8 *Fine Industrial Commodities* v *Powling* [1954]71 RPC 253 (288).

9 *Lister & Co.* v *Stubbs* [1890]45 Ch D 1 (CA), where the court rejected a claim to investments made by an agent out of secret commissions. *Powell & Tomas* v *Evans Johes & Co.* [1905]1 KB 11.

not be regarded as belonging in equity to the company unless they followed from a use of the company's property.[10]

As regards the character of confidential information whether it can be treated as company's property or not, jurists differ in their views. The information confidential to the company is deemed to be the company's property, in almost every case in which directors are liable to account for profits there will have been a use of the company's property.[11] Thus, on this basis not merely the profits made but the shares acquired themselves were held to be recoverable in *Regal (Hastings) Ltd.* v *Gulliver*[12] and in *Phipps* v *Boardman.*[13] In *Peso Sliver Mines Ltd.* v *Cropper*[14] the Canadian Supreme Court clearly assumed that confidential information is a property of the company. But in *Phipps* v *Boardman,* the members of the House of Lords had no unanimity in this regard. But those who held that confidential information is not an asset of the company seem to under estimate its proprietary characteristics. A third party may clearly be restrained from using confidential information,[15] and apparently may be made to restore benefits derived from it by means of an action *'in rem'* at any rates if he knew that the information was confidential.[16] Equity certainly seems to come very close to treating confidential information to the company as the company's property and hence recoverable by it. Recovery here is in the form of proceedings *'in rem'* as opposed to recovery *in personam* as in the case of suit for compensation or account of profits. Thus suit for restoration can be sought against third parties also.

8.6 Recession of contracts

It is a statutory duty on the part of the directors to disclose their interests in contracts which they are proposed to be entered into by

10 Goff & Jones, *The Law of Restitution,* pp. 459-460.
11 For cf. *Bell Houses* v *City Wall Properties Ltd.* [1966]2 QB 656 (CA), where knowledge of sources of finance was held to be an asset of the company.
12 [1942]1 All ER 378.
13 [1967]2 AC 46 (HL).
14 [1966]58 DLR 1.
15 *Cranleigh Precision Engineering Ltd.* v *Bryant* [1965]1 WLR 1293 (supra). There the third party and another controlled by thedirector; but the same principle applies to an independent third party: *Saturian Engineering Ltd.* v *Campbell Engineering Ltd.* [1963]3 All ER 413 (CA); *Printers & Finishers Ltd.* v *Hollway* [1965]1 WLR 1.
16 *Saltman Engineering Ltd.* v *Campbell Engineering Ltd.* (supra); *Peter Pan Manufacturing Corpn.* v *Corsets Silhouette Ltd.* [1964]1 WLR 96.

the company. An agreement with the company which breaks the rules relating to contracts in which directors are interested may be avoided[17] provided that the rights of *bona fide* third parties have not hurt.[18] Again *restitutio in integrum* must be possible.[19]

Since the directors owe a duty of disclosure to the company, the primary remedy against him in the event of breach is for the company to bring proceedings for recession of any contract with him or in which he is interested or for the recovery of any secret profits which he has made. So far as the right to rescind is concerned, this must be exercised on normal contractual principles, that is to say the company must have done nothing to show an intention to ratify the agreement after finding out about the non-disclosure or misrepresentation[20] and *restitutio in integrum* must still be possible.[1]

However, in view of the wide powers not exercised by the courts to order financial adjustments when directing recession, it is doubtful whether the *restitutio in integrum* operates as a real restraint, at any rate where the director has been fraudulent and where he himself is responsible for the dealings alleged to have resulted in restitution being impossible.[2] The only circumstance where this requirement seems likely to impose a serious limitation is where innocent third parties have acquired rights to the property concerned, and even there a monetary adjustment will often enable the third parties rights to be discharged.[3] The mere fact that the company is in liquidation does not prevent it from rescinding the contract. However, as regards rescission of an allotment of shares in the company the rules are very

17 Section 297(5).

18 *Transval Lands Co.* v *New Belgium (Transval) Land & Development Co.* [1914]2 Ch 488 (CA).

19 *Re Leeds & Hanley Theatre of Varieties* [1902]2 Ch 809 (CA); *Steedman* v *Frigidaire Corpn.* [1933]1 DLR 161 (PC); *Dominion Royalty Corpn.* v *Goffatt* [1935]1 DLR 780.

20 *Lagunas Nitrate Co.* v *Lagunas Syndicate* [1899]2 Ch 392 (CA). Here again "the company" must mean the members or an independent board; clearly ratification by puppet directors cannot be effective.

1 *Re Leeds & Hanley Theatre of Varieties,* Ibid.

2 *Erlanger* v *New Sombrero Phosphate Co.* [1878]3 App Cas 1218 (HL); *Spence* v *Crawford* [1939]3 All ER 271 (HL). These cases suggests that the courts have more restricted powers of financial adjustment when there is no fraud: *Amstrong* v *Jackson* [1917]2 KB 822.

3 As in *R. Leeds & Hanley Theatre of Varieties,* Ibid, where theproperty has been mortgaged to a Bank.

strict.[4] Again, the mere fact that the contract had been performed never seems to have destroyed the right to rescind a contract of this type.

Further, if the contract is rescinded the directors' secret profit will also disappear as a result, but if he has made a profit on some ancillary transaction there is no doubt that this too may be recovered. Moreover, a secret profit may be recovered although the company elects not to rescind the contract.[5]

8.7 Account of profits

The remedy of account of profit arises from a breach of an equitable or statutory right. Most commonly, the remedy will encompass an order for the payment of money closely akin to restitution, such as a trustee who uses trust funds for their own purposes. A fiduciary has to account for profits earned in breach of duty even where the fiduciary has acted honestly and reasonably.[6] Unauthorized gains have to be accounted and to be restored according to the nature of breach and particular relationship and the manner it was breached.[7]

The fiduciary position of directors enjoins an obligation not to make any secret profit by using that position. If they make any secret profit, they are strictly liable to account for such profits to the company. This liability may either arise out of a contract made between a director and the company,[8] or as a result of some contract or arrangement between the director and a third person.[9]

In the case of contract made between the directors and the company, accounting is an additional remedy available besides the avoidance of the contract in question and is normally available whether or not there is rescission.[10] But if the director has sold his own property to the

4 *Oakes* v *Turquand* [1867] LR 2 HL 325.

5 *Gluckstein* v *Barnes* [1900] AC 240 (HL). Also *Jubilee Cotton Mills* v *Lewis* [1924] AC 958 (HL).

6 *Warman International Ltd* v *Dwyer* [1995]182 CLR 544 (577); [1995] HCA 18.

7 http://www.sclqld.org.au/lu/items/articles/588, visited on 04.06.2012.

8 *Imperial Mercantile Credit Asson.* v *Colemarn* [1873] LR 6 HL 189.

9 *Regal (Hastings) Ltd.* v *Gulliver,* Ibid.

10 *Gluckstein* v *Barnes*, Ibid.

company the right to an account of profits will be lost if the company elects not to rescind or is too late to do so.[11]

As regards the profit arises out of a contract between the director and a third party there will be no question of rescinding that contract at the instance of the company, since the company is not a party to the contract. Here account of profit is the sole remedy. But in either case the proof of any loss suffered by the company is not required for the recovery of profit. It is recoverable not as damages or compensation but because the company is entitled to call upon the directors to account to it.[12] The liability to account is an equitable one.

8.8 Summary dismissal

The relations subsisting between the company and its directors are neither one of master and servant nor of a principal and Agent. Hence, the right which a master or a principal to dismiss a servant or an agent, as the case may be, who has been guilty of serious misconduct has no application to a director as such. However, he can at any time be dismissed from his directorship by an ordinary resolution in the general meeting subject to compliance with the provisions, s. 284.

On the whole, s. 284 provides a comparatively less cumbersome process for the removal of directors from their office. According to this section a company may remove a director before the expiry of his period of office by an ordinary resolution in the general meeting.[13] A special notice shall be required for this purpose.[14] Again the director shall be entitled to be heard[15]and is also entitled to make representations.[16]

Where the directors attempt to avoid their removal by omitting to call a meeting or by not attending with a view to create a situation

11 *Re Ambrose Lake Tin Co.* [1880]11 Ch D 390 (CA); *Re Cape Breton Co.* [1885]29 Ch D 795 (CA); *Cavendish Bentinck* v *Fenn* [1997]12 App Cas 652 (HL), *Ladywell Mining Co.* v *Brookes* [1887]35 Ch D 400 (CA); *Re Lady Forrest (Murchison) Gold Mine* [1901]1 Ch 852; *Borland* v *Earle* [1902] AC 83 (PC); *Jacobus Matter* v *Marley* [1913]85 LJPC 167; *Robinson* v *Randontien Estate* [1921] AC 168 (A.Afr.S.C.); *P&G Steam Navigation Co.* v *Johnson* [1938]60 CLR 189 (Aus HC); *Hely Hutachinson* v *Brayhead Ltd.* [1968]1 QB 549 (CA).

12 *Boston Deep Sea Fishing & Ice Co.* v *Ansell* [1888]39 Ch D 339.

13 Section 284(1) of the Companies Act 1956.

14 Section 284(2) of the Companies Act 1956.

15 Section 284(3) of the Companies Act 1956.

16 Section 284(4) of the Companies Act 1956.

of 'no quorum', the Company Law Board may convene the necessary meeting under s. 186.[17] Again it was held that a permanent director, who is entitled to hold office for life under the articles of the company, can also be removed.[18]

However, nothing in this section shall be taken as depriving a person removed there under of any compensation or damages payable to him in respect of the termination of office.[19] Compensation or damages can be claimed not only for the termination of the office, but any other office which will be terminated along with that office, such as that of managing director. The amount will be calculated with reference to his last income taking into account his liability to income-tax, super-tax etc.[20]

Again, this section does not affect the power of the Board of Directors to revoke the appointment of a managing director or any other officer of the company, made by the Board.[1]

In the absence of a special contract, where a managing director or manager is appointed as per the Articles of a company, the removal of such person or the termination of his service in accordance with the Articles or the Provisions of the Act does not give rise to an action for damages for wrongful dismissal on the ground that he has not been given reasonable notice.[2] However, a company cannot, after entering into a contract of service, bring about a breach of it by changing its articles.[3]

The provisions of this section are mandatory and clearly cannot be dispensed with because it is alleged that the director has been guilty of misconduct. It would be possible to provide in the articles of the company that his office shall be vacated in the event of misconduct but the more usual and effective provision is one to the effect that this shall occur if the board call upon him to resign.

17 *Re El Sombrero Ltd.* [1958]3 All ER 1 (Ch D).

18 *Tarlok Chand Khanna* v *Rajkumar Kapoor* (1983)54 Comp Cas 12 (Del).

19 Section 284(7)(*a*).

20 *British Transport Commission* v *Gourley* [1965]3 All ER 796 (HL); *Beach* v *Reed Corrugated Cases Ltd.* [1956]2 All ER 652 (QBD); *Phipps* v *Orthodox Unit Trusts Ltd.* [1987]3 All ER 305 (CA).

1 *Major General Shanbha Sharnsher* v *Kamani Bros.* AIR 1959 Bom 201.

2 *Reed* v *Astoria Garage (Streatham) Ltd.* [1952] All ER 292 (CA).

3 *Shindler* v *North Raincoat Co. Ltd.* [1962]2 All ER 269; *Southern Foundries Ltd.* v *Shirlaw* [1940]2 All ER 445 (HL).

If all these remedies are taken together, dismissal from office seems to be a real deterrent to fraudulent directors. But it is only a punitive one. Suit for compensation and recovery of property are seemed to be the best remedies for a breach of trust by the directors of a company.

8.9 Conclusion

Where there has been a breach of trust, the trustee is personally liable for the loss caused to the trust estate. Directors are supposed to act with honesty and good faith in their official capacity and they are not supposed to act against the interest of the company. The fiduciary relationship with the director and the company is paramount and at the same time the interest of the shareholders has to be protected by the directors. If the directors are doing anything in breach of their duty, the affected person can approach the court for various remedies like injunction, compensation, restoration of property, rescission of contracts, account of profits, etc.

9

Directors in the 21st Century—The Companies Bill 2012

9.1 Introduction

The Indian Companies Regulation history starts with the Indian Companies Act 1866; the Indian Companies Act 1882; the Indian Companies Act 1913; the Registration of Transferred Companies Ordinance 1942; the Companies Act 1956. The Companies Bill 1997 was introduced in the Rajya Sabha on 14th August 1997 and pending therein, and the Bill was referred to the Department Related Parliamentary Standing Committee on Finance. Pending the Bill, the Companies (Amendment) Ordinance 1998 was promulgated on 31st October 1998. Subsequently, the Companies Amendment Bill 1998 was introduced in the Lok Sabha on 22nd December to replace the Ordinance. But it could not be passed, another Ordinance called Companies (Amendment) Ordinance 1999 was promulgated on 7th January 1999. The Ordinance was on similar lines as Companies (Amendment) Bill 1998. All these Bills were referred to Department-Related Parliamentary Standing Committee on Home Affairs headed by its Chairman, Pranab Mukherjee, which the Committee contains 15 members from Rajya Sabha and 30 members from Lok Sabha. The Committee considered all the Bills and submitted its Report to Rajya Sabha on 27th July 2000 which was also laid in Lok Sabha on 27th July 2000. Companies (Amendment) Bill 2002 was passed to transfer all the powers of the Company Law Board to the National Company Law Tribunal. The 2008 Bill re-introduced in the Parliament as the Companies Bill 2009 completely repealed the entire 1956 Act in order to enable the Indian companies to compete in a globalized world. The Bill was not passed by the Parliament due to many reasons and pressure tactics from

Indian industry. In December 2011, the Law Minister introduced the "new" bill in the Parliament again. When compare to the Companies Act 1956, the new Bill is with only 420 clauses (700 sections were in the 1956 Act). There were drastic changes made to the existing provisions in order to match the international standards as claimed by the Government. The Companies Bill 2011, introduced in Lok Sabha on 14th December 2011, was referred to the Standing Committee on 5th January 2012. The Standing Committee submitted its report on 26th June 2012. Incorporating recommendations of the Standing Committee, the Companies Bill 2012 was introduced and passed in Lok Sabha on 18th December 2012. After 56 years, the Companies Act 1956 has going to be repealed. The proposed Act is divided into 29 chapters, 470 clauses and seven schedules.

9.2 Companies Bill 1997

The Companies Bill 1997 seeks to remove existing lacunae in the Companies Act 1956 and streamline some of the existing provisions for better working and administration of the Companies Act. In view of the extensive changes proposed to be made in the Companies Act 1956, the Bill seeks to repeal and re-enact the said Act.

The main objective of re-enacting the Companies Act is to facilitate a healthy growth of the Indian Corporate Sector under a liberalized, fast changing and highly competitive environment while redrafting the law, an Endeavour has been made to adopt a balanced approach that recognizes an international trend, i.e., flexibility and greater self regulation by Companies subject to better disclosure, more efficient enforcement of law, and prompt and stringent punishments to those who violate the law. The core object of the Companies Bill is to provide effective protection to the different participants leaving management free to direct its energies to the pursuit of the Company's objectives.

The Bill provided in clause (*xi*) limiting the age up to Seventy-five years for all directors in public companies, Clause (*xiii*) providing that a public company may have a maximum of 15 directors, clause (*xix*) constituting the Company Law Tribunal in place of the existing Company Law Board and vesting the Tribunal with more function and powers and providing it with wider jurisdiction. Certain provisions of the Companies Bill 1997 have been taken out of that Bill and incorporated in the Companies (Amendment) Bill 1999.

It provides certain salient changes in the duty of directors. Clause 54 provides for civil liability for misstatement in prospectus. Clause 222 provides for a number of Directorships of Companies. Suggestion came from various parts of Industry to modify it as "Directorship in subsidiaries should be exempted. Directorship in holding and subsidiary companies to be treated as one directorship. Performance of subsidiary is clubbed by way of equity consolidation". This suggestion is accepted by the Government and the clause is dropped to such extent. Clause 224 provides for retiring age for directors it is deleted as by the recommendation of the Committee. The Committee cleared both the Bills after acceptance of suggestions from various bodies and discussions.

9.3 The Companies (Second Amendment) Bill 1999

As on 1st January 2000 a total number of 5,32,580 Companies were at work and their estimated paid up capital was ₹ 2,72,865 crore. India was in the forefront of the Company Law. The first Companies Act was enacted in 1913. Certain Amendments were passed in 1936 and 1951. The present Act was enacted in 1956 as a result of industrial policy resolutions and federalization of corporate laws in different States, pursuant to the integration of princely states in the Union of India. The Act has been amended seventeen times till 1999.

There is an imperative need to further amend the Companies Act pursuant to the New Economic Policy announced in 1991, rapid economic developments taking place globally, liberalization of economies, access to world market, WTO etc. Further amendments to the law are necessary to facilitate healthy growth of Indian Corporate Sector under liberalized and highly competitive environment. Greater flexibility, transparency, disclosure, efficient enforcement, tougher penalties, better investor's protection is the felt needs of the time. U.K., USA, Australia, Canada, EU etc., had already updated their Company Law. A working group was appointed by the Government in 1996 and submitted their report in 1997. The Companies Bill 1999 is in essence the reflection of the report.

The highlights of the Bill are: To provide transparency and good corporate governance, investor protection; stringent penalties; repeal of redundant provisions. The Committee accepted suggestions from various organizations and bodies. Regarding the Directors Cl. 122 provides that small shareholders can elect at least one Director in each Board of

Directors of Companies with a paid up capital of ₹ 5 crore or more having 1000 or more small shareholders.

The suggestions to omit the provision for representation of small shareholders by electing at least one among them on Board of Directors cannot be accepted because of small shareholders do not have a voice to represent on Board of Directors as on date. The election will take place in the manner as may be prescribed. The Government is proposed to include an explanation that for the purpose of ascertaining 1000 number of shareholders and 5 crores or more paid up share capital, the basis shall be the date of issue of notice.

It provides for Directors report to include a Directors Responsibility Statement. In view of giving representation to the small investors in the Board of Directors, Committee recommended, "Since a large number of women professionals are entering the arena of corporate management, giving them adequate representation in the Board of Directors".

In the General observations made by the Committee notes that the nomenclature of the Companies Act was framed almost a century ago. In the present day corporate parlance, corporate governance is being talked about. In this context, the Government may deliberate on the need for changing the nomenclature of the Companies Act to "Corporate Governance Act" because the whole purpose of the amendments sought to be made through the two Bills and those enforced by the Companies (Amendment) Act 1999, is to ensure that there is transparency, efficiency, competitiveness and effectiveness which are the hallmarks of good corporate governance. It is the apt time for emancipation and revolutionizes the Companies Act itself.

9.4 Companies (Amendment) Bill 2000

The Union Cabinet has approved the Companies (Amendment) Bill 2000, which seeks to ensure better corporate governance, investor friendly transparency in working of Companies and protection to shareholders and depositors. The Bill incorporates almost all the provision of the Companies (Second Amendment) Bill 1999 as approved by the department related Standing Committee of Parliament.[1]

Under the new Bill, the contentious cl. 122 in the 1999 Bill, that seeks to insert a provision to sub-section (1) of s. 252 of the Companies Act 1956

1 *The Hindu,* New Delhi, 18th August 2000.

to provide for mandatory representation from small shareholders in the board of directors has been deleted from the new Bill.

In the Bill, it has been decided to retain the Company Law Board. The Bill also envisages giving adequate representation to women on boards of directors. Other features include capital market related provision to be administration by SEBI—a person cannot be a director in more than fifteen companies; the directors report to include directors responsibility statement and introduction of postal ballot for certain important matters which are crucial to corporate governance. The numbers of directorships in companies were restricted to 15. Section 276 whereby a person who is Managing Director or whole-time Director can also be Director in only 10 other companies.

In the light of the new Acts the fiduciary duties of directors are in a high point in the Era of Liberalization and Globalization in the past. The stringent penal provisions will act as a check and balance system by the director itself in discharging their duties.

9.5 Companies (Amendment) Bill 2002

The 2000 Bill prematurely died and again re-introduced in 2002. The bill provides for transfer of all powers enjoyed by the Company Law Board (CLB) to the newly constituted National Company Law Tribunal. Rehabilitation and Revival Fund for companies were provided in the Companies (Second Amendment) Act 2002.

9.6 Companies (Amendment) Bill 2003

The Bill aims to provide adequate protection to investors, shareholders, creditors, employees and persons appointed by governmental agencies to ensure quick and effective rectification of corporate wrongs.

Various new issues have been raised by this new Amendment. Important among them is the concept of Independent Directors. By insertion of new s. 252A, persons ineligible for appointment as such have been laid down. Compulsory training of directors in an Institute notified by the Central Government is an another new initiative introduced in the Bill.

With this Bill of 2003, new ss. 629B and 629C have been inserted for the benefit of investors. As per s. 629B, if a company fails to credit to IEPF (s. 205C), amounts specified under s. 205C, then the Company and every officer of the Company in default shall be punishable with a fine not less than the amount not deposited. In addition the Officer in default shall also be punishable with imprisonment for a period of not less than 3 months which may extend to 2 years. Again it has been provided under s. 629C that the Central Government in the interest of investors or security market may by order on an application made by Judicial Magistrate of first class having jurisdiction, attach bank accounts of any intermediary or any person associated with securities market who in any manner is involved in the violation of any of the provisions of this Act. It has been provided further that only accounts or transactions which relate to the proceeds actually involved in the violation shall be allowed to be attached. Stringent measures have been incorporated for adequate protection of investors.

The concept of Chief Accounts Officer (CAO) was introduced under s. 215A. Under the new Bill there are certain services which cannot be provided by the Statutory Auditors in respect of their employer companies under s. 226A. Primary among them are:

- Accounting and book–keeping services relating to the accounting records or financial statements.
- Internal audit services.
- Financial information systems design and implementation.
- Actual services.
- Broker or as intermediary referred to s. 12 of the SEBI Act 1992.
- Out–sourced financial services etc.

Thus under s. 383A role of Company Secretaries has been clearly defined and enhanced considerably. However, vide changes were proposed in the Bill, has never passed even though there were vast changes happened in the Indian corporate sector.

9.7 Companies Bill 2008 and 2009

In October 2008, Shri Gupta, Minister of Company Affairs had withdrawn the Companies (Amendment) Bill 2003 which was introduced in the Rajya Sabha on 7.5.2003 as the said Bill was not in tune with the present day requirements of corporate situation in India.[2] This is an initiative of the Government to promote the development of the Indian corporate sector through enlightened regulation.

2 http://www.pib.nic.in/release/release.asp?relid=44114, visited on 22.04.2009.

The comprehensive revision of the Companies Act 1956 was taken up by the Ministry since not only had the number of companies in India expanded from about 30,000 in 1956 to above 8 lakhs,[3] the Indian corporate sector had also transformed itself in a manner that was unimaginable even a decade ago. Today, Indian companies have expanded and grown into global entities, continuously entering into and bringing new activities into the fold of the Indian economy. In doing so, they are emerging internationally as efficient providers of a wide range of goods and services while increasing employment opportunities at home. The 1956 Act is neither equipped to meet the aspirations of the Indian corporate sector nor is it equipped to meet the eventualities of the corporate fraud in the 21st Century. This was proved by the 7000 Crore fraud revealed by its chairman of "Satyam."

The Act is a voluminous piece of legislation which is in force since 1956 consisting of 658 sections, 6 Tables, 14 Schedules and it has become both complex and complicated due to successive amendments numbering about 24, over a period of little more than half a century. During this period a lot of changes have taken place in the economic milieu, both in India and abroad. The business in India has been freed from diverse, complex regulatory framework.

The new Bill seeks to work the Indian companies in a new regulatory environment at par with international standards on corporate governance that foster entrepreneurship, investment and growth. The New Bill aims at simplification of Company law by (*i*) segregating and deleting the procedural laws from the substantive law, (*ii*) procedural laws to be prescribed by the Central Government in the form of Rules, (*iii*) clubbing of existing provisions, (*iv*) retaining some of the provisions of the Act which are considered relevant and useful, and (*v*) harmonization of company law with some of the provisions of SEBI governance norms.

The Bill reinforces shareholders democracy, facilitates e-Governance in company processes, recognizes the liability of Boards, directors and senior management personnel of companies, provides for a new scheme for penalties and punishment for non-compliance or violation of the law, harmonizes corporate regulation with action by sectoral regulators, incorporates a new framework for mergers and

3 *Ibid.*

amalgamations of companies and provides an extensive Insolvency Code based on the latest principles recommended by the United Nations Commission on International Trade Law (UNCITRAL).

The 2008 Bill was lapsed due to the dissolution of the 14th Lok Sabha. The new Government again introduced the Companies Bill 2009 in the Lok Sabha on 3rd August 2009 at the backdrop of Satyam Services multi crore scam. The said Bill was referred to the Parliamentary Standing Committee on Finance for examination and report and the Committee gave its Report on 31st August 2010. A new draft has been introduced in the parliament in December 2011 with the suggested changes. The Companies Bill 2011, introduced in Lok Sabha on 14th December 2011, was referred to the Standing Committee on 5th January 2012. The Standing Committee submitted its report on 26th June 2012, the new bill has been introduced in the Lok Sabha on and passed on 18th December 2012. The provisions relating to the company directors are only analyzed below.

9.8 The Companies Bill 2011 and the Bill 2012

Objective of the Bill

1. In view of large amendments to the Companies Bill 2009 arising out of the recommendations of the Parliamentary Standing Committee on Finance and suggestions of the stakeholders, the Central Government decided to withdraw the Companies Bill 2009 and introduce a fresh Bill incorporating therein the recommendations of Standing Committee and suggestions of the stakeholder. The 2012 Bill simply wants to consolidate and amend the law relating to companies.

2. Articulation of shareholders democracy with protection of the rights of minority stakeholders, responsible self-regulation with adequate disclosures and accountability. Reduction of Government control over internal corporate processes.

3. Relaxation of restriction limiting the number of persons in associations or partnerships, etc., to a maximum of one hundred, with no ceiling as to associations, or partnerships, formed by professionals regulated by special Acts.

4. Easy transition of companies operating under the Companies Act 1956, to the new framework as also from one type of company to another. Freedom with regard to the numbers and layers of subsidiary

companies that a company may have, subject to disclosures in respect of their relationship and transactions or dealings between them.

Definitions

5. CLAUSE 2(10). Clause 2(10) provides that "Board of Directors" or "Board," in relation to a company, means the collective body of the directors of the company.

6. CLAUSE 2(18). Clause 2(18) "Chief Executive Officer" means an officer of a company, who has been designated as such by it.

7. CLAUSE 2(34). "Director" means a director appointed to the Board of a company.

8. CLAUSE 2(41). Clause 2(41) seeks to introduce a uniform financial year for all companies from April to March of every coming year. Even though it is a welcome step, now a day more and more foreign companies are following current year as the financial year. They will find it very difficult to consolidate its subsidiaries in India have a different financial year. But if the subsidiary of a foreign company wants to follow a different financial year, they can approach the Tribunal and if it is satisfied such request can be granted by the Tribunal to keep in consolidation with the foreign company. But such companies should synchronize their financial year with the new bill within a period of two years.

9. CLAUSE 2(47). Clause 2(47) provides that "independent director" means an independent director referred to in sub-sec. (5) of s. 149.

10. CLAUSE 2(49). "Interested Director" means a director who is in any way, whether by himself or through any of his relatives or firm, body corporate or other association of individuals in which he or any of his relatives is a partner, director or a member, interested in a contract or arrangement, or proposed contract or arrangement, entered into or to be entered into by or on behalf of a company.

11. CLAUSE 2(51). "Key managerial personnel", in relation to a company, means—

(*i*) the Chief Executive Officer or the managing director or the manager;

(*ii*) the company secretary;

(*iii*) the whole-time director;

(*iv*) the Chief Financial Officer; and

(*v*) such other officer as may be prescribed.

The Companies Bill 2011 had excluded whole-time directors from the definition of "key managerial personnel" on the premise that in cases where a company has a managing director in place, whole-time directors do not exercise substantial powers of management and accordingly should be kept outside the ambit of the definition. In its report on the Companies Bill 2011, the SCF, differing from the views of the MCA, had elaborated that "whole-time directors, being important functionaries in a company with substantial role in decision-making, cannot be kept outside the purview of KMPs". As a mark of deference to the observations of the SCF, the Companies Bill 2012 has now included whole-time directors under the definition of "key managerial personnel".

12. CLAUSE 2(53). "Manager" means an individual who, subject to the superintendence, control and direction of the Board of Directors, has the management of the whole, or substantially the whole, of the affairs of a company, and includes a director or any other person occupying the position of a manager, by whatever name called, whether under a contract of service or not.

13. CLAUSE 2(54). "Managing Director" means a director who, by virtue of the articles of a company or an agreement with the company or a resolution passed in its general meeting, or by its Board of Directors, is entrusted with substantial powers of management of the affairs of the company and includes a director occupying the position of managing director, by whatever name called.

14. CLAUSE 2(59). "Officer" includes any director, manager or key managerial personnel or any person in accordance with whose directions or instructions the Board of Directors or any one or more of the directors is or are accustomed to act.

15. CLAUSE 2(60). *OFFICER WHO IS IN DEFAULT.* "Officer who is in default", for the purpose of any provision in this Act which enacts that an officer of the company who is in default shall be liable to any penalty or punishment by way of imprisonment, fine or otherwise, means any of the following officers of a company, namely:

(*i*) whole-time director;

(*ii*) key managerial personnel;

(*iii*) where there is no key managerial personnel, such director or directors as specified by the Board in this behalf and who has or have given his or their consent in writing to the Board to such specification, or all the directors, if no director is so specified;

(*iv*) any person who, under the immediate authority of the Board or any key managerial personnel, is charged with any responsibility including maintenance, filing or distribution of accounts or records, authorises, actively participates in, knowingly permits, or knowingly fails to take active steps to prevent, any default;

(*v*) any person in accordance with whose advice, directions or instructions the Board of Directors of the company is accustomed to act, other than a person who gives advice to the Board in a professional capacity;

(*vi*) every director, in respect of a contravention of any of the provisions of this Act, who is aware of such contravention by virtue of the receipt by him of any proceedings of the Board or participation in such proceedings without objecting to the same, or where such contravention had taken place with his consent or connivance;

(*vii*) in respect of the issue or transfer of any shares of a company, the share transfer agents, registrars and merchant bankers to the issue or transfer.

16. CLAUSE 2(94). "Whole-time director" includes a director in the whole-time employment of the company.

17. CLAUSE 2(62). ***ONE PERSON COMPANY (OPC).*** Clause 2(62) provides that "one person company" means a company which has only one person as a member. To encourage individuals with entrepreneurial activity, the Bill introduces a new entity in the form of One-Person Company (OPC) as a legal entity that would be separate and distinct from the promoter of the company. As the name suggests OPC shall have only one member and can have only one director. And OPC need not have to hold an annual general meeting. The allotment of shares, securities, debentures management and administration will be separate and distinct from other companies under the Act. For transactions entering into OPC

and the director should be in writing and entered into a register and recorded in the first minutes of the board of director s meeting. The last letters of the company should be "OPC Limited" Memorandum of One Person Company shall indicate the name of a person who shall become member, in the event of death, disability or otherwise of the single disability or otherwise of the single member. The companies formed under this clause may be limited by shares or limited by guarantee or an unlimited company. Conversion of a private company or a One Person Company into a public company or a One Person Company or a public company into private company with the approval of members through special resolution and approval of the Tribunal will be required for conversion of a public company into a private company or OPC.

18. EXPLANATION TO CLAUSE 32(4). "Red herring prospectus" means a prospectus which does not include complete particulars of the quantum or price of the securities or class of securities included therein.

19. The 2012 Bill defines unlimited companies as "a company not having any limit on the liability of its members".[4] The Bill retains the concept of Producer Companies, while providing a more stringent regime for not-for–profit companies to check misuse. No restriction proposed on the number of subsidiary companies that a company may have, subject to disclosure in respect of their relationship and transactions between them.[5]

20. CLAUSE 2(85). *SMALL COMPANY.* A small company would other than a public company whose paid up share capital is not more than ₹ 50 Lakh and shall not exceed five crore rupees. The annual turnover also should not be more than ₹ 2 crores or such higher amount as may be prescribed which shall not be more than 20 crore rupees. But a holding of subsidiary company, company formed for charitable purposes, company or body corporate formed by the Government under special Act does not come under the definition of a small company.

21. CLAUSES 2(88) & 54. "Sweat equity shares" means such equity shares as are issued by the company to its directors or employees at a discount or for consideration, other than cash, for providing their know-how or making available rights in the nature of intellectual property rights or value additions, by whatever name called.

4 Clause 2(92) of the 2012 Bill.
5 http://www.taxguru.in, visited on 15.06.2012.

22. CLAUSE 8. *NON-PROFITABLE COMPANIES.* Clause 8 deals with non-profitable companies like s. 25 of the Companies Act 1956 which empowers the Central Government to register an association as limited company having charitable objects to promote commerce, art, science, sports, education, research, social welfare, religion, charity, etc., without adding to its name the words "Limited," "Private Limited" or "OPC Limited." Payments of dividends are prohibited and the profits can be used for further development of the company. In contravention of these provisions, the Central Government can revoke the license and order wound up the company. Speedy incorporation process, with detailed declarations and disclosures about the promoters, directors etc., at the time of incorporation itself. Every company director would be required to acquire a unique Director Identification Number (DIN).

23. *NUMBER OF DIRECTORS.* Relaxation of restrictions limiting the number of partners in entities such as partnership firms, banking companies etc., to a maximum 100, with no ceiling as to professional associations regulated by Special Acts.

24. CLAUSE 149(3). Every company shall have at least one director who has stayed in India for a total period of not less than 182 days in previous calendar year.

25. CLAUSE 149. *INDEPENDENT DIRECTORS.* All listed companies are required to appoint independent directors.

- Such other public companies as may be prescribed by the Central Government shall also be required to appoint independent directors.
- At least one-third of the Board of such companies should comprise independent directors.
- Nominee director appointed by any institution, or in pursuance of any agreement, or appointed by any Government to represent its shareholding shall not be deemed to be an independent director.
- Only an independent director can be appointed as alternate director to an independent director [first proviso to Clause 161(2)].
- The independent directors shall abide by a code provided in Schedule IV to the Bill.

- Independent directors shall hold office up to two consecutive terms. One term is up to five consecutive years.
- Eligible for appointment in same company after cooling period of three years.

26. CLAUSE 166. *DUTIES OF DIRECTORS.* First time the duties of the company directors are defined in the Bill and penalties are prescribed for its contravention.

The duties of the company directors are:

(*i*) He should act in accordance with the articles of the company.

(*ii*) Act in good faith in order to promote the objects of the company for the benefit of its members as a whole, and in the best interests of the company, its employees, the shareholders, the community and for the protection of environment.

(*iii*) Exercise his duties with due and reasonable care, skill and diligence and shall exercise independent judgment.

(*iv*) Not involve in a situation in which he may have a direct or indirect interest that conflicts, or possibly may conflict, which the interest of the company.

(*v*) Not achieve or attempt to achieve any undue gain or advantage either to himself or to his relatives, partners, or associates and if such director is found guilty of making any undue gain under sub-sec. (7), he shall be liable to pay an amount equal to that gain to the company.

(*vi*) Not to assign his office and any assignment so made shall be void.

If a director of a company contravenes the provisions of this section such director shall be punishable with fine which shall not be less than one lakh rupees but which may extend to five lakh rupees.

27. CLAUSE 173(2). Participation of board meetings through audio/ video visual means.

28. CLAUSE 177(2). *AUDIT COMMITTEE.* An Audit Committee shall be constituted with minimum of three directors with independent director forming a majority. The persons in the committee should be able to understand the financial statements.

29. CLAUSE 178(1). *NOMINATION AND REMUNERATION COMMITTEE.* It is mandatory to constitute a nomination and remuneration committee for listed companies. The Committee shall consist of three or more non-executive directors, out of which not less than one half shall be independent director. The Committee shall formulate a policy and criteria for determining qualification and remuneration of key managerial personnel.

30. CLAUSE 178(4). *STAKEHOLDER'S RELATIONSHIP COMMITTEE.* If the combined membership of the shareholders, debenture holders and deposit holders and other security holders is more than one thousand during a financial year, the company shall constitute a relationship committee with a non-executive director as its chairman.

31. CLAUSE 197(7). Independent directors may not get any share options, but they may get payment of fee and profit linked commissions. The Central Government has to fix the fees rather than the company deciding the remuneration for independent directors.

32. CLAUSE 149(8). Independent director shall not be entitled to any stock options, but is entitled to get payment of fees and profit subject to the specified limits as remuneration. In a direct conflicting provision in clause 49 of the listing agreement applicable to all listed companies allowed shareholders to fix the maximum number of stock options to be given as remuneration to an independent director. Thus, there is a direct conflict between Companies Bill 2012 and the listing agreement.

33. CLAUSE 173. *BOARD MEETINGS.* At least seven days' notice has to be given to all directors. Meetings can be convened with shorter notice if there is at least one independent director shall be present at the meeting. Any such decision taken at the meeting in the absence of an independent director should be ratified by at least one independent director to take effect.

34. CLAUSES 118(10) & 205. First time, secretarial standards are prescribed in the Companies Bill 2012. Every company shall observe secretarial standards in general and board meetings prescribed by the Institute of Company Secretaries of India.

35. A new clause 121, seeks to provide report on each annual general meeting including the confirmation to the effect that the meeting was convened, held and conducted as per the provision of the Act and the rules made there under. A copy of this report shall be filed with the Registrar.

36. CLAUSE 108. Provides for electronic means of voting rights in the general meeting or proxy voting is permitted.

37. CLAUSE 204. Secretarial Audit is introduced: Every listed company and other categories of companies should annex with its board report a Secretarial Audit Report prepared by a qualified company secretary in practice.

38. CLAUSE 148. The concept of Cost Auditing Standards being made mandatory.

39. CLAUSE 73. *ACCEPTANCE OF DEPOSIT.* A company can accept deposits only after fulfilling the following criteria:

- Passing of a resolution in a general meeting;
- Issue of circular to members on the financial position of the company, the credit rating obtained, the total number of depositors, and the previous deposits accepted by the company;
- Certification by the company that they had not defaulted in the repayment of deposits.
- An amount not less than 15% of the deposits maturing during a financial year shall be deposited in deposit repayment account.

40. *ACCEPTANCE OF DEPOSITS & INSIDER TRADING.* Companies are not allowed to raise deposits from the public except on the basis of permission available to them through other Special Acts. The Bill prohibits insider trading by company directors or Key Managerial Personnel and declares it as an offence with criminal liability (Clause 195);

41. CLAUSE 149. *WOMAN DIRECTOR.* At least one women director being made mandatory in the prescribed class of companies. The appointment and qualification of directors has been dealt in other chapters.

Clauses 149(9) and 149(10) of the Companies Bill 2012, an independent director shall hold office for a term up to five consecutive years on the board of the company provided that he can hold office for two consecutive terms.

42. CLAUSE 135. *CSR.* Every company having net worth of rupees five hundred crore or more or turnover of more than 1000 crore or more or net profit of five crore or more during any financial year *shall* constitute a Corporate Social Responsibility (CSR) Committee of the

Board consisting of three or more directors, out of which at least one director shall be an independent director. The committee shall recommend a CSR policy to the company and its approximate expenditure per year. As a result of the amendment, the CSR clause would now make it mandatory for a company with a (*i*) net worth of ₹ 500 crores; or (*ii*) turnover of ₹ 1,000 crores; or (*iii*) net profit of ₹ 5 crore, in a fiscal year, to conduct CSR activities.

Every board of directors should make it sure that at least two per cent of the net profits of the company made during the immediately preceding three years. If the company fails to spend such amount, it should specify the reason for not spending such amount. The duty of the CSR Committee is as follows:

(*a*) formulate and recommend to the Board, a Corporate Social Responsibility Policy which shall indicate the activities to be undertaken by the company as specified in Schedule VII;

(*b*) recommend the amount of expenditure to be incurred on the activities referred to in clause (*a*) and

(*c*) monitor the Corporate Social Responsibility Policy of the company from time to time.

CSR is not mandatory in most of the countries. On the other hand some the countries like Saudi Arabia, where companies are required to pay amounts equal to 2.5 percent of the income to the revenue department, which then distributes the amounts to the needy around the country. But in India, the CSR is left to the discretion of individual companies to determine the manner in which the amounts are deployed in accordance with Schedule VII of the Companies Bill 2012.

43. CLAUSE 194. Director and key managerial personnel of a company are prohibited from forward dealing in securities of the company. Clause 203(1) of the Companies Bill 2012 does not permit the same person to be appointed as the chairperson as well as the MD or CEO unless where the articles of association clearly provide so or in those cases where the company does not carry on multiple businesses. Further, the restriction of appointing the same person to be the chairperson as well as the MD or CEO has also been eased in the case of those classes of companies engaged in multiple businesses and which have appointed one or more CEOs for each such class of businesses. Such appointments should be reported to the Central Government.

44. CLAUSE 46(5). If a company intends to defraud, issues a duplicate certificate of shares, the company shall be punishable with fine which shall not be less than five times the face value of shares involved in the issue of duplicate certificate but which may extend to ten times the face value of such shares or ₹ 10 crore, whichever is higher.

45. CLAUSE 247. *REGISTERED VALUERS.* This is a new provision included for the first time. If a valuation is required in case of any property of a company, stock, shares, debentures, securities or goodwill shall be valued by a person with such qualifications act as a valuer in accordance with the directions of the Audit Committee or director board.

46. CLAUSE 245. *CLASS ACTION SUITS.* For the first time provisions were included for class action suits by members or depositors was of the opinion that the affairs of the company are being conducted in a manner prejudicial to the interest of the company, members or depositors can file an application before the Tribunal for a series of actions:

(*i*) To restrain the company from an act which are *ultra vires* the articles or memorandum of the company.

(*ii*) To restrain the company from committing breach of any provisions of the company's memorandum or articles.

(*iii*) To declare a resolution altering the memorandum or article of the Company as void if a resolution was passed by suppression of material facts or obtained by mis-statement to the members or depositors.

(*iv*) To restrain the company from doing an act which is contrary to the Companies Act or any other law?

(*v*) To restrain the company from taking action contrary to such resolutions passed by the members.

47. CLAUSE 465. The provisions of Part IXA of the Companies Act 1956 shall be applicable *mutatis mutandis* to a Producer Company in a manner as if the Companies Act 1956 has not been repealed until a special Act is enacted for Producer Companies.

48. CLAUSE 26. *PROSPECTUS AND ALLOTMENT OF SHARES.* Clause 26 specifically prohibits the issue of prospectus before its publication. No statement of an expert shall be included in the prospectus.

49. CLAUSE 31. *SHELF PROSPECTUS.* A shelf prospectus can be filed with the Registrar of Companies with a validity of not more than one year from the date of first offer. No further prospectus is required during the validity of such prospectus. "shelf prospectus" means a prospectus in respect of which the securities or class of securities included therein are issued for subscription in one or more issues over a certain period without the issue of further prospectus.[6]

50. CLAUSE 32. *RED HERRING PROSPECTUS.* Red herring prospectus means a prospectus which does not include complete particulars of the quantum or price of the securities included therein. A company can issue a red herring prospectus prior to the issue of a prospectus. It will carry same obligations as are applicable to a prospectus and any variation between the red herring prospectus and a prospectus shall be highlighted as variations in the prospectus.

51. CLAUSE 34, 35 & 36 READ WITH CLAUSE 447. *PUNISHMENT.* If any person, either knowingly or recklessly makes any statement, promise or forecast which is false, deceptive or misleading, or deliberately conceals any material facts, to induce another person to subscribe to shares, or securities shall be punishable with imprisonment for a term which may extend to three years and with fine which shall not be less than one lakh rupees but which may extend to fifty lakh rupees. If any person abets these offences shall be punishable with imprisonment for a term which may extend to three years and with fine which shall not be less than fifty thousand rupees but which may extend to fifty lakh rupees.[7] Clause 34 provides for criminal liability for mis-statement in prospectus. The purview of this Clause is expansive as it has been drafted to bring within its scope not only those parties related to the company but, also include, any person not having any co-relation to the company.

Clause 35 talks about civil liability for mis-statement in prospectus and Clause 36 provides for punishment for fraudulently inducing persons to invest money. Clause 35 cast responsibility upon the following persons for mis-statement in the prospectus:

(*a*) director of a company at the time of issue of the prospectus;

6 *Explanation* to Clause 31(3) of Companies Bill 2012.
7 Clauses 34, 35 & 36.

(*b*) authorized person named in the prospectus as a director of a company;

(*c*) promoter of a company;

(*d*) who authorized the issue of a prospectus.

Clause 127 provides that once the company has declared the dividend and has not been paid within 30 days from such declaration, every director of the company shall be punishable with an imprisonment which may extend to two years and fine which shall not be less than one thousand rupees for every day of default.

52. *Share Capital and Debentures.* The share capital of the companies is limited by two kinds of shares, equity share capital and preferential share capital. Where a share capital of the company is divided into different classes of shares, the rights attached to the shares of any class may be varied with the consent in writing of the holders of not less than three-fourths of the issued shares of that class or by means of a special resolution passed at a separate meeting of the holders.[8] Where any calls for further share capital are made on the shares of a class, such calls shall be made on a uniform basis on all shares falling under that class.[9] No company limited by shares can issue non-redeemable shares after commencement of this Act and also a limited company cannot grant a loan to buy its own shares unless permitted by the Act. The buy-back of its own shares is restricted under clause 70 of the Bill. If any company accepts deposits with the intent of defrauding depositors or for any fraudulent purposes, every officer of the company is personally liable for losses or damage to the depositors.

53. *Accounts and Audits.* Clause 133 read with clause 148 has introduced auditing standards in addition to accounting standards. Statutory recognition of audit, remuneration and stakeholders relationship committees of the Board and the Chief Executive Officer (CEO), the Chief Financial Officer (CFO) and the Company Secretary to be as Key Managerial Personnel (KMP). Bill also provides for an advisory body known as National Advisory Committee on Accounting

8 Clause 43.
9 Clause 49.

and Auditing Standards to advice the Central Government to advice on accounting standards. The role, rights and duties of the auditors defined so as to maintain integrity and independence of the audit process. Consolidation of financial statements of subsidiaries with those of holding companies is proposed to be made mandatory.

Director's Responsibility Statement according to clause 134(5) should be filed and this statement should contain:

(*a*) in the preparation of the annual accounts, the applicable accounting standards had been followed along with proper explanation relating to material departures;

(*b*) the directors had selected such accounting policies and applied them consistently and made judgments and estimates that are reasonable and prudent so as to give a true and fair view of the state of affairs of the company at the end of the financial year and of the profit and loss of the company for that period;

(*c*) the directors had taken proper and sufficient care for the maintenance of adequate accounting records in accordance with the provisions of this Act for safeguarding the assets of the company and for preventing and detecting fraud and other irregularities;

(*d*) the directors had prepared the annual accounts on a going concern basis; and

(*e*) the directors, in the case of a listed company, had laid down internal financial controls to be followed by the company and that such internal financial controls are adequate and were operating effectively.

(*f*) the directors had devised proper systems to ensure compliance with the provisions of all applicable laws and that such systems were adequate and operating effectively.

54. CLAUSE 177. The Audit Committee shall consist of a minimum of three directors with independent directors forming a majority and at least one director having knowledge of financial management, audit or accounts. The Chairman of an Audit Committee shall be an independent director.

55. CLAUSE 394. In case of financial statements, auditor of holding company can access records of subsidiaries. The auditor has to make a report to the members on that accounts, financial statement or other documents required to be laid in general meeting give a true and fair view of the state of the company's affairs and such other matters as may be prescribed. The report shall state reasons for negative and qualified remarks. The clause also provides the manner in which audit report of a Government company shall be finalized by the Comptroller and Auditor General. This clause also provides to notify the auditing standard by the Central Government.

56. CLAUSE 168. This clause is a new one and seeks to provide that a director may resign from his office by giving a notice in writing to the company and the Board shall, on receipt of such notice take note of the same and the company shall intimate the Registrar and place such resignation in the subsequent general meeting of the company. The resignation of a director shall be effected from the date on which the notice is received by the company.

57. CLAUSE 184. Clause 184 provides that every director shall make disclosures of his concern or interest in any company or bodies corporate, firms, or other association of individuals. It also stipulates that every director of a company who is concerned or interested in a contract or arrangement shall disclose the nature of his concern or interest at the meeting of the board and shall not participate in such meeting. The clause further provides that a contract or arrangement entered into by the company without disclosure or with participation by a director who is so concerned or interested shall be voidable at the option of the company.

58. CLAUSE 192. Clause 192 is a new clause which seeks to provide for the manner in respect of regulation of arrangements between a company and its directors in respect of acquisition of assets for consideration other than cash. The clause provides that such arrangements shall require prior approval by a resolution in general meeting and if the director or connected person is a director of its holding company, approval is required to be obtained by passing a resolution in general meeting of the holding company. The clause also provides the circumstances when an arrangement entered into by a

company or its holding company in contravention of the provisions is voidable at the instance of the company.

59. CLAUSE 193. Clause 193 is also a new provision which provides for contracts between One Person Company (OPC) and its sole member. It provides that where a One Person Company Limited by shares or by guarantee enters into a contract with the sole member of the company who is also director, the company shall, unless the contract is in writing, ensure that the terms of the contract or offer are contained in a memorandum or are recorded in the minutes of the first Board meeting held after entering into the contract and every such contract shall be informed to the Registrar.

60. CLAUSE 194. Clause 194 prohibit whole-time director or any of its key managerial personnel from buying certain kinds of future contracts in relation to securities of the company and also prohibits dealing in securities of a company, procuring or communicating, directly or indirectly, about any unpublished price-sensitive information to any person.

61. CLAUSE 195. No director can enter into an insider trading, contravention will attract a punishment which may extend to five years imprisonment and a fine which shall not be less than five lakh rupees but which may extend to 25 crore rupees or three times of the amount of profit made out of insider trading, whichever is higher, or both.

62. CLAUSES 211 & 212. Clauses 211 & 212 are new clauses which seek to provide that the Central Government shall constitute Serious Fraud Investigation Office (SFIO). The SFIO will be headed by a director and will consist of experts from various disciplines. The Central Government shall also appoint a Director in the SFIO not below the rank of Joint Secretary and may also appoint such experts and other officers as it considers necessary for efficient discharge of functions. This is a welcome move to investigate frauds in the companies. Statutory recognition has been given to Serious Fraud Investigation Office. Investigation report filed by SFIO will be considered as a report filed by a police officer.

63. CLAUSE 233. *MERGER AND AMALGAMATIONS.* This is a new clause which seeks to provide for merger or amalgamation between two or more small companies or between a holding company and its wholly-owned

subsidiary company or prescribed class or class of companies by giving a notice of the proposed scheme inviting comments or objections or suggestions by both the transferor and the transferee company and Registrar, Official Liquidator or persons affected by the scheme. The Central Government is empowered to make rules for merger and amalgamations.

64. CLAUSE 246. *CONTEMPT OF TRIBUNAL.* This clause seeks to provide that cls. 337 to 341 (both inclusive) relating to power to punish for contempt of the Tribunal, etc., shall apply in relation to a fraudulent application made to the Tribunal for oppression and mismanagement.

65. CLAUSE 251. *PENALTY FOR FRAUDULENT APPLICATION TO REMOVE A COMPANY NAME FROM REGISTER.* This is a new clause seeks to provide penalty in case anybody made a fraudulent application for removal of name of the company from the register of companies with the object of evading the liabilities of the company or with the intention to deceive the creditors or to defraud any other persons.

66. CLAUSE 259. *DATA BANK OF ADMINISTRATORS.* This is a new clause seeks to provide that the interim administrator or company administrator shall be appointed by the Tribunal from a databank maintained by Central Government in a manner as may be prescribed consisting of the names of company secretaries, chartered accountants, cost accountants, or other professionals. The Tribunal may direct the company administrator to take over the assets or management of the company to assist him in the management of the company. The company administrator may engage the services of suitable experts with the approval of the Tribunal.

67. CLAUSE 284. *CO-OPERATION WITH LIQUIDATOR.* This is a new clause seeks to provide for co-operation by the promoters, directors, officers and employees, past and present, of the company to the company liquidator in discharge of his functions and duties. This clause further seeks to provide that if any of the aforesaid people fails to discharge his obligations, he shall be punishable with imprisonment which may extend to six months or with fine which may extend to fifty thousand rupees or with both.

68. CLAUSE 286. *LIABILITY FOR FURTHER CONTRIBUTION.* This is a new clause and seeks to put obligations on directors and managers of limited

company whose liability is unlimited and seeks to provide that such a director or manager, shall, in addition to his liability to contribute as an ordinary member, be liable to make further contribution as if he were at the commencements of winding up a member of an unlimited company.

69. CLAUSE 342. *PROSECUTION BY TRIBUNALS.* This clause corresponds to s. 545 of the Companies Act 1956 and seeks to empower the Tribunal to prosecute the delinquent officers and members of the company for being guilty of offence in relation to the company. The clause also provides for fine on the part of person who fails or neglect to give assistance.

70. CLAUSE 435. *SPECIAL COURTS.* This is a new clause which deals with the establishment of Special Courts by the Central Government in consultation with the Chief Justice of the High Court within whose jurisdiction the Judge is to be appointed. It further provides that person so appointed as Judge of Special Court shall be one who immediately before such appointment was a Sessions Judge or an Additional Sessions Judge.

71. CLAUSE 436. *JURISDICTION OF SPECIAL COURTS.* This is a new clause which seeks to provide that all offences under this Act shall be triable by the Special Courts. If any person is produced before the magistrate, he shall forward the case to the Tribunal.

72. CLAUSE 437. *APPEAL AND REVISION.* This is a new clause which provides that High Courts shall have the power of appeal or revision as if special courts were Court of Session trying cases within the local limits of the jurisdiction of the High Court. Special courts will be deemed to be a court of session and the Code of Criminal Procedure 1973 will be applicable to the courts.

73. CLAUSE 442. *MEDIATION PANEL.* In this clause Central Government is authorised to maintain a panel of experts to be called as 'Mediation Panel' for mediation between parties during the pendency of any proceedings before the Central Government or Tribunal. The clause further provides that any of the parties to proceeding or Central Government or Tribunal *suo moto* refer any matter pertaining to proceeding to such number of experts from the mediation panel.

74. CLAUSE 455. *DORMANT COMPANIES.* This is a new clause and seeks to deal with dormant company. It provides that a dormant company shall be one which has not been carrying any business or has not made any significant accounting transaction in the last two financial years. Such a company may make an application to Registrar for obtaining the status of a dormant company.

The Companies Bill 2012 is a welcome step towards enacting a modern company law.

10

Rethinking the Fiduciary Duties and Liabilities of Directors

10.1 Fiduciary duties of Directors—redefining

Corporate financial frauds are not new to India or elsewhere in the world. Big companies like Enron exposed and the Satyam followed the suit. The instances of fraud had increased in the recent past especially; financial frauds are the single biggest corporate threat in India. The trustworthiness of the companies has gone on drains after these frauds. The track record of penal prosecution on such illegal acts is not clear in India. A study by the consulting firm KPMG reveals that 87% of Indian companies are hit by financial fraud.[1] Most of the managers who organize such frauds use the loopholes in the law to scot free at the end. Rajat Gupta's conviction in the US for insider trading exposed the personal responsibilities attached to corporates. But in India corporate offences are not taken seriously by the courts as well. The poor level of personal liabilities of company managers and lack of clarity on their fiduciary duties will store more skeletons in the cupboard of Indian Inc. There has been a sea change in the governance of Indian companies in the recent past. But a little change has been made to the Companies Act 1956. Lack of statutory reforms preventing the Indian companies from overhauling their activities in accordance with international standards.

The Securities and Exchange Board of India (SEBI), the corporate regulator, failed to stop multi-crore fraudulent transactions in the Industry. This led to the massive corporate accounting scandals like

1 http://www.livemint.com/2010/04/06222658/Financial-fraud-hit-87-of-Ind.html, visited on 07.07.2012.

happened in 'Satyam' in 2009. The Satyam scandal forced the Government of India to investigate the case and replace the director board with Government nominees. The intense debate on statutory reforms going on in the aftermath of Satyam accounting scandal and later on in the mega 2G spectrum scam rocked the Indian political circles and a handful of big corporate houses involved in the scam worth lakhs of crores of rupees. The Time magazine listed this as the second "top 10" abuses of power next to the Watergate scandal. The Companies Bill 2011 is in place, but the Government failed to convert it into a legislation. Personal accountability is a key to answer the question of corporate financial frauds in the country. The duties of directors have to be defined clearly in order to fix the liability.

This work has focused on the fiduciary duties of directors and their liabilities in breach of such duties. These duties are owed by the directors directly or indirectly to the company, shareholders, creditors and the society at large. The fiduciary duties to the company jurisprudence are evolved clearly through a number of precedents within India and other parts of the world. The duty to the shareholders and creditors are still evolving and the judicial decisions differ on this point. While there are several issues need to be sorted out by Indian courts on fiduciary duties and liabilities of directors. This work has sought to try and clarify many of the unclear aspects of law that covers the responsibilities of company directors in India. But the arguments made in this book are justified from a normative perspective. It has been submitted that many a times there is no clarity on prosecution of directors both in the statute and in case law. The common law principles of duty to take care, loyalty and due diligence of company directors were left unanswered in the Companies Act 1956 and in the Companies Bill 2011 as well. The 2011 Bill should address these issues when it will be presented it in the parliament soon. The Indian industry also wants more clarity on the role of independent director's duties and their liabilities. If the liabilities are not clearly defined, many experts may not be willing to join as independent directors in companies. It is very pertinent to take note that more than 800 independent directors resigned in the aftermath of 'Satyam' scam in 2009 and it is mandatory to appoint independent directors under the 2011 Bill.

The affairs of a company are run by specially trained people with special knowledge and skill known as company directors. Every director is bound by a statutory and common law duty known as "fiduciary duty"[2] to the company. Every director's duties rest upon individual responsibility. The fiduciary duty is likewise not owed directly to creditors, employees or other stakeholders of the company, although there is a range of circumstances in which a director may, by virtue of the neglect of his fiduciary duty to the company, be held personally liable to the company's stakeholders. Individuals in positions of trust within a company are often tempted to abuse their position in different ways. Directors and 'Director Board' is an integral part of the company and they are expected to provide advisory and other important functions. These directors are selected based on their skill and expertise they offer to the company. The responsibilities of directors are distinct and separate from its management. They are expected to direct the company in right direction and ensure integrity in financial transactions.

Directors have a legal duty to act in the interest of the company and shareholders. Directors are appointed to promote the success of the company. Directors derive their powers, duties and liabilities from the Companies laws available in the country. The Companies Bill 2011 provides ample provisions to explain the powers of directors in the statute as well as derived from the memorandum and articles of a company. The management powers of directors must be exercised in accordance with fiduciary duties and for the benefit of the company. Directors can be removed in the general meeting if they act against the company and the shareholder's interests. When a company be found guilty of indulging in criminal activities, the director who is in charge or directly responsible for such activities should be prosecuted. The trend is in the upward in fixing civil and criminal liability of directors in India in the background of recent scams in the Indian corporate sector including what happened in the 'Satyam scam" discussed earlier.

This fiduciary duty includes duty of care; duty of loyalty, duty not to delegate and duty of disclosure. Duty of care requires that a director makes his decisions with due diligence and deliberations by using his skill as a reasonable person of knowledge and experience.[3] The duty

2 The term 'fiduciary' being derived from the Latin 'fiduciarius' meaning 'of trust'.

3 *Re Brazilian Rubber Plantations and Estates Ltd.* [1911]1 Ch 425 (437).

of care extends to all directors in the company.[4] The terms 'care' and 'skill' should not be used interchangeably, because they refer to different standards of liability. 'Care' refers to the pains and perception that a reasonable man would apply in handling his own affairs. 'Skill' is the profession of art, the holding out of a special ability. This varies with the type of agent employed, the client's expectations of him based on his qualifications and experience, and the custom and practice of the particular business.[5] The extent of director's duty and care depends on the company's nature of business and any particular responsibility assigned to him. The strictness of fiduciary obligation of company directors has been improved to some extent by the statutes and by the courts. Under the established law, directors may not divert to themselves corporate opportunities.

A director specifically appointed, however, because he professes and is required to display some special skill or calling, will be liable in negligence for failing to meet the objective standard of care set by the notional reasonably competent exponent of that craft.[6] As noted above, a distinction exists between skill and care. For the standard of care, an objective test is set, namely, that to be expected of a reasonable man. He is expected to exercise the care which can reasonably be expected from a person with knowledge and experience in that field. The director's must take decisions and to act in good faith to make prudent, considered, and informed choices. The duty of loyalty and care requires the directors to act in the best interests of the company. The personal interests must be fully disclosed and should abstain from doing anything against the company. The numerous cases in India with related to the breach of directors duties and consequent judgments from the courts reveal that the duty of care, loyalty, skill and care remains the essential standard of directors in the fiduciary duties.

They cannot act against the company intentionally or in bad faith. In *G.D. Bhargava* v *Registrar of Companies,* the High Court of Allahabad ruled that protection under s. 633 of the Companies Act shall not be available, where the negligence of the director amounts

4 *Jorchester Finance Co. Ltd.* v *Stebbing* [1989] BCLC 498.
5 See Chitty on *Contracts,* 31st Ed., vol. 2, paras 31-115–31-116.
6 Re *Macro (Ipswich) Ltd.* [1994]2 BCLC 354; [1994] BCC 781.

to an offence so as to attract the provisions of the IPC relating to fraud or forgery.[7]

The duty of loyalty addresses conflict of interest. It requires any interest of the director in any transactions should be disclosed. He should refrain from taking any advantage of his position as a director. If a director purchases property in his name first and then sold it to the company and thus made profits, he should account to the company for such profits.[8] He cannot escape from the duty to report by resigning from the company after obtaining the profits.[9] In the case of *P.K. Nedungadi* v *Malayalee Bank Ltd.,* it was observed that, where any director has misapplied or retained money or property of the company or has been guilty of breach of trust or misfeasance, the court may examine into his conduct and order to him to repay or restore the money or property to the company or to pay compensation.[10] The law sets an objective standard in relation to directors by virtue of the position of trust that they occupy over company property which they are empowered to manage.[11]

A director is an agent and in a fiduciary position to his principal and as such he must act *bona fide* and must not allow his interest to conflict with his duty.[12] Conflicts of interest must be resolved in favour of the company. If any agent or officer of a company or firm makes a profit for himself without having disclosed his dealing, he is liable to account to his principal for the money received.[13]

But it was observed that "it would be proper to relieve directors of consequences of defaults and the breaches unless they are directly involved in the acts or omission complained of or have otherwise not acted honestly or reasonably or have financial involvement in the

7 *G.D. Bhargava* v *Regitrar of Companies* (1970)40 Comp Cas 664. See also *Re Railway and General Light Improvement Co., Marzetti's* case (1880)42 LT 206 (CA).

8 *Burland* v *Earle* [1902] AC 83 (PC).

9 *Industrial Development Consultant Ltd.* v *Cooley* [1972]2 All ER 162; [1972]1 WLR 443.

10 AIR 1971 SC 829; (1972)42 Comp Cas 120 (SC).

11 *Re Produce Marketing Consortium Ltd.* (No 2) [1989] BCLC 520; 5 BCC 569.

12 *Kelly* v *Cooper* [1993] AC 205; [1994]1 BCLC 395.

13 *Cook* v *Deeks* [1916]1 AC 554; [1916] UKPC 10.

company."[14] If the director can prove that he acted in the best interest of the company, nothing preventing him from taking decisions in good faith.

As per Denning, MR in *Boulting* v *Association of Cinematograph, Television and Allied Technicians*:

> 'There is nothing wrong in it. It is done every day. Nothing wrong, that is, so long as the director is left free to exercise his best judgment in the interests of the company which he serves.'[15]

The potential conflict of interest should be reported to the company and shareholders. The duty of honesty requires that the management should transfer material information to the shareholders. In the case of *Nanalal Zaver* v *Bombay Life Insurance Co. Ltd.,* it was observed that, if the power to issue further shares is exercised by the directors not for the benefit of the company but simply and solely for their personal aggrandizement and to the detrimental of the company, the court will interfere and prevent the directors from doing so.[16]

A director has a positive duty to apply a degree of discretion to the resources under his control and manage them to advantage. A failure to 'manage' is therefore in theory a breach of duty but courts have been reluctant to apply the benefit of hindsight to overturn decisions made in the course of operating the business and in good faith, even though the consequences are unsatisfactory for the company.[17]

The directors are bound by the rule "*delegatus non potest non delegare*" is a latin maxim which means that a delegated authority cannot further delegate. This principle is applicable to company directors because the company reposes trust and confidence in him to carry out on his behalf a particular transaction or to act for him generally. As a company director is directly appointed by the shareholders, they are entitled to assume that the directors will not hand over their responsibilities and discretions to others, unless the articles provide for delegation to a managing director or any other

14 *Om Prakash Khaitan* v *Shree Keshariya Investment Ltd.* (1978)48 Comp Cas 85 (Del).

15 [1963]2 QB 606 at 626 (CA); [1963]1 All ER 716.

16 AIR 1950 SC 172; (1950) SCR 391.

17 *Lagunas Nitrate Co* v *Lagunas Syndicate* [1899]2 Ch 392; 68 LJ Ch 699 (CA); *Howard Smith Ltd* v *Ampol Petroleum* [1974] AC 821 (832); [1974]1 All ER 1126; [1924]2 WLR 689.

person. But if there no express authority has given delegation is not possible.[18] Personal performance of the duties is inevitable in the absence of express provisions.[19]

Duty of good faith and duty of care are two pillars in the role of a director. He assumes two roles, one as an agent of the company and other as a trustee who controls the assets of the company. The fiduciary duties can be summarized as follows:

- To act in good faith towards the company and shareholders.
- To act only within their powers and use their powers only for purposes which benefit the company. Directors who act outside their powers bind the company to the transaction but may be held personally liable if a loss results.
- Director has to file returns of share allotment.
- Not to use for personal gain any information acquired in their capacity as a director from the company or outside.
- To act in the best interests of the company and to avoid a conflict between personal and company interests. The director may never act on his own interest over the company interests. If he acts against the interest of the company, it is not binding on the company.[20]
- To disclose any interest accrued from the sale of company property.
- To disclose receipt of compensation from transfer of shares.
- Duty to attend board meetings.
- To convey annual general meetings and special annual general meetings.
- To exercise independent judgment in decision-making. A director who is appointed to represent an interest group, for example employees, is nevertheless obliged to act in the best interests of the company as a whole.
- If a director sits in board of more than one company, he must have distinct duties towards both companies. In such a situation

18 *De Bussche* v *Alt* [1878]8 Ch D 286; 47 LJ Ch 381 (CA).

19 *Re County Palatine Loan and Discount Co.*, *Cartmell's* Case [1874]9 Ch App 691; 43 LJ Ch 588.

20 *Raj Cylinders & Containers* v *Hindustan General Industries Ltd.* AIR 1988 Del 418.

if there is a conflict of interest between two companies, he must resign from one board.

- The duty of care and skill of the director in specific areas should be used for the benefit of the company.
- Directors have a duty to act within their powers prescribed in the memorandum and articles of association and to monitor the activities of the management within its powers.
- Directors are individually and severally liable for any financial loss to the company due to their decision making beyond their powers.
- Breach of trust or a wrongful act by a director is liable for criminal prosecution and punishment.
- Directors have a right to inspect the accounts of the company.
- Claims reimbursement of his expenses.
- Discharge of duties without interference from any other directors.
- Reasonable period of notice of company meetings.

A description of the legal and equitable rules relating to directors' duties appears to show that their duties of honesty and good faith are exceptionally strict. This picture is, however, somewhat misleading. In practice, their fiduciary duties do not weight too heavily upon them because there are many limitations in enforcing these duties. The undue adherence to the corporate entity principle, exclusion clauses in the articles of the company, growing professionalism in the management of the company, everything works in the way of enforcing these duties. Again the legal procedures for invoking these rights do not seem to be very much effective. The purpose of this chapter is to discuss the limitations in enforcing these duties and making a conclusion of the study on director's rights, duties, liabilities and punishment for their violations.

10.2 Lifting the corporate veil

"A corporation is an artificial being, invisible, intangible and existing only in contemplation of law."[1] The company does not have a mind or

1 Marshall, J in *Trustees of Dartmouth College* v *Woodward* [1819]17 US 518 (636).

a body to work or take decisions. These are done through human beings appointed to manage the affairs of the company known as directors. They act as agents of the company and selected by the shareholders in company meeting. Directors are described sometimes as agents, sometimes as trustees and sometimes as managing partners. But each of these expressions is used not as exhaustive as of their powers and responsibilities, but as indicating useful points of view from which they may for the moment and for the particular purpose be considered.[2] The position of directors is not easy to define. They act as agents of the company, but they are not servants of the company.[3] Overall, they are fiduciaries of the company when it comes to their duties and liabilities.

Though incorporation of a company solves many procedural problems, it does not wholly remove those which arise when there is a dispute within the company, indeed, it may render them intractable. If one partner breaking the duties which he owns to his co-partners the latter can call him to account. When, however, the directors of an incorporated company are breaking their duties, the other members of the company normally have no "*locus standi*". The duties are owed not to them but to the company itself; and therefore it is the company itself which should sue. But those against whom the action is to be brought themselves is the appropriate organ for instigating proceedings in the company's name. Thus interests of those persons who are really the true owners of the company are often disregarded.

It is fairly recognized that if the duty to be enforced is one owed to the company, then the primary remedy for its enforcement is an action by the company against those in default. If, the directors have broken their duties of honesty and good faith, the company is the proper plaintiff in an action against them.[4]

The above said famous rule in *Foss* v *Harbottle* was extended right from its pronouncement to cover all cases where what is complained

2 *Imperial Hydropathic Hotel Co.* v *Hampson* [1882]23 Ch D 1; 49 LT 150.

3 *Moriarty* v *Regent's Garage & Engg Co.* [1921]1 KB 766.

4 *Foss* v *Harbottle* [1843]2 Hare 461; 67 ER 189; followed by *Gray* v *Lewis* [1873] LR 8 Ch App 1035; *Russell* v *Wakefield Waterworks Co.* [1875] LR 20 Eq 474; *Duckett* v *Gover* [1877]6 Ch D 82; *Borland* v *Earle* [1902] AC.546 (PC); *Foster* v *Foster* [1916]1 Ch 532; *Pavlides* v *Jensen* [1956] Ch 565; [1956]2 All ER 518; *Birch* v *Sullivan* [1957]1 WLR 1247; *Heviting* v *Dupont* [1964]1 WLR 843 (CA).

of is some internal irregularity in the operation of the company;[5] for example to dispute the validity of the appointment of some of the directors,[6] or to attack the refusal to call a poll at a meeting.[7] Though the courts often describe these actions as wrongs done to the company, it is far from clear why they should not instead be regarded as breaches of the rights of each shareholder under the contract established by the memorandum and articles. And, in fact, where the breach is one which could not be remedied by an ordinary resolution of the company, the courts should recognize that it is an infringement of the personal rights of the member in respect of which he can therefore bring an action.[8]

10.3 Conflict of personal interest

It is a basic equitable principle that, as fiduciaries, directors must not place themselves in a position in which there is conflict between their duties to the company and their personal interests. This equitable principle finds statutory recognition when it has been made obligatory on the part of the directors to disclose their interest in the contracts in which the company is a party.[9] Again, it is provided further that where no such disclosure is made the director concerned shall be punishable.[10]

However, in actual practice these fiduciary duties cannot be weighed too heavily upon the directors, this is because of the fact that these strict rules are not acceptable to the business community.

10.4 Director's positions–changing scenario

Directors fiduciary duties, except in so far as they depend on statutory provisions expressly limited to directors, are not so restricted but apply equally to any officials of the company who are authorized to act on its behalf and in particular to those acting in a managerial capacity. Thus those who are the company's agents or managers stands in a

5 *Moseley* v *Alston* [1847]1 PL 790; *Mac Dougall* v *Gardiner* [1875-76]1 LR Ch D 13; *Cambel* v *Australian Mutual Provident Society* [1908]77 LJ PC 117; *Cotter* v *National Union of Seamen* [1929]2 Ch 58 (CA).

6 *Mozlcy* v *Alston*, ibid.

7 *Mac Dougall* v *Gardiner*, ibid.

8 *Render* v *Lushington* [1877]6 Ch D 70; *Edwards* v *Halliwell* [1950]2 All ER 1064 (CA); [1950] WN 537 (CA).

9 Section 299(1).

10 Section 299(4).

fiduciary position towards it, as opposed to those who are merely its servants, who do work for it but do not act on its behalf and in particular to those acting in a managerial capacity. Thus those who are the company's agents or managers stands in a fiduciary position towards it, as opposed to those who are merely its servants, who do work for it but do not act on its behalf. The duties of these agents who act on behalf of the company are more extensive than those of mere servants.[11] Servants do not occupy any fiduciary position. But servants too owe duties of fidelity which in most respects amount to the same.[12] However, these depend upon the normal law of master and servant and present no peculiarities in the company law field.

This is a matter of considerable practical importance now, that it is common for the management of public companies to be delegated by the board to a smaller body. At present the managers to whom the directors delegate their powers are likely themselves to be managing and other full time service directors. But the modern tendency seems to be towards a clearer distinction between the management which runs the business and the board of directors which oversees the management and lays down broad lines of policy. This may lead to the practice of delegating managerial powers to professional managers without seats on the board. The result is that the real control of the company comes within the hands of some few people who have nothing at stake except their remuneration. Moreover the duty they owe to the company is lesser when compared to the directors. They are only servants of the company and not trustees. Their duties extend to care and skill and also honesty in their activities on behalf of the company. They owe no fiduciary duties. Thus, the company comes under the control of certain self-proclaimed professionals. In this field legislative innovations seem to be inevitable. Again, the power of delegation may also be given to the general meeting instead of the board.

10.5 Role in breach of trust

It is now well settled that a third person who knowingly participates in a breach of directors' fiduciary duties are liable as the directors themselves. Thus a controlling shareholder may be liable if he knowingly participate in a breach of trust by the directors. He will

11 *Bell* v *Lever Bros.* [1932] AC 161.
12 *Cf. Reading* v *Att.-General* [1951] AC 507 (HL).

equally be liable if without lawful excuse he induces the directors to break any contractual obligations which they owe to the company.[13] The controller, therefore, cannot with impunity install men of straw as dummy and use them to bleed the company.

However, this liability of the controlling shareholders for the acts of the directors falls far short of imposing on the true controllers' general liability for the acts and defaults of the directors. In practice it will be difficult to prove that in any particular transaction the directors have acted merely as puppets for others who have pulled the strings.[14] Thus, those who are responsible for the drafting of the Companies Act seem to have disregarded the notion of shifting responsibility on to the shoulders of the true masters of the company's vesting since the word 'director' is defined as 'any person occupying the position of director by whatever name called'.[15] The truth lies in the fact that the Act makes no serious efforts to define their position.

Again the provisions relating to the registration of directors' share holdings and to the publication of the particulars of the directors result that the company may be under a duty to hold out someone to the outside world as a director at all. It need not be considered what effect of this would be on the person concerned, for it is in the highest degree unlikely that any company will ever admit that its directors are accustomed to act on another's instruction. Thus it is not always the directors who actually direct. A possible solution to this problem is that persons holding majority of shares may be held liable. This would also ensure-responsibility of the directors to the real owners of the company.

The directors are liable civilly for breach of trust in managing the company's affairs. They can also be held liable for committing crimes like fraud and other offences mentioned in the Act. They are not only subjected to the corporate law, but the general law prevailing in the country as well.

13 *Jasperson* v *Dominion Tobacco Co.* [1923] AC 709 (PC); *Torquay Hotel Co. Ltd.* v *Cousins* [1969]2 WLR 289 (CA); *Boulting* v *A.C.T.A.T.* [1962]2 QB 606 (CA).

14 *Belanger United Rubber Estates Ltd.* v *Cradock (No. 3)* [1968]2 All ER 1073.

15 Section 2(13).

10.6 Directors' duty of accountability

By virtue of the controlling interest, the majorities of shareholders to some extent releases the directors from their duties and enable them to retain the benefit without being accounted.[16] The general meeting can permit them to enter into contracts with the company, to profit from their offices, or otherwise to place themselves in a position where their interests may conflict with their duty.[17] But the directors has to disclose their interests to the company, the disclosure shall be made at the first meeting of the Board itself. Similarly it can ratify an act by the directors in excess of powers conferred on them.[18] The non-disclosure will visit with a penal provision punishable with fine. They have duty to attend the board meetings.

However, a resolution of the general meeting cannot either prospectively or retrospectively, authorize the directors to act in fraud of the company.[19] Here the word 'fraud' is used in a wider sense than deceit or dishonesty. If the directors have acted in their own interests or those of a third party rather than in the interest of the company,[20] or have not directed their minds to the question whether what they are doing is in the best interests of the company[1] a resolution of the general meeting will not protect them.

Thus, when the directors appropriate the company's property, it seems that their action can be ratified by a resolution of the company if they can show positively that this was passed *bona fide* in the interests of the company it seems to be impossible to ratify.[2] Thus, not only the acts of the directors but the resolution ratifying such acts must also be in the interest of the company. Even a resolution not suing the directors for a past breach of duty may be a *bona fide* one in the interests of the company. However, while it might be in the interest

16 *Kaye* v *Croydon Tramways Co. Ltd.* [1898]1 Ch 358 (CA); *Tiessen* v *Henderson* [1899]1 Ch 861.

17 *Boulting* v *A.C.T.A.T.,* Ibid.

18 *Irvine* v *Union Bank of Australia* [1877]2 App Cas 366 (PC); *Grant* v *U.K. Switchback Rys.* [1888]40 Ch D 135 (CA); *Bamford* v *Bamford* [1969]2 WLR 1107; [1969]1 All ER 969; [1970] Ch 212.

19 *Atwood* v *Merryweather* [1867] LR 5 Eq 464.

20 *Mason* v *Harris* [1879]11 Ch D 97 (CA).

1 *Re W.&M. Roith Ltd.* [1867]1 WLR 432; *Alexander* v *Automatic Telephone Co.* [1900]2 Ch 56 (CA); *Millers (Invercargill) Ltd.* v *Maddams* [1938] NZ LR 490 (CA) (NZ); *Naguh Ltd.* v *McCann* [1954]90 CLR 425 (Aust HC).

2 *Bamford* v *Banford,* Ibid.

of the company not to spend its money on litigation, it is difficult to show how it can be in its interests to release the directors from liability so as to protect them from suit by an individual member suing at his own expense on behalf of the company.[3] Thus, a resolution not to sue even a fraudulent director may also, therefore, conceivably is valid if it can positively be shown to have been passed the test of bonafideness in the interests of the company. These provisions for ratification seem to have virtually destroyed the efficiency of enforcing the fiduciary duties of directors so these provisions are to be modified within possible limits.

10.7 Procedural limitations

It is a plain truth that legal duties are valueless in the absence of effective procedures for invoking them before the court. The corporate entity principle incorporates the idea that the directors owe their duties to the company and not to the shareholders.[4] Thus, when the directors of an incorporated company are breaking their fiduciary duties, the other members of the company normally have no '*locus standi*' to sue the directors.[5] This is because of the notion that the duties are owed not to the individual shareholders but to the company itself. But often the wrong-doers themselves will be the appropriate persons for instigating proceedings in the name of the company. Hence, some alternative means of enforcement have been made available in certain circumstances as a result of intervention by courts and legislature.

It is now well established that in certain circumstances an individual shareholder or group of shareholders can institute proceedings as plaintiffs instead of those proceedings having to be instituted in the name of the company. It is generally stated that a suit by a shareholder instead of by the company is allowed in the following circumstances:[6]

(*i*) When it is complained that the company is acting or proposing to act *ultra vires*.[7]

3 *East Pant Du Lead Mining Co.* v *Merryweather* [1864]2 HQ M 254.
4 *Percival* v *Wright* [1902]2 Ch 421.
5 *Foss* v *Harbottle* [1843]2 Hare 461; 67 ER 189.
6 *Edwards* v *Halliwell* [1950]2 All ER 1064 (CA).
7 *Bagshaw* v *The Eastern Union Ry.* [1849]7 Hare 114; *Simpson* v *West Minister Palace Hotel Co.* [1860]8 HLC 712; *Hoole* v *G.W. Ry.* [1867] LR 3 Ch App 262; *Russell* v *Wakefield Waterworks Co.* [1875] LR 20 EQ 474; *Hutton* v *W. Cork Ry*. [1883]23 Ch D 654; *Yorkshire Ministers' Asson.* v *Howden* [1908] AC 256 (HL).

(*ii*) When the act complained of, though not *ultra vires* the company, could be effective only if resolved upon by more than a simple majority vote,[8] i.e.; where a special or extraordinary resolution is required and (it is alleged) has not been validly passed.

(*iii*) Where it is alleged that the personal rights of the plaintiff shareholder have been infringed or are about to be infringed.[9]

(*iv*) Where those who control the company are perpetrating a fraud on the minority.[10]

(*v*) Any other case where the interests of justice require that the general rule, requiring suit by the company, should be disregarded.[11]

Apart from these equitable remedies, a series of statutory remedies are available to shareholders. The provisions of such remedies has resulted in a considerable extension of the protection afforded to members of the company, and thereby has imposed a greater duties on the controllers and made all their duties more readily enforceable.

First is the winding up of the company. Any member can move to the court for winding up of the company in case of an oppression of minority.[12] Again, any member of the company can apply to the

8 *Baillie* v *Oriental Telephone Co.* [1915]1 Ch 503 (CA); *Cotter* v *National Union of Seamen* [1929]2 Ch 58 (69,70); *Edwards* v *Halliwell* [1950]2 All ER 1064 (CA); *Campbell* v *Australian Mutual Provident Society* [1908] LT PC 117; *Normandy* v *Ind Coop & Co. Ltd.* [1908]1 Ch 84.

9 *Johnson* v *Lyttle's Iron Agency* [1877]5 Ch D 687 (CA); *Pender* v *Lushington* [1877]6 Ch D 70; *Wood* v *Odessa Waterworks Co.* [1889]42 Ch D 636; *Salmon* v *Quin & Axtens* [1909] AC 442; *British America Nickel Corpn.* v *O'Brien* [1927] AC 369 (PC); *Edwards* v *Halliwell* [1950]2 All ER 1064; *Hayes* v *Bristol Plant Hire Ltd.* [1957]1 WLR 499. Further List of Illustrations, Ref: Cam LJ (1957) at pp. 210-211.

10 *Atwool* v *Merryweather* [1867] LR 5 Eq 464n; *Merrier* v *Hooper's Telegraph Works* [1874]9 Ch App 350; *Manson* v *Harris* [1879]11 Ch D 97 (CA); *Spikes* v *Grosvenor Hotel* [1897]2 QB 124 (CA); *Alexander* v *Automatic Telephone Co.* [1900]2 Ch 56 (CA); *Borland* v *Earle* [1902] AC 83 (PC); *Cooks* v *Decks* [1916]1 AC 554 (PC).

11 *Russell* v *Wakefield Waterworks Co.* [1872] LR 20 Eq 474; *Heyting* v *Dupont* [1964]1 WLR 843 (CA).

12 *Loch* v *John Blackwood Ltd.* [1924] AC 783; [1924] All ER Rep 200 (PC); *Re Tivoli Freeholds* [1972] VR 445; *R. Sabapathy Rao* v *Sabapathy Press Ltd.* AIR 1925 Mad 489.

Company Law Board (CLB) for relief in cases of oppression[13] and mismanagement.[14]

Thus, a member now has an impressive array of remedies at his disposal, especially where fraud or oppression is alleged. But an effective sanction against breach of the controlling director's duties of care and skill is still lacking. Again the rule in *Foss* v *Harbottle* will normally be a bar against shareholders actions. Further, it is not clear that any of the other remedies will be available to a minority. The relative laxity of these duties, in comparison with the duties of loyalty is reflected in the procedural sphere also.

The New Company Law (Amendment) Bill 1997, (Second Amendment) Bill 1999, and Company Law (Amendment) Bill 2000 are not even tried to define directors. The new 2011 Bill provides the inclusion of women on boards of directors will change the arena of corporate management. The directors report to include director's responsibility statement and 2000 Bill vest more powers with the Department of Company Affairs for effective enforcement of the provisions by enhancing the penalty for contravention will act as a check and balance system and the new Bill is in tune with the era of globalization and liberalization. The 2011 Bill is a path breaking one in its letter. But the Bill is not passed according to its spirit so far by the Government.

The paramount fiduciary duty of directors, by way of analogy with the duties owed by a trustee to his '*Cestui Que Trust*', is to exercise their powers bonafidely for the benefit of the company. They must not place themselves in a situation where their duties and personal interest conflict or may conflict, nor must they allow themselves to be placed in a situation where the exercise of their powers for the company's benefit is in any way fettered. Even a "nominee", "alternate", "puppet" or "stooge" director owes his duties to the company he serves, and not to the interests responsible for his nomination.

If a director is directly or indirectly interested in a contract entered into or proposed to be entered into by the company, he must disclose the nature and the extent of his interest to his fellow directors and the company. In addition, material interests of directors in contracts of

13 Section 397.
14 Section 398.

significance with the company have to be disclosed. More over a director is not permitted to vote on a contract in which he is interested at a Board meeting, though lie may vote on it as a shareholder at a general meeting. The service contracts of directors are open to inspection by the members of the company. The company in general meeting may reward its directors with bonuses, but the directors may not make presents to themselves. A director may not make secret profits for himself, nor may he, without the approval of the general meeting, use for his own advantage, or appropriate to himself, assets, confidential information or opportunities which property belong to the company or which only present themselves to him by reason of his office. And even a general meeting cannot permit a director to take corporate property or opportunities for himself where this would amount to a fraud on the minority. Further, directors are not expected to take benefits out of a takeover or a merger. As fiduciaries they must perform their duties fully and entirely for the best of the interests of the company in good faith and *bona fide*.

Thus, in exercising their powers the directors must always bear in mind that they are in a fiduciary position and must exercise their powers for the benefit of the company, and for that alone. The court has intervened to prevent the abuse of a power to forfeit shares,[15] to make calls,[16] to refuse to register transfers,[17] and to issue shares.[18] But directors acting in their personal capacity as purchasers of shares or property are not trustees of individual shareholders.[19] However, where directors have discretion and are *bona fide* acting in the exercise of it, it is the habit of the courts to interfere with them.[20] Again, where the articles vest the power of carrying on the business of the company, in the directors, the company in general meeting cannot override the directors' powers of carrying on the business by prescribing a regulation or passing a resolution inconsistent with the articles.[1] But the company

15 *Richmond's* case 4 KI 305 (325).
16 *Gilbert's* case 5 Ch App 569; *Alexander* v *Automatic Telephone Co.* [1900]2 Ch 56 (CA).
17 *Re Gresham Life Assurance Society, Ex Parte Panney* LR 8 Ch App 446 (449).
18 *Punt* v *Symons & Co. Ltd.* [1903]2 Ch 506; *Piercy* v *S. Mills & Co. Ltd.* [1920]1 Ch 77.
19 *Percival* v *Wright* [1902]2 Ch 421.
20 *In Re Gresham Life Assurance Society* (ibid).
1 *Automatic Self-Cleansing Co.* v *Cuninghame* [1906]2 Ch 34; *Gramophone & Typewriter* v *Stanley* [1908]2 KB 89; *Salmon* v *Quin and Axtens* [1909]1 Ch 311 (CA).

in general meeting may determine whether or not an action shall be commenced in the name of the company.[2]

The directors as fiduciaries may be held liable for various kinds of misfeasance or breach of trust. The term "breach of trust" is generally confined to some misapplication of the funds of the company and the term "misfeasance" to other breaches of duty which does not involve such misapplication. For instance, to apply the funds of the company to *ultra vires* purposes,[3] or to pay dividends out of capital[4] is a breach of trust; to allot shares knowingly to an infant[5] or to take a bribe;[6] to give a creditor a fraudulent preference, or to commit a breach of the articles resulting in loss to the company. In cases of misfeasance or breach of trust the delinquent director has no right of set off[7] nor can be rely on a release in general terms.[8]

However, the efficacy of the equitable and statutory provisions describing the fiduciary obligations of directors and their liability for breach of trust are considerably being mitigated by the provisions for the insertion of exemption clauses in the articles of a company. It has for many years been usual to insert a clause in the articles of Association, protecting the directors from liability for losses to the company except in the case of their "willful default" or except in the case of their dishonesty. Directors were held to be protected by such a clause in many cases in the past.[9] This protection is now partly removed by Companies Act 1956, s. 201, which provides as follows:

> Section 201(1). "Save as provided in this section, any provision, whether contained in the the articles of association of a company or in an agreement with a company or in any other instrument, for exempting any officer of the company or any person employed by the company as auditor from, or indemnifying him against any liability which by virtue of any rule of law, would otherwise attach to him in respect of any negligence, default,

2 *Marshall's Valve Gear Co.* v *Manning, Wardle & Co.* [1909]1 Ch 267.
3 *Cullerne* v *London & Co. Society* 25 QBD 484.
4 *Fliteroft's* case 21 Ch D 419.
5 *Ex parte Wilson* 8 Ch App 45.
6 *Person's* case 5 Ch D 336.
7 *In re Anglo-French Co-operative Society* 21 Ch D 492; *In re Carriage Supply Association* 27 Ch D 322; *Fliteraft's* case 21 Ch D 519.
8 *Re Joint Stock Trust Co.* (1912)56 SJ 272.
9 For eg. *In Re Brazilian Rubber Estates Ltd.* [1911]1 Ch 425; *Re City Equitable Fire Insurance Co.* [1925] Ch 407; [1924] All ER Rep 495 (CA).

misfeasance, breach of duty or breach of trust of which he may be guilty in relation to the company, shall be void":

> "Provided that a company may, in pursuance of any such provision as aforesaid, indemnify any such officer or auditor against any liability incurred by him in defending any proceedings, whether civil or criminal, in which judgment is given in his favour or in which he is acquitted or discharged or in connection with any application under section 633 in which relief is granted to him by the Court".

The above said provision must be read with s. 633 of the Companies Act which provides as follows:

> Section 633(1). "If in any proceeding for negligence, default, breach of duty, misfeasance, or breach of trust against an officer of a company, it appears to the court hearing the case that he is or may be liable in respect of the negligence, default, breach of duty, misfeasance or breach of trust, but that he has acted honestly and reasonably, and that having regard to all circumstances of the case, including those connected with his appointment, he ought fairly to be excused, the court may relieve him, either wholly or partly, from his liability on such terms as it may think fit".

Again sub-sec. (2) of s. 633 further says:

> "(2) Where any such officer has reason to apprehend that any proceeding will or might be brought against him in respect of any negligence, default, breach of duty, misfeasance, or breach of trust, he may apply to the High Court for relief and the High Court on such application shall have the same power to relieve him as it would have had if it had been a court before which a proceeding against that officer for negligence, default, breach of duty, misfeasance, had been brought under sub-section (1)".

From the whole discussion the fiduciary duties loyalty and good faith of directors as described by the legal and equitable rules appear to show that they are exceptionally strict. This picture, i.e., however, somewhat is misleading. In practice their fiduciary duties do not weigh too heavily upon them because fiduciary and other duties of directors could be discharged without liability so long as the directors have control over the voting. These duties of loyalty and good faith are again, largely waived by the articles of the company in connection with contracts between them and their companies where at most good faith is required. Often all that remains is a general duty to disclose their interests in the most general terms, and to disclose it in advance, merely to their fellow directors, and only after the contract is concluded to the true beneficiaries, the shareholders. Again the corporate entity principle also brought with it the idea that the directors and other managerial personnel owe their duties to the company alone and not to individual shareholder. The logical sequence of the idea is that the individual shareholders will not have any *locus standi* where the company is the proper plaintiff. Besides this there are a number of procedural limitations in the way of effective enforcement of the directors' fiduciary the new Companies Bill 2011 provides for tremendous changes in the Companies Act 1956 to ensure better governance, transparency in working of companies and in order to meet the requirements of liberalisation, deregulation, simplification, changing economic scenario and international corporate market make it necessary to amend the Company Law.

10.8 The Companies Bill 2012—highlights

To provide transparency and good corporate governance;

- Introduced investor democracy and addresses public concern over corporate accountability;
- The scope of officer under default has been broadened;
- Stringent penalties;
- More powers to Auditors and changing of Auditors every 5 years;
- Duties of directors are specified and breach of duties are penalised;
- Accounting standards are prescribed;
- The mandate and role of independent directors defined along with the term of their office as maximum 10 years;
- The maximum number of members, which a Private Company can have, is increased from 50 to 200;
- Compulsory appointment of at least one women director is provided;
- The concept of one person company has been introduced;
- Introduction of provisions to set up Serious Fraud Investigation Office (SFIO);
- Valuation of assets of the company should be done by a registered valuer;
- Limited the number of holding companies;

- Severe restrictions on companies to act as groups;
- Borderline for remuneration of directors to be decided by Remuneration Committee;
- Separate positions of Chairman and Managing Director;
- Corporate funding of political parties and NGOs are introduced;
- Clear provisions of corporate governance;
- Mandatorily a Corporate Social Responsibility (CSR) Committee of the Board should be constituted for formulating a CSR policy of the company;
- Shifting of jurisdiction of High Courts in company matters to the National Company Law Tribunal (NCLT);
- Class action by shareholders introduced in the Bill;
- Winding up procedure made simple but the grounds for winding up specified;
- Insider trading of company directors made it as a criminal offence;
- Repeal of Redundant provisions.

Provisions for Director's report to include Director's Responsibility Statement will ensure and strengthen the fiduciary duties of directors by a cross check. A person cannot be a Director in more than 15 Companies; this will increase the working time of Directors in each company which will ultimately beneficial for the system itself and the company. Adequate representation of women on the boards of directors will help the entry of a large number of women professionals in the arena of corporate management. Whatever may be the change in the new Act the fiduciary duties of directors will always exist, without which the company cannot exist and we may hope that the new Act will fill the gaps in the law.

10.9 Suggestions

- Codify the standard of fiduciary duties like standard of care, skill, and due diligence.
- Improve disclosure of company information requiring public.
- Strengthening auditor's powers to obtain sufficient information from the company to discharge his duties.

- Stringent provisions for formation of subsidiaries and control by parent company.
- The Bill should specify the number of companies in which an individual/firm may be appointed as an auditor.
- Liabilities of audit firm should be specified and penal provisions should be included on erring firms and individual responsibility should be fixed.
- Auditors should be appointed every year in the general meeting for more accountability than appoint them for five years.
- Stricter provisions to be included for protecting the interests of minority shareholders.
- Reduce the time frame for winding up of companies in order to reduce the realization of capital and distribution to shareholders.

Index

***